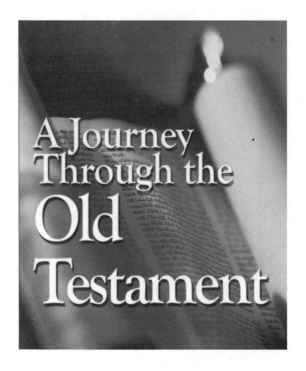

A Journey Through the Old Testament

Contributors:

R. Jerome Boone, D.Min.
Mike Chapman, D.Min.
Hannah Harrington, Ph.D.
Rickie D. Moore, Ph.D.
David C. Cooper, D.Min.

Edited by Homer G. Rhea, L.H.D.

Church of God School of Ministry
Cleveland, Tennessee

Paul L. Walker, Ph.D.
Chancellor, Division of Education

Donald S. Aultman, Ed.D.
Vice Chancellor, Division of Education
Director, School of Ministry

Homer G. Rhea, L.H.D.
Editorial Director

ISBN: 0-87148-050-6

Printed by Pathway Press
Cleveland, Tennessee
United States of America

TABLE OF CONTENTS

Foreword

This survey of the Old Testament began as an effort by the School of Ministry in developing its curriculum for the Certificate In Ministerial Studies. The process was initiated with a series of 42 video lessons which were taught by two pastors and two professors—the primary contributors to this work. This was followed by editing the video lessons to place the Old Testament survey in a textbook format.

The School of Ministry is indebted to R. Jerome Boone, whose book, *Survey of the Old Testament,* provided the basis for the initial video presentations. The contributors to the video lessons were given the opportunity to vary their presentations from the original Boone material to more completely follow their individual interests in the Old Testament record. The final video lessons made it evident that a textbook, which followed the video-lesson presentations more precisely, was needed.

While this introduction to the Old Testament is limited to some of the contributors' favorite Old Testament portions of scripture, the work done by Mike Chapman, D.Min., Hannah Harrington, Ph.D., Rickie D. Moore, Ph.D., and David C. Cooper, D.Min., is a significant contribution to a knowledge of the

Old Testament as a basis for effective ministry. This survey will contribute significantly to an understanding of Old Testament literature—thirty-nine remarkable books that are the Word of God.

Donald S. Aultman, Ed.D.
Director, School of Ministry
Vice Chancellor, Division of Education
September 2001

PREFACE

Much of what is written in the New Testament has its roots in the Old Testament. Indeed, many New Testament passages cannot be fully understood without information related to them in the Old Testament. Jesus and the apostle Paul are both found quoting from the Old Testament on numerous occasions. After all, as a popular writer has recently observed, this is the Bible Jesus read.

The Old Testament is rich in biographical information, historical perspective, poetry, wisdom, and inspirational writings. The sovereign work of God is found throughout. Archeological studies have confirmed many accounts that critics have called into question. The contributors to this volume have made use of the latest scholarship and the finest works on the Old Testament to bring an informed analysis of this portion of the Bible. Their insight makes plain the eternal truths set forth in this ancient, but modernly applicable, book.

Old Testament Survey by Jerome Boone, published by the Lee University External Studies Program, provided the outline for the videos upon which this textbook is based. For additional information relative to the Old Testament, students are encouraged to purchase a copy of *Old Testament Survey* from Lee University.

A Journey Through the Old Testament is based on a video series bearing the same name. Its greatest value will come from reading it in conjunction with the videotapes. It is offered as part of the Certificate In Ministerial Studies program originated by the School of Ministry.

At the time of this writing, the contributors to this volume are actively involved in ministry. Jerome Boone serves as dean of the School of Religion at Lee University in Cleveland, Tennessee; Michael Chapman is pastor of the City Church of God in Chattanooga, Tennessee; Hannah Harrington holds the position of chairperson of the Biblical and Theological Studies Division of Patten College in Oakland, California; Rickie Moore is professor of Old Testament Studies at the Church of God Theological Seminary in Cleveland, Tennessee; and David Cooper serves as pastor of the Mount Paran Central Church of God in Atlanta, Georgia.

Several people have been involved in bringing this project to a successful completion. The Media Resource Group (MRG) is responsible for the production of the videotapes upon which this book is based. Abigail Hughes had the arduous task of transcribing the videotapes so the editors could put them into book form. No one was more valuable to this project than Nellie Keasling whose handiwork is seen in the graphics for the videotapes and copyediting of the book. Sam McGraner designed the cover, flowed the copy and formatted the book. Hoyt E. Stone, editor extraordinaire, did the initial editing on several chapters. The staff at Pathway Press are responsible for the printing of this material. Donald S. Aultman has offered guidance throughout. This entire project is the brainchild of Paul L. Walker who has given it his wholehearted support. To each of these I extend my deepest appreciation and acknowledge that this project would not have been possible without their assistance.

The School of Ministry offers this volume in the hope that its contents will increase the knowledge of those who read its pages concerning the most important book ever written—the Bible. May they learn from the experiences of those who lived in the pages of this magnificent book and may they live out its principles day by day.

Homer G. Rhea, L.H.D.
Editorial Director
School of Ministry
Cleveland, Tennessee
September 2001

1 Introduction to the Old Testament

By R. Jerome Boone, D.Min.

The body of literature commonly recognized in Christianity as the Old Testament also constitutes the sacred writings of Judaism. These books were the sacred Scripture of the early church and were ultimately included in the Christian canon because they predict and give witness to the messsiahship of Jesus Christ.

Paul said of these writings, "For everything that was written in the past was written to teach us, so that through endurance and the encouragement of the Scriptures we might have hope" (Romans 15:4, *NIV*). He described them as instructive (2 Timothy 3:15-17) because they reveal the moral will of God. Although he understood that salvation comes through faith in Jesus Christ alone, he also knew that God revealed many important truths about His will for His people in the Old Testament scriptures. Paul applied those truths to the Christian faith as he wrote his epistles, often quoting from the Old Testament.

The nature of the Old Testament as witness to Jesus Christ and revelation of the moral will of God is the reason for this study. This journey through the Old Testament will focus on God's revelation of Himself and His plan of redemption for humankind. This first chapter will examine the Old Testament as it relates to the New Testament and God's plan of salvation.

God's Plan of Salvation as Revealed From Genesis to Revelation

The Old Testament begins with God's creation of the heavens, the earth and ultimately humankind. He created humankind in righteousness and placed them in the Garden of Eden to have fellowship with them. According to the Genesis account, God came down and walked with Adam and Eve in the cool of each day (see Genesis 3:8).

God had given Adam and Eve perfect liberty in the Garden with only one restriction. His rules for them were explicit and easily observed. There came a day, however, when they decided to exercise their own wills in direct disobedience to God's instructions, and by this single disobedience, sin entered into the world. From that point on, the Old Testament tells the story of God's work in redeeming humankind back to Himself—a story that leads to the Gospels and the coming of Jesus Christ.

On the heels of the fall of humankind in Genesis 3:15, the first prophecy was given of a coming Messiah, the seed of woman who would defeat the seed of the enemy, bringing redemption to humankind. Though Adam and Eve were cast out of Eden, God did not forsake them. He made a way of atonement for their sins. Though pronouncing judgment upon them, He demonstrated mercy toward them and promised a Redeemer to their descendants.

Most of the Old Testament tells the story of God's relationship with Abraham and his descendents. In calling Abraham into a covenant relationship, God made a fresh revelation of Himself and His will to humankind. For Abraham, it was a time of obedience and faith. The Bible says of Abraham, "And he believed in the Lord, and He accounted it to him for righteousness" (Genesis 15:6, *NKJV*). And also in Romans 4:3 the Bible says, "For what does the Scripture say? 'Abraham believed God, and it was accounted to him for righteousness'" (*NKJV*).

As the descendants of Abraham eventually formed the nation of Israel, God began to reveal His moral will to them through Moses on Mt. Sinai. From the law of Moses to the ministry of the prophets, God revealed His message to the world through Israel. The end and aim of this Old Testament message was the advent of the Messiah and Savior Jesus Christ.

Jesus Christ was a son of Abraham and a descendent of King David. Yet, born of the Virgin Mary by the Holy Spirit, He was God incarnate—a flesh revelation of God for the world. Throughout the New Testament period that revelation was propagated through the apostles and New Testament writers.

At the end of the Bible in the Book of Revelation, human history comes full circle. God will bring the world back to the same righteousness that He started with in Genesis. There will be a new heaven and a new earth created in the righteousness of Eden. God's plan of salvation, ultimately, is to restore the righteousness of this world that was first created in Genesis.

Israel and God's Plan of Salvation

Adam and Eve became the father and mother of the entire human race. The development of human-kind eventually formed a line of righteous people and a line of sinful people. Seth, the third son of Adam and Eve, became the father of a line of righteous people, and Cain, their firstborn, became the father of a line of unrighteousness people.

By Genesis 6, the wickedness of the world had become so pervasive in its influence that even the righteous descendants of Seth had been overcome by the wickedness of the world. Only Noah and his family were righteous enough to avoid God's wrath. God entered into judgment with humankind and destroyed them all, with the exception of Noah, his wife, and his family.

In the Genesis flood, God judged wickedness. The descendants of Adam and Eve were wicked and they died. Just as Paul said to the Romans, "The wages of sin is death" (Romans 6:23). But just as God is not willing for the righteous to perish with the wicked, He made a way of escape for Noah and his family. God not only judged wickedness, He preserved righteousness.

Noah and his family were once more given the commandment, just as Adam and Eve, to be fruitful, multiply and fill the earth. Again, God began to multiply the human race.

After the Flood, things were very much like they were before. Noah and his wife had a righteous son, Shem who preserved a line of righteous people in the earth. The other sons of Noah, however, seem to have followed in the ways of Cain, and wickedness again predominated. Just as it was before the Flood, as humankind increased, sin increased. As they multiplied and filled the earth, sin multiplied. Again, sin became so prevalent that even the righteous descendents of Shem began to be influenced by it. Because of this wickedness, God intervened in human history again, not with a flood or other forms of destruction, but with a new revelation of Himself to Abraham.

God called Abraham, a descendant of Shem, when he lived in Ur of Chaldees. He asked Abraham to come out from among his country and kinsmen and travel to a land that He would show him—the land of Canaan. There, God used Abraham to bring up a righteous people—a nation that would preserve the chronology of God in the earth. From Abraham, God brought forth the nation of Israel, a "kingdom of priests and a holy nation" (Exodus 19:6, *NKJV*).

Israel represented God to the world and the world to God. This was more clearly revealed as God spoke to Israel through the prophet Isaiah, "I, the Lord, have called You in righteousness, and will hold Your hand; I will keep You and give You as a covenant to the people, as a light to the Gentiles" (Isaiah 42:6, *NKJV*). God intended to work through Israel to bring all the nations of the earth to Himself in covenant relationship.

Unfortunately, that did not happen. Because of Israel's own disobedience they eventually followed the same pattern of degradation and sinfulness of earlier generations. As the nation of Israel increased, sin increased.

However, throughout the Old Testament, God often speaks of a righteous remnant that remained faithful to Him. Out of that righteous remnant, God broke into the history of humankind once again in the person of Jesus Christ—God incarnate.

The birth of Jesus marked a boundary between the Old Testament and the New Testament. He brought a conclusion to the Old Testament and inaugurated the New Testament. It is through Jesus Christ that God continues to work out His plan of salvation and purpose for the world. Just as God said to Israel, "And you shall be to Me a kingdom of priests and a holy nation" (Exodus 19:6, *NKJV*), He reiterated to the church, "But you are a chosen generation, a royal priesthood, a holy nation, His own special people, that you may proclaim the praises of Him who called you out of darkness into His marvelous light" (1 Peter 2:9, *NKJV*).

The Great Commission given in Matthew 28:19, 20, expresses God's purpose for the church: "Go therefore and make disciples of all the nations, baptizing them in the name of the Father and of the Son and of the Holy Spirit, teaching them to observe all things that I have commanded you; and lo, I am with you always, even to the end of the age" (*NKJV*). God is now at work in the church just as He was in Israel in the Old Testament.

There is coming a time, however, when God is going to bring human history to a close. At that point, God will take His people out of this world briefly and return with them to establish His millennial kingdom—a thousand years of righteousness under the authority of Jesus Christ. God's plan will have come full circle. Just as the story started in Genesis with a righteous creation in complete submission to God, the story ends with all creation again submitted to God in righteousness.

This plan established continuity between the Old and New Testaments. God did not do something brand new in the New Testament; it was prefigured in the Old. This is why Paul said the Old Testament is like a tutor leading mankind to Jesus Christ (see Galatians 3:24, 25). God has always been at work in the world, preserving knowledge of, faith in, and obedience to Himself.

The Story of Israel

The third perspective on the Old Testament focuses on the story of Israel from Genesis 12 to Malachi 4. This story can be viewed in four phases:

1. The formation of Israel as a nation
2. The development of Israel as a kingdom
3. The destruction of Israel as a kingdom
4. The restoration of Israel as a nation, not as a kingdom.

The first phase takes place primarily in the books of the Bible known as the Pentateuch—Genesis through Deuteronomy. In the Pentateuch, the formation of Israel as a nation unfolds from the call of Abraham out of Ur of the Chaldeans to the call of Moses to lead Abraham's descendants out of Egypt. As a small family, they moved from Ur of the Chaldeans, but as a great nation, they were delivered from Egypt. As God brought Israel out of Egypt and into Canaan, two of God's promises to Abraham were fulfilled: to make Abraham a great nation and to give him the land of Canaan as a heritage.

After God had multiplied Israel into a great nation and given them the land of Canaan, He moved them toward becoming a kingdom. That was a time when God was transforming Israel the nation into

Israel the kingdom that would rule over other nations under David and Solomon.

At that point God's purpose for Israel could have been fulfilled, but it was not. Perhaps the nations could have been brought to Jerusalem to worship God at the Temple and then have gone back to their respective homes, taking the knowledge of God with them—the knowledge of God filling the earth. What could have happened did not because of the sinfulness of Solomon and Israel.

In the last years of his kingship, Solomon fell into idolatry and sinned before God. He also allowed idolatry to develop throughout the land. At his death, the kingdom of Israel came to an end in civil war, dividing the kingdom into Israel, the Northern Kingdom, and Judah, the Southern Kingdom.

Because of the sinfulness of Israel, God brought judgment upon both of these kingdoms. The Assyrians destroyed the Northern Kingdom in 722 B.C. The Southern Kingdom lasted a bit longer, surviving until 586 B.C., when the Babylonians destroyed Jerusalem and took the people to Babylon as captives. However, God in His mercy eventually brought Israel out of the Babylonian captivity and returned them to Canaan and there restored them as a nation. That was the nation of Israel that extended into the New Testament period, the same nation into which Jesus Christ was born.

These four phases are key elements of Israel's history. In this text, each of these phases will be developed as one gains an overview of the Old Testament.

2 The Pentateuch

By Mike Chapman, D.Min.

The Bible is the most exciting book in all of human history. It is the Word of God; and as such, it is His communication to this world, revealing messages about Him, hope, life and love.

This journey through the Old Testament begins with the study of the Pentateuch. The word *Pentateuch* literally means "five books" and refers to the first five books of the Old Testament—Genesis, Exodus, Leviticus, Numbers and Deuteronomy. These books form a foundation for the study of the rest of the Word of God.

The Hebrew Bible is divided into three units— the Law, the Prophets, and the Writings. The Law, also called the Torah, is the Pentateuch. The Pentateuch has also been called the Books of the Law or the Five Books of Moses.

The term *canonicity* means "the authority of a book or books to claim to be divinely inspired Scripture." Down through the ages, the people of God— Israel in the Old Testament and the church in the New Testament—have sought to determine which books were from God and could claim divine inspiration. Some books have faced extreme scrutiny to determine whether they should be included as Scripture. The Pentateuch, however, has never been questioned as to its canonicity. As a literary unit, these books provide a foundation for both the Old and the New Testaments.

Authorship of the Pentateuch

Traditionally, Christians and Jews have believed that Moses was the author of these five books. That is why they are often called the Five Books of Moses. The Pentateuch itself supports this view, claiming Moses as being essentially responsible for its authorship. Moses was personally involved in the deliverance of Israel from Egypt and leading them to the Promised Land. He was also personally involved in the receiving of the Law. Consequently, he would have firsthand knowledge of the events and developments that took place in the Pentateuch. He probably used scribes to help record some of this information, but one must keep in mind that Moses was indeed responsible for the authorship.

Moses would have been careful to ensure that a written record of the Law and the history was maintained, because the children of Israel were commanded to keep the Law. If they were going to keep the Law, they had to have it written down. They were also commanded to not forget the events of their deliverance from Egypt or their wanderings in the wilderness. Therefore, Moses would have been careful to make sure a written history, as well as a written law, was maintained. Consequently, reason dictates the Mosaic authorship of at least Exodus through Deuteronomy.

But how did Moses write the Book of Genesis? Or, where did he get his information? The Book of Genesis predates Moses by thousands of years. Abraham would have been born as many as 800 years before Moses, yet he recorded the history of Abraham's period. Genesis spans a tremendous amount of time all the way back to the first moments of Creation. How did Moses know those things? How did God cause him to write the Book of Genesis?

First of all, Moses was well qualified to write about the events in the Book of Genesis because he was raised in Pharaoh's Court. At the time of Moses, Egypt had the most advanced civilization in the world. Trained in the courts of Pharaoh, Moses undoubtedly knew Egyptian, probably Babylonian and his native Hebrew language as well. He would have had access to, and been able to read, the various historical literatures and ancient writings of the Middle East—sources that have long since been lost. Oral traditions—stories and historical records that were passed on and repeated over and over again—perhaps also supplemented these historical records. Therefore, it would be safe to say that Moses knew more about world history prior to his day than anyone today knows about that particular time.

Most important to Moses' writings, however, was the divine enablement of the Holy Spirit. The Bible says, "All Scripture is given by inspiration of God" (2 Timothy 3:16). The Greek word translated *inspiration* in this passage is *theopneustos*, which literally means "God breathed." God breathed upon these men through His Holy Spirit so that the words they penned were the very words of God. The Holy Spirit superintended and watched over them so that their writings are inerrant and completely trustworthy.

In the 20th century, a type of scholarship arose from liberal theologians called higher criticism. Higher criticism basically analyzed Bible texts and made subjective judgments as to whether these texts of the Bible should be considered authentic. It challenged the authorship of many Old Testament writers, including Moses' authorship of the Book of Genesis, as well as the other books of the Pentateuch.

Higher criticism claimed the Book of Genesis to be a composite of writings from three priests identified as J, E, and P. The J writings emphasized the name Jehovah or *Yahweh* for God; the E writings preferred the word *Elohim*; and P was considered the author of all other Genesis passages. Further, higher criticism claimed that the Pentateuch was not written in the time of Moses but during the time of David and Solomon.

In spite of this type of criticism, there is strong support—both internal and external—for the Mosaic authorship of the Book of Genesis, as well as the other four Books of the Pentateuch. Throughout the Bible—both Old and New Testaments—Moses is recognized as authoring each Book of the Pentateuch. Jesus recognized the authorship of Moses, as did Paul. The books themselves were commonly called the Books of Moses.

Two reasons higher-criticism scholars rejected Mosaic authorship of the Pentateuch were the presence of historical information and the use of particular literary styles, both considered more normative to the 8th century B.C. than the 14th century B.C., the era of Moses. However, in 1929, the Ras Shamra tablets were discovered on the coast of Syria, and in the mid-1970s, the Ebla tablets were discovered in northern Syria, both containing the same historical information and using the same literary styles questioned in the Pentateuch. Both discoveries were dated to around 1400 B.C., effectively silencing those higher-criticism arguments against Mosaic authorship.

Archaeology has again and again come to the support of the Scripture. Nelson Gurack, a noted archaeologist and expert in ancient documents, said, "There has never been an archaeological find that has controverted a Biblical text." The more archeological discoveries that are made, the more confirmation is given that the Word of God is true and inerrant.

Chronology of the Pentateuch

The Pentateuch falls naturally into three historical eras, which lend themselves easily to an outline for study. The first can be called the Creation Era (Genesis 1-11), because it deals with the creation of the universe, the creation and fall of man, the flood of Noah and the Tower of Babel. This era is foundational to the study of God's plan of redemption and His working with man from that era until now.

The second period is the Patriarch Era (Genesis 12-50). The word *patriarch* means "father." As God began the nation of Israel, He chose Abraham to father a family, and eventually a nation, through which God would bring Jesus Christ into the world. Each of those recognized as Israel's patriarchs—Abraham, Isaac, Jacob, and Joseph—contributed significantly to God's plan of building that great nation.

The third period is called the Exodus Era and spans the Books of Exodus, Leviticus, Numbers and

Deuteronomy. This era covers the life of Moses, the Exodus of Israel out of Egyptian bondage, the giving of the Law and the wandering of Israel in the wilderness for 40 years.

These five books of the Pentateuch fit together as a historical record of the birth of Israel, the nation, guided by the revelation of God's laws for that nation as His chosen people. Actually, there are three historical records—Genesis, Exodus and Numbers—that provide the chronology of the Pentateuch. The Books of Leviticus and Deuteronomy are set chronologically in the same time frame as Exodus and Numbers, but they are composed of the various religious, civil, and customary laws God gave to Israel through Moses.

Geography of the Pentateuch

Any study of the Old Testament should also include the geography of the area in which all of those events took place. Not only the events of the Pentateuch, but also every event of the Old Testament took place in an area roughly the size of Texas. Landmarks, such as bodies of water—the Red Sea, the Dead Sea, the Sea of Galilee, and rivers, such as the Nile, the Jordan, the Tigris, the Euphrates— should become increasingly familiar to the student of the Old Testament. Knowledge of the geographic location of each enhances the mental perception of the location of each story.

Another way of becoming familiar with the geography of the Old Testament is to compare the locations of modern nations with their Biblical counterparts. For instance, modern Iraq corresponds with Biblical Babylon, Iran with Persia, and Syria with

Assyria. This gives a modern perspective to Biblical geography.

A Pattern of Study for the Pentateuch

Thus far, an overview of the Pentateuch has been given with regard to authorship, structure, chronology and geography. The following chapters will give attention to the three eras mentioned previously in more detail. In approaching each of these eras, a summary will first be given, including the central figure(s), the main location, and a chronological setting for the story-line summary (a one-sentence statement that summarizes the main theme of the period).

Second, a brief study of a map will take place, focusing on where the events of the era occurred. Following the map study, there will be an expansion summary, breaking down the era and its events more precisely. Finally, a simple overview will be given of the book or books that cover and/or were written during the era. Essentially, this will not be a book-by-book study of the Pentateuch but an era-by-era study of the times, persons and events contained in those books.

This pattern may be better explained with a brief look at the Creation Era. The key figure in the Creation Era was Adam; the key location was the Garden of Eden; and the time frame was from the Creation to approximately 2100 B.C., the birth of Abraham. A one-sentence, story-line summary for this era is, "Adam is created by God, but sin destroyed God's original plan for man." Key words in this sentence are *created, sin, destroyed* and *plan*. This, in essence, reveals what the study will be covering. This study will focus on Creation, the first sin, the results of that first sin, and the plan that God had in mind.

The map study for the Creation Era can focus only on where Eden possibly was. According to the Bible, a river that flowed through the Garden of Eden became the head of four rivers (Genesis 2:10-14). Those rivers were the Pishon, Gihon, Tigris and the Euphrates. The first two of these rivers are not in existence today. They may have simply dried up or could have been absorbed into the Tigris and/or Euphrates rivers as they expanded over time. However, one can still assume that Eden was at the headwaters of the Tigris and Euphrates rivers.

THE BEGINNING

The very first words in the Old Testament are "In the beginning God." God's existence is an accepted fact of Scripture. The Bible never makes an attempt to prove His existence. In fact, the Bible indicates that it is the height of foolishness to refuse to believe in God. Therefore, it is stated emphatically and without apology: "In the beginning God created the heavens and the earth" (Genesis 1:1).

One of the oldest statements of the Christian faith is the Apostle's Creed which states: "I believe in one God, the Father Almighty, Maker of heaven and earth." That is the fundamental affirmation of the Christian faith—God is the Creator. He was before the beginning of time, and He is the Initiator of human existence.

3

Genesis:
The Six Days
of Creation

By Mike Chapman, D.Min.

By way of review, this study focuses on the Creation Era—Genesis 1-11. The key figure is Adam, and the setting is the Garden of Eden. The time line is from the beginning of time until approximately the year 2100 B.C.

Genesis 1:1 says, "In the beginning God created the heaven and the earth." The Hebrew word for God is *Elohim*. The *el* in Hebrew means "like God." For example, a name like Michael or Daniel means "one who is like God." Also, the word *Elohim* is plural. Some think it is a reference to the Trinity; others think it is the Hebrew way of recognizing God as Almighty. Since the Hebrew language has no capitalization, there is no way to show a proper noun unless it is pluralized. Thus, *Elohim* would be called the plural of excellence or the plural of supremacy.

Creation and the Bible
The Biblical account of Creation, initially revealed in Genesis, is found throughout the Bible in both

the Old and New Testaments. For instance, in Hebrews 11:3, the Bible says, "Through faith we understand that the worlds were framed by the word of God, so that things which are seen were not made of things which do appear." This passage indicates that the visible was birthed out of the invisible—the physical world from the spirit world.

Isaiah 40:28 affirms the creativeness of God at the beginning: "Do you not know? Have you not heard? The Lord is the everlasting God, the Creator of the ends of the earth" (*NIV*). Jeremiah said, "He has made the earth by His power, He has established the world by His wisdom, and has stretched out the heavens at His discretion" (10:12, *NKJV*). Jeremiah understood Creation as an act of the power and wisdom of God.

John affirmed the power of God in Creation—specifically in the person of Jesus—when he said, "All things were made through Him, and without Him nothing was made that was made" (1:3, *NKJV*). This passage says two important things. First, it clearly says that Jesus is God and as God, took part in the Creation. Secondly, it says that there was nothing made without His involvement.

Paul said, "For by Him were all things created that are in heaven and that are on earth, visible and invisible, whether they are thrones or dominions or principalities or powers. All things were created by Him and for Him" (Colossians 1:16, *NKJV*). God not only created the visible world but also the invisible world. More importantly, Paul said that all things were created not just *by* Him, but *for* Him as well.

Nehemiah said, "You alone are the Lord. You made heaven, the heaven of heavens, with all their host, the earth and everything on it, the seas and all that is in them, and You preserve them all. The host of heaven worships You" (9:6, *NKJV*). The Book of Revelation also states, "The twenty-four elders fall down before Him who sits on the throne and worship Him who lives forever and ever, and cast their crowns before the throne saying: 'You are worthy, O Lord, to receive glory and honor and power; for you created all things, and by Your will they exist and were created'" (4:10, 11, *NKJV*).

It is interesting that one of the foundations of the worship God receives in heaven is the fact that He created all things. Nehemiah said that all of creation is to worship God; Paul said all things were created by Him and for Him; and Revelation indicates that His creative power is the foundation of the worship of God, even in heaven. He is worthy because He is the Creator. Obviously, the creation story is not exclusive to Genesis. It is a doctrinal reality throughout the Bible, both Old and New Testaments.

Defining Creation

A theological definition of *creation* could be stated as follows: "Creation is that free act of God whereby He, according to His sovereign will and for His own glory, in the beginning brought forth the whole visible and invisible universe without the use of preexisting materials; and thus gave it an existence distinct from Him yet always dependent on Him." This theological definition expresses seven facets of the doctrine of creation.

First, it describes Creation as a free act of God, indicating that it was not a necessary act—something God had to do. God was in no way obligated to create, but it was His free choice—His desire to do so.

Secondly, this definition describes Creation as an act of God, not a matter of chance. The origin of the universe was not random or accidental; it was an intentional act of God.

The third statement in this definition is of vast importance to one's understanding of Creation. It states that God created for His own glory. The glory of God is the highest end of all things. God—the Supreme Being, the Perfect One—would have to choose the highest ends for whatever He does. There is no higher goal for anything in the universe than the glory of God. Therefore, the aim of Creation was for His glory.

Fourth, this definition states God created in the beginning. Such a statement begs the question: The beginning of what? Obviously, the answer must be: The beginning of time. Often the concepts of time and eternity are viewed as being connected in some way—as though eternity is simply endless time. In reality, time and eternity have nothing in common. Eternity is not endless time, but timelessness—the suspension of time.

Time, by definition, could be called a succession of moments—one moment after another. Time is measured in small units—seconds, minutes, hours, days, weeks, months, years—each unit basically defined as a succession of moments. With that definition, eternity could never be looked upon as an endless succession of moments. Eternity is timelessness and defies measurement; it is one eternal, constant present tense. For example, when God revealed Himself to Moses from the burning bush,

He identified Himself as "I Am," because He is eternal.

The succession of moments means change. However, change is a word that can never be applied to God. He does not change. Therefore, when considering the phrase "In the beginning," it is understood that at some point a moment existed when there was no succession of moments. Then God said, "Let there be . . ." and at that moment, time began. The Bible seems to indicate that somewhere in the future time will end. Thus, eternity is timelessness.

Fifth, this definition says that God created both the visible and invisible worlds. Genesis 1:1 says, "In the beginning God created the heavens and the earth" (*NIV*). Included in the phrase, "the heavens" is an invisible realm of reality. Paul was cognizant of this and said, "For by Him all things were created that are in heaven and that are on earth, visible and invisible" (Colossians 1:16, *NKJV*).

Often in his writings, Paul referred to a realm of reality that he called the heavenlies, the spirit realm or heavenly places (see Ephesians 1:3, 20; 2:6; 3:10). He was not simply making reference to the sun, moon, planets and stars; he was talking about an actual heavenly or spiritual realm. This realm is separate and distinct from the physical or visible realm. Consider the example of angels. They are beings created by God who dwell in that spirit realm. The Bible says "The angel of the Lord encamps all around those who fear Him, and delivers them" (Psalm 34:7, *NKJV*). Just because they are not visible does not mean they are not there. They are in that invisible, spirit realm.

Paul gives an example of the two realms of reality in 2 Corinthians 4:18: "We do not look at the things which are seen, but at the things which are not seen. For the things which are seen are temporary, but the things which are not seen are eternal" (*NKJV*).

Sixth, this definition says that God created everything without the use of preexisting material. The theological term for this is *ex nihilo*, a Latin term meaning "out of nothing." Before God said "Let there be," there was nothing but God. The material world was birthed out of the Word of God and nothing more. Hebrews 11:3 says, "The things which are seen were not made of things which are visible" (*NKJV*). In a void of time and space, God said, "Let there be," and the universe came forth.

Finally, the seventh statement of this definition of creation says that God created a world distinct from, yet dependent upon Him. Distinct means that God and the universe are not the same. Eastern religions teach pantheism, which says the universe is God; no difference is recognized between the substance of the universe and the person of God. In other words, everything is God.

Christianity, however, teaches that God created a universe that is distinct from Him and that He is transcendent. He transcends the universe, but at the same time, He is present in His universe. God is both transcendent and eminent—above the universe yet in the universe.

God is big enough to encompass everything, yet He inhabits the space between the electrons, protons and neutrons of the atom. There is not one space that He does not fill nor one star or galaxy He does not transcend in this entire universe.

This is the doctrine of creation. So God created the world as a free act for His own glory; at the beginning of time; a visible and invisible world; out of nothing; but a world in which He rules, He reigns, and He is present in all things.

Creation Controversy

There has been a controversy over the years concerning the way the first and second verses of Genesis 1 has been interpreted. Three opposing views have been proposed which focus on the difference in tone and wording between these two verses. The first view is that verse 1 should be considered a title for the narrative that follows—a thematic statement expounded upon in the following verses.

The second view has been called the gap theory or the restoration theory. This theory claims the existence of a pre-Adamic world, spanning eons of time during which the dinosaurs could have existed. At some point in time, that world was destroyed by some catastrophic event, leaving the earth formless and void—absent of any life forms. A new beginning was then inaugurated in verse 2 when the Bible says, "And the Spirit of God moved upon the face of the waters." God is portrayed as brooding over this destroyed world, restoring and refreshing it with new life.

The cause of the catastrophic gap has been postulated to be the fall of Satan. Satan's fall introduced sin into the original created order and so devastated everything that the original creation was destroyed. Verse 2 would then serve as a gap, lasting an untold space of time before God began His work of restoration in verse 3.

Several things concerning this passage and the entire Bible combine to cast doubt upon the gap or restoration theory. First of all, several words used in the translation can be confusing. In verse 1, Is the Bible saying that the created world *was* or *became* without form and void? Since the word used can be translated both ways, a closer look must be taken. The Hebrew word used in that passage most often means *was*, and only occasionally means *became*. Also, other words more appropriately used to relate the meaning of *became* were not used. The result of this word study casts doubt upon the gap theory by indicating that God's initial creation *was* formless and void in the process of creation and did not *become* so later.

The most convincing argument against the gap theory or restoration theory is that no other reference to it occurs throughout the Bible. It would seem that something of that magnitude would have other references somewhere in the Scripture. Because of these facts, few scholars accept the gap or restoration theory.

The third view is that Genesis 1:1 is the original creation of time and matter, and verse 2 begins the story of how God formed the matter. It could be said that verse 1 tells how God created the materials and verse 2 begins to tell what God did with the materials He had created. This simple yet concise statement seems to give the best interpretation of those scriptures.

The Seven Days of Creation

The seven days of creation can be divided into two categories or sections. The first three days could be called the days of preparation, and the last three days could be called the days of decoration.

On the first day, God created original matter and light. On the fourth day, He created the light bearers—the sun, the moon and the stars. Prior to the creation of these heavenly lights, God himself was the source of all light in the universe. On the second day, He separated the waters—in essence, He created the seas and the atmosphere. On the fifth day, He created the inhabitants of the waters and the atmosphere—fish and birds. On the third day, dry land appeared, and on the sixth day, came the creation of land animals and man.

On the seventh day, the Bible says God rested. That does not mean that God was tired. When it says He rested, it simply means that He ceased His labor—He stopped working on the project of creation. He pronounced His creation good and turned His attention to sovereignty and the providential role of watching over His creation. He is running His world. He is active in all of His creation.

The seven days of creation basically say that God does things in an orderly way. He has a plan and works in all things according to the plan He has designed. Just as His plan was perfect and successful in those seven days, so is His plan for His creation today.

4 Genesis: The Theories of Creation

By Mike Chapman, D.Min.

This chapter continues the study of the Creation Era of the Old Testament, with focus specifically on the creation week of God. Because understanding the creation week is so vital, extra time is given to this subject in the first three chapters of Genesis.

Bible scholars have devoted much time to the study of the days of creation. The basic question usually narrows down to this: Were these days literally and actually seven 24-hour periods? The word *day*, as used here, is the Hebrew word *yom*. There are four ways one can view this question, or four views of creation.

Creation Views and Genesis Controversy

1. *View one says these days were literally 24-hour days.* This is the traditional view held by most conservative Christians. Giving credence to this view are the repeated phrases "the evening and the morning," certainly implying a traditional way of thinking

in the Jewish mind, or within a Jewish context. Among the people of Israel, a new day began with sunset, not sunrise or midnight. Thus, the "evening and morning" would be a common expression, meaning these were 24-hour days.

2. *View two says these days were six time periods of indefinite length.* The word *yom*, just like our word *day*, can be used, and was used, in the Old Testament to refer to a period of time that may be more or less than a 24-hour period. For instance, one could say right now, living at the beginning of the 21st century, that we are living in the Day of Technology or the Day of Global Economics. Thus used, the word *day* refers not to a specific day of the calendar but to a period of time. So, some would say the word *yom* means six periods of time or six stages of time.

3. *View three says these days were revelation days.* This means that God explained or told Moses about His creation during a six-day period. For instance, on day one, God told Moses He created light, on day two, the next thing. This was not necessarily the sequential order in which God created so much as how God told Moses about it. Moses got this revelation in six days, and on the seventh day God said, "That's it. I've told you the whole thing."

4. *View four says the creation story is a religious myth.* The creation story is to be seen figuratively. It is a religious story, teaching some truths and some ideas, but none of this portion of Scripture is to be taken literally. This view, of course, is rejected by just about all Evangelical, conservative Christians. Most Evangelicals have a problem with the third view

as well, believing the context of Genesis simply does not support it.

The serious question here is between the other two views—seven literal days or seven periods of time.

There are two very practical arguments in favor of the seven periods of time theory. First, God created Adam and Eve on the sixth day, with Adam being created first. Adam was given responsibility for tending the Garden and naming all the animals. Scripture goes on to say Adam became lonely because there was no companion for him. It seems that it would take longer than 24 hours both to do the task and to become lonely. Twenty-four hours seems a very short period of time for all those things to have taken place.

The second reason has to do with the seventh day. God rested on the seventh day. In essence, one might say God is still in the seventh day in that God no longer creates. He simply remains Lord over His creation. This leads one to conclude that the seventh day was certainly longer than a 24-hour period.

One might also argue that, since the sun and the moon were created on the fourth day, and a day is judged by the rotation of the earth on its axis, there is no basis for judging a day until the fourth day.

Since this point is merely a matter of discussion and not one pertinent to salvation, what one believes here ought not to be considered as a matter of heresy. God will reveal the full truth in heaven. Many sincere, honest Christians believe the "day" mentioned does actually refer to a 24-hour period, but it appears that in all likelihood a larger number of people now lean toward the indefinite period of time concept. The important thing is to recognize God as Creator.

Another controversy revolves around the Genesis 1 and the Genesis 2 question. Some scholars consider these to be two separate accounts of Creation, one by the E author, the other by the J author, as discussed in an earlier chapter. There is, however, a more plausible explanation.

In Genesis 1, the emphasis is on the entire six days of Creation. Genesis 2 focuses on the sixth day only. The sixth day is when Adam and Eve were created. In Genesis 1, the name used for God is *Elohim*. In Genesis 2 the name used is Jehovah. Genesis 1 sets forth the power of God. Genesis 2 presents the personal nature of God—God who walks in the Garden with Adam. Jehovah is God's personal name. When the people in the Old Testament asked what God these Hebrew people served, they answered, "Jehovah," the English translation of the Hebrew word *Yahweh.*

Genesis 2 presents God in covenant with man. Jehovah is always God's covenant name. Thus viewed, there is really no controversy between Genesis 1and Genesis 2. It is simply two different emphases telling the same story.

The Creation of Man

The Bible says God created man. He created both male and female, meaning, of course, that He created mankind. As used here, the word *man* is to be understood as gender neutral. It means male and female.

The creation of man differed from other aspects of the universe. God's creation acts, until he came to man, were based on His spoken Word. God said, "Let there be . . ." and there was. However, God did not say, "Let there be humans," or "Let there be a man." God chose a special involvement in creating man. He formed man's physical body from the elemental dust—the clay of the earth. While there are different theories as to why God chose this creation method, all speculation seems to indicate the great concern and special involvement God had in creating the human race.

Moreover, God did not simply form a human body; He created both body and soul. The word *Adam* means "of the red earth or dirt man." But after God formed Adam's body, the Bible says that God breathed into it the breath of life and man became a living soul (see Genesis 2:7). Here was something unique. In this one creation, God blended two elements—the physical and the spiritual.

As noted earlier, the words *breath* and *spirit* are synonymous. There is but one word in both Hebrew and Greek, the Hebrew word *ruach,* meaning "spirit, breath, or wind"; and the Greek word *pneuma,* meaning "spirit, breath and wind." Thus, one can just as easily read, "God breathed into man a spirit." God was saying, "I'm making man in My image." When God breathed into man, He put into human beings something from Himself. He put into man a spirit.

In a former chapter, it was noted that God created two realms of reality: the physical world and the spiritual world. God created humans with the ability to communicate with, and live in, both worlds. With the physical body, human beings relate to the physical world around them. Animals also are physical and they relate to the world about them. But unlike animals, human beings have a spirit. They commune with, communicate with, and are constantly aware of a spiritual dimension.

A good example of this physical and spiritual reality existing side by side, is found in the Book of Revelation. John wrote: "I . . . was on the island of Patmos because of . . . [my] testimony of Jesus " (1:9, *NIV*). In other words, physically, John was on an island. But John also wrote, "On the Lord's Day," which would have been Sunday, "I was in the Spirit" (1:10, *NIV*). His body was in a physical place called Patmos, but his spirit was in touch with the spirit world. God created human beings for both.

The Trinitarian Concept

We must note also that the Bible indicates a divine council prior to the creation of man. These are the words, "And God said, Let us make man in our image and after our likeness" (Genesis 1:26). Then the next verse records, "So God created man in his own image, in the image of God created he him; male and female created he them" (v. 27).

Of course, the question is, "With whom was God talking? To whom was He saying, 'Let *us* make man in *our* image?'" Some have speculated God was talking to the angelic hosts, but there is no hint anywhere in the Bible that angels were involved in Creation. In fact, angels are themselves created beings. So, to whom was God speaking?

In these words are revealed the very first Bible affirmation of the Trinitarian concept of God. The divine council was one that took place between God the Father, God the Son, and God the Holy Spirit. "Let us make man in our image." In the next verse when God did create man, He didn't say, "We made him after Our image," but rather He said, "In His image He created him" (see v. 27). This is a return to the singular, a strong indication here that there is one God, one Divine Being, existing within a plurality of Father, Son, and Holy Spirit.

The Image of God

What precisely does it mean that man (humankind) is created in the image of God? First, this reference certainly does not mean a physical image. God does not physically look like man. The Bible tells us "God is a Spirit" (John 4:24). After His resurrection, Jesus told the disciples they could touch Him, noting, "A [spirit] does not have flesh and bones" (Luke 24:39, *NIV*). So, spirit means nonphysical. God does not have a body. Thus, any reference to God's image in man refers to something other than the physical body.

Some will ask, "What about those Bible passages that refer to the hand of God, the eye of God, the ears of God, and so forth?" These are what is referred to in literature as *anthropomorphisms*, a mouthful of a word, which simply means "to explain something in human terms." There are occasions in the Bible, especially in the poetic works, where these anthropomorphisms are used to help explain God, who acts, sees, and hears. From the human perspective, one cannot help but think *hand* (instrument of action), *eye* (instrument of sight), and *ear* (instrument of sound).

Nevertheless, God in His essence does not have a body. This understanding highlights and makes all the more dramatic the incarnation (to be made flesh) of Jesus Christ, when He came to earth. He took on a human body, meaning He did not have one before. He even noted in prayer, according to Hebrews "a body you prepared for me" (Hebrews 10:5, *NIV*).

The image of God in man is a personal, spiritual and moral image. Man has the quality of personhood, like God. Human beings have longings; they are rational creatures (in other words, they can think); they have will, volition, and can make choices; and they are emotional with feelings. These are all characteristics of divinity. God breathed into man a different dimension, making him into a spiritual being with the capacity to commune with God.

Interestingly, the Greek word for man is *anthropos*, from which the word anthropomorphism comes. Another derivation from *anthropos* is the word *anthropology*, normally meaning "the study of man," but also "one who walks upright." Man is thus able to look up into the face of God.

Man's ability to look up into the face of God means more than the raising of one's physical head. It means one's ability to be conscious or aware of that which is transcendent. Man is the only created being aware of his own mortality. Animals do not discern this truth. They are not aware that one day they will die. In this aspect also is reflected God's image—a spiritual and moral consciousness.

The Moral Dimension

At the height of all Creation, God made man in true righteousness and holiness. Man was created perfect and innocent, and he was given a twofold responsibility.

First of all, man was given the responsibility, or the privilege, of communing with God. With man, God established a personal relationship. Every human being has this ability to commune with God. Secular science that views man only as "another animal" in the creative scheme of things always comes up short, unable to understand or explain much of the reality that makes up human life. Understanding of what it means to have a relationship with God brings to the human heart a sense of security not found elsewhere. A great relationship with God produces a sense of great security.

Man's assigned responsibility in the Garden was to rule over the lower creation, to bear offspring, and to fill the earth. Basically, man's responsibility was to extend the Garden throughout the world. Although it was noted earlier that the Garden of Eden is thought to have been located in a certain place on the world map, that was not supposed to be the end of the Garden of Eden. The Garden was supposed to be expanded to the entire world so that the glory of the Lord would fill the earth. The word *Eden* means "delight." God wanted His glory and His delight to fill the earth. It was man's responsibility to do that—expand the glory of the Lord to the whole world.

When Jesus gave the Great Commission to the disciples and said, "Go and make disciples of all nations" (Matthew 28:19, *NIV*), He expressed a New Testament version of what Adam and Eve were originally charged with doing. Their roles and responsibilities were indeed significant. Adam and Eve were created in perfect security and with significant responsibilities.

This truth makes it all the more poignant that when Adam sinned, so very much was lost. In Adam, man lost his security, his perfect and pure communion with God, his holy relationship, and he was driven from the Garden into a world where everything was hostile to him and his existence.

Human beings still yearn for the kind of security and significance that was known in the Garden of Eden. All human beings strive for what they were originally created to have, and to become the person whom they were created to be. In essence, the story and the struggles of all humanity is neither more nor less than the desire to get back to the Garden, to find once again that lost security and significance. In the good news of Jesus Christ, man has God's revelation of His pathway back to Him.

Creation Versus Evolution

No Christian study of Creation can be complete without mention of what has come to be known as the creation-evolution controversy. In this modern, so-called scientific age, those who embrace creationism as a credible theory may think of themselves as being viewed as dummies or simple-minded people. To believe that "In the beginning God created the heavens and the earth" may be a simple concept, but it is not a simple-minded one. Basically, the creationism theory contends that the universe does not hold within itself an explanation for its own origin or for its own existence. Many brilliant minds, true scientists in every sense of the word, agree with this idea.

This chapter will conclude with a look at the first of two very basic scientific laws that lend credence to the theory of creationism. All natural science is based upon two laws—laws so basic that if these two laws were not true, no natural science whatsoever could exist.

THE LAW OF CAUSALITY

This scientifically recognized law states that every result is the effect of a cause and no effect is greater than its cause. The finite must be caused. *Finite* means "that which has boundaries; that which has a beginning; that which has an end; that which is limited." In essence, everything other than God is finite. This means everything has to have a cause.

Philosophically, it is impossible to have an endless series of cause and effect. If one moves backward from one effect to its cause, and keeps moving backward, one will eventually come to something that is an uncaused cause. In other words, one comes to that which caused everything after it, but which was itself not caused. Philosophically, one has to come to that. When this uncaused cause is reached—no matter how long it takes, how many the steps or the stages or the light years—one eventually comes to something that is no longer finite.

What does that mean? It means that at some point one crosses a line, moving from the finite to the infinite. *Infinite* means "that which has no boundaries." The infinite is not bound by time; it has always been; it is not bound by space; it is everywhere (omnipresent). *Infinite* means "without boundaries of any type; transcendent." Thus, the uncaused cause is an infinite cause. This says that by the law of

49

causality, there is an infinite cause. By definition, God is infinite; God has no boundaries.

One's understanding of this truth is further aided by recognition that it is impossible to have two infinites. One cannot conceive of two infinite beings or of two infinite entities. How could one tell them apart? Where would one stop and the other begin? By definition, there can be only one infinite.

If the uncaused cause is infinite, then that uncaused cause must be a being that is called God. This also says something else: When one crosses the line between the caused and the uncaused, then one moves from the natural to the supernatural. The word *supernatural* simply means "something that is over the natural; it means infinite; it means God."

Thus, the cause of the universe has to be an infinite cause. It has to be a supernatural cause. The uncaused cause must be God, the prime mover, as it is so often referred to scientifically.

The next chapter will continue this discussion and open with a look at the second of the two basic scientific laws.

5

Genesis:
Sin and Its
Consequences

By Mike Chapman, D.Min.

Chapter 4 concluded with the broad heading, "Creationism Versus Evolution," and specifically with the first of two scientific laws that tend to confirm creationism as a valid theory of the universe. The first law, already discussed, is called the law of causality, which says, "every effect has to have a cause."

This chapter opens with an examination of the second scientific law—the law of uniformity— which says, "whatever caused some effect in the past will cause that same effect in the future." Both these laws are foundational in terms of modern science and recognized by virtually all scientific authorities. The question is, What does this second law mean and how does it relate to creationism?

Specified Complexity
There is a scientifically recognized type of order called specified complexity. This order is *complex*, meaning "it consists of a variety of parts, but it also has specific purpose." For example, one could say

51

the human body is a specified complexity. It has a variety of parts, but each part serves a specific purpose in terms of the whole.

Science says that anytime one sees a specified complexity there must be intelligence behind it. There is just no way to have specified complexity without intelligent intervention. That is not a preacher or a teacher talking; that is true scientific theory.

For instance, a person is walking on the seashore. Along the beach can be seen all the items normally found on a beach—rocks, seashells, a few dead starfish, wood, plastic debris, and other litter. This scene does not represent specified complexity. It may be complex, but it has no specific purpose, meaning it all just happened. No intelligent being arranged it.

However, suppose this person walking along the seashore comes suddenly upon a sand castle. It makes no difference whether the sand castle is elaborate, such as one built by a group of college art students, or very simple, such as one built by a three-year-old child, the sand castle represents a specified complexity. The same would be true if, on down the beach, the person noticed a drawing in the sand—a stick- or finger-drawn heart within which are the words, "Jimmy loves Susie." This is a specified complexity. It is complex, made up of different parts, but it has a specific purpose.

Upon seeing that heart in the sand, one knows an intelligent person did it. One does not have to speculate whether the ocean waves caused the sand castle and the drawn heart, nor does one wonder if the wind blew them into existence. One knows an intelligent mind was behind both the castle and the drawing.

Specified complexity always indicates intelligence—that is scientific law. This statement, of course, leads to the following question: When one looks at the universe, when one beholds all the beauty and intricacies of plant and animal life on this earth, when one glances in the mirror or examines the human body, is one beholding a specified complexity? Or, do these things represent a mere random happening such as litter on the beach? A rather stupid question, is it not? The answer is obvious. Wherever one sees a specified complexity, one sees intelligent intervention.

The law of uniformity says, "whatever caused some effect in the past will always cause that same effect in the future," and "whatever causes specified complexity will always cause specified complexity." And that is intelligence.

Thus, these two laws of science affirm the following: (1) the beginning of the universe had an infinite cause, and (2) that infinite cause had to have been an intelligent cause, not a random force. Christian believers, of course, well understand that the intelligent cause is simply another way of making reference to Almighty God.

Other Theories

Over the years, several concepts have been given as alternatives to creationism.

DUALISM

Dualism claims there are two infinites. God and the universe are both eternal, and the world has always been. A variation of this would be, the spirit world and the physical world have both always existed.

EMANATION

The emanation theory comes from pantheism, discussed in an earlier chapter, and claims the physical universe *is* God, or that God and the world are one. Therefore, the world had no beginning; it has always been. In this view, God is not personal. God is a kind of infinite force that permeates everything.

EVOLUTION

The most prominent view, however, especially in the Western world, is evolution, or spontaneous generation, a theory in opposition to creationism.

Evolution claims basically that "through a series of gradual changes, caused by random, but inherent forces, the universe came into existence." Evolutionists talk of "the big bang" from which all things originated, or they speak of something smaller than the atom from which, in time, all things now existing came to be.

First, it should be remembered that the theory of evolution is bad scientific theory. The two basic scientific laws just previously discussed prove it to be a bad scientific theory. In fact, most evolutionists know, and many evolutionists admit, that gaps exist in their theory. Bring up the theory of evolution to an avowed proponent and ask a question, virtually any question, and the evolutionist will invariably come back with something like this, "We know, but given enough time, anything could happen."

No less a well-known and credible scientist than George Wahl, Professor Emeritus at Harvard University, winner of the Nobel Prize in Biology, 1971, says,

There are only two possibilities as to how life arose. One is through spontaneous generation, a rising evolution. The other is through a supernatural act of God. There is no third possibility. Spontaneous generation was scientifically disproved 120 years ago by Pasteur and others. This leaves us with only one logical conclusion: life arose as a supernatural act of God.

However, Professor Wahl goes on to say,

I will not accept that philosophically, because I do not want to believe in God. Therefore, I choose to believe in what I know, I choose to believe in that which I know is scientifically impossible.

Here is a man who is a respected scientist, a man who says the evolutionary theory cannot be true; and yet a man who vows to hold to a false theory because he does not wish to believe in God. That says much about the root of today's popular evolution theory. If one rejects evolution, the only rational alternative is creationism. So, evolution struggles on.

A great gap exists between nothing and something. A big gap exists between matter which is seen and life which is not seen. A gap exists between animal life and human life. Evolution struggles with how to fill the gaps.

THEISTIC EVOLUTION

Theistic evolution concludes: "Well, God created the world, but He used evolution, or what is called evolution, as His method for doing it." This is, quite obviously, an attempt to bridge or merge a belief in God with a so-called scientific theory. Proponents would either see Genesis 1 as an allegory—a literary idea, but not a literal idea—or as a myth, something which describes a religious truth. Even though a number of good people have adopted this theory, it seems to have serious problems.

Worldview

These past two chapters have allotted much space to the subject of creation. Why? Because an individual's worldview is formed by what one believes about the origin of the universe. A worldview determines perspective, how one approaches life, and how one sees the issues of life. In fact, every individual's worldview can be rather succinctly portrayed with personal answers to four key questions:

1. Where did I come from?
2. Why am I here?
3. How should I live?
4. Where am I going?

How one answers the first question—the question of origin—will establish boundaries for how one answers the other three.

If indeed evolution is true, and if there were no God at the beginning . . . if the earth, the universe, and human beings are here by some kind of random chance . . . then the second question is moot. It is a dead issue. If evolution is true, people are here for no reason at all.

The passion of every human heart is to find meaning. Take God out of the beginning and there is no meaning. Take God out of the beginning and there is no morality. How can one possibly know right from wrong? How can there even be a right or wrong, without God in the beginning? The interesting flip side of that question is, If there be no God, then where does the human concept of morality and ethics come from in the first place?

> I visited the Ukraine not long ago, and I asked a group of college and university students, all raised under communism, "What is the purpose of life if there is no God in the beginning?" From a group of about 40 very intelligent, sharp students, I received blank stares. I phrased the question again: "What did your communist teachers tell you about the purpose of life?" Finally, they answered, "We were told the purpose of life is to be good and serve the government."
> "Well, where do you get that theory?"
> "It was imposed on us."
> "By whom?"
> "By communism."
> "What gave them the right to make such an imposition?"

That brings up the third question, of morality. If there is no God, then man becomes the measure of everything. Any morality is forced by the one who has the greatest power. In other words, the biggest guy, or the guy with the biggest stick or gun, rules. If there is no God at the beginning, then there is no meaning, there is no morality, there is no hope, no future, or eternal destiny.

Sin Enters the World

Genesis 3, gives the first presentation of sin. This chapter introduces "the evil one," Satan. Although in this account, he is referred to only as the Serpent, other passages, both in the Old and New Testaments, verify the serpent as Satan.

Adam and Eve sinned by breaking the one prohibition God placed on them—"Do not eat of this tree. You can eat of every other tree, but not this tree" (see v. 3). Satan's temptation of Eve was typical of all sin. He made her to question God's integrity, to question whether God actually said, or actually meant, what He said.

Eve and Adam both ate of the forbidden fruit from the tree "of the knowledge of good and evil" (2:17). They broke the covenant God made with them and they came under the curse of God's judgment. The immediate result of their sin was death, meaning immediate separation from God, meaning physical death of the body, and meaning ultimately the second death—hell, the bottomless pit.

There was a threefold consequence of this death.

1. *Guilt.* Adam stood condemned before God in a broken covenant relationship. Every human being inherits Adam's sin and Adam's debt. Every person is therefore born guilty and in sin, condemned before God.

2. *Depravity.* That word simply means moral pollution. No one has to teach a child how to sin. The knowledge and the penchant for sin is there at birth. One never has to teach a child to lie. Sin is inherent. Depravity means moral pollution.

3. *Inability.* Human beings are helpless and totally unable to change or remove themselves from

this sinful condition. Try as one may with human strength, one remains the same—a sinner. The beauty of God's salvation in Jesus Christ is that He offers a cure for all these inherent consequences of sin. For guilt, God's plan offers justification. For depravity, God provides sanctification. For inability, God gives the miraculous strength of new birth through regeneration.

Driven from the Garden, Adam and Eve lost their security. They began life under the curse of sin, facing undreamed of difficulties. Their shame was immediately expressed when they hid themselves. They made excuses and blamed others for their problems. They learned the meaning of fear. The very thing that was supposed to be a joy for Adam, his work, now became his curse, demanding the sweat of his brow. God's blessing upon Eve, childbearing, now became for her tainted with sorrow and pain. Tensions entered the picture, and the curse was expanded through the words, "Your desire will be for your husband, and he will rule over you" (Genesis 3:16, *NIV*). Though some may view the husband's rule over the wife as a blessing, all should remember it was part of the curse of sin and it brings trouble, not blessing. Satan himself was placed under the curse and will eventually be destroyed.

As a result of sin, the whole universe was placed under a curse (Romans 8:18-22). The whole creation longs for redemption, and one day God will create new heavens and a new earth and there shall be no more curse (Revelation 22:3).

Promised Savior

In Genesis 3, in the midst of this terrible situation, God speaks the first proclamation of the gospel—the good news. God said to Satan, " I will put enmity between thee and the woman, and between thy seed and her seed; it shall bruise thy head, and thou shalt bruise his heel" (v. 15). This was the first promise in the Bible that a Savior, a Messiah, a Redeemer would one day come.

This passage truly relates some very interesting things. First, it says the "seed of the woman." That sounds strange because one usually thinks of the "seed of the man." Many scholars believe this early passage is a foreshadowing of the virgin birth of Jesus, the seed of woman rather than man.

Second, the passage speaks of spiritual warfare. There was going to be strife between the followers of Satan and the followers of the seed of the woman. All humanity was going to be divided into two groups, some of the seed of the woman, some of the seed of the serpent.

Third, it also says the day will come when the head of the serpent, the authority of Satan, is going to be crushed, and the instrument of that crushing will be the bruised heel of the seed of the woman. Satan bruised His heel, but He crushed Satan's head.

Had God left out the third chapter of Genesis, man would have no idea, no explanation, for the existence of evil on this earth. Had God not told man about this sin, he would not know where evil came from.

Judgment for Sin

Genesis 4 gives the story of Cain and Abel and the first murder. Then a third son, Seth, was born. All of his descendants and all of mankind can be divided into two categories—the God rejecters, generally thought of as the line of Cain, or the seed of the serpent, and the God followers, the line of Seth, or the seed of the woman.

The Bible speaks of the sons of God marrying the daughters of men and some have speculated this to have been a kind of demon/human sexual union that produced a strange hybrid being. Such an idea does not make a whole lot of sense. A far more likely interpretation is that the references "sons of God" and "the daughters of men" mean the descendants of Seth and the descendants of Cain. Intermarriage between the God followers and the God rejecters eventually led to unabated wickedness in the land.

This quick overview leads to Genesis 6 and the story of Noah and the Flood. By the time of Noah, God could find only eight righteous people (God followers) on the earth—Noah and his wife, their three sons, and their wives.

God chose to destroy the world by a great flood—a flood which was both the mercy and judgment of God. Here one begins to see a more detailed introduction of the concept of God's judgment, a detailing of the fact that God judges sin. The Flood was judgment on the God rejecters. The Flood was also mercy and grace, a merciful surgery on the human race which cut out the evil, cancerous tissue in order to allow the healthy tissue to restore itself.

Some people would have one believe the Old Testament is all about law, and not about grace; but the story of the Flood also tells of God's grace. "Noah found grace in the eyes of the Lord" (Genesis 6:8). For 120 years Noah worked on the ark. That time span was a period of grace. While he was building the ark, Noah was a preacher of righteousness.

During that time, any one of the God rejecters could have become a God follower just by accepting Noah's message.

What a message it must have been when the animals came marching to the ark. Noah did not go out and round up the animals. God sent them. Even after they were on the ark, and Noah and his family were there, the Scripture says there were seven more days during which the door was open. God was saying, "Anyone else can come on board. This is your chance. The door is open." Was that not a door of grace? At the end of seven days, God closed the door. That was God's way of saying the day of my favor, of my mercy, is over.

The rain came. It rained for 40 days and 40 nights. Then, for 150 days the waters covered the earth. Bible scholars figure that Noah, his family and the animals, were on the ark for approximately one year before it finally came to rest on the mountain of Ararat.

One interesting thing to note is that following the Flood, Scripture indicates a dramatic decrease in the life expectancy of people on earth. Prior to the Flood there is a record of people living for 600, 800, and even 900 years. After the Flood, the life expectancy began to go down. Some speculate the Flood brought an ecological change, with more ultraviolet rays getting to the earth and reducing the life span. Others suppose God allowed early generations to live longer in order to populate the earth. Whatever the reason, there was a dramatic drop off. Abraham seems to have lived a very long time, about 175 years, but by David's time, one is fortunate and blessed to live 70 years.

Beginning of the Nations

The final point to be covered in the Creation Era is the beginning of the nations, a recounting of what happened after Noah's sons left the ark. According to Scripture, all ethnic groupings of people upon the earth are the descendants of Noah's three sons—Ham, Shem, and Japheth.

The descendants of Japheth seemed to have gone north and northwest and later, perhaps, into Europe. The descendants of Ham tended to go south and southwest to Egypt, Africa, Arabia and the eastern coast of the Mediterranean Sea. The descendants of Shem settled in the Near East, with some groups going south to Arabia and southeast to Persia.

Basically, the Flood gave mankind a fresh start. Man failed again. This time man built a tower, an ancient temple. It was a place of worship. Instead of God's way, the Tower of Babel once again represented failure, and God confused the languages so nations of the earth would be formed.

6

Genesis: The Patriarch Era: Part 1

By Mike Chapman, D.Min.

The traditional understanding of the Book of Genesis is that Moses was the author, and it was written around 1440 B.C. during the Israelites' wandering from Egypt to Canaan. The word *Genesis* simply means "beginning." In step with its meaning, the Book of Genesis records the beginning of the universe, man, sin, prophecy, nations, languages, and of the Hebrew nation.

The key geographic locations mentioned in the Book of Genesis are Eden, Mount Ararat, and Babel. The key people are Adam, Eve, Cain, Abel, Seth, Noah, Japheth, Shem, and Ham.

In the first 11 chapters of Genesis, the human race was tested three times—in the Garden of Eden, at the time of the Flood, and at the Tower of Babel—and each testing ended in failure.

This chapter shifts from the Creation Era to the Patriarch Era, and God's continuing efforts to establish a relationship with mankind.

Historical Backdrop

The Patriarch Era covers the lives of four men—Abraham, Isaac, Jacob and Joseph. Their stories constitute the greater part of the Book of Genesis (Chapters 12 through 50), beginning with the call of Abram. Just as Adam was the key person in the study of the Creation Era, so Abraham is the key person in the Patriarch Era. The location of this study is primarily in Canaan, and the time frame is somewhere between 2100 and 1870 B.C. The story-line summary for this study is simple: Abraham is *chosen* by God to father a *people* to *represent* God to the world. Those three highlighted words—*chosen, people, represent*—establish the key concept for the Patriarch Period.

TIME OF ABRAHAM'S BIRTH

All events prior to Abraham fall into a time period rather difficult to pinpoint, but the birth of Abraham is easier. Here is the reasoning by which a fairly certain date is established.

Solomon began his reign around 970 B.C., a date historically verifiable through accounts other than the Bible. He began construction of the Temple in the fourth year of his reign, or 966 B.C. First Kings 6:1 states the Exodus occurred 481 years before the beginning of the construction of the Temple. Jacob and his family went into Canaan 430 years prior to the Exodus, and Scripture reveals that Abraham entered Canaan 215 years prior to Jacob and the family, about 2091 B.C. Abraham was 75 years old at that time, making his date of birth approximately 2166 B.C.

PLACE OF ABRAHAM'S BIRTH

Abraham's home was Ur, probably not far from the original Garden of Eden, in the land of the Chaldeans, later known as Babylon. Abraham began his journey from Ur to Haran, from which he followed the natural curve of the Fertile Crescent down to Canaan, a distance of approximately 1,500 miles. With the exception of periodic sojourns in Egypt, all studies in this chapter take place within this geographic location.

Abraham's birthplace was a very prominent city, blessed with what one might call an ancient university with a large library of clay tablets. Commerce was well developed, serviced by ships from the Persian Gulf. Since the main god of the people of Ur was the moon god, Nana, one can surmise that Abram was raised a pagan. Nevertheless, God in His wisdom and sovereignty spoke to, and called Abram—a perfect example of divine election. God always chooses men before men choose God. By faith Abram followed God.

EXPANDED SUMMARY

Abraham's call is detailed in Genesis 12–23, with references also found in the New Testament—Acts 7:2-4 and Hebrews 11:8-12. His father was Terah, who moved his family to Haran in northern Mesopotamia, about 600 miles northwest of Ur. In those days families were like clans, a Bedouin-type nomadic, extended family. Scripture indicates Abram stayed in Haran until his father died. His two brothers Haran and Nahor were there as well.

After the death of Terah, God came personally in some form to Abram and called him. Abraham responded and made his way into the strange and unknown land of Canaan. One does not know for sure how God communicated with Abram, but one thing is known for sure from Scripture, and that is, Abram knew he followed God's leading. The writer of Hebrews stated it this way: "By faith Abraham, when he was called to go out into a place which he should after receive for an inheritance, obeyed; and he went out, not knowing whither he went" (11:8).

On the journey to Canaan, Abram came to know God in a more intimate manner. He came to know who God was and something of His purpose. Thus, the journey to Canaan was more than a mere trip; it was also Abram's time of getting to know God.

The Abrahamic Covenant

The God of all creation is a covenant God. He had a covenant with Adam. He formed a covenant with Noah. In Genesis 12, the Abrahamic covenant is revealed. Scripture records Abram's call and God's promise in this manner:

> Now the Lord had said unto Abram, Get thee out of thy country, and from thy kindred, and from thy father's house, unto a land that I will shew thee: and I will make of thee a great nation, and I will bless thee, and make thy name great; and thou shalt be a blessing: and I will bless them that bless thee, and curse him that curseth thee: and in thee shall all families of the earth be blessed (Genesis 12:1-3).

This covenant with Abraham was the beginning of the people of Israel—the nation of Israel. God promised to bless Abram, to make his name great, and to make of him a great nation; furthermore, He also promised to bless all the families of the earth through Abraham, a reference to the coming of the promised Messiah, Jesus Christ. Through Messiah, all nations of the earth would be blessed.

God's purpose for Israel was fourfold:

1. To witness to the rest of humanity of the nature and reality of God. Israel was to be God's people—servant-witnesses in the world.

2. To be a repository of His revelation. Through Israel, God would reveal Himself as Almighty God in acts, in judgments, and through the scriptures of the Old Testament. The scriptures of the Old Testament came through the Jews—the national repository into which God poured the revelation of Himself.

3. To be a channel for the Messiah, Savior, and Redeemer.

4. To be a channel of blessing for the entire world.

Believers in Jesus Christ today are chosen for the same purpose, to be servant-witnesses of God's grace. To speak of the people of Israel and the people of God today as "chosen" is not to place on them a mere title to wear or some badge of honor to display to the world, but it means they are chosen for God's purpose.

God's covenant with Abraham included the sacrifice of animals. Therefore, it was a blood covenant, a binding covenant: "And he (God) said to him (Abram), take me an heifer of three years old, and a she goat of three years old, and a ram of three years old, and a turtledove, and a young pigeon " (Genesis 15:9).

In Genesis 17, the covenant was more firmly established through the rite of circumcision, which God described as "a token of the covenant betwixt me and you" (Genesis 17:11). Circumcision is a continuing religious ritual among Jews. Every Jewish male child is circumcised on the 8th day of birth as a sign of the covenant people of God. However, the Bible stresses that this physical circumcision is far less important than circumcision of the heart (the removal of sin from one's heart). In the New Testament, circumcision was replaced by water baptism as a sign of the covenant and as a sign of one's entrance into the people of God.

This was also the occasion at which God gave Abram a new name, changing it from Abram to *Abraham*, meaning "a father of many nations" (Genesis 17:5).

The Testing of Faith

The faith of Abraham was tested time after time during the next 25 years as he waited for the promised son through whom he was to become the father of many nations. Many have speculated on all those long years of waiting, and of wandering, but the Bible says God renewed His covenant with Abraham and then miraculously gave him Isaac, the son of promise.

The pivotal event in development of Abraham's faith came some years after Isaac was born. God spoke to Abraham in these words, "Take now thy son, thine only son, Isaac, whom thou lovest, and get thee into the land of Moriah; and offer him there for a burnt offering upon one of the mountains which I will tell thee of" (Genesis 22:2).

Abraham demonstrated his willingness to obey. In all likelihood, Isaac was a full adult. Obviously, he was no child because of the conversation that took place between him and his father as they make their way up the mountain. This incident is used often, and properly so, to demonstrate the faith of Abraham; but it should be noted that it also demonstrates the faith of Isaac, second of the Patriarchs, for he gave no resistance to Abraham's commandment from God.

God's covenant promises are always put to the test. His covenant with Adam was tested by the Tree of Knowledge of Good and Evil; His covenant with Noah by the command to build an ark; and here the covenant is tested by Abraham's faith, couched in terms of his being told to sacrifice his only son.

In these modern times, it seems strange, almost unthinkable, that God would make such a request of a father. However, the truths become more obvious as the whole story comes into focus.

First, one must keep in mind that God was testing Abraham's faith in His integrity. God intervened and rescued Isaac, but only after Abraham had proven his willingness to obey. The story bears this out. Abraham said to his servants who had gone with him to the foot of Mount Moriah, "Stay here with the donkey while I and the boy go over there. We will worship and then we will come back to you" (22:5, *NIV*). Those words prove Abraham fully expected that, even if he went through with this sacrifice, his son would be raised from the dead.

The Book of Hebrews elaborates even further on this theme (11:17-19).

Second, it is significant that Abraham took Isaac to Mount Moriah, the very mountain which, according to tradition, would later become the Temple Mount in the city of Jerusalem. At the moment Abraham was prepared to sacrifice his son, an angel appeared, saying, "Abraham, Abraham . . . Lay not thine hand upon the lad, neither do thou any thing unto him: for now I know that thou fearest God, seeing thou hast not withheld thy son, thine only son from me" (Genesis 22:11, 12). Abraham looked over and saw a ram caught in a bush. Abraham proved his faith: God provided the sacrifice.

JEHOVAH-JIREH

Abraham named the place *Jehovah-Jireh*, meaning "my Lord will provide." The words *Jehovah-Jireh* literally mean "God who sees ahead of time." He is saying, "God is a provider, but He has provided a long time before the need ever arose." In other words, from Abraham's perspective, God knew at that moment he would need a substitute sacrifice and, before he even came to the top of the mountain, God ensnared a ram by his horns. This God— Jehovah, the Almighty—is Jehovah-Jireh.

When God's people today claim the provision of God and say, "Oh Lord, you are Jehovah-Jireh," they are essentially saying, "God, you have seen the need before it even arose. You knew this need would be here and You are the One who has already made provision." Jesus himself confirmed this when He said, "your Father knoweth what things ye have need of, before ye ask him" (Matthew 6:8).

72

This story presents a most interesting situation. Abraham was going up one side of the mountain with Isaac; while going up the other side of the mountain, unknown to Abraham and Isaac, was a ram, God's prepared sacrifice. Both were moving toward the place of sacrifice at the same time, both moving at the will and behest of the Almighty, and the meeting was to be both symbolic and prophetic of the coming central event of history.

What a phenomenal picture! Here is humanity, cloaked in sin, going up one side of history to this place of sacrifice; while, on the other side of history, unseen by human eyes, God is sending the sacrificial Lamb (His only begotten Son) to atone for the sin of the world. And the meeting place is Calvary. What a graphic picture God portrays to help people fully understand what is really taking place through the gift of His Son.

God's People

The blessing of Abraham was transferred through his family and would eventually be received by all people of faith. In other words, all the descendants of Abraham are recipients of the Abrahamic covenant. Each believer, each one who has faith in Christ, is of Abraham's seed (Galatians 3). Each is a descendant of Abraham. That means the Abrahamic covenant is also the believer's covenant today. That means that when one speaks of the chosen people of God, one refers to the Jewish people through whom came the Messiah, Jesus Christ, and all who believe on His name. Every believer in Jesus Christ is part of that group, a chosen individual, heir of the covenant of God.

The apostle Paul writes about this in three chapters of the Book of Romans: 9, 10, 11. He writes of the root and the trunk of the tree. He mentions the natural branches of the tree, which were Israel, but goes on to say that, because they did not believe on Jesus, they were cut off and God chose some wild branches, the Gentiles, and grafted them into the tree. God also promised that, when all these Gentile branches are grafted in, He is going to go back to the natural branches and bring them back. God's covenant with Israel is eternal, and history has yet to show precisely how it will all work out. Paul does give a warning to believers, however, by noting that one must be careful in terms of how he lives and respects this covenant. If God can remove the natural branches of the tree, then how much easier can He remove those grafted in if they fail to keep His commandments.

According to the Scriptures, there is yet to come a restoration of multitudes of Jewish people who believe upon and accept Jesus as the Messiah.

Christian believers today need to understand what Paul made very clear. God does not have two groups of chosen people. Those who contend there is an Old Testament chosen people, Israel, and a New Testament chosen people, the church, have failed to understand the Abrahamic covenant as fulfilled in the coming of Messiah. They have failed to grasp the way of faith as revealed in the story of Abraham.

The Bible says He has made both one, breaking down the wall of petition. There is one people of God, one new creation in Christ. Note these words from the Book of Ephesians:

> For we are his workmanship, created in Christ Jesus unto good works, which God hath before ordained that we should walk in them. Wherefore remember, that ye being in time past Gentiles in the flesh, who are called uncircumcision by that which is called the circumcision in the flesh made by hands; that at that time ye were without Christ, being aliens from the commonwealth of Israel, and strangers from the covenants of promise, having no hope, and without God in the world: but now in Christ Jesus ye who sometimes were far off are made nigh by the blood of Christ. For he is our peace, who hath made both one, and hath broken down the middle wall of partition between us; having abolished in his flesh the enmity, even the law of commandments contained in ordinances; for to make in himself of twain one new man, so making peace (Ephesians 2:10-15).

Gentile believers and the church have not replaced Israel in terms of the Abrahamic covenant, but they have joined them and there will be a restoration of many Jews who will come to know Jesus as Messiah sometime in the future.

The Abrahamic covenant forms the foundation of two other special covenants as well: the Palestinian covenant (Deuteronomy 30), which relates to God's promise that the land of Palestine would be the heritage of Israel forever; and the Davidic covenant (2 Samuel 7), which establishes the throne of David forever and which is fulfilled through Messiah who sits upon that throne.

The Two Sons of Abraham

Abraham had two sons, Ishmael, the son of Hagar, and Isaac, the son of promise. He later had other sons by another wife.

Ishmael was the product of Abraham's taking things into his own hands. He seems to have said to himself, "Now God, you told me I was going to have a child and my wife Sarah is barren and I am getting old, so I guess I am going to have to figure out something on my own." He therefore fathered a son by Sarah's servant, Hagar. Abraham was 86 years old when Ishmael was born, meaning he had waited 11 years from the time of the promise.

What Abraham did was not an uncommon custom in ancient times. It was done with his wife's agreement. From this union with Hagar, through Ishmael, has come the Arab people found in the Middle East to this very day. Two groups of people—Jews and Arabs—both the offspring of Abraham, still have conflict to this very day.

There was jealousy and tension between Sarah and Hagar from the very beginning. Sarah was jealous that Hagar had a son and she did not. This continued until Ishmael was 16 years old and was sent away. Interestingly enough, while they were in the desert and it appeared they were near death, Scripture records the appearance of one called the angel of the Lord. This was a special messenger from God that instructed Ishmael and Hagar how they could survive, led them to safety, and made them a promise.

Many people mistakenly think Isaac was given everything and Ishmael nothing; but, if one reads closely in Genesis 16, one discovers that God made promises concerning a future inheritance to the descendants of Ishmael. Ishmael loved his father Abraham and, when Abraham died, both he and Isaac buried him.

Abraham was 100 years old and Sarah was 90 when Isaac was born. The name *Isaac* means "laughter," referring to the fact that Sarah laughed at the thought she would have a child at her advanced age. Since Sarah died at the age of 120, she lived long enough to see her son Isaac become a grown man.

Abraham, according to Scripture, married a second wife, Keturah, and she bore him six sons later. Abraham died at the age of 175. He was buried in a place called Machpelah, in the ancient city of Hebron, which still exists today.

In time, Isaac and Jacob, along with their wives, would also be buried there, making Hebron a very special place to the Jews today.

7

Genesis: The Patriarch Era: Part 2

By Mike Chapman, D.Min.

The last chapter introduced Abram, the first patriarch of Israel, with his amazing migration from Ur to Haran and eventually to Canaan. God made a very special covenant with Abram and changed his name to *Abraham*, meaning "the father of many nations." God's covenant with Abraham was a covenant of blessing, not only for Abraham but for the whole world. As a parallel to the account of Abraham, it was noted how all Christian believers today are part of that covenant, for they are the spiritual descendants of Abraham through Jesus Christ.

The chapter closed with two pertinent observations: First, God has only one people, and they are represented in the Abrahamic covenant in which Israel was the chosen channel through which the Messiah, Jesus Christ of Nazareth, would be introduced to the world. God has always loved Israel and has promised to draw the people of Israel back into the fold in the end time, when they will come to accept Christ as the Messiah. Second, even as Isaac, the son of promise, became father of the Jewish nation, Abraham's other son, Ishmael (born to Sarah's handmaiden Hagar), became father of the Arab nations.

Abraham and Melchizedek

Genesis 14 suddenly introduces a mysterious man by the name of Melchizedek. The introduction of this man comes in only three verses, but they reveal some important truths which are referenced later in the Book of Psalms and especially by the writer of Hebrews:

> And Melchizedek king of Salem brought forth bread and wine: and he was the priest of the most high God. And he blessed him, and said, Blessed be Abram of the most high God, possessor of heaven and earth: And blessed be the most high God, which hath delivered thine enemies into thy hand. And he gave him tithes of all" (Genesis 14:18-20).

Melchizedek was from a very small city called Salem, thought by many to be the root beginning of what eventually became the city of Jerusalem. He was both king and priest of the city of Salem. That in itself is something very unique.

Since Abraham's encounter with Melchizedek took place long before the time of Moses, there had been no priesthood instituted, no Ten Commandments delivered, no law of God established, and no Tabernacle. Yet there was a priest who predated, by hundreds of years, the very first priest in Israel, who would be Aaron.

Melchizedek, this unique figure that appeared out of nowhere, became legendary in Jewish mentality. Many began to think he was an appearance of God. Bible scholars know little of the circumstances surrounding this meeting, nor of how Abraham came to know Melchizedek, but the scriptures indicate he paid him special homage. Not only that, but Abraham gave ten percent of all his possessions to Melchizedek, the first incident of tithing recorded in the Bible.

Melchizedek is mentioned in Psalms with a prophetic reference to the Messiah: "The Lord hath sworn, and will not repent, Thou art a priest for ever after the order of Melchizedek" (110:4). In the New Testament, the writer of Hebrews has even more to say about Melchizedek (Hebrews 5, 6 and 7). Many believe the appearance of Melchizedek was a theophany, an Old Testament appearance of Jesus Christ.

Whether that be true or not (there are good arguments among Bible scholars for both views), one does know for sure that Melchizedek was a type of Christ. A *type* is terminology used for "example or prototype," someone who helps one see what Messiah would be like prior to His coming. In fact, the writer in Psalms and the writer of the Book of Hebrews make it very clear that Jesus was a "priest for ever after the order of Melchizedek."

When Moses instituted the priesthood under the direction of God, it was an Aaronic priesthood, a spiritual dynasty under the line of Aaron. But the Melchizedek priesthood preceded that, meaning

Jesus was priest before there ever was an earthly priest. Jesus was always the true high priest of God. Aaron was but an object lesson of Christ's eternal priesthood. So, Jesus was a priest after the order of Melchizedek, an eternal priest, not like human priests, but a priest forever. This priest either appeared or was personified in the person of Melchizedek during the life of Abraham.

The Angel of Light

Another unique occurrance in the life of Abraham was an appearance of the angel of light— the angel of the Lord. Sometimes one can mistakenly read this passage in the Bible and just assume it refers to another angel, but most Bible scholars believe anytime one sees the full phrase "the angel of the Lord," that it is not just an angel or just some men in white, but it is a theophany. The angel of the Lord in the Bible was indeed God in a manifest way— it was God manifested in a human way. The first Old Testament appearance of the angel of the Lord, believed to have been Jesus Christ, occurred during the life of Abraham.

It was an angel of the Lord that appeared to Hagar and Ishmael and these appearances were repeated throughout the Patriarch Period and even into other periods of Old Testament history. One of the most dramatic appearances came in the life of Jacob where he wrestled with the Lord. Initially, Scripture said he wrestled with an angel, but when it was all over, it said he wrestled with God. Most conclude Jacob's encounter was with God in the form of an angel, a unique and special angel that really was not an angel at all. Jacob wrestled with God.

Righteousness by Faith

Another important revelation from the life of Abraham is the principle of righteousness by faith. The Bible says that Abraham believed God and it was accounted to him as righteousness (Genesis 15:6). In the Book of Romans, Paul says Abraham is the father of all those who are made righteous by faith (4:1-3). That simply means Abraham taught the principle of imputed righteousness by faith rather than righteousness by works.

Justification by faith became a major theme of Paul's writings, especially in Romans and Galatians. All human efforts and good works fall short of making any individual righteous in the sight of God. It is only through faith in the atonement of His Son Jesus Christ that any sinner is made righteous. By trusting in Jesus, by believing in Him, believers are accepted, forgiven, and adopted into the family of God. Abraham was the first example in which the Bible sets forth this marvelous truth.

ISAAC, THE SECOND PATRIARCH

One might say that Isaac is the second father of promise. His story is found in Genesis 24–26. Isaac chose his wife, Rebekah, from his homeland and married at about the age of 40. He continued to live in the Land of Promise, becoming even more prosperous than his father, Abraham. The Bible describes how Abraham and his extended family lived basically in tents. By the time of Isaac, they were becoming more established as permanent residents of the territory.

The Bible does not give a very detailed account of the life of Isaac, but he was faithful to the God of

Abraham; therefore, God renewed for him the promise He had made to his father: "I will make thy seed to multiply as the stars of heaven, and will give unto thy seed all these countries; and in thy seed shall all the nations of the earth be blessed" (Genesis 26:4). Isaac died a very old man, best remembered as being the father of twin sons, Jacob and Esau.

Jacob, the third patriarch

Jacob occupies a most favorable spot in the patriarchal lineup. Since his name was changed from Jacob to Israel, every reference to the nation of Israel, even today, honors his memory.

Jacob had two wives, Leah and Rachel, both daughters of his Uncle Laban. From the beginning, Jacob was in love with Rachel; however, he was tricked into marrying the older sister, Leah, first, and then he had to work seven more years for Rachel (Genesis 29).

Scripture records that Jacob had two very important encounters with God. Jacob's first encounter took place when he fled home and was making his way to the house of his Uncle Laban (Genesis 28). This was the occasion of Jacob's dream of the ladder set up from earth to heaven, with descending and ascending angels. It was on this occasion that God confirmed the Abrahamic covenant to Jacob:

> And he dreamed, and behold a ladder set
> up on the earth, and the top of it reached
> to heaven: and behold the angels of God
> ascending and descending on it. And,
> behold, the Lord stood above it, and said, I

am the Lord God of Abraham thy father, and the God of Isaac: the land whereon thou liest, to thee will I give it, and to thy seed; and thy seed shall be as the dust of the earth, and thou shalt spread abroad to the west, and to the east, and to the north, and to the south: and in thee and in thy seed shall all the families of the earth be blessed. And, behold, I am with thee, and will keep thee in all places whither thou goest, and will bring thee again into this land; for I will not leave thee, until I have done that which I have spoken to thee of (vv. 12-15).

One significant aspect to this dream is its indication of activity going on in the spirit world between heaven and earth. God was wanting Jacob to know His blessing was coming to him, the very same covenant promise that God had made to his father, Isaac, and to his grandfather, Abraham. Jacob named the place Bethel. Today's pronunciation is Bethel, but Jacob probably called it *Beth,* meaning "house" and *el,* meaning "God," or together "the house of God."

Jacob's second important encounter with God occurred many years later, after his sojourn with Laban, when he had become very wealthy, and when he was about to be confronted by his twin brother, Esau. Through deceit, Jacob had laid claim to the birthright which should have gone to Esau, the first-born of the twin brothers. Although it had been revealed to both Isaac and Rebekah that Jacob, not Esau, would be the son of promise, Jacob and his mother had not been willing to wait for God to work things out. They had schemed to take the birthright, the result of which caused Jacob to be forced to flee home and caused the continuing strife between the two brothers. Esau, in fact, threatened to kill his brother.

Even after many years, when the heart of Jacob yearned for reconciliation with Esau, the occasion of meeting was tense. With anguish of soul, and at another place similar to Bethel, Jacob wrestled with God. It is amazing how God uses all kinds of people. Jacob was not a good guy; he was a schemer, a deceiver, a thief. Nevertheless, through the years, God worked a great change in the heart of Jacob. This is dramatically noted in the words of his prayer shortly before meeting with Esau:

> And Jacob said, O God of my father Abraham, and God of my father Isaac, the Lord which saidst unto me, return unto thy country, and to thy kindred, and I will deal well with thee: I am not worthy of the least of all the mercies, and of all the truth, which thou hast shewed unto thy servant; for with my staff I passed over this Jordan; and now I am become two bands. Deliver me, I pray thee, from the hand of my brother, from the hand of Esau: for I fear him, lest he will come and smite me, and the mother with the children. And thou saidst, I will surely do thee good, and make thy seed as the sand of the sea, which cannot be numbered for multitude (Genesis 32:9-12).

Out of this humility and in response to God's voice, Jacob chose a very generous gift in hopes of reconciliation with Esau.

Basically, though, the issue was not how good or how bad Jacob was. The issue was God's veracity and the covenant He had made with Abraham. God always keeps His covenant. The night before Jacob was to meet his brother Esau, he wrestled with the angel of the Lord at a place called Peniel. Initially, as noted earlier, the scripture does not say Jacob wrestled with the Lord, but it says so later. *To wrestle* means "to be stubborn and tenacious." Jacob would not let go. He needed reassurance, and he was determined to find it. As the night wore on and dawn neared, the angel touched Jacob's thigh, and it was knocked out of joint. The angel of the Lord blessed Jacob and changed his name to *Israel*, meaning "a prince with God." "And he said, thy name shall be called no more Jacob, but Israel: for as a prince hast thou power with God and with men, and hast prevailed" (Genesis 32:28).

From that time on, Jacob walked with a limp. Nevertheless, the miracle of God's blessing was immediately seen in the encounter with Esau. What had at first promised to be a fierce battle, with perhaps many lives being lost, turned into a peaceful meeting, with two brothers settling their differences in a notable manner: "And Esau ran to meet him, and embraced him, and fell on his neck, and kissed him: and they wept" (Genesis 33:4).

Jacob was the father of 12 sons. Each son became the head of one of the 12 tribes of Israel or the children of Israel.

JOSEPH, THE FOURTH PATRIARCH

Joseph's story is told in Genesis 37–50. Of all the 12 sons of Jacob, Joseph was the most committed to the Abrahamic covenant. He was also one of the two sons of Rachel, Jacob's favorite wife, the other being Benjamin. Jacob showed his love for Joseph with the presentation of a coat of many colors. Joseph shared his dreams with his brothers, dreams in which they paid him homage, and which they did not appreciate. His jealous brothers at first wanted to kill Joseph, but later they agreed to a scheme through which they sold him to Midianite slave traders on their way to Egypt and then lied to their father by pretending Joseph was indeed dead.

Upon arrival in Egypt and through circumstances the Scripture clearly indicates to be the providential care of God, Joseph became the prime minister of Egypt, or as one popular movie called him, the prince of Egypt. Highlights of Joseph's story involve service in the home of Potiphar, betrayal by Potiphar's wife when he refused her sexual advances, and imprisonment.

While Joseph was in prison, he interpreted dreams for two key officials of Pharaoh's palace, a cup bearer and a butler. One had a good dream, the other a nightmare. Joseph told the butler he was going to die, and three days later, he was hanged. He told the cup bearer he was going to be set free and restored to his position. Joseph also asked the cup bearer to remember him when he was back in the presence of the Pharaoh. However, the cup bearer forgot about Joseph for two years. Then, when Pharaoh had a dream, the cup bearer remembered a man in prison who was good at interpreting dreams.

Joseph interpreted the Pharaoh's dream which was about seven years of plenty to be followed by seven years of famine. As a result, Joseph was released from prison, put in charge of storing the grain, and of preparing the entire nation for the coming famine. Joseph became what one would probably refer to today as the prime minister of Egypt.

The famine was so severe it affected all the surrounding nations, including Canaan. While others suffered, Egypt had food. Joseph's family came to Egypt, seeking food, with no suspicion it was their brother Joseph who was in charge of the store houses of grain. A great family reunion took place. All the family moved to Egypt. Joseph held no bitterness, because he saw in all these circumstances once again the providential working of God. He told his brothers, "But as for you, ye thought evil against me; but God meant it unto good, to bring to pass, as it is this day, to save much people alive" (Genesis 50:20).

Jacob's family numbered about 70 when they all moved to be with Joseph, thus beginning a 430-year sojourn in the land of Egypt.

Joseph died at the age of 110. At his death, all the children of Israel were in Egypt. They enjoyed certain privileges while Joseph lived and even while he was remembered, but they eventually lost their favored status. Joseph wanted his family to know that Egypt was not to be their permanent home. They would one day return to Canaan, and he made them promise that, when they returned, they would take his bones with them. Later, one of the most moving scenes of the Exodus took place when the bones of Joseph were dug up and carried back to the land of Canaan.

Before Jacob died, he blessed the two sons of Joseph, Manasseh and Ephraim, noting that they would receive a double blessing when the nation of Israel would be formed. On a map of the 12 tribes of Israel, there is no tribe of Joseph. But there are two tribes—Manasseh and Ephraim—which represent his double portion as prophesied by his father, Jacob.

The Bible records this genealogy. Terah was the father of Abraham. Abraham fathered Isaac, the son of promise. Isaac had two sons, Jacob and Esau, with Jacob being the son of promise. Jacob, in turn, fathered 12 sons: Rueben, Simeon, Levi, Judah, Issachar, Zebulun, Naphtali, Dan, Asher, Gad, Joseph and Benjamin. Those became the 12 tribes.

One final note of interest. Since Joseph's two sons each became a tribe, one would think there would be 13 tribes rather than 12. However, the tribe of Levi was chosen to be the priestly tribe, serving a spiritual function and with no geographic inheritance, thus leaving only the traditional 12 tribes of Israel.

8

The Exodus Era: Part 1

By Mike Chapman, D.Min.

The Book of Genesis has been the topic of study thus far. Another book written during this period was Job. While there will be more said about the Book of Job later, it is important to note Job's chronological place in Scripture. Job is generally believed to have been a contemporary of the patriarchs, maybe even of Abraham. While the author of the book of Job is unknown, some have attributed it to Moses, yet others to Solomon. The Book of Job is categorized as one of the poetic books of the Old Testament—a three-volume set of books called wisdom literature. The other two books of wisdom literature are Proverbs and Ecclesiastes. Wisdom literature basically tells how men ought to live in order to have a meaningful life.

The big question raised in the Book of Job is, "Why do the innocent suffer?" The book details the extraordinary suffering of Job. The point to be made here is that Job was a real man and a contemporary of the patriarchs.

Israel's Exodus From Egypt

When Jacob and his family entered Egypt, they numbered about 70. During the next 430 years, this Hebrew clan grew to an estimated 2-3 million people. Eventually, however, these once-favored kindred to Joseph became an enslaved and persecuted people. Persecution sharpened the spiritual hunger of the Hebrews, and they cried out to God for deliverance.

This state of affairs introduces the third era of the Pentateuch—the Exodus Era. The Exodus from Egypt was no small trip. Moses led 2-3 million people, not counting cattle and other livestock, on a trek from Egypt to Canaan. It is estimated that, when they crossed the Red Sea, walking 100 abreast, the line was about 50 miles long. Truly amazing! Communication alone was a major undertaking. Moses accomplished this mammoth task by organizing the people first by tribes and then by smaller family units. Communication was made with flag or hand signals or by word of mouth. Viewed from any perspective, the Exodus was no small feat. It ranks as one of the greatest historical events of the ancient world.

The key figure in the Exodus was Moses. The central geographic location was Egypt to begin with and then the wilderness within the Sinai Peninsula. The time frame for the Exodus was about 40 years— 1440-1400 B.C. Under God's direction, Moses delivered the Hebrew people from slavery in Egypt and gave them the Law.

A historical overview of the Pharaohs of Egypt helps one to understand that this Bible story relates to real people in a real place and at a specific time. The Israelites entered Egypt at what is known as the Middle Kingdom Era of Egyptian history, somewhere between 2000-1780 B.C. During that period, the Pharaohs were known as the shepherd kings. They were of Asiatic descent, actually foreign kings, rather than ethnic Egyptians. This fact may well account for the cordial and more ready acceptance of Joseph and his kindred. Joseph's entry into Egypt probably occurred when the second of these shepherd kings reigned from 1897-1878 B.C. When Jacob and his family arrived in Egypt, the third shepherd king had come to power from 1878-1840 B.C. In 1570 B.C., native Egyptians rebelled, driving out the foreign shepherd kings and restoring an ethnic Egyptian dynasty. Thus, a new group of Pharaohs, rulers that did not know Joseph and who were not friendly to these foreigners, came to power.

The Bible says, "There arose a Pharaoh who did not know Joseph" (see Exodus 1:8). This Pharaoh probably reigned from 1570-1542 B.C., with his daughter being the one who found Moses in the Nile River. The Pharaoh of the oppression is usually thought to have been Thutmose III, sometimes called the Napoleon of Egypt. He reigned from 1482-1450 B.C., and his son, Amenhotep II, was most likely the Pharaoh of the Exodus.

These references to well-established historical documents and people are quite valuable to the Bible scholar and to every Christian believer. They silence the skeptics who claim the scriptures are but myth or religious writings that ought not be taken seriously. They build faith among believers by verifying that Moses was indeed both a called prophet of God and an educated scholar (educated in Egypt), quite

93

capable of writing his record of events in the best medium known to man at that time.

A Bible map reveals the full area in which these events took place, starting with Egypt and the land of Goshen where the Israelites were concentrated. Under the leadership of Moses and Aaron they traveled southeast to the upper edge of the Red Sea and made their miraculous crossing into the plains section of the Wilderness of Shur. From there the Israelites followed the relatively smooth plains south past Marah and then due east into the Wilderness of Sin. Then they moved farther south into the more desolate area of Mt. Sinai with its surrounding wilderness area that makes up the lower Sinai Peninsula and remains a very rugged territory even to this day. After a generation in this wilderness area, the Israelites eventually made their way up the eastern side of the Sinai Peninsula all the way to Kadesh-Barnea from where they sent spies into the land of Canaan. Once again, the point needs to be made that all Moses wrote is easily related to fairly exact places known even today to exist in the Sinai Peninsula. This is a study of history, accurately recorded and preserved for later generations by a sovereign God. In spite of all the efforts of religious skeptics, Moses' account holds up.

The following is an expanded summary of the Exodus Era: Under the Pharaohs, the Israelites were reduced to slave existence (Exodus 1). Their bondage became very severe and they cried out to the God of Abraham for deliverance. Hearing their cry, and in fulfillment of His sovereign covenant with the patriarchs, God chose Moses to be their deliverer.

Moses, God's Deliverer

The life of Moses divides into almost three equal parts, each revealing God's sovereign plan. He was raised, educated, and trained in Pharaoh's palace for about 40 years before choosing to acknowledge his relationship with the Israelites and being cast out. Moses then spent 40 years in Midian, a desert wilderness area, caring for the flocks of his father-in-law and learning survival in a harsh climate totally opposite to what he had known in Egypt. Finally, Moses spent the last 40 years of his life leading the Israelites through the wilderness to Canaan.

It is totally amazing how Moses was so uniquely prepared, trained, and divinely equipped for his life's work. It is equally amazing that Moses understood none of this, had no hint of what God was doing in and through him until that morning when, in Midian, he saw a burning bush that was not consumed and came face-to-face with Jehovah God. God spoke to Moses, and Moses understood he was chosen for a unique and special task.

Moses made excuses, but God convinced him that he was to deliver his people out of Egypt. It is here that God's name, Jehovah, first appears—"I Am That I Am." Of course, the name Jehovah appeared earlier in Genesis but that was because Moses authored the book and used the name earlier, although he discovered the name at the burning-bush experience.

The name Jehovah

Moses asked God a very simple question, "When I stand before the Pharaoh of Egypt, whom shall I say sent me?" (see Exodus 3:13). God answered,

"Tell him, I Am" (v. 14). In Hebrew, *I am* is the verb "to be." From this comes the Hebrew name Yahweh, and Yahweh becomes Jehovah in English. God told Moses to tell Pharaoh, "Jehovah sent me."

Other names are used for God throughout the Old Testament but none so prominent as Jehovah. Earlier in this study reference was made to *El* and *Elohim,* meaning "the strong and mighty God, the Creator, the One to be feared." Another name often used is *El-Elyon,* meaning the Exalted One, the Most High. Almost every time one comes across this passage in Scripture, "Most High God," it is the translation of *El-Elyon.* Another name for God is *Adonai,* most often translated in the Old Testament English Bible as Lord, with a capital L and the rest of the letters small. *Adonai* means "the owner and ruler of all things," and it is the most frequently used name for God in the Old Testament. Also, there is the name *El-Shaddai,* meaning "the God who is almighty, the God who is more than enough, who brings blessing and comfort to His people."

One ought to remember, however, that God's proper name is Yahweh or Jehovah. This is his covenant name. It is the name signifying He enters into covenant with man. It is His most sacred and holy name. He is the God of grace, the God of covenant, the God Jehovah. Bible translators have attempted to convey the significance of this fact. When one reads the English version of the Bible, the name Yahweh is often translated LORD (all caps). Most Jewish scribes chose to refer to God as *Adonai,* rather than Jehovah because they did not want to take God's name in vain.

DELIVERANCE

Moses stepped forth to deliver the children of Israel armed only with the rod of a shepherd. In a certain sense this rod represented the failure of Moses. He gave up the splendors of Egypt, and he fled as a murderer to take up the rod of a shepherd in the wilderness. How fitting that God turned this symbol of his failure into a staff of victory.

Israel's deliverance came through a series of 10 plagues against the Egyptians: (1) water turned into blood, (2) the plague of frogs, (3) the plague of lice, (4) the swarms of flies, (5) the plague upon Egyptian cattle but not upon the cattle of Israel, (6) the boils, (7) the hail and fire everywhere except in Goshen, (8) the locusts, (9) darkness over the land for three days, and (10) the death of every firstborn son in Egypt.

Great significance was attached to the rituals surrounding the last plague, especially the steps required of every Israelite family in order to make sure the death angel did not come to the firstborn of their homes. Moses instructed every family to kill a lamb and take the blood of the lamb and put it on the doorposts of the home. Jewish historians record that they put the blood on the door by taking a type of a plant, dipping it in the blood of the lamb, and then striking the doorpost, first vertically, and then horizontally to form a cross. When the death angel came, he passed over all the homes with blood applied to the door. This event was the beginning of the Jewish festival of Passover, still recognized and observed today.

In the New Testament, the apostle Paul calls Jesus our Passover Lamb. When Jesus appeared on the banks of the Jordan River, John the Baptist pointed Him out to the crowd and said, "Behold the Lamb of God, which taketh away the sin of the world" (John 1:29). The Bible refers to Jesus Christ as the "Lamb slain from the foundation of the world" (Revelation 13:8). Thus, the Egyptian ritual was a symbol, a prototype of the coming of Christ and His dying for the sins of the whole world. God instituted Passover as a festival for the Jews to remember their deliverance from Egypt. He led Israel through the miraculous crossing of the Red Sea and prepared them for a wilderness journey, during which time they would come to know God Jehovah in a more personal manner.

Israel's deliverance is presented as a story with two very difficult events: first, getting all the Israelites out of Egyptian bondage; second, getting them through the wilderness and into the land of Canaan. In all likelihood it took about three months for Moses and the 3 million people to make it to the area of Mt. Sinai. This was not a quick trip. This was no longer a family of 70 people, but a nation. An important ingredient to being a nation is having a law. At Sinai, God gave His Law to Moses. The children of Israel stayed in the Mt. Sinai area for at least one year. Much needed to be done. Moses had to get the Law, and he had to write it down. The Law had to be encoded. The Tabernacle had to be built, along with the ark of the covenant. At Mt. Sinai, through God's covenant with the Israelites and in the giving of the Law, Israel first began to take on a national identity.

TEN COMMANDMENTS

Moses received the Law directly from God. He received the Ten Commandments upon the top of

Mt. Sinai. He received the other laws as God spoke to him from the door of the Tabernacle.

Why, one might ask, was so much of the Law expressed in negative terms? There was a reason. The Law, quite correctly, presupposes the existence of sin and evil in every heart. It had been that way since Adam. God had to explicitly say "do not" because it is man's natural disposition to do evil.

Basically, there are four purposes for the Law:

1. *The Law is to reveal the holiness of God.* When God gave His Commandments and the details of His Law, He pointed to His holiness. He is a righteous God, and these Laws reflect His absolute and unique holiness.

2. *The Law reveals the sinfulness of the human heart.* An understanding of the holiness of God always highlights the contrast between Him and the sinfulness of man's heart.

3. *The Law reveals how much man needs salvation.* Salvation simply means deliverance from a condition from which man cannot rescue himself. The Law makes people more aware of the human dilemma and of their inability to correct it.

4. *The Law is designed to preserve the chosen people of God.* It was given to preserve Israel as a nation, to establish and safeguard their unique status. The Ten Commandments, given to Moses on top of Mt. Sinai, are recorded in Exodus 20 and in Deuteronomy 5. Moses was also given approximately 600 other commandments, things to govern the civil life, the religious life, and the everyday life of the people of Israel.

During the time Moses and the people of Israel were at Mt. Sinai, Moses was also given instructions on how the Tabernacle was to be built, on the institution of the priesthood, the feast days of Israel, and the sacrificial system. These were to govern the religious life of Israel.

THE TABERNACLE

The Tabernacle was sometimes called the Tent of Meeting, the gathering place for times of religious and spiritual celebrations. The Tabernacle represented the presence of God among His people, and it became the center of life for Israel as they moved through the wilderness. God displayed His presence with a pillar of fire above the Tabernacle during the night and a pillar of cloud by day. The Tabernacle consisted first of an open courtyard 150 feet long and 75 feet wide. The Tabernacle proper, a tent-like structure, was 15 feet by 45 feet, consisting of a front part called the Holy Place and a second part known as the Holy of Holies, 15 feet by 15 feet. The entire Tabernacle was not huge by any stretch of the imagination.

There was only one gate or entrance to the Tabernacle, located on the eastern side. The first thing one came to upon entering the courtyard was a bronze altar on which a fire burned continually. Burnt sacrifices were made on this altar. There was also a laver of water in which the priests could wash themselves before entering the Holy Place. Those were the only two items in the courtyard.

Moving into the Holy Place, the first part of the Tabernacle proper—which was covered—revealed a room with three objects: a golden candlestick that burned, a table of shewbread where 12 loaves were placed every week (representing each of the 12 tribes of Israel) for the priests to eat, and the altar of incense just in front of the veil that separated the Holy Place from the Holy of Holies. The altar of incense represented the prayers of the people going up to God.

Only the high priest was permitted to enter the Holy of Holies. He did so one day a year, on the Day of Atonement. Only one item was in the Holy of Holies—the ark of the covenant. This ark was four feet long, two feet wide, and two feet deep—not large, but very ornate. It was a chest totally overlaid with gold. According to Hebrews 9:4, three items were placed in the ark—the original tablets of stone on which the Ten Commandments were written, a jar of manna God had sent to feed them in the wilderness, and Aaron's rod that budded (Numbers 17). On top of the ark were two angels—cherubim—whose wings touched to form almost a triangle. The top of the ark became known as the mercy seat and it was here the glory of the Lord was revealed.

On the annual Day of Atonement, the high priest entered with the blood of a sacrifice to make atonement for the sins of the people.

Since the whole Tabernacle represented the presence of God with His people, Moses was given meticulous instructions on how to build it—the colors, the materials to be used, and all the important details. The Temple that King Solomon built later was based on this same structure built by Moses.

Moses' brother, Aaron, was the first high priest of Israel, thus beginning a long line of what is known as the Aaronic priesthood. Later, the tribe of Levi was chosen as the special tribe to be priests unto God.

Thus, Israel was delivered from Egyptian bondage to become a nation, the Tabernacle was built, the Law was given, and the priesthood was established.

The next chapter will examine festival days, details of the sacrificial system, and Israel's continuing journey into the Promised Land.

9

The Exodus Era: Part 2

By Mike Chapman, D.Min.

During the year that Moses and the children of Israel camped at Mt. Sinai, God gave them detailed plans for the Tabernacle, the priesthood, and the tribe of Levi. Moses also received instructions from God relative to holy days and feast days. These will introduce this final study on the Pentateuch, and the study will come primarily from Leviticus 25.

Jewish Holidays

The first and best known of Jewish weekly holidays to be established was the Sabbath. It began at sundown on Friday and lasted until sundown on Saturday. During this period of time, the Israelites were commanded to rest, not work. The Sabbath reflected back to the creation week and to God's having created the world in six days and resting on the seventh. The Hebrew word for Sabbath is *Shabbat,* meaning "to be with one's family." It was a time to reflect upon God and to rest.

The Israelites also had a Sabbath Year—one year in seven. They were to prepare for this year in advance, permitting the land to rest from any cultivated crops. Today, the scientific value of this is well understood. Land planted year after year is depleted of minerals and produces less and less.

A third Jewish celebration was the Year of Jubilee which was to be observed every 50 years. During the Year of Jubilee, all debts were to be cancelled, indentured slaves were to be set free, and all property returned to its original owner. Spiritually, the Year of Jubilee hints of the time of Jesus. In Luke's Gospel, when Christ said the Spirit was upon Him and He was to preach "the acceptable year of the Lord" (Luke 4:19), He was, in all probability, making reference to the Year of Jubilee. One might also note that when Jesus comes into an individual's heart, the sin debt is cancelled, jubilee has come, and the believer is restored to a rightful place in the inheritance of God.

A final celebration to be mentioned here was the New Moon Festival. The Jewish calendar ran from new moon to new moon, a 30-day month. The Israelites celebrated at the beginning of every new month.

FESTIVALS OF ISRAEL

In addition to these holidays, several Jewish festivals are set forth in Leviticus 23. Central to the heart of God, to Moses, and the early leaders of Israel was the need for seeing that faith passed from one generation to the next. Most of these holidays were for the younger generation—the children. It is an ideal method for instructing them in the truths of God and in the history of Israel. These times were truly festivals; they were fun times. Believers today ought to think more seriously and positively about the next generation. The best gift any parent can pass along to his/her children is the knowledge of God's covenant with man through Jesus Christ. When children know who they are and what they are in God, they develop into happy, responsible, productive citizens.

Festival of Passover. Passover began the Jewish religious year by celebrating Israel's deliverance from Egyptian bondage. Passover, the oldest continuing religious ritual in the world, is also a phenomenal portrayal of Jesus Christ. Many Bible scholars believe that God will some day use the Passover as one means for opening the eyes of the Jews to the reality of Christ as Messiah. It was while eating the Passover that Jesus instituted what today is called Communion. He said, "This bread, the bread of affliction, is My body. This cup, the cup of redemption, is My blood" (see Luke 22:17-20).

Festival of Unleavened Bread. The Festival of Unleavened Bread began the day after Passover and lasted for seven days. During this time the people of Israel made special offerings unto God.

Festival of Firstfruits. The Festival of Firstfruits began with the barley harvest when an Israelite presented a sheaf of the first barley as a wave offering to God. This sheaf presentation was more than a token, it was the firstfruits of the harvest, presented as thanksgiving and in confidence that God would bless the remainder of the harvest. Tithing is often referred to as the firstfruits—giving unto God the first 10 percent of income in covenant expectation that He has promised to bless the rest.

Festival of Pentecost. Pentecost came 50 days after Passover, a one-day festival celebrating the gathering of the whole harvest. Sometimes Pentecost is called the Festival of Weeks, because it was 50 days after Passover. Added to this joyous harvest celebration later was also the commemoration of the giving of the Law to Moses on Mt. Sinai.

Festival of Trumpets. The Festival of Trumpets was a one-day holiday, celebrating the beginning of the civil year just as Passover began the religious year. This festival, New Year's Day for the Jews, is known today as Rosh Hashanah which is still celebrated by Jews around the world.

Day of Atonement. The Day of Atonement came 10 days after the Festival of Trumpets. It was a day of fasting and atonement for the collective sins of the nation. This was not necessarily a joyous festival, but a time of prayer and spiritual dedication. It is known today as Yom Kippur, meaning the Day of Atonement.

On this day in the Old Testament, the high priest entered the Holy of Holies to sprinkle blood on the mercy seat as atonement for the sins of the people. On this same day, the priest would take a living sacrifice, a goat, anoint it and send it out into the wilderness, symbolically placing on this scapegoat the sins of all the people.

Festival of Tabernacles. This final festival that God gave to Moses took place five days after the Day of Atonement and lasted for seven days. This festival eventually became known as the Feast of Booths, when later, Jewish families would leave their homes and actually live in tents nearby as a reminder of the time their ancestors wandered through the wilderness and had no permanent dwelling place.

Those were the feast days—the holidays—God said would be on the calendar of the Israelites. Later, two others were added.

Festival of Purim. The Festival of Purim celebrated the events that took place in the Book of Esther.

Festival of Lights (Hanukkah). The Festival of Lights celebrated the rededication of the Temple (about 200 years before Christ), after it had been desecrated by Antiochus IV who replaced the altar of Jehovah with one for Zeus, instigating the rebellion of the Maccabees.

In addition to all these holidays and the feast days, various sacrifices were set forth in Leviticus 1-5.

Sacrifices or offerings of Israel

The burnt offering. This offering was always placed on the brazen altar in the Tabernacle. It represented total surrender. The entire animal, or the entire offering, was consumed. The burnt offering was a voluntary act of worship, done at a certain point in worship and for atonement of sin.

The meal offering. This offering was so named because it was a vegetable rather than an animal. It was given in recognition of God's goodness and provision. The individual brought grain or meal as an offering unto God.

The peace offering. This offering was an act of worship, signifying one wanted to have fellowship with God. This sacrifice had to be an animal without blemish or physical defect.

The sin offering. This offering was presented for certain sins. If a high priest was giving this offering, he brought a young bull. If one was a leader among the people, he brought a male goat. If one was a common citizen, he brought either a female goat or a lamb. If one was poor, he brought a pigeon or a dove, but if one was very poor, he brought flour. All of these could be offered as atonement for specific sins.

The trespass offering. Finally there was the trespass offering, sometimes called the guilt offering, given not only when one had sinned against God but also against an individual. This offering had to be either a ram or a lamb; furthermore, one had to make restitution to the individual who was wronged.

These many laws, sacrifices, festivals, and offerings present a remarkable foreshadowing of Jesus Christ the Messiah. Any in-depth study of the Tabernacle, the sacrifices, and even of the holidays will reveal more and more who Jesus is and what Jesus came to do.

Three of the feast days of Israel came to be recognized as journey feasts—Passover, Pentecost, and Tabernacles—requiring travel to the holy city of Jerusalem. Every Jewish male was asked to travel to Jerusalem, if possible, on these feast days. This explains a crowded Jerusalem during the days of Christ on earth. In time, however, as the Jewish people became more dispersed throughout the world, travel to Jerusalem became more difficult.

KADESH-BARNEA

After Israel had been at Mt. Sinai for approximately one year, they moved out and marched north up the eastern side of the Sinai Peninsula to Kadesh-Barnea. The name of the place means rebellion or failure. Kadesh-Barnea was an oasis, considered the southern gateway into Canaan. Moses chose 12 key individuals, one from each of the 12 tribes, to go spy out the land. The 12 returned with a glowing report: "The land is beautiful, the land is fantastic, everything is great." However, that was quickly overshadowed by fear and doubt when 10 of the spies said, "The Canaanites are powerful, they are strong like giants, and we are like grasshoppers in their sight" (see Numbers 13:26-33).

Two of the spies, Joshua and Caleb, agreed with the positives of the other 10, but they added a note of faith: "Yes, the men are big, but God has said the land is ours. We can take it with His help" (see Numbers 14:6-9).

This was Israel's moment of great failure. They believed the majority report and refused to follow Moses into Canaan. In this instance, the majority was not right. God's judgment came upon Israel, and they were forced to wander in the wilderness for 40 years, usually considered a generation. The purpose of this severe judgment was for that entire generation of faithless ones to die in the wilderness. The two exceptions to this judgment were Joshua and Caleb. Because of their faith, they were allowed to live throughout the entire period and enter into the land of Canaan.

This time of wandering in the wilderness is used repeatedly in the New Testament to talk about how Christians, through faith, can lay claim to the possessions of God. A failure of faith destines one to wander in the wilderness of defeat.

Eventually a new generation arose. The children of the Exodus generation grew up and became the adults who would lay claim to the land of Canaan. One might call these people the Joshua generation.

Moses led Israel north of the Dead Sea, to a spot near Jericho, but he was not allowed to enter into Canaan. Now a very old man—120 years old—Moses died, and the Bible says God buried the body of Moses on Mt. Nebo (Deuteronomy 24:5, 6). The people did not know where his burial site was. Thus, the wilderness wandering of the Israelites ends as they stand on the threshold of their Promised Land.

Books of the Exodus Era

Perhaps it will be helpful at this point to look more closely at the books of the Exodus Era.

EXODUS

The author of the Book of Exodus was Moses. This book covers a historical period beginning about 400 years after Joseph's death and concludes with the Israelites at Mt. Sinai. Exodus covers the entire period in which Moses is trying to convince Pharaoh to let the children of Israel go. It covers the call of Moses, the deliverance of Israel from Egypt, the journey to Mt. Sinai (a journey that took about three months), the giving of the Ten Commandments, and the requirements for building the Tabernacle.

LEVITICUS

Moses is the author of the Book of Leviticus. This book takes its name from the tribe of Levi, the priestly tribe. This tribe was given the responsibility of executing the religious laws of Israel. It was written primarily during the year the Israelites camped at Mt. Sinai and contains the full revelation of the law of God, often called the holiness code. In Leviticus one often reads, "Do this because I the Lord your God am holy" (see 19:2).

God wanted the people of Israel to know these were not arbitrary laws. These were not mere casual rules He gave them. These laws were designed specifically to help them understand the holiness of His very nature. That is why Leviticus has sometimes been referred to as the holiness code. The commandments of this book fully established the nation of Israel and their unique character as a people. When the Israelites left Mt. Sinai with the Book of Leviticus in hand, they were no longer just a group of former slaves; they were a nation. They had law, and they had rules that governed the conduct of daily life.

NUMBERS

Moses wrote the Book of Numbers as well. The first 10 chapters of the Book of Numbers occurred during the year at Mt. Sinai; the second part (Chapters 11-36) records the rebellion at Kadesh-Barnea and subsequent wanderings in the wilderness. The book is well named, since it deals with numbers. Moses took two censuses while the children of Israel were in the wilderness: the first at Mt. Sinai before the wilderness wandering began, and the second at the end of that 40-year period. The census let Moses know how many people they had and how many fighting men were available.

The first census revealed that there were 601,730 fighting men. Except for Joshua and Caleb, and because of unbelief, all those would die in the wilderness. The second census, taken at the end of the wilderness wandering, revealed that there were 603,550 soldiers or fighting men, essentially the same number as before when they first had opportunity to move into the land of Canaan.

DEUTERONOMY

Moses is considered the author of Deuteronomy, although Joshua probably wrote the last part which dealt with Moses' death. The word *Deuteronomy* means "second law." The book consists of four major addresses given by Moses to the Israelites at the end of their wandering. He speaks to a new group of fighting men. The older ones have died in the wilderness. This is the Joshua generation, and they are preparing to move into Canaan.

In characteristic fashion, Moses, the elder, reminds the younger generation of their heritage, of all God has done for Israel these many years, and of all God has promised. An overview of the four speeches can be given as follows:

1. Moses rehearses the past, and he challenges the new generation to obedience in the future.
2. Moses repeats the Ten Commandments, given nearly 40 years previously.
3. Moses explains the entire Law.
4. Moses then reminds Israel of their covenant relationship with God. God keeps His covenant, and Israel must keep hers.

Surely that was a powerful moment! A white-haired, elderly Moses, his life coming to an end, instructing a new generation in their covenant relationship with Almighty God. Every minister and spiritual leader today, including parents who basically are family priests, must understand this spiritual responsibility for passing along the "good news" of redemption to the next generation. The future depends on it.

Moses named Joshua as his successor, the very same Joshua who had been with him for so many years. In a sense, Moses commissioned Joshua to carry on his work. There was never a marking for the grave of Moses since God buried his body, but there is another appearance of Moses. He is mentioned in the New Testament where he appears on the Mount of Transfiguration with Jesus and the prophet Elijah.

Thus ends an overview of the Pentateuch—the foundation for the rest of God's Word.

10

Joshua

By Hannah Harrington, Ph.D.

This chapter will examine the personal stories in the Book of Joshua in light of the theme of faith and compromise. God promised His people Israel a special land—the land of Canaan. This theme was the underlying thesis of their deliverance from Egypt, their stay at Sinai, and their wandering in the wilderness. This book further reveals God's veracity of always keeping His promises.

When one examines the Book of Joshua, he discovers something very interesting. God told Joshua, "Every place that the sole of your foot will tread upon I have given you, as I said to Moses" (Joshua 1:3, *NKJV*). These words reveal that, even though the land had been promised to Israel, they had to do something themselves—they had to walk the land—the length and breadth of it. In other words, Israel had to take action in order to claim God's promise.

A look at the map of Canaan reveals that Israel entered the land at its southern end—at Jericho—only a few miles above the Dead Sea. Jericho was the first battle for the land. Ai was the second. With those two victories, Jericho and Ai, Israel made a central thrust into the land, dividing it north and south. Canaanite forces were divided into a Northern coalition and a Southern coalition. One might call Joshua's strategy one of dividing and conquering. With central victories which divided the land, followed by southern victories and then a northern victory, Joshua and the Israelites had broken the military back of the Canaanites.

The Battle of Jericho

Jericho was strategically located for a city of its day. It was the first outpost when entering the land of Canaan from the southeast. The city had plenty of water from the Jordan River. It sat astride trade routes east to west and easily connected up with the king's highway which was a busy north-south trade route.

The Bible account reveals Jericho was protected by very high walls. Modern archaeologists have uncovered a lot of remains from this ancient city, although it is not altogether clear which stratum of excavation actually goes back to the time of Joshua. Archaeologists have uncovered 23 levels of civilization at Jericho, and they consider it one of the older cities in the world.

One thing was very clear as Israel approached the city of Jericho—this wandering band of wilderness nomads could not possibly conquer a great walled city like Jericho in their own power and strength. Nevertheless, God had promised to give them cities they did not establish. God's promise to Joshua was reiterated time and again: "Be strong and of good courage. I will not fail you" (1:5-7).

Joshua sent out spies. Significantly, Joshua sent only two spies, not 12, as Moses had done. Most likely he remembered there was no use sending 12 if only two of them would return with a positive report. Joshua chose two trusted men and sent them into the city. But Joshua did not leave the matter there; he also spoke with the Commander of the Lord's army. This individual was, most likely, Jesus himself, because He accepted worship. Angels in the Old Testament always declined worship and insisted that the person worship God instead." This individual, however, accepted worship.

To human understanding, the strategy for the battle of Jericho was bizarre indeed. Walk around the city one time each day for six days. Do not talk; just walk. One can easily imagine what this silent ritual did to the people of the city—its psychological impact surely generated a feeling of unease. After all, these people had heard of the God of Israel and of the mighty things He had done for them when He brought them out of Egypt. There was no question in the minds of the people of Jericho—Israel had a powerful God. This truth was revealed more explicitly in the words of Rahab to the spies: "We know you will win this battle" (see Joshua 2:9).

On the last day of the week, the seventh day, the people walked around the city walls seven times. Then the silence was broken. Seven priests walking before the ark of the covenant, put their lips to seven trumpets of ram's horns and blew with a mighty blast. Here is how the Bible tells the story:

> So the people shouted when the priests
> blew the trumpets. And it happened when

> the people heard the sound of the trum-
> pet, and the people shouted with a great
> shout, that the wall fell down flat. Then
> the people went up into the city, every man
> straight before him, and they took the city.
> And they utterly destroyed all that was in
> the city, both man and woman, young and
> old, ox and sheep and donkey, with the edge
> of the sword (Joshua 6:20, 21, *NKJV*).

What an amazing victory! How excited the people of Israel must have been! God was truly with them.

God made the point, explicitly, from the very beginning of the battles in Canaan, that all the glory must go to Him. He required that the people not benefit from the riches of this city. Jericho was to be a firstfruits city of the battles of Canaan. All the precious metals from the city were to be put into the Tabernacle treasury. Everything else was to be destroyed. The Hebrew word used here is *charam,* meaning "devoted to God." In this case, Israel was to prove her devotion through obedience by totally destroying Jericho. Basically, God was saying to Israel, "If you can experience a victory such as this and then destroy everything, then you will have proven your devotion to me." Proven devotion comes with actions, not mere words.

All Israel was rejoicing. None could stand before such a God. They were ready for the next battle. Excitement was at fever pitch.

The Battle of Ai

Joshua and the army of Israel attacked the people of Ai with all the confidence that naturally comes in the wake of a victory such as Jericho. However, their attack was rebuffed and many Israelite soldiers killed. What went wrong? What happened to the miraculous God who was with them so awesomely at Jericho?

Joshua and the elders went to prayer, but God stopped the prayer, telling them, "There is sin in the camp" (Joshua 7:11). No point in praying as if nothing is wrong when there are spiritual matters to be set straight. A man by the name of Achan had stolen some of the precious goods from the city of Jericho. They found his treasure buried under his tent. These items were supposed to have been ear-marked for God and utterly destroyed. This had been God's explicit command. Achan and his whole household were then stoned to death.

Israel went back into battle, and this time God gave them another miraculous victory. In this second battle, Joshua took but a small troop, only 5,000 men, up to the city of Ai. Seeing such a small number, the residents of Ai rushed out of the city for a quick kill. What they did not realize was that a larger Israelite army, 30,000 men, had gone around to the back of the city. The soldiers of the city of Ai went out chasing the 5,000-man troop while the larger Israelite troop marched into the city and burned it.

This was the second amazing victory for the Israelites. With these two victories, Israel had made a definite, central thrust into the land, thus dividing the Canaanites into a southern and a northern camp.

The Southern Campaign

The people of Gibeon occupied land near the city of Ai. Having seen what happened to Jericho and Ai, they were scared. To them, it was one thing to fight a battle with a normal foe, but it was quite another to fight with one whose God rolled back the waters of the Jordan River and caused the city walls of Jericho to fall down. They sent emissaries to Joshua who pretended to be from a far country. Their clothes were worn, and they had moldy bread. They said, "We just want to be your slaves. We have no interest in fighting you. In fact, we've heard of your fame in our far country" (see Joshua 9:8-15).

According to Israelite law, residents outside of the Promised Land were not under the ban of God's wrath. Thus, it was possible to make a peace treaty with them. One cannot be sure if they knew of this law or not. In any case, they may have, and the Israelites would have had no problem with them if they had indeed been from a far country.

One discovers from the Bible, however, that the Gibeonites were no small foe. Gibeon was actually called a royal city, and they were strong and powerful. Joshua did not consult God about Gibeon; he just went ahead and made a treaty with them.

The southern cities were infuriated at Gibeon for selling out like this. This action reduced morale considerably, and it also caused the remaining cities to band together. They thus came, not to fight against Israel, but against Gibeon for her betrayal. Since Joshua was now committed by peace treaty to protect the Gibeonites, his forces marched 25 miles overnight from Gilgal to Gibeon, and God gave the victory. Any reading of this campaign lets one know it was God who gave the victory. It was hardly more than a mopping up campaign to the Israelites.

Three things are obvious from the Bible account: (1) God sent a general panic into this coalition,

(2) God sent hailstones upon the enemy only, and (3) God stayed the sun in its orbit for a full day just so the Israelites could continue the fight and accomplish full victory.

At the conclusion of these events, Joshua reiterated God's Word, confessing: "Fear not, nor be dismayed, be strong and of good courage: for thus shall the Lord do to all your enemies against whom ye fight" (Joshua 10:25). With these events, the Southern coalition of Canaanites was completely in disarray—many soldiers dead, kings killed, people frightened before an Israelite army whose God assisted them through such miracles. Israel had taken control of the South, and Joshua now turned his attention to the North.

The Northern Campaign

By this time the Northern Canaanites understood that no single city was able to withstand these Israelites, so they formed a coalition around the city of Hazor, located just north of the Sea of Galilee. Hazor had a very strong military fort. Archaeological digs have been performed at Hazor, and one can visit this site even today.

In this situation, God was also at work. He hardened the hearts of the Canaanites, and they thought theirs would be an easy victory. They had confidence in their strength and their army. Perhaps they reasoned, "The South just wasn't organized."

One sees God's providence in these events, because the Northern people allied with Hazor, Joshua and his troops were able to conquer the North in a single battle. Otherwise, they would have had to go city by city. Joshua and the people of Israel went into Hazor, Scripture says, and burned the place down. God kept His promise to Joshua: "And the Lord said unto Joshua, 'Be not afraid because of them: for to morrow about this time will I deliver them up all slain before Israel: thou shalt hough (hamstring) their horses, and burn their chariots with fire'" (Joshua 11:6).

Phase Two

In Chapter 13, God speaks to Joshua in a very different manner. Age is always a fact with which human beings must reckon, but few would enjoy hearing God say, "Thou art old and stricken in years, and there remaineth yet very much land to be possessed" (Joshua 13:1). Those were God's precise words to Joshua. God was not trying to discourage Joshua, but he was directing him to prepare Israel for another phase of responsibility.

The time came for each of the 12 tribes of Israel to move into their allotted areas of Canaan. It was time for them to settle down and take over all the land. It was one thing for everyone to be running around together under the banner of a very strong leader like Joshua, but it was quite another for each tribe to continue in faith with what God had said to do.

God had divided up the land many years earlier, under Moses, giving each tribe a specific place to settle. God reminded Joshua the time had come. The military backbone of the Canaanites had been broken. God had worked miracles. Most of the frightened people who were left in the land were just glad to be alive. However, there were many pockets of resistance which needed to be neutralized. That was to be the responsibility of each tribe in its particular area.

The rules for these engagements had also been set forth by Moses years earlier. They were the same for every tribe. The Israelites were to show no mercy. They were to destroy every one of the Canaanites. Otherwise, as God said, they would influence Israel and turn her away from Him.

Unfortunately, on their own, the tribes did not exhibit the strong faith of Joshua. Some of them looked at the situation and said, "Why should we kill these Canaanites? They can just pay us taxes and provide a good income." In other cases, as with Ephraim and Manasseh, the Israelites made slaves out of the Canaanites. They reasoned, "Why kill a good work force?" Compromises seeped in. In the case of Asher, Israel actually moved in with the Canaanites.

In the case of Dan, assigned to the rugged Southwest area where there yet remained a strong Philistine presence, the Israelites abandoned the area completely and chose to move into the North. God had just worked miracles, but nonetheless, Dan did not have faith to believe the same God could help them defeat the Philistines and take over their tribal allotment.

Judah conquered most of its goal, but not all, finding itself powerless against the iron chariots of the Canaanites. These compromises ate through the hearts of the Israelites like a cancer, keeping the tribes away from true victory.

Caleb

In the midst of all these failures, the Bible gives one outstanding example of the kind of faithfulness

God expected from all the tribes. Caleb was an 85-year-old man as Israel came into her promised inheritance. Caleb and Joshua were about 25 years older than the other fighting men because of all the deaths in the wilderness. The Bible says Caleb was a man completely filled up with God. He had so much faith that he believed, even at the age of 85, he could go with his clan into the impregnable fortress of Mount Hebron and win the victory. His now immortal words to Joshua still ring today, "Give me this mountain" (Joshua 14:12).

Hebron was 30,000 feet above sea level, and the cities were walled forts. Also, Anakite, the giant, lived there. Now, Caleb was not a foolish man; he saw these obstacles just like everybody else. Caleb simply knew that God would help him overcome all obstacles. Caleb's words were "if so be the Lord will be with me, then I shall be able to drive them out, as the Lord said" (Joshua 14:12). And so, based on God's promises, Caleb and his clan attacked Hebron, won a great victory over all the inhabitants, and settled the area.

Conclusion

What truths are most obvious from these events? First, strong leaders are needed, men full of faith like Joshua and Caleb.

Second, each Christian must learn to know God personally. Leaders are to guide Christian believers, but they cannot replace one's personal relationship with God. One can go to conferences, to church services, to workshops, but none of these are enough when the going gets really tough. Each individual must prove God for himself and be able to rely on Him completely through faith.   Regular communication with God, and obedience to Him will create spiritual health.

Each one of God's children has a Promised Land. This reference is to heaven ultimately, but it also means a land to conquer on this earth and in this present life. Each has a task to fulfill and each needs God's help and direct intervention. Each has dreams and visions which can come to pass through God's strength and provision.   Through these particular tasks and missions, one proves either faithful or unfaithful in terms of the special relationship God wishes for each of His children.

With trust in God, each one can end life like Caleb—spiritually strong and full of faith.

11

Judges

By Hannah Harrington, Ph.D.

If one can say the Book of Joshua is about victory through faith, then one is correct in saying the Book of Judges is about failure through compromise.

Judges was written about 1000 B.C. and describes the period of Israelite history between the time of Joshua and the time of Saul, the first king of Israel. The period takes in a timeline of about 350 years and is called the period of the Judges.

Political and Religious Conditions

The period of the Judges was not a good time in Israel's history, but a time characterized by general disorder, compromise, lack of devotion to God, and very little noteworthy central leadership. There were a few bright spots, however, a few men and women of God who had faith to believe that Jehovah could overcome all obstacles.

Interestingly enough, the political and social situation everywhere in the land of Canaan during

127

this period (1400 to about 1050 B.C.) was also very chaotic. Extra Biblical sources help contribute to one's understanding of this period in ancient history. Technically speaking, Egypt had control over the area. One never hears about Egypt in the Book of Judges; therefore, one can safely assume their control was rather weak. It seems that no one had real control over the land, but one can learn some interesting things from Egyptian sources.

One Egyptian source, around 1300 B.C., describes Israel as a land laid waste. Also, in the 13th century B.C., an Egyptian inn boy who was traveling through the land reported: "The land of Canaan is overgrown, there are plants and trees all over the roads. You can't even get through. Lions are numerous. Thieves run around. In fact, thieves stole my horse." He goes on to say he was robbed on two occasions. The land was unsafe and out of control.

Another Egyptian report, this one in the 11th century B.C., comes from a temple official named Wenamon, who was sent on official business from Egypt to Biblos. To get to Biblos he had to travel through the land of Canaan. On this trip, he too was robbed. He tried to meet with the local kings in the land of Canaan and got absolutely no cooperation.

The Book of Judges does not mention any of these reports because that is not its topic. It is interested in Israel and her relationship with God Jehovah. Nevertheless, the Book of Judges is about chaos and religious chaos. More than once the author says, "In those days there was no king in Israel, but every man did that which was right in his own eyes" (17:6).

In Judges 2, one finds that God was very upset, because the Israelites had adopted the Canaanite way of life and the Canaanite religion. A number of specific Canaanite gods are mentioned. The most prominent is Baal, the main fertility God of the Canaanites. Three female goddesses are also mentioned: Asherah, Ashtoreth, and Anat. Another male god mentioned is Dagon, probably a god of grain or the harvest.

In the Hebrew and Canaanite dialects, *Ba-al* means "lord and master." Just as God predicted they would, the Israelites compromised with the local population. The Canaanite way of life influenced the Israelites, and they were soon adopting Canaanite religious practices.

Again, extra Biblical sources reveal some things about Canaanite religion. The scriptures record over and again about Israel going "after other gods." This phrase, of course, is metaphorical in the sense that Israel had left her true love, Jehovah, and had gone to worship other gods, but it also has a more literal meaning as well. Worship at a Canaanite shrine was nothing like worship in a church today. Worship at a Canaanite shrine was an abomination to God. Women gave themselves to the temple as prostitutes, and men worshiped through blatant sexual activities with these priestesses of the temple. There was nothing holy about it; it was a sensual religion, catering to fleshly appetites.

When Israel became caught up in these fertility rituals and sexual practices, God was infuriated: "And the anger of the Lord was hot against Israel; and he said, because that this people hath transgressed my covenant which I commanded their fathers, and have not hearkened unto my voice; I also will not henceforth drive out any from before them of the nations which Joshua left when he died" (2:20, 21).

Thus, the result of Israel's disobedience was God's absence and God's judgment. The book presents a recurring cycle in Israel's relationship with God—a cycle that reveals the human propensity to sin. Israel would fall into sin. God would respond by raising up some oppressor who would afflict them, torment them, enslave them, or overtax them. Israel would cry out to God, asking forgiveness, more to get rid of the oppressor than to reestablish relationship with Jehovah. Then, God would raise up a judge, a deliverer, somebody who would lead the people to victory. So ran the cycle—sin, oppression, repentance, a judge, deliverance, and then back into sin. During most of this period, as stated earlier, Israel was under oppression; but there were a few bright lights. These were men and/or women whom God raised up to lead Israel to victory and establish peace and godliness at least for a while. Some of the bright lights of this period were Deborah, Gideon, Jephthah, and Ehud. Their stories are familiar.

Religious Syncretism

The term *religious syncretism* is used to focus on that which is not exactly hypocrisy, not exactly idol worship, but is not at the same time true, pure worship of God Jehovah. Syncretism represents an effort to put the two together, to try to make both work. There were things about the Canaanite religion that were attractive to the Israelites and they tried to mingle those with what they knew about true religion and the Mosaic law. One knows, of course, that in God's eyes that does not work.

This brand of neither fish nor foul religious syncretism—this mingling of beliefs—is a very dangerous thing, because one deceives himself or herself into thinking that somehow because one is still worshiping everything is all right. One begins to think the God of Israel will go along even though there are the trappings of other religions around or maybe there is a fertility god in the backyard.

In all manner of ways, people from the beginning of time have rationalized the mixing of beliefs—intermingling God's ways with the ways of the world. The Book of Judges gives several graphic examples of this type of compromise.

SOCIAL INTERACTION

First, as noted from the very beginning, the Israelites moved in with the Canaanites. They ignored God's command to completely destroy them. This meant that, physically, there was a social mingling between God's people and the Canaanites.

GIDEON'S FAILURE

As one reads further, failures become more shocking. For instance, following the beautiful chapter about Gideon and how God brought miraculous victory for the Israelites, one discovers that this same Gideon, at the end of his life, set up a golden ephod (a priest's garment). Sure enough, Israel began to worship that idol. Had one asked those Israelites who God was, they would have answered, "Yahweh." Had one asked them who their great heroes of the faith were, they would have said, "Moses, Joshua." But they just had this little thing on the side, this little something borrowed from the Canaanites, to help with their visual expression of worship.

JEPHTHAH'S DAUGHTER

Jephthah offers the reader yet another example. He brought miraculous victory for Israel over the Ammonites (Chapters 11, 12). It is amazing what God did for him. Still, he was so tainted with Canaanite influence that he ended up sacrificing his only child. Some Bible scholars do not think Jephthah actually sacrificed his daughter—they speculate he just committed her to the temple—but the scriptures make it very clear. He vowed (foolish vow or not) that he would offer as a burnt offering the first thing that came out of his house to greet him after the battle. His only daughter was the first one to come and greet him and the Scripture says, "He did to her as he vowed" (11:39).

Although Jephthah's story is a very sad one, it dramatically illustrates what is meant by religious syncretism—the mixing and intermingling of ideas from one religion with another. Among the Canaanites, child sacrifice was an accepted practice, along with body mutilation, snake worship, and cult prostitution. These influences were creeping into Israel's social and religious life, and God was not pleased.

MICAH'S FALSE PRIESTHOOD

A more subtle and extended example of religious syncretism is presented at the end of the Book of Judges. It is in many ways a little known story—not one of the greats, not a bright light, and not one found in the roll call of faith in Hebrews. The story takes place after the last of the judges—Samson—in Chapters 17-21.

The Micah of this story is not Micah, the prophet. This Micah is one trying to mix Canaanite ways with the true worship of God and, as the story progresses, one realizes it is not working. Micah was of the tribe of Ephraim. He did a terrible thing when he stole 1,100 pieces of silver from his mother. Later though, perhaps feeling guilty, he confessed his theft to his mother. She was so happy to receive the money back that she promised to devote it to God. She was referring to the God of Israel because she called Him Yahweh. In 17:3 she said, "I solemnly consecrate my silver to the Lord for my son to make a carved image and a cast idol" (*NIV*).

The money was given to a silversmith who made two idols with it. Micah then made a golden ephod for these idols and set up a shrine in his house. Remember, all this was being done with the idea of worshiping Jehovah. There is no mention of Baal, just the use of a little something extra to improve the worship. Micah's next thought was, "We need a priest. Maybe my son could do the job" (v. 5). So, Micah installed his own son to be a priest at his own shrine, before his own idols, in his own house—and that was religion for him.

Some while later a Levite passed through looking for work. Micah offered him some wages, thinking how nice it would be to have a real priest at his shrine. Believe it or not, the Levite agreed. Micah said, "Now I know Yahweh will prosper me because I've got a Levite to be my priest" (v. 13). Of course, the many problems with this arrangement are obvious.

The second part of this story has to do with the tribe of Dan. As noted previously, the Danites refused to accept their allotted territory because of the Philistines, choosing instead to move into the mountainous region of the North—as far away as they could get from the area God had given them.

First, the Danites sent five trustworthy men northward to spy out another area for them. Passing by the home of Micah, the men recognized the voice of the Levite inside and asked him for blessing and a prophecy. The Levite went through some ritual and assured them, "God is with you" (18:6). The men continued on to the northeastern corner of the land and found some very friendly, carefree people, completely unsuspecting of any harm. They had no entrenched military leader, and they were quite isolated from the rest of the Canaanite population.

The scouts returned home elated, reporting that the land would be easy to take. The tribe of Dan sent 600 armed soldiers to conquer the newly found territory. As these soldiers passed the home of Micah, the five scouts suggested, "Why don't we stop here? This man has religious stuff that may be useful to us." So, they stole Micah's idols. They also told the Levite he would be better off working for them, so he stole even more religious objects and joined them.

Micah confronted the men but it did no good. They more or less threatened him and sent him back home with his loss.

The men from Dan went on to Laish, killed all the people there, burned the town to the ground, and renamed the place Dan. From that day, throughout the Israelite monarchy, repeated references are made to Israel being from Dan (in the north) to Beersheba (in the south).

Why is this story important? Certainly there are more famous stories in the Book of Judges. But this one reveals the level at which the Israelites had accepted pagan ways and tried to mix them with God's ways. Micah and his mother clearly felt like they were worshiping the one true God, Yahweh, the one who worked miracles in Israel's behalf. Micah's mother donated the silver to Yahweh. Micah thought Yahweh would bless him because he employed a Levite. Even more shockingly, the Levite was thrilled to work at Micah's idolatrous shrine and just as happily joined the men of Dan who were clearly refusing God's will for their lives. In the end, Micah lost everything.

What are the lessons to be learned here? Are there things like this in the church today? Some in the church today want to include as much of the world as possible within the bounds of Christianity to make it more appealing. Religious syncretism is an effort to make everybody happy, regardless of God's truth as revealed in the Word. Worship is still seen as the way to Christ but the means have been intermingled with ideas completely contrary to the Christian faith and holiness.

For example, one student told of attending a Christian service in which the minister handed out his card with a phone number for receiving a Bible reading. Others have told of Christian fellowship meals at which participants drink alcohol and become drunk. Yet other efforts are still being made to make Christianity more appealing, more popular, more modern.

It will not work. As the period of the Judges reveals, God does not bless any kind of mixture of his laws with popular demand. He does not accept any of the compromises many have made in terms of their faith. He has been clear about what He requires, and He expects obedience.

Conclusion

Today, as well as in the time of Israel's judges, many do not know exactly what God requires. Truth has been so diluted, both inside and outside the church, that many young people are growing up without a clear moral code. As a result, this places greater responsibility on the church and every Christian to realize:

1. God will not bless those who reject Him for other gods.
2. God will not bless any mixture of faith and sin.
3. People must be taught the truth so they can live it.

All ways do not lead to God. If they did, His commandments and His revelation would not be necessary.

It is up to the church—the people of God on earth today—who know the truth, to teach it to others without compromise.

12

Ruth

By Hannah Harrington, Ph.D.

The story of Ruth took place during the period of the judges. The book is unique because it gives a woman the central role. More striking perhaps, is the fact that the woman was a foreigner—a Moabite. In her story, Ruth not only becomes an Israelite, but she is clearly in the genealogy of King David, and therefore in the lineage of Jesus the Messiah. For a Gentile to be included in this special bloodline was quite remarkable.

The Book of Ruth is a lesson in faith. In this case, it is the faith of an outsider who sees in one person, Naomi, that Israel's God is real. As one will see, Naomi had her times of doubt; nevertheless, when she made the decision to return to the Land of Promise to do God's will, Ruth was affected enough to want to go with her and to become one of her people.

The book breaks down easily into four parts, corresponding to its four chapters: Ruth's journey, Ruth's gleaning, Ruth's appeal, and Ruth's marriage.

Ruth's Journey

A great famine came upon the land of Canaan. The severity of the situation is well illustrated by what happened to the family of Elimelech and his wife, Naomi. They became so desperate for food that the only solution they could think of was to leave the Promised Land and move to the land of Moab.

A quick look at any Bible map will show one the geography involved in this story. In the southern part of the country, near Jerusalem, is Bethlehem. Directly east is the Jordan, and across the river is what is known as the Trans-Jordan. At the time of this story, opposite Bethlehem in the Trans-Jordan, was the country of Ammon. A little south, directly east of the Dead Sea was the country of Moab.

One sees a certain irony in the idea that an Israelite family must move out of the Land of Promise because of famine and go to a pagan area where no one worshiped the true God. The idea may have made sense on the surface, and it was in all likelihood the excuse Elimelech used, but it should be noted that this man and his family certainly did not prosper in Moab. They only ran into more trouble. Nothing in the Book of Ruth implies that God told Elimelech to take his family to the land of Moab, and Naomi's latter lament certainly hints that she realized they should never have left the Promised Land.

Elimelech and Naomi may have found food in Moab, but they were confronted with idolatry and their sons intermarried with foreign women, even though such was explicitly forbidden in the law of Moses—"An Ammonite or Moabite shall not enter into the congregation of the Lord; even to their tenth generation shall they not enter into the congregation of the Lord for ever" (Deuteronomy 23:3).

Moab was not good to this family. First the father, Elimelech, died. Then the two sons also passed away, leaving Naomi a poor widow with only her two daughters-in-law, Orpah and Ruth. Surely one of the most telling statements of this family's journey to Moab fell from Naomi's lips upon her return to the land of Judah. She said to her friends, "Call me not Naomi (meaning pleasantness), call me Mara (meaning bitterness): for the Almighty hath dealt very bitterly with me. I went out full, and the Lord hath brought me home again empty" (Ruth 1:20, 21).

The last phrase is quite an interesting one. One would have thought she went away empty, not full. After all, the land was in a famine. She had gone to Moab, supposedly, to find fullness. Naomi faced herself honestly. She did not blame others, or the situation. She did not make excuses. She honestly faced herself. She and her husband had made the wrong decision, and God afflicted them for it.

Now, however, she made the right decision—to return to the Land of Promise, to where God's blessing could be experienced, to where she should be. And it is at that point where the reader is introduced to Ruth, one of her daughters-in-law, who sees something in her mother-in-law she admires.

Ruth's decision can be better understood if viewed from her perspective. From ours, one might be led to think: *Well, Ruth was living in Moab. She ought to have wanted to go to the Land of Promise.* But think about it from Ruth's point of view. She was not an Israelite. Moab was her home; her people lived there, and she had been taught all about the gods of Moab. It was not a small thing for Ruth to say, "I will go with this lady to her land. I will live there. I will die there. I will be buried there. Her God will be my God, her people my people" (see 1:16, 17).

The full significance of Ruth's statement meant, "I do not wish to be a Moabite anymore." Ruth was renouncing everything she knew as home. She was turning her back on her people, her land, and her god. She did not really know this God Jehovah, of whom Naomi spoke, but she did see something in her mother-in-law that made her want to go with her.

Ruth was returning with her mother-in-law to the Land of Promise, but she faced a problem. That problem is summed up in Israel's ancient law of inheritance known as the *levirate*. The *levirate* was not merely an Israelite custom, but one found in other societies as well. It was designed for two purposes: first, to protect and project the family name so that the linage did not run out; and secondly, to protect the family's land heritage.

If one of the sons in a family dies prematurely or without a son to inherit the family land, the levirate comes into play to ensure that his name will continue, and his land will be taken care of. If, for example, the second son of a family marries, goes off to war and is killed, leaving a widow with no children—without an heir—the man's name will cease and his land inheritance will be lost. According to the levirate, the man's brother could step into the picture, take care of the widow, and even father a child by her. That child would continue the linage

140

of the dead man, in name and with the inheritance of land. That is what one sees portrayed in Naomi's conversation with her two daughters-in-law.

In today's world, land inheritance is not the big deal it was in the land of Israel. It was totally different in Israel. There, if someone could not afford to keep his land and had to sell it, the nearest relative had both the option and the obligation to buy it. This ensured that family land allotments remained constant. The nearest relative who stepped forward and performed this duty to a kinsman is called a *levir,* and from this, one gets the word *levirate.*

In the case of Naomi and Ruth, it is clear that both are aware of the levirate tradition. One would expect Naomi to have known. She either explained it to Ruth or Ruth, too, understood it from her own land. Ruth's husband was dead. Naomi tells her, "Look. I don't have any more sons, someone else who can step in and help you. I am old and will have no more sons, so don't look to me to solve your problems. I can't offer you any hope. If you come with me, you will be coming with trouble. There is no hope and I am a bitter woman" (see 1:12, 13).

Nevertheless, Ruth saw something desirable in Naomi. She refused to leave her even when her sister-in-law changed her mind. Ruth said, "Where you go I will go, and where you stay I will stay. Your people will be my people and your God my God. Where you die I will die, and there I will be buried" (1:16, 17, *NIV*).

Naomi took action. She and Ruth began the long and difficult journey back to Judah, back to Bethlehem, a walking distance of at least 75 miles. They had to go around the Dead Sea and make their way down into the Jordan Valley and then climb up to Jerusalem. This latter part of the journey would be the famous trip "from Jerusalem down to Jericho," to which Jesus referred in His story of the Good Samaritan. It was difficult under the best of circumstances, but almost impossible for two women traveling alone. Nevertheless, Ruth and Naomi made the journey together and arrived eventually in the city of Bethlehem, not far from Jerusalem.

Ruth's Gleaning

A very wealthy landowner named Boaz was a distant relative of Elimelech. He had never left the land, not even in the time of famine, and God had been good to him. Scripture says, as well, that Boaz was a godly man. He was kind, and he was law abiding.

The Book of Leviticus instructs that when a farmer reaps his harvest, he is not to gather up everything all the way to the borders of his property. Neither is he to strip his vineyard bare. He is to leave something for the stranger and the poor. He is supposed to be generous. Boaz was such a man. So much so that he was called *gibor hayil*, meaning "man of valor or a man of worth."

Boaz was a strong man, with character. He is also portrayed in Chapter 2 as a good employer. Look at the exact words: "And, behold, Boaz came from Bethlehem, and said unto the reapers, The Lord be with you. And they answered him, The Lord bless thee" (Ruth 2:4).

Would not anyone be pleased with a greeting like that from an employer?

Boaz also asked, "Who is that new girl out there?"

The servant answered, "She is the Moabite girl, returned with Naomi." One can imagine different reasons why the servant responded this way. Perhaps Ruth dressed a little differently. Perhaps she had an accent. Perhaps the servant was prejudiced toward the Moabites. Whatever, the taint of being Moabite was placed on Ruth with the opening introduction.

Boaz also heard about the kindness of Ruth to Naomi and he rewarded her for it. He told the reapers, "Pull out good sheaves—not just the ones that accidentally drop and not just the normal leavings as the law demands—but I want you to take out some good sheaves and purposefully leave them for Ruth" (see 2:15, 16).

Ruth was utterly amazed by this generosity. She said to Boaz, "You are so good to me, and I am a Moabite" (see v. 10). She was well aware of her status—a stranger in a foreign land. She was not at all surprised at the servant referring to her as a Moabite. She expected that. But she did not expect such kindness and generosity from the wealthy Boaz. His attitude and treatment were viewed as marks of real favor, noticed by Ruth and more fully appreciated by Naomi.

Ruth's Appeal

Ruth came home to Naomi, who wanted to know how everything went. "Did you meet Boaz? What did he say? What did he do?"

Ruth had with her a big, long shawl, the kind women wore in the country, and it was full of grain. Naomi realized that alone meant things had truly gone well. Her excitement grew.

"You know what Ruth?" she said. "Boaz is related to my husband's family. There is a chance here for you, and what I want most for you is a home."

Then, quite the mother-in-law, Naomi advised Ruth in very specific ways.

"Obviously, Boaz liked you. You must see him again. I want you to take a bath. I want you to put on some nice perfume, and dress up. Then go see Boaz. Now, don't just rush in there. Just wait until he's finished his day, until he's had a good dinner, and calmed down. No doubt many kinds of things go on between employer and employees during the day for a man like Boaz. So you wait until everything is all settled down and then go and talk to him" (see 3:1-5).

Ruth did not hesitate or offer any excuses. She obeyed Naomi and did exactly what she suggested.

Indeed, Boaz was in a cheerful mood when he lay down for the night and went to sleep. However, in the middle of the night, Boaz awoke to find a woman lying at his feet. In the darkness he did not recognize her and his first words were, "Who are you?" (3:9).

Ruth was not put off by this at all. She stayed calm, it seems, and she identified herself as Ruth. Then she said something that seems rather radical to us but which Boaz understood right off, "Spread your robe over your handmaid for you are a redeeming kinsman" (v. 9).

In Hebrew, the word used here is *kanaph,* meaning "spread your robe," and referring to the corner of a man's garment. It is also the word for wing. Literally Ruth said, "Take me under your wing," which may be translated even more directly as, "Marry me."

Boaz did not interpret Ruth's action or her words as being loose, or inappropriate. Note how he reacted. He said, "Blessed are you that you didn't go after the young men" (v. 10). Then he commended her that she would want her kinsman to care for her, and called her an *eshet hayil*, a word meaning "his counterpart in the community." Of course, Ruth was not a woman of substance. She had no money— no earthly possessions at all. But Boaz was so approving of her that he called her his counterpart and recognized she was a woman of character.

Ruth returned home to a very anxious Naomi who was, no doubt, wondering how her plan for Ruth was working. Ruth told her mother-in-law what happened, and Naomi's reaction was, "You know what, Ruth? That man will not rest until he has settled this matter. Things are looking good" (vv. 16-18).

Ruth's Marriage

Boaz did indeed take Ruth to be his wife.

The context and details of business in the ancient world is most strikingly set forth in Chapter 4 of this book.

First, one notes that business is conducted at the city gate. A gate, as referred to here is not just an iron gate on hinges that swings open, nor is it simply an entranceway to a city. The gate of a city is a whole complex of shops, courts, and other places of civic business. In this case, one is dealing with someone who is going to be a redeemer figure. The Hebrew word used here is *goel*, meaning "redeemer— someone who is going to step forward and take care of the widow." The first thing to be decided in this

145

public court at the gate is who Ruth's closest kinsman really is and whether he is willing to become a
goel (redeemer). The closest kinsman must be given
first opportunity to marry her. In this case, Boaz
was not the nearest kinsman, so his rights had to
be settled before a forum of 10 elders, known as the
meizon. To this day, in Jewish society, a *meizon* is
needed even for public prayer.

Boaz had a strategy worked out. It is clear from
the beginning that he wanted to marry Ruth. He
first brought up the issue of Naomi's land, asking
the nearest kinsman if he wanted to take over
Naomi's property. This relative was very excited
about taking over the land because that would have
added to his own wealth. Then Boaz asked, "Are
you willing to take responsibility for Ruth, the
Moabite?" (see 4:5).

It is most interesting that Boaz used the phrase
"Ruth the Moabite," realizing this would probably
dampen the kinsmen's interest. And Boaz was right.
The kinsman would not agree—land, yes, but not
the widow.

Upon the nearest kinsman's refusal, Boaz declared
himself as next of kin and gladly stated he would
take Ruth to be his wife in the presence of all the
witnesses. In time, Ruth became the mother of a
male child who was a great blessing to Naomi in her
old age. And Naomi's neighbors all rejoiced with
her saying, "A son is born to Naomi" (v. 17). Naomi
had reclaimed her husband's rights in the community and, through Ruth, she had preserved his land
and his name.

Through the faith and courage of Ruth, along
with the kindness and generosity of Boaz, a royal,

Messianic line continued through the Old Testament. In fact, Ruth was the great-grandmother of King David, also making her and Boaz ancestors of the future King of kings to be born to Mary and Joseph years later in the little town of Bethlehem.

Conclusion

What are the lessons of this beautiful story?

First, God is gracious. Naomi made a big mistake in her life by going to Moab in the first place. She paid a terrible price for this, but she was honest with God. She confessed her mistaken judgment, and returned to the land of her fathers. God gave her an unusual daughter-in-law in the person of Ruth, graciously protected her, and brought her back to the Promised Land. The women of Israel later said to her about Ruth, "[she] loves you and . . . is better to you than seven sons" (4:15, *NIV*). God is always gracious, eager to lift one out of despair, doubt or disaster; and He can turn seemingly hopeless situations into good.

Second, faith can indeed move mountains. Ruth had the wrong identity—she was of the wrong people, the wrong religion, the wrong land. She had no family other than a bereaved sister-in-law and a mother-in-law who was planning to leave her. However, Ruth found faith in her heart. She recognized in Naomi the path to true life through Jehovah, and God rewarded her.

Finally, one notes that God rewards generosity. Those who give of themselves generously find themselves receiving from God, in turn, much more than they have ever given. This is seen in Ruth, giving of herself to Naomi, and in Boaz's obvious respect and kindness. He is rewarded with a heritage he could never have anticipated—a place in the royal line of King David and Jesus Christ.

13

1, 2 Samuel

By Hannah Harrington, Ph.D.

This new period of study in Israelite history focuses primarily on the monarchy. The period of the Judges lasted from about 1400 B.C. until about 1050 B.C. The period known as the Israelite monarchy was divided into three sections: the first included the whole nation and covered about three generations—Kings Saul, David, Solomon, and Rehoboam—the second dealt with a kingdom divided between Israel in the North and Judah in the South that lasted until 722 B.C.; and the third dealt with only Judah in the South that lasted until 586 B.C.

The one key issue of this study will be Israel's demand for a king. When one reads 1 Samuel 8, one gets the clear impression that asking for a king was a bad idea. Samuel was not in favor of it, and God was not in favor of it. The question is, Why? After all, was not Moses a kind of king? Israel did not call him a king, but he was a very authoritarian leader, as was Joshua.

149

Obviously, according to Scripture, there was something not immediately seen going on—something that demands a closer look.

Israel's Demand for a King

The leaders of Israel stated several reasons why they wanted a king, though they did not mention all of them at first. They pointed out that Samuel was getting old. They also reminded him that, although he had been a very good leader, his sons were simply not fit to take his place. Significantly, Samuel did not argue that point. He too was disappointed in his sons.

Later in the chapter, the leaders pointed out that all the other nations had a king, so why should they not have one as well. It is this statement that is key to the whole problem.

Egypt had a king. What was he like? The Egyptian kings were the most powerful, famous and popular of the ancient world. They were called *pharaohs*, a word meaning "big house." Pharaoh had absolute power and authority; for one reason—he was considered to be divine, a god. The Egyptians worshiped many gods, but one was the god Horace, represented by the falcon, and Pharaoh was Horace incarnate. Thus, when the pharaoh issued a decree, the people viewed it as coming from a god, not from another human being.

This knowledge makes one view more significantly the ten plagues God brought upon the land of Egypt, especially the last one—death of the first-born throughout the whole land. When Pharaoh lost his firstborn son, it meant the next Horace incarnate lay dead in his bed at the hand of Moses,

the prophet of the great I Am. This was God's declaration of Himself as God, King of the universe, while
Pharaoh was but another human being.

Other cultures recognized the king as supreme
authority, unquestioned and absolute. He was the
military commander in chief who led into battle. He
had power to draft men into his service, no questions asked. He declared war at will, and against
whom he chose, for good reasons or merely on a
whim. The king in the ancient world could also draft
people to work for him—to build him a house, or to
erect a massive tomb such as the Egyptian pyramids. Historians have given various opinions as to
the science of how these pyramids were built, but
one thing is certain—they came about on the backs
of massive numbers of slaves. These pyramids were
built for giant burial vaults, designed to preserve
the bodies of the pharaohs and to supply their needs
in the afterlife.

Another common practice among kings of the
ancient world was the confiscation of land, either
for the personal use of the king or for those whom
he wished to honor and reward.

The Hittites provide an even more extreme
example. In the Hittite kingdom, the king owned all
of the land, and the people were like tenant farm-
ers, required to produce a certain amount of produce for the king.

Not only did kings conscript soldiers for war,
enslave people for labor, and confiscate land at will,
but they held absolute power over children and
women. Sons and daughters could be taken as
household servants and any woman could be taken

by the king as a wife or mistress. Since the king held absolute power and authority, personal liberty was virtually unknown and always at risk.

These are reasons why Israel's demand for a king is a serious departure from what God had planned. God had given strict demands for leaders in Israel. He had mandated equal rights for all and demanded that Israel be fair to strangers in the land that accepted God's law.

In Israel, land was acquired by divine allotment. God first revealed this to Moses. He told Joshua, "I have given you this land. Take it" (see Joshua 1:2, 3, 13). Further, God allotted the land according to the 12 tribes of Israel, each with specific areas. Therefore, land allotment was not in human hands when it came to Israel. God owned the land, and He had allotted it to His people—a total contrast to the idea of the king owning the land.

In Israel, marriages were respected. Women were never to be kidnaped or mistreated. There were definite laws on those subjects.

One troubling reference to the subject of a king in Israel is found in Deuteronomy 17. The passage describes the model for a king in Israel and may lead to the question, "How does one deal with this apparent contradiction?" Close reading of Chapter 17 reveals that the model for a king in Israel had no resemblance to those models described earlier. The Israelite king was not supposed to multiply wives, horses and chariots, and excessive wealth. He was to be guided by the Mosaic Law, faithfully observing every word of it.

Note the precise wording:

Thou mayest not set a stranger over thee, which is not thy brother. But he shall not multiply horses to himself, nor cause the people to return to Egypt, to the end that he should multiply horses: forasmuch as the Lord hath said unto you, Ye shall henceforth return no more that way. Neither shall he multiply wives to himself, that his heart turn not away: neither shall he greatly multiply to himself silver and gold (Deuteronomy 17:15-17).

More specifically note:

When he sitteth upon the throne of his kingdom, that he shall write him a copy of this law in a book out of that which is before the priests the Levites: and it shall be with him, and he shall read therein all the days of his life: that he may learn to fear the Lord his God, to keep all the words of this law and these statutes, to do them: that his heart be not lifted up above his brethren, and that he turn not aside from the commandment, to the right hand, or to the left: to the end that he may prolong his days in his kingdom, he, and his children, in the midst of Israel (Deuteronomy 17:18-20).

Such a leader as that would have been a good leader, not at all like the kings previously discussed in the ancient Near East.

Slavery was unacceptable among the children of Israel. God told His people to remember what it was like to have been a slave in Egypt and never to enslave their fellow Israelites. All authority in Israel came from the divine law, not from human whim.

The people of Israel knew these things. Deuteronomy was part of their Bible. Nevertheless, Israel wanted a king—a king like other nations, a king to prevent military losses. This displeased Jehovah, because He knew they were removing Him from that central position in their lives. In all likelihood, one should view Israel's first excuse for a king—the fact that Samuel's sons were corrupt—as a mere smokescreen. Samuel always wanted godly leadership over Israel.

Israel's third reason for wanting a king—to prevent further military losses—did not surface until the end of the chapter where Samuel was trying to reason with them. Note what Samuel told them:

> This will be the manner of the king that shall reign over you: He will take your sons, and appoint them for himself, for his chariots, and to be his horsemen; and some shall run before his chariots. And he will appoint him captains over thousands, and captains over fifties; and will set them to ear his ground, and to reap his harvest, and to make his instruments of war, and instruments of his chariots. And he will take your daughters to be confectionaries, and to be cooks, and to be bakers. And he will take your fields, and your vineyards, and your oliveyards, even the best of them, and give them to his servants. And he will take the

tenth of your seed, and of your vineyards,
and give to his officers, and to his servants.
And he will take your menservants, and
your maidservants, and your goodliest
young men, and your asses, and put them
to his work. He will take the tenth of your
sheep: and ye shall be his servants. And
ye shall cry out in that day because of your
king which ye shall have chosen you; and
the Lord will not hear you in that day (1
Samuel 8:11-18).

The people of Israel listened to that sobering exhortation and still said, "We must have a king like other nations, to rule over us, and to go out at our head and fight our battles" (see 1 Samuel 8:19, 20). The military issue was definitely on their minds.

One cannot help but wonder what was really behind the complaint. After all, under the leadership of Joshua and more recently the leadership of Samuel, Israel had experienced victory after victory. Most recently, the Philistines had been defeated simply because Samuel prayed. So, what was really behind this demand for a king?

When ancient Near Eastern kings fought battles, they went forth with military strength, using armor and the latest weapons. Israel fought by faith, based on obedience to God's Word; and believe it or not, often without weapons. One knows this from a Bible account that relates how in Saul's army, only he and his son Jonathan had spears (1 Samuel 13:20-22). The others had only their farm implements with which to engage the enemy.

The map shows that the Philistines occupied the southwestern portion of the land. Not only were they a powerful people but they also held a monopoly on iron. So strong was the Philistine hold on iron that the Israelite farmer had to go to the Philistines just to get his farm implements sharpened. This meant that God had to work a miracle for the Israelite army to win any battles at all. That, of course, was exactly what God wanted. He wanted His people to depend on Him, and He had proven Himself more than willing to fight their battles.

Israel defeated the Amalekites miraculously as Moses raised his hands in prayer. Israel took the walled city of Jericho through miraculous help from God. Scripture gives many other examples to show battles were not fought in Israel as they were fought in other countries. God gave victories, but He demanded that there be no sin in the camp. In other words, Israel's strength lay in God rather than a powerful standing army. Israel had to have faith in God, courage enough to face the enemy, and obedience to God's law which demanded ethical living and abstinence from sin and idolatry.

What one discovers here with Israel in the time of Samuel is that they were tired of this arrangement. They were tired of trusting God for miracles. They wanted to get rid of their moral obligation, their need for faith. They wanted a king. In essence, Israel was saying, "Why can't we just have a king like other nations, and a standing army that can take care of these military problems? Why does our behavior in daily life have to determine whether we have victory or not? Nobody else operates like this. Nobody else has to be so introspective, so self-analytical, so conscientious. This idea of winning battles by prayer and obedience and impeccable moral behavior and faith—it is so risky. Besides it is expecting too much. Why can't we just have a king and a standing army to take care of everything?"

In those words, and in those attitudes, one comes to understand more fully the underlying problem with Israel's request for a king.

Being the sterling prophet that he was, Samuel simply could not believe his ears. He was absolutely overwhelmed. He went to God in prayer, and God strengthened him. "The people have not rejected you, Samuel," God said, "but they have rejected me. Let them have their king" (1 Samuel 8:7). What a sad day indeed when God lets people have what they demand even when it is not good for them!

Israel's Kings

Samuel anointed a king according to God's direction. This first king of Israel was, one might say, the people's choice. Saul was handsome and of a very striking appearance. The scriptures called him a *gibor hiyal,* a term encountered in the Book of Ruth, with a baseline meaning "that which has to do with strength." Saul was viewed as a hero, most likely a military hero. He was a head and shoulders taller than everybody else in Israel. He looked like someone who really could fight wars, someone who would definitely command a position of leadership in battle.

God gave the people what they wanted. The Bible says that God's Spirit turned Saul into another man (1 Samuel 10:6). Saul did not start with the qualities Samuel would have chosen, but God worked with him. This demonstrated God's grace to Israel even in these circumstances. He was willing to work with Saul, to help this new king if only Saul would be obedient.

The history of Israel confirms Samuel's fears. Saul did not turn out to be a good and obedient king. Looking two generations forward to King Solomon, one finds a king characterized more like other kings of his day—living lavishly, taxing the people heavily, and taking many wives at will. The Bible tells us Solomon had 700 wives and 300 concubines (1 Kings 11:3), and they turned his heart away from God.

From the beginning of his reign, Saul drafted the strong young men for his army. David, though a good king, never seemed to get out from under the constant demand of war. All these things happened just as Samuel said they would.

In wicked King Ahab, one finds demonstrated rampant idolatry and also an example of greedy land confiscation. Ahab had everything he needed, but next door, lived Naboth who had a beautiful and fruitful vineyard. Ahab wanted Naboth's vineyard for a vegetable garden. Naboth would not sell. In Israel, land was a person's rightful possession and, according to law, not even the king could touch it. His answer to the king was, "This land is my divine inheritance. I cannot sell it to you." Ahab pouted. His wife Jezebel could not understand Ahab's attitude. She said to him, "You are the king. If you want it, take it" (see 1 Kings 21:3-16). That is exactly what happened: Ahab stole Naboth's vineyard and came under the severe judgment of God.

Solomon made people work in unbelievable ways. His work days were so excessive that the Israelites spent one month out of every three just working on his special building projects.

All Samuel's fears were definitely confirmed. The rod of authority changed in Israel from its rightful place in God's hands—just, beneficent, wise—into the hands of a greedy human king. Most pathetic of all is the way the people eagerly raced to follow their king to their own destruction.

Conclusion

What does all this have to do with the Christian's life in today's world? Believers today are really not in the business of choosing kings.

These truths graphically remind Christians that God has to remain in charge of their lives. He must be at the helm. Contemporary Christians too often depend on things, on material wealth, to take care of problems. Many today, just like Israel, desire some institution to lead the way and make decisions simple, thus avoiding that close personal relationship with God and the responsibility that goes with it.

One can far too easily conclude that if there were more money readily available, there would not be the constant need for prayer and the seeking of God's face. If one but had that new job, that expanded salary, then one would not have to constantly struggle to pay the bills and to make sure everything was right with God in order to have Him bring the miracle solution. If one only had unlimited material resources, then one would not have to worry all the time. Such thoughts and attitudes portray that one is not very concerned with God or with His opinion, only with self. Such was the attitude of Israel, was it not?

But God wants His children to bring daily problems and decisions to Him. He wants daily acknowledgment that He is King—the only King of all life.

Since money is measurable, it gives one a sense of security and comfort, at least on the surface. But only God gives the peace that passes all understanding. Only He is able to give real security. Only He can be counted on to win every battle, to give directions as to which battles to fight, to lead and guide around every obstacle. In short, the Christian life always requires faith. There is no such thing as finally making it to a point where faith is no longer required and to where an individual no longer needs God's grace and guidance.

Ethics, as well as sensitivity and obedience to God, has always been and will continue to be necessary for spiritual success. The Christian life is a constant battle against the forces of evil that try to swerve one from God's perfect will. Satan constantly tries to tempt believers with greed, selfishness, pride, and many other things designed to divert one's attention from Christ. Yet, only He remains as Lord of the believer's life.

14

King Saul

By Hannah Harrington, Ph.D.

This chapter will discuss the career of King Saul, who was the people's choice, both in terms of their demand for a king and in terms of his physical bearing. The last chapter noted reservations about Saul, but it also ended on something of a positive note by pointing out that God's Spirit came upon Saul and changed his heart. God's mercy and grace are always available for individuals, even for a man like Saul, and there was reason to believe this arrangement would work if Saul would give heed to the voice of God.

The historical record of King Saul highlights his major battles. These reveal his attitudes, character, and overall methods for handling the responsibilities of a king. They also give an early hint as to whether or not things are going to work out for Israel with Saul as their king.

The Major Battles of Saul

Saul engaged in four major battles: (1) with the Ammonites, (2) with the Philistines, (3) with the Amalekites, and (4) with the Philistines again—the battle in which he died. Attention will be given to the first three, because they offer vivid indications of Saul's spirituality, or lack of it, with applications for living today.

THE AMMONITE BATTLE

The *Bible Atlas* shows the people of Ammon living east of the Jordan River, an area normally referred to as the Trans-Jordan, between the Dead Sea and the Sea of Galilee. Faced off against the Ammonites, on the west side of the Jordan, were the Israelites.

The Ammonites, under their leader Nahash (a Hebrew word meaning snake), threatened to lay siege to the city of Jabesh-Gilead. In the ancient Near East, wars usually began with a siege, designed to close up a city and starve the people into submission. It so happened in this situation that the people in Jabesh-Gilead gave up rather quickly. They requested a peace treaty and offered to serve the Ammonites.

King Nahash thought he could get a better deal than that. He offered to make peace, but he added, "We will also put out the right eye of every person in the city" (see 1 Samuel 11:2). To Nahash's way of thinking, that would solidify the treaty in a manner the people could never forget. That proposition was not what the people of Jabesh-Gilead had expected. They said, "Give us a week to think about it and we will get back to you " (see v. 3).

162

They immediately sent word to King Saul who had set up his capital at Gibeah, in the very heart of Israelite territory. Saul was certainly not pleased. He called for all the tribes of Israel to unite, setting forth a policy that ran something like this: "We're responsible for each other, all for one and one for all. Our kindred have been threatened, so we need to come to their aid." The Bible says that the Spirit of God gripped Saul. His anger flared in righteous indignation that anybody, any enemy, would threaten the people of God in such manner (see v. 6).

Saul cut up a yoke of oxen and sent the pieces throughout the land of Israel with a warning: "Here is what will happen to your oxen if you do not show up for battle with Saul and Samuel against the Ammonite King Nahash" (see v. 7). Saul showed respect for Jehovah by including His prophet Samuel in his recruitment message. He showed faith and refused to compromise. Rather, he insisted that the people of Jabesh-Gilead stand firm and publicly declared he was not going to let King Nahash threaten the armies of Israel in such manner. Thus, God gave Israel a complete victory.

The battle over, the Israelites celebrated. The people offered sacrifices to God and were so thrilled and pleased with their new King that they had an inauguration banquet. Throughout all Israel, the people were happy.

If one were to judge Saul's actions in this first test of his power, one would have to give him an A plus. He did the right thing. He insisted on unity, and he worked in cooperation with God's prophet. He showed courage by believing God for the victory.

163

He did not let the enemy of God's people get away with anything.

After this victory and before the next war, Samuel gave something of a farewell address to the people of Israel. Basically, he reminded them that their request for a king had not been a good thing, but he went on to reassure the people. "Don't be afraid," he told them, "Serve God with all your heart. If both you and the king who reigns over you will follow the Lord, things will work out. God is gracious. He will work with you and with the king" (see 1 Samuel 12:14).

Unfortunately, as has been noted so often, power does corrupt. When one does not keep God in the forefront, when one does not truly honor Him for the victory, then power will definitely corrupt.

Saul, victorious over the Ammonites, next had to join battle with a more persistent enemy—his own soul and human weaknesses.

THE PHILISTINE BATTLE

To understand Israel's ongoing conflicts with the Philistines, one must first pinpoint their location geographically. Primarily, they were entrenched in the southwest corner of the land of Canaan. Today, their land would approximate what newspapers refer to constantly as the Gaza Strip. That was their primary territory, their headquarters and their five main cities.

The Philistines were sea people, traders, and looters. They had come originally from the island of Crete, or the Greek islands, some by sea and some by land around through the land of the Hittites and down through what is today Lebanon. Their intentions had been to loot the cities of the land of Canaan and move on down to confront mighty Egypt. However, when they finally met up with the armies of Egypt, they were stopped in their tracks. There is a secular record of this confrontation, written by the Egyptian pharaoh, telling about how he was able to stop this migration of sea people.

Unable to move farther south, the Philistines settled into the southwest corner of the land of Canaan and built strong cities. They grew even stronger militarily because of their monopoly on iron and their skill at fashioning what were then modern weapons of warfare. One should realize, as well, that the Philistines tended to move out from their southwest corner and infiltrate over into land claimed by the tribes of Israel. At the time of Saul, they had moved up into Israel as far as Bashan.

The Philistines, with weapons of iron and body armor, presented an awesome sight. The latter story of David and Goliath reminds one of what they were like. Goliath was armored and protected everywhere except his forehead. Unquestionably, the Philistines were a major threat to Israelite peace and to their occupancy of the Land of Promise. It was a threat the new King Saul could not ignore for long.

Saul prepared for battle with the Philistines by taking an army of 2,000 chosen men with him and, at the same time, putting 1,000 good men under the leadership of his son Jonathan.

Almost immediately, Jonathan took down a Philistine garrison. God gave him a victory. Saul advertised the victory, but did not mention it as Jonathan's. Saul then rallied all the Israelite forces at Gilgal.

At Gilgal, Saul waited for Samuel to come and offer the opening sacrifices. That was the proper procedure—God would be acknowledged first, and He would be asked, "Is this your will?" But Samuel was delayed. When the prophet did not show up right away, Saul grew fearful the people would scatter and go home. Saul thought he could not afford to let that happen, so he proceeded to offer a sacrifice to God on his own.

Samuel arrived just as Saul finished the sacrificial offering. What a terrible moment! Saul was a soldier, a warrior with blood on his hands. He was not a priest, and he certainly was not supposed to be offering sacrifices unto Jehovah.

"What have you done?" Samuel asked (see 1 Samuel 13:11).

That was a wonderful opportunity for Saul to confess and say, "I'm sorry, Samuel." But he did not respond that way at all. Rather, he said, "Well, you know, the people started scattering and you hadn't come. I thought the Philistines might march down and trample me. So I forced myself to go ahead and offer this burnt offering" (see vv. 11, 12).

Samuel's next words weighed heavy with judgment and prophetic warning, "God would have worked miracles with you, Saul. Obedience is better than sacrifice. Now, your kingship will not last. God will give it to another" (see vv. 13, 14).

As was emphasized earlier, battles in Israel were won by faith and obedience, not military power. In the midst of all this, Jonathan, Saul's son, proved to be a sterling example of faith. His heroism inspired the battle in the first place, because Saul was frightened. Jonathan and his armor-bearer took out a whole garrison of Philistines. The incident is recorded like this: "And Jonathan said to the young man that bare his armour, Come, and let us go over unto the garrison of these uncircumcised: it may be that the Lord will work for us: for there is no restraint to the Lord to save by many or by few" (1 Samuel 14:6). What a wonderful statement of faith. Jonathan acknowledged it made no difference to God how many there were. God could give the victory. The armor-bearer's faith was expressed when he said, "You lead the way and I will follow" (see v. 7).

Jonathan tested his armor-bearer yet further by saying, "When we get close to that garrison, we will see if they talk to us, and what they say. If they invite us to come on up, we will know the Lord is going to give us victory" (see vv. 8-10).

The Philistines did indeed come out, and they actually mocked them by saying, "Look here. Some Hebrews have come out of their holes. Why don't you guys come on up here? We will teach you a lesson" (see v. 12). That challenge, rather than frightening Jonathan, only confirmed that God was going to give them victory.

Jonathan and his armor-bearer went against that garrison and actually took out 20 men. The Bible says God sent an earthquake to terrorize the whole lot of them. Following that incident, Saul and his company were more than happy to join Jonathan. They pursued the enemy and won the victory.

Saul does another foolish thing when he makes a very rash oath by saying, "Nobody here is allowed to eat anything until I have had vengeance on my enemies" (see v. 24). There is definitely something wrong with that statement: too much "I" language. It makes one wonder, whose battle this is anyway.

Jonathan had not heard about the oath. Being hungry, he found a beehive, scooped out the honey and ate it (see v. 27). Jonathan would have been put to death had not the people intervened on his behalf.

Saul's oath had yet further consequences: when the Israelite people got hungry, they just started slaughtering and eating animals right on the spot. They did not wait to slaughter the animals properly, and to drain the blood as prescribed in Levitical law. They just yielded to their appetites, slaughtered, and ate (see v. 32). This was definitely a violation of the law. God was very angry, and Saul knew it, so he quickly set up an altar and had sacrifices offered to God.

Scripture gives another interesting comment about Saul, about his character: "The same was the first altar that he built unto the Lord" (v. 35). Basically, Saul was not a praying man; this was the first altar for him to build.

Through these events, one begins to see a different Saul, to realize that the A plus given him before this battle with the Philistines may have been premature. Too much self is coming through in Saul, too much pride, too much arrogance.

THE AMALEKITES

The third of Saul's battles was with the Amalekites. One cannot know for sure just where the Amalekites were situated geographically. They seemed to have moved around. However, it is known that they were descendants of Esau, and they decided to come up against Israel in battle.

God told Samuel, and Samuel told Saul that these Amalekites were to be totally destroyed. This was to have been a holy war with everything dedicated to God Jehovah, and Saul was to take no booty and no reward. The Amalekites were to be obliterated from the face of the earth.

God's anger against Amalek went all the way back to when Israel encountered Amalek in the wilderness of Sinai. There, Amalek had attacked Israel from the rear and for no good reason. Israel was just peacefully marching through the desert, not bothering anybody. God now promised the prophet Samuel that He was going to settle the score with Amalek (see 1 Samuel 15:1-3).

Israel went into battle, and again Saul made a big mistake by absolutely disobeying God's Word. Rather than destroying all the Amalekites and their possessions, Saul spared the animals and even the life of the wicked King Agag. According to the scriptures, Saul destroyed only what was cheap and rather worthless (see vv. 7-9).

Does this not sound like the same problem Joshua had with Achan who greedily looked upon, and then confiscated for himself, some of the treasure of Jericho? Achan brought sin into the camp and paid with his life.

The prophet Samuel came to Saul obviously unhappy. Saul went out to meet Samuel, giving him a cheerful greeting: "Blessed be thou of the Lord: I have performed the commandment of the Lord" (v. 13). His was blatant hypocrisy and straight out lying. Not only that, but he was also lying to the prophet of God, and acting like everything was all right.

169

Samuel knew better. He asked, "What meaneth then this bleating of the sheep in mine ears, and the lowing of the oxen which I hear?" (v. 14). Again, one would hope that Saul would confess, acknowledging he is in the presence of God's prophet. But, no. He denied all responsibility, and he blamed the people by saying, "They spared the best oxen and the best sheep, Samuel. They spared them in order to make a great sacrifice unto the Lord your God (see v. 21).

Again, something is strange here. Why did Saul say "the Lord *your* God?" Where was Saul's God?

Samuel placed the blame right where it belonged. He spoke sharply with his rebuke: "Just stop, Saul. Stop right there. I do not need any more of your garbage. Just stop it." Then Samuel went on with, "Let me tell you what the Lord said to me last night. You are no longer a small and irresponsible man. You are king and head of the tribes of Israel. This is all your responsibility. Why have you disobeyed the Lord and swooped up the spoil in defiance of God's will?"

There is no way a person can hoodwink God. God always knows exactly who is at fault. He knows every deed, every attitude, precisely why one does whatever he decides to do. God knows every motive of the heart. Human excuses go over today no better than they did with Saul and his pathetic argument that the people did it.

Saul expressed the epitome of pride. He did not confess the sin. He tried to explain it away, to rationalize. He did not humble himself before God's prophet. He just kept trying to worm his way out of the blame. Even after Samuel told him to stop, Saul kept on: "But I did obey the Lord. I took care of the mission on which the Lord sent me."

Samuel's response was, "Rebellion is as the sin of witchcraft. . . . Because thou hast rejected the word of the Lord, he hath rejected thee from being king" (v. 23). Spiritually, Saul just did not get the picture. It was time to stop the argument and fall on his face before God in repentance.

Finally, Saul tried to confess, but it was too late. As Samuel turned from him, Saul admitted he was wrong but he added, "Please honor me in the presence of the people" (see v. 30). His confession was obviously superficial. It lacked the deep ring of genuine contrition. It seemed more of a quick fix, the saving of face before the people rather than godly sorrow. Note the words, "Samuel, just honor me."

Samuel ignored everything Saul said. He took a sword and personally executed King Agag. One would think that, had Saul been really confessing and truly repenting, he would have taken care of Agag. Scripture says that Samuel never saw Saul again to the day of his death (see v. 35). He was directed of God to anoint David to take over the kingdom.

Saul's death came a few years later in a final battle with the Philistines. It was a most shameful death, with his head left to hang on the walls of Beth-shan. His epitaph should properly read: "A man who tried to do it his way, tried to get his own honor, tried to sidestep what God commanded."

Conclusion

What lessons are to be learned from this unfortunate man?

First of all, God did not hold Saul accountable for Israel's unwise choice of a king. Rather, God was willing to work through Saul, to bless him. He even put His Spirit upon Saul, so much so that the people at one time asked, "Is Saul among the prophets too?" Even they were surprised at God's Spirit on Saul. In grace and His mercy, God was willing to work with Saul. These stories clearly show that God gave Saul opportunity after opportunity to mend his ways.

As a king, Saul turned out to be a disaster. He could not accept criticism—he had to fight it, reject it, and put the blame elsewhere. Some people today are like that. They just simply cannot admit they made the wrong choice and did the wrong thing. They cannot honestly and from the heart say, "Lord, I'm sorry. I made the wrong decision. Forgive me. Help me." Such individuals, like King Saul, are to be pitied. Saul's life is a graphic example of gradual deterioration, unwise decisions, and outright rebellion.

If one wants God's grace and blessing, he must be genuine in terms of honesty and character. One must accept honest criticism and be humble before God and His servants. One must constantly examine motives and actions, asking God to turn the searchlight of His Word on every deed and thought. One must seek purity and refuse to cover up faults and to blame others. Finally, power corrupts when God is left out of the picture. Saul, by his disobedience to God, was taking God's place in Israel.

In every generation, the Christian must walk humbly in submission before God. Christian leaders are especially susceptible to these errors, thinking themselves in authority, when it is really God Jehovah who holds success and failure, life and death in His hands.

15

King David

By Hannah Harrington, Ph.D.

God told Samuel He had turned from Saul to another. He was turning to a person who would be after His own heart—King David (1 Samuel 16:1-7). An interesting comparison between these two men can be made from Scripture: Saul was the people's choice, but God moved on him and changed his heart (a change which did not last); conversely, David was God's choice—one who loved God from the beginning.

Man sees the outside of a person. So Saul, in all appearances, looked like the right choice, but he simply would not follow God. David was not just the people's choice; he was God's choice. This contrast will be highlighted throughout this chapter. David had a very unusual combination of qualities: he was sensitive, a musician who played the harp and wrote songs, and he was also a courageous warrior. This chapter will portray David's life in four settings: (1) his preparation, (2) his kingship, (3) his troubles, and (4) his life in comparison to Saul's life.

David's Preparation

When the sovereign God wishes to use people, He prepares them. He does not just hand someone a task without equipping him to do it right. The Scripture is very clear on this. God prepared David for service long before he became king of Israel. He perfected his skills as a musician while yet a shepherd boy, developing such a reputation that when King Saul was depressed and struggling with his inner demons, capital courtiers recommended that he call David to play soothing music. Because David was very good at playing the harp, his music calmed Saul's troubled spirit. One might wonder what would have happened in Saul's presence if some of the so-called musicians of today had been called before him.

Those with musical gifts and talents need to develop them. They need to be responsible stewards of the gifts God has given them.

David was equally good in terms of his warrior's ability. He was courageous enough to confront Goliath with only a sling and some stones. Furthermore, he was wise enough to cut off Goliath's head afterward, proving he knew how to use a sword. His skill with weapons may seem somewhat surprising in light of what is known of the period and how difficult it was to acquire them. In spite of this, David learned about weapons, and he became skilled in their use.

David's uniqueness is portrayed in a merging of the musician's sensitivity with the courage and strength of a warrior.

David's spirituality is seen in his great faith in God. Goliath was 9.5 feet tall, fearsome in appearance, and so armored for battle that none would accept his challenge to fight. As was customary with armies of that day, the Philistines had chosen Goliath as their representative, their champion. They sent him out to challenge the opposition to a one-on-one confrontation—a fight to the death. They believed their gods fought with them. Thus, Goliath was a threat and a challenge not only to the army of Saul but also to the God of Israel. The man who won the duel thus represented the strongest god.

When Goliath stepped out before the Philistines to challenge Saul's army, he expected a worthy opponent. Understandably, when he saw only a boy with a sling coming toward him, he was highly insulted. His reaction was, "Am I a dog, that thou comest against me with staves?" (1 Samuel 17:43). He went on to say he would feed David's flesh to the birds (v. 44).

David's response was classic faith, not in himself, but in the God of Israel:

> Then said David to the Philistine, Thou comest to me with a sword, and with a spear, and with a shield: but I come to thee in the name of the Lord of hosts, the God of the armies of Israel, whom thou hast defied. This day will the Lord deliver thee into mine hand; and I will smite thee, and take thine head from thee; and I will give the carcases of the host of the Philistines this day unto the fowls of the air, and to the wild beasts of the earth; that all the earth may know that there is a God in Israel. And all this assembly shall know that the Lord saveth not with sword and spear: for the battle is the Lord's, and he will give you into our hands (1 Samuel 17:45-47).

This whole incident was quite an indictment against the army of Israel. Where was their faith? Nevertheless, David did not care who was with him or who was against him. He knew God could bring him victory.

After such a great battle and the people's praises of David, he had to run from the jealous rages of King Saul, thus becoming a fugitive in the land. There were even times when David had to leave Israel and hide in enemy territory. One may have difficulty seeing purpose in the fugitive years of David's life. After all, would it not have been better for David to have been made a captain over Saul's army, so he could lead them to more victories? However, God had a plan and a purpose for David not yet revealed. God knew what He is doing.

Quite surprisingly, David and a small band of men who joined themselves to him, actually ended up in the southern Philistine camp. Though the Philistines were the biggest enemy of Israel, David found more safety there than in Israelite territory under the leadership of Saul. God knew what He was doing. During the time David spent in the Philistine camp, he learned their military strategy, their production and use of arms, their organizational abilities, and their skills as warriors. Most likely, he also learned about their capacity, number of troops, administration, concerns, threats, and other enemies, all knowledge he would put to use later in life.

David's band of political outcasts was made up of 400 men. Scripture describes them as men disgusted with life. They were men who found in David the leader they wanted. One should note also that as David and his men raided along the borders of Israel, David always prayed and sought the blessings of God (2 Samuel 5:19). He never got ahead of God. The Bible says that David had a prophet with him. When he prayed, God sometimes said "yes," and sometimes God said "no." David listened to the voice of God and his victories continued, along with his fearsome reputation as a warrior. Although Samuel anointed him king as a youth, it was actually more than 20 years before David came to the throne of Israel.

David's Reign as King of Israel

As king, David was a very wise administrator.

Recently, archaeologists have uncovered new evidence of David's kingdom. From a dig in Tell Dan in 1993, has come a stone about a foot high which commemorates a military victory. Words on the stone include the phrase *Bayith David*, meaning *house of David*. Bible believers have known for years about David, but now for the skeptics, there is hard historical evidence to back up the Bible's claim for the greatness of David.

David extended Israel's borders to the North and to the South. He subjugated all of the enemy neighbors, including the Philistines. These included Syria to the North, Ammon to the East of the Jordan, and Moab to the South, thus giving him control over the whole Trans-Jordan.

David also made the decision to choose Jerusalem as the capital, a promising city on the border between the tribes of Judah and Benjamin. This choice showed great wisdom. Jerusalem was a border town, inhabited mostly by Jebusites. Neither Judah nor Benjamin claimed it. The Jebusites had lived in Jerusalem all through the Period of the Judges. No Israelites had ever been able to conquer the mountainous fortress, thus leaving a pocket of the enemy within the land of Israel. David, with great faith and courage, took his men up against Jerusalem and won a total victory. He rightly claimed that Jerusalem was his city.

Finally, David showed wisdom and spiritual sensitivity in his desire to build God a house. He told God, "I have a beautiful house. Your presence is represented by a tent" (see 2 Samuel 7:2). He wanted God to have a house.

David's Troubles

One may not really enjoy talking of David's troubles, especially his sins (it is a sordid tale and terrible blot on an otherwise beautiful life), but it is necessary to fully understand God's grace and mercy. God deals with human beings, not perfect people. His objective is redemption and restoration through repentance and trust. Here, too, David presents a sterling example of what God can do and will do for the repentant heart.

The story began during a time of war. On this occasion, David was not with the troops. His general, Joab, was in charge. At home, David saw Bathsheba bathing and desired her. He invited her to his house and initiated a sexual relationship. However, Bathsheba was married to Uriah, one of the soldiers fighting with Joab. Sometime later, David's problem increased significantly when it turned out he had gotten Bathsheba pregnant.

As is characteristic of men and women in trouble, David looked for a human way out. He called Uriah from the battlefront, intending that he go home, spend time with his wife, and thus cover up the sin. Uriah came home all right, but refused to sleep with Bathsheba. He was a soldier engaged in a holy war, and thus forbidden to have sexual relations until the battle was won. David had certainly not counted on that reaction from Uriah. The faithful soldier stayed on the doorstep of David's palace, rather than at home with his wife.

David sent Uriah back to the battle with a letter to Joab, instructing him to see that Uriah was placed on the front line of battle to make sure he would be killed. That is how David the king, David the man after God's own heart, became David the adulterer and David the murderer. Sin is a terrible taskmaster.

The prophet confronted David with God's judgment, telling him, "The child is going to die. Trouble and strife will always rest upon your house. Your wives will be shamed publicly. You sinned in secret, but you will be shamed openly" (see 2 Samuel 12:10-12).

The prophecies all came to pass. The child died. David's family became dysfunctional: rape, murder, and insurrection in his family. Absalom broke David's heart over and over again. He was the son who connived to take over the government, who openly showed no respect for his father, and who ended up dying a violent death. David's greatest heartaches came, not from outside enemies, but from within his own household.

David's Life Compared to Saul's Life

A comparison between Saul and David notes some striking points. Both were kings, both were warriors, both had faults, both committed sin, and both knew what it was to have the Holy Spirit of God move on them. So, why is there admiration when one speaks of David and pity and disdain when Saul is mentioned?

David had a sincere love for God and for God's people. Saul did not. In fact, he was concerned for himself. God and His people were way down Saul's list of priorities.

A look into the Book of Psalms gives a better understanding of David; they reveal the depth of his spiritual commitment. He said of God, "I delight to do thy will, O my God: yea, thy law is within my heart" (40:8). He said to the people, "Love the Lord, all ye his saints" (31:23). And he wrote, "One thing have I desired of the Lord, that will I seek after; that I may dwell in the house of the Lord all the days of my life" (27:4).

David sinned, yes. But his penitence was genuine. He did not ask God to honor him anyway, as did King Saul. David prayed, "Have mercy upon me, O God. . . . For I acknowledge my transgressions: and my sin is ever before me. . . . Create in me a clean heart, O God; and renew a right spirit within me. . . . Then will I teach transgressors thy ways; and sinners shall be converted unto thee" (Psalm 51:1, 3, 10, 13). On yet another occasion David prayed, "Keep back thy servant also from presumptuous sins; let them not have dominion over me" (Psalm 19:13).

Compare Saul's attitude to David's words concerning sacrifice: "Oh God, you have no delight in sacrifice. Were I to give you a burnt offering you would not be pleased. The sacrifice acceptable to God is a broken spirit. A broken and a contrite heart, O God, you will not despise" (see Psalm 51:16, 17).

On another occasion David prepared to worship God and present a sacrifice when a friend stepped forward and offered to give the sacrifice himself. David replied, "How can I offer God that which has cost me nothing?" (see 2 Kings 24:24).

Those are words many Christians today need to consider. How easy it is to desire God's love and blessings, His grace and mercy, His guidance and leadership, while at the same time costing the believer nothing. Christian believers never purchase God's grace and mercy (they are beyond human reach), but believers show their dedication through willingness to place life and all it represents on the altar of service to God.

Attitudes can differ among Christians, it seems. Some say, like David, "I will give what I owe because He's given so much to me." Others say, like Saul, "Well, let's just get through this. I realize I did the wrong thing, but let's just get through this. Honor me anyway."

Most surprisingly, the scriptures reveal that David always respected King Saul, even when his enemy wanted to kill him. Only God in the human heart can make that possible!

David's love for his troops was so strong that, on one occasion when they risked their lives to go get water for him, he poured the water out, saying, "This water is too sacred to drink because men risked their lives for it" (see 2 Samuel 23:15-17).

The writer of the Book of Acts puts David's life into perspective with these words: "David . . . served his own generation by the will of God" (Acts 13:36).

David's love for Saul's son Jonathan is proverbial (they were lifelong friends), but less well known is David's love and concern for the physically handicapped Mephibosheth whom David honored and promised, "You will always have a place at my table" (see 2 Samuel 9:7).

David loved and honored his parents as well, at one point moving them from Canaan into Moab to make sure they were safe.

When both Saul and Jonathan died, David genuinely mourned their deaths, saying, "You daughters of Israel, weep over Saul, who clothed you daintily in scarlet" (2 Samuel 1:24). In short, David truly had a heart for God. He was human, with human weaknesses and foibles, but he had a sincere heart that yearned to know God intimately and personally.

Conclusion

So, what does one learn from the life of David?

First, God is sovereign. He prepared David in advance for his role as king over all Israel. To the human eye, that preparation seems bizarre, through circumstances one could hardly visualize as advantageous. Nevertheless, when God's time came, David was ready and he became a great king and servant of Jehovah, honored to this day.

Upon coming to the throne, David ruled wisely, and he was a good administrator. He was uncompromising but fair, both with his people and with his enemies.

David sincerely loved God and God's people. He combined sensitivity with strength, and music with battle. God blessed David, because David put God first in his life.

God rewarded David for his faithfulness and gave him an eternal dynasty through the Messiah Jesus Christ who came later. Even after he sinned, David's love for God proved genuine. His repentance was honest, and God accepted it, even as God accepts sincere penitents today.

16

1, 2 Kings— Solomon and the Temple

By Hannah Harrington, Ph.D.

The focus for this chapter will be the establishment of Solomon's temple. The first point to be considered will be why Solomon needed to build the Temple. Next will be a description of Solomon's temple, and who worked there, along with their qualifications. Finally, there will be an overview of Solomon's dedication service.

The Scripture clearly indicates God's approval of animal sacrifices. In the ancient world, many people other than the Israelites sacrificed animals in their worship rituals. With Israel each part of the sacrificial system was accompanied by rules that taught certain principles about God. These principles remain in effect today even though Christians do not offer animal sacrifices. Animal sacrifices typified Christ, the supreme sacrifice, who died on the cross for the sins of the world. Since Christ, no further animal sacrifices have been necessary. Nevertheless, certain principles and truths involved in worship in ancient Israel teach lessons that are valuable today.

The phrase *ancient Israelite cult* is a technical expression in Old Testament studies that means "a sacrificial system," including a temple and a priesthood. One might just as easily speak of the Egyptian cult or the Babylonian cult. This refers to a Babylonian or an Egyptian sacrificial system with a temple and a priesthood rather than a *religious cult* in today's society.

God's Temple

God is a holy God; He cannot tolerate evil. The question to be considered here is how a holy God could have fellowship with the flawed, frail, backsliding people of Israel. God's solution was to have His own house of worship. God must have a place the people of Israel would recognize as especially holy, respected, and honored. God wished His people to come into His house with the proper attitude and respect, that which befitted a meeting with the holy God. God is so holy and so powerful that He must be mediated. He is too holy, too powerful, too overwhelming to be experienced directly. This understanding explains the construction of the Tabernacle in the time of Moses. The Tabernacle was simply a big tent—with special rooms, furniture, and functions—in the midst of all the little Israelite tents.

David, because of his love for God, decided to build God a house. His reasoning was, "Lord, I have a nice house. These people have built a beautiful house for me, using the best wood and the best materials. They have honored me, the king, but if anybody is to be honored, it should be You. So, I want to build You a house." God was pleased with David's heart and David's intention. He thought it was a good idea, but He said to David, "You shall not build a house for My name, because you have been a man of war and have shed blood" (1 Chronicles 28: 31, *NKJV*).

God also told David that, because he wanted to build a house for Him, He would honor him with a house not made with hands. God would establish the house of David forever. His would be an eternal dynasty. And, as believers now know, this promise came true through the Messiah, Jesus Christ, who extends the royal line of David forever.

CONSTRUCTION OF THE TEMPLE

It took King Solomon seven years to build the Temple. He used only the finest of materials and the most skilled of workmen. The basic floor plan, the center of the Temple, was similar to that of the Tabernacle. The Temple was made of stone. The floors and walls were made of pure cedar—the finest wood in the ancient East. The furniture was overlaid with gold, and some of it was made of solid gold. That was the heart of the Temple—beautiful to behold.

Surrounding this center of the Temple was a three-story annex which was divided into store rooms, a treasury, and chambers to be used for various purposes. In the main sanctuary were two rooms, the smaller—approximately 30 by 30 feet— the Holy of Holies, and the larger—approximately 30 by 60 feet—the Holy Place. The Holy of Holies was considered God's special room, His throne room. Here rested the ark of the covenant.

Within the ark of the covenant were the tables of stone which God gave to Moses at Mt. Sinai, and upon which were written the Ten Commandments.

189

Next to the ark of the covenant were two golden cherubim, each with a wingspan half the width of the room. The two cherubim together overshadowed the ark of the covenant. In the ancient Tabernacle, two small cherubim rested on top of the ark. Solomon enhanced, expanded, and elaborated on the original design, making everything even more beautiful.

Three things dominated that section of the Temple known as the Holy Place. First, there was an altar of incense, which provided a fragrant smell in the room. Second, there was a table, on which rested 12 loaves of bread—one for each of the tribes—to supply food for the priests on duty at the time. And finally, there were 10 golden lampstands. In the Tabernacle, there had been one golden lampstand. Here again, Solomon followed the design, but he enhanced and elaborated on it.

Outside the Holy Place and the Holy of Holies was the outer court, as with the Tabernacle. The small laver of the Tabernacle was expanded in the Temple to 15 feet in diameter, made of bronze. This was used for purification of the temple vessels. Anything that needed to be washed was washed there. Also in the outer court was the altar of burnt offering where the sacrifices were made unto God. That was the basic floor plan and the basic furnishings of Solomon's temple.

Had one lived in Israel in that day, however, one could not have gone into the inner part of the Temple. The average Israelite could not go into the Holy Place either. Only the priests were allowed. They could go into the Holy Place, but only the high priest could go into the Holy of Holies. Furthermore, he could go in there only one time a year to offer special atonement for the people of Israel.

THE PRIESTS

How did one become a priest? There were very, very strict requirements. First, one had to be born into the proper bloodline—of the tribe of Levi, and in the specific family of Aaron. Only men were allowed to be priests. They served God at the Temple. One might wonder how it was possible for every son of Aaron, every grandson, great grandson, right on down the line to fit in there. Well, they did not all work at once. Other Jewish writings reveal, and there are also clues in the Bible, that the Levites worked in shifts, usually a two-week shift out of every year.

One might think that was quite a job, working only two weeks out of the year, but the rest of the year their job was to teach God's law to the people. Religious education started right from the beginning in Israel. The priests, as well as all the Levites, would teach throughout Israel most of the year. Two weeks in the year the priests worked in the Temple.

Solomon used only the very best when he built the Temple. The best builders in the ancient world were the Phoenicians. They had the best craftsmen, and they had best wood. Although very few are left today, in that day the cedars of Lebanon were famous throughout the world. Solomon ordered the best. Inside the Temple, artisans carved and crafted ornate cherubs, palm trees, flowers, and intricate designs, all beautifully proportioned.

THE PERSONNEL

When it came to work personnel, there were restrictions, of course. The priests worked inside. Any Levite was allowed in the court, but not into the sanctuary. The Levites were there first to protect the sacred house. They were the guardians. They made sure nothing unholy came in. This included people, because no person was allowed in particular areas: not for any reason. The priests were the mediators between God and Israel at His house. The priests were God's agents, so when the people saw them, they thought of holy people—God's special representatives.

Though not allowed to offer sacrifices or go into the sanctuary, the Levites were guardians of the whole Temple complex. They were also skilled musicians, playing instruments and singing songs, thus beautifying the service and directing the people's hearts to the worship of God. In the Book of Psalms, it is revealed that certain Levites had the special function of writing music or hymns, thus making the worship even more beautiful.

The high priest performed his duties under a very strict set of rules. He wore a golden diadem on his forehead that said *Holy,* meaning "holiness unto the Lord," reminding all that he was God's agent. On his breastplate, he wore 12 gemstones, each representing a different tribe in Israel. These reminded the people that when the high priest went into the Holy Place, and even into the Holy of Holies, he was taking them before God. The high priest was every Israelite's mediator with Jehovah. He represented Israel before the throne of God, and at the same time, he represented God to Israel.

THE SACRIFICIAL SYSTEM

The priests also officiated the sacrificial system, which was rather complex. Some sacrifices were for sin, but not all. When a person sinned, he/she brought an animal before God, saying in effect: "I have violated the commands of holy God. I deserve to die. But God in His mercy has allowed me to bring this substitute animal to die in my place." The sinner then killed his own animal sacrifice. This taught Israel both the seriousness of sin and the mercy of God. Of course with this sacrificial act, one had to be repentant and offer confession. The Scripture is very clear on this point in the Book of Numbers. If one sinned "with a high hand" (Numbers 15:30, RSV)—in other words, deliberately—then one could not simply send a servant with a sacrifice and get forgiveness. One had to genuinely confess and repent. Otherwise, one was to be cut off from Israel.

There were other sacrificial offerings, such as peace offerings, grain offerings, and burnt offerings. The peace offering could also be translated as the fellowship offering. These sacrificial offerings were brought to God, not because one had sinned but because one was grateful for all God had done. The Scripture says that one had only a day in which to eat these thanksgiving offerings. The reason for this is that the family was supposed to invite their friends, their whole family, making it a time of fellowship and a festive occasion. Thus, one sees that God ordained fellowship right from the beginning—fellowship in His house, fellowship in His presence. The best portions of the animal were given to the priests who were officiating—in effect, like giving the best portions to God—but most of it was eaten with family and friends.

Dedication of the Temple

The details of Solomon's dedication service are recorded in 2 Chronicles 5, 6, and 7. This is the first service ever to be conducted in the new Temple. Solomon seems to have had in mind only one thought: *Lord, I sure hope You are going to be happy.*

What, precisely, was the order of things?

First, 120 Levite musicians lined up with trumpets. Miraculously, the Scripture records, they played in unison. Then came a group of Levite singers—the choir—to sing hymns. They were all dressed in white linen: the first Scriptural reference to choir robes. They too had instruments in their hands—cymbals and harps—praising the Lord, saying, "For he is good; for his mercy endureth for ever" (2 Chronicles 5:13).

And what happened? God was so pleased that His presence filled the house. Scripture says He filled the Temple with a cloud. The priests could not minister in the house because of the glory of God. What a wonderful occasion! Best of all, when they placed all the sacrifices on the altar, fire came down from God and incinerated the sacrifices with all the people watching. The fire was real. The people knew God was pleased. It was indeed a wonderful occasion! This fire was important because it was going to consume Israel's sin offerings and guilt offerings. This was the fire that was going to purge the evil out of Israel and it would be the responsibility of the priests to keep this holy fire burning on the altar. Scripture says they offered a burnt offering every morning and a burnt offering every evening for the whole state of Israel.

This sets forth a wonderful teaching principle for all of God's people today. When believers come to Christ for salvation and the fire of God begins to burn in their hearts, it is a miracle—a wonderful, exciting, born-again miracle. Then it becomes the Christian's responsibility to keep that fire burning—through prayer, through constant communication and fellowship with the Lord.

At Solomon's dedication of the Temple, God was definitely present. His presence remains the most important element in any worship service. For example, What if one were invited to meet the queen of England at beautiful Buckingham Palace in London, and upon arrival, admired the gardens, saw the palace guards, watched various parades and displays, and saw the ornate decorations of the buildings, yet never got to meet the queen? Something would be missing. It is the same thing—though far more important—with God. Unless He is in the house, present when one worships, what point is there to all these choirs and musicians, and all the other rituals? What is the point if God is not present?

The Temple dedication reminds one that, from the very earliest of times, God saw His house as a meeting place with His people. It was where He and His could meet, converse, and fellowship; and it was to be a sacred place, honored and revered in the heart.

There was yet more to Solomon's dedication. He had things to tell God—very beautiful things. Solomon stood before the altar of the Lord, in front of the whole congregation of Israel, and spread forth his hands. On a bronze platform, before all the people, he first stood and then knelt to offer a most beautiful prayer (2 Chronicles 6:12, 13). In summary, he acknowledged he had fulfilled David's wishes to build God a house. He acknowledged

God's promises and God's goodness in keeping His promises to David. Then he acknowledged that, when one thinks about it, one knows that God, the Creator of the universe, cannot be confined to any building.

Solomon beseeched God to always listen to the prayers prayed in this house. Whether those prayers be repentance for sins committed, whether for enemies that threaten God's people, whether because of famine, drought, disease, or any other disaster or crises, Solomon wanted God to hear the prayers offered in this dedicated Temple. Even if a stranger came by and prayed, Solomon wanted God to hear the prayer and answer from heaven.

Since God's name was on this house, Solomon prayed for God's eyes to be open night and day to the needs of His people. God said, "This is My house" (see 2 Chronicles 7:16), meaning one can come here to talk to God, to know He is present. In the ancient world, to know someone's name meant to have access to him. So it is with God and His house. Christians today honor God and go to Him in the name of His Son, Jesus Christ.

God's response to Solomon's prayer was most beautiful. Fire came down and consumed the sacrifices. Smoke filled the Temple. Following the dedication, the people celebrated for a whole week, their faces reflecting the glory of God.

God appeared to Solomon in the night with His response:

> And the Lord appeared to Solomon by night,
> and said unto him, I have heard thy prayer,

and have chosen this place to myself for an house of sacrifice. If I shut up heaven that there be no rain, or if I command the locusts to devour the land, or if I send pestilence among my people; if my people, which are called by my name, shall humble themselves, and pray, and seek my face, and turn from their wicked ways; then will I hear from heaven, and will forgive their sin, and will heal their land. Now mine eyes shall be open, and mine ears attent unto the prayer that is made in this place. For now have I chosen and sanctified this house, that my name may be there for ever: and mine eyes and mine heart shall be there perpetually. And as for thee, if thou wilt walk before me, as David thy father walked, and do according to all that I have commanded thee, and shalt observe my statutes and my judgments; then will I stablish the throne of thy kingdom, according as I have covenanted with David thy father, saying, There shall not fail thee a man to be ruler in Israel (2 Chronicles 7:12-18).

Those words present quite a challenge for believers today. Can God say the same thing about Christian churches today? Is God's heart always there? Do God's people bear His name?

Conclusion

The dedication of Solomon's temple has definite applications for Christians attending church today. Some people do not see why God's people should have a church building at all or why they

197

should have a weekly service. They would as soon stay home and watch worship on TV, or just pray at home. After all, God is everywhere. In the Old Testament, the Israelites also knew God was everywhere. That was not the point. A special, beautiful building was set apart just to honor God. It was to get away from the everyday work place, away from the family home, to think of God himself. It was a place to assemble and offer praise and worship.

Today, Christians recognize Christ as the supreme sacrifice, offered once and for all for the sins of the world. Animal sacrifices are no longer necessary. But, from the Temple, one also learns of other aspects of worship. One learns of fellowship, praise, prayer, and sacred ritual. One learns the temple or church is an earthly meeting place which God honors and agrees to fill with His presence. Worship services are important. They should be holy. One should not rush thoughtlessly into God's presence, but should come with respect and reverence. The church building bears God's name and it is a sign to all passing that God is honored in this place. God hears prayer at His house. Those working at His house, whether ushers or musicians or ministers or teachers, should be exemplary and direct the congregation to God.

Finally, it is important for the Christian to consider motives when entering church. They should expect the fire of God's Holy Spirit to burn in their hearts and to sense His divine and glorious presence.

17 Praise and Lament: The Poetic Books— Psalms, Song of Solomon, Lamentations

By Hannah Harrington, Ph.D.

Throughout the poetic books of the Bible, especially in the Psalms, one often encounters the themes of *praise* and *lament*. This chapter will focus on these themes.

The Book of Psalms is very special because the writings are so personal in nature. Reading them, one can sense the writer's heart and soul being poured either into a praise to God or a lament for some crisis situation. The reader can easily identify with this personal, reflective type of writing. Hassell Bullock says, "To read and pray the Psalms is to join the voices of numberless people who too have read and prayed them, have felt their joy, anguish and indignation." Thus, reading the Psalms is always a very personal and intimate experience.

Bible scholars have traditionally identified many types of psalms: hymns, penitential psalms, wisdom psalms, and messianic psalms. There are even imprecatory psalms which call for evil or a curse upon the enemy. There are enthronement psalms to be used when the king is being installed. Of course most of the time, the writers of the psalms are talking about God as King on His throne. Some scholars, however, have concluded that basically all these can be categorized as either praise or lament. This study will follow that concept.

The Praise Psalm

The word *praise* has many synonyms, as used in Scripture: "to exalt, to lift up, to honor, to extol, to give homage, to worship, to serve and to glorify." C.S. Lewis, the English writer and theologian, said: "Praise is joy expressing itself in speech." To truly glorify God is to enjoy Him. When individuals enjoy something, they tend immediately to praise it. A masterful piece of art, a melodious rendition of music, a delicious dinner: if one enjoys these, he automatically expresses praise. Praise comes out of, and continues, because of the enjoyment.

The same is true in one's relationship with God. When one enjoys Him—His presence . . . being with Him—one just spontaneously praises Him. If one does not enjoy Him, the praise is rather meaningless. If one did not really enjoy the dinner, then saying it was a good dinner would not make it so. Praise of God is lifeless and dead, if one does not really enjoy Him.

What is true praise? One cannot truly praise something that is not being enjoyed. The next logical question might be: Why does God demand praise? Is that not a little arrogant? What if individual people went around demanding praise? Would one not conclude, "They really think they are something"?

Yet, God demands praise. Does God need it? Has He an ego problem? Does God need our approval? Certainly not. He is the only perfect, pure, totally self-sufficient Being in the universe. It is not that God needs praise, but that His people need to give it. Praise establishes priorities. Praise invites God into one's innermost being. The scriptures advise: "The righteous are glad when they praise him" (see Psalm 68:3). They also say, "The soul that's in despair must begin to praise him" (see Psalm 42:11). God wants His children to enjoy Him, to invite Him into every event of the day. In the process of praise, the omnipotent God makes His presence known. He comes into man's limited world. Quoting C.S. Lewis again: "To praise God is to appreciate and enjoy the most beautiful, the most satisfying Person or Object in the world."

Somebody has said, "Never to have been in love is never to have lived." That may or may not be true; but, not to praise God and so never have enjoyed His presence is certainly never to have been spiritually alive. It means never to have been awake, and somehow to have missed the greatest experience given to humankind. Spiritually speaking, not to praise God is to be dead.

How does one praise God properly? A look into the Book of Psalms gives some clues. First, praise includes reflection on who God is. One finds many descriptions of who God is in the Psalms. He is described as both father and mother (27:10). He is described as a shepherd (23:1). He is described as water for the thirsty (42:1, 2; 63:1, 2). He is described as a bird protecting her young (91:4). He is described as a judge (50:4, 6), as a fortress (27:1; 91:2), a shield and buckler (91:4), as the King of the whole earth (47:7), as the awesome Creator (33:8, 9), the omnipotent One (91:1).

Thus, praise begins with reflection on just who this marvelous God really is and on how awesome He really is. Then one moves on to reflect on what this marvelous, omnipotent God has done. Here one discovers personal attention from the great and almighty God of heaven and earth. What an awesome thought! The Creator of the universe is personally concerned with what is happening at the moment in an individual's life. God is so magnificent, so big and awesome, and yet He is concerned for those little, daily problems of a single life! Though transcendently awesome, God is yet close to each individual. He rules the universe, and yet he personally intervenes in each life on planet Earth. He is the Creator of all things, and yet He has given mankind His earth and promised His backing and support.

The psalmist says, "Whom have I in heaven, but thee? And there is none upon the earth that I desire beside thee" (73:25). So, when people praise God, they reflect on who He is and then they reflect on what He has done for others and for them.

The results of praise are most exciting. A person who praises and worships God is oriented and focused and fixed on God. Such an individual cannot fail. One may have down times and periods of depression, but in the overall race of life, that person cannot lose. There is only victory in the godly life of true praise.

Likewise, the individual who is full of praise to God will have a healthy self-esteem. Praise of its very nature authenticates self-identity and self-worth. It is virtually impossible to maintain a low view of self when one begins to read the Psalms carefully and to praise God. Knowing that God the Creator is concerned with what is happening at the moment, in this present day and time, even in one's daily activities, simply lifts the human spirit. Reflecting on Him and on His mighty acts, one is supplied with the meaning and purpose of personal existence.

None should denigrate that very thing on which God is focusing His personal attention. Note the following lines; they reveal this truth:

> The angel of the Lord encampeth round about them that fear him, and delivereth them. O taste and see that the Lord is good: blessed is the man that trusteth in him. O fear the Lord, ye his saints: for there is no want to them that fear him. The young lions do lack, and suffer hunger: but they that seek the Lord shall not want any good thing." (Psalm 34:7-10).

Note yet another verse: "The eyes of the Lord are upon the righteous, and his ears are open unto their cry" (Psalm 34:15).

See what is meant. How can one possibly denigrate oneself when the Creator of the universe has His ears open, just listening for a cry? It is truly amazing when one thinks about it. "The righteous cry and the Lord heareth and delivereth them out of all their troubles" (v. 17). "The Lord is nigh unto them that are of a broken heart; and saveth such as be of a contrite spirit" (v. 18). "The Lord redeemeth the soul of his servants: and none of them that trust in him shall be desolate" (v. 22).

When one reflects on who God is and how much He is concerned for His people, it will make one feel better. Nevertheless, every experience in life is not an "up" experience. There are low points and definite down times. The psalmist knew that, perhaps better than most.

The Lament Psalm

The Psalms give many examples of laments. The lament is recognized by certain specific elements. These elements of formal structure will include . . .

1. An introductory cry to God, called an invocation.
2. A complaint: the description of some kind of crisis.
3. A petition or supplication to God.
4. A statement of confidence in God.
5. A vow to praise God.

The classic example of the lament in the Old Testament is found, not in the Psalms, but in the Book of Lamentations itself. It is found in its own separate book, known by that title.

The Book of Lamentations is traditionally ascribed to Jeremiah. Scholars do not know for sure, and there are different opinions, but Jeremiah is probably the most likely author. The book was written shortly after 586 B.C., a very dark period in the history of the people of Judah. As noted earlier, the

Israelite kingdom had split into a Northern Kingdom and a Southern Kingdom. The Northern Kingdom had been carried into captivity in 722 B.C., leaving only one kingdom—God's people in the South, known as the Kingdom of Judah.

Then, in 586 B.C., the great Babylonian army under the leadership of Nebuchadnezzar came westward and conquered various countries along the Mediterranean coast. Judah was the last of those countries, and she too came under Babylonian siege. The Babylonian army completely devastated Jerusalem. One might think God would have stood up for His house, since He talked so much about how precious and honorable it was. He did not. He let it collapse. He let the Babylonians come in and desecrate it, because there had been sin in the camp. There had not been just a single sin, but sin on top of sin, sin continually, and sin in spite of all warnings from God and His prophets. So, God's punishment for Israel's sin was this scourge of a Babylonian army that took two waves of exiles from Judah into Babylon.

In 586 B.C., the Babylonian army completely destroyed the city of Jerusalem, leaving only the very poorest of the poor in the land. On that date, Solomon's great Temple was also destroyed. Lamentations is a lament for this disaster. Note a few of the verses with which the book opens:

> How doth the city sit solitary, that was full of people! how is she become as a widow! she that was great among the nations, and princess among the provinces, how is she become tributary! She weepeth sore in the

> night, and her tears are on her cheeks: among all her lovers she hath none to comfort her: all her friends have dealt treacherously with her, they are become her enemies. Judah is gone into captivity because of affliction, and because of great servitude: she dwelleth among the heathen, she findeth no rest: all her persecutors overtook her between the straits (Lamentations 1:1-3).

It was a very dark time for the people of God. They especially lamented the destruction of the Temple. That Temple represented the key for the people of God. And God let the Temple be destroyed, let it burn to the ground. Scripture makes it very clear that God was the one who was against them. It is one thing to go through difficult moments of trouble, but it is quite another to know trouble comes at the hand of God himself. That concept is very much a concern in the Book of Lamentations.

The extent of the depression in the city is shown in Lamentations 5:1-16, where one finds these key phrases:

- "Behold our reproach."
- "Our heritage has passed . . . to aliens."
- "Our homes to strangers."
- "We are orphans and fatherless."
- "Our mothers are as widows"
- "We must pay to drink our own water."
- "Our wood is sold unto us"
- "Our necks are under persecution."
- "We labor, and have no rest."
- "We are slaves in order to get bread" (paraphrase).

- "Our fathers have sinned . . . and we have borne their iniquities."
- "Servants have ruled over us."
- "We [get] . . . bread [at] the peril of our lives."
- "Our skin was black like an oven because of . . . famine."
- "They ravage our women and our maids" (paraphrase).
- "Princes are hanged . . . by their hands."
- "[Our] elders were not honored."
- "Our young men are made to grind at the mill" (paraphrase).
- "[Our] children fell under the [weight of the] wood."
- "[Our] elders have ceased from the gate."
- "The young men no longer play music" (paraphrase).
- "The joy of our hearts [has] ceased."
- "Our dance [has] turned into mourning."
- "The crown is fallen from our heads."
- "Woe unto us, that we have sinned."

The book ends with a plea for God to take them back. The book truly is depressing—lament of the first order. No such disaster had ever before taken place in Jerusalem.

Still, this is a very interesting Biblical lament, very unique, and also composed tightly from a literary point of view. The form and the artistry of Lamentations is exceptional. Here are some of the unique features the reader will discover. The Book of Lamentations has five chapters. Each of the five chapters, except for the middle one, has 22 verses. When one reads chapters 1, 2, and 4 (if read in Hebrew), one finds that each verse starts with the next letter of the alphabet. For the English alphabet, it would be like chapter 1, verse 1 starts with "A," using the word "All." The second verse would start with "B," like the word, "Better." And the third verse with "C," like the word "Count." This pattern continues verse by verse right through to the end of the alphabet. It would be nice if some artist could literally do these chapters in English. Understandably, it would take time and talent to display that degree of artistry.

Chapters 2, 4, and 5 follow the same style and pattern. Interestingly, though, the chapter sandwiched in between these two front chapters and the two last chapters—Chapter 3—has 66 verses. In Chapter 3, the first verse starts with "A," the second verse starts with "A," and the third verse starts with "A." But, when one gets to verse 4, it starts with "B." So do verses 5 and 6. That is the pattern, three verses for each letter of the alphabet because there are three times the number of verses in this chapter. What is this supposed to mean? Of course, it could mean there is an artist at work here since the words are arranged in a very sophisticated manner. More likely, though, there really is a message. For example, the writer is trying to draw attention to Chapter 3, hinting there is something very special about it.

So, one should look more closely at Lamentations, Chapter 3. Is it any different from the other chapters? Chapter 1 was depressing. Although no quotes have been shared from Chapters 2 and 4, they also are depressing, gloomy, heavy chapters. A long quote was shared from Chapter 5 earlier, with specifics, and those words gave descriptions of which any human would feel concern. Chapter 3 says, "I am the man that hath seen affliction by the rod of his wrath" (v. 1). That sounds like a lament. "My flesh and my skin hath he made old; he hath broken my bones" (v. 4). Look at verse 16: "He hath also broken my teeth with gravel stones, he hath covered me with ashes." This man is very, very low in spirit. He is very, very depressed.

But, if one keeps reading, something amazing begins to emerge. In the middle section of Chapter 3, starting at verse 22, are these words:

> It is of the Lord's mercies that we are not consumed, because his compassions fail not. They are new every morning: great is thy faithfulness. The Lord is my portion, saith my soul; therefore will I hope in him. The Lord is good unto them that wait for him, to the soul that seeketh him. It is good that a man should both hope and quietly wait for the salvation of the Lord (Lamentations 3:22-26).

How can this man say in the middle of such disaster, "Great is God's faithfulness"? One could say that hope never shines more brightly than when perceived by inspiration right in the middle of darkness. The situation was the same. Everything was just as had been described. The opening chapter and the closing chapter present absolute hopelessness. Yet in the middle, the words of Chapter 3 shine forth: "Great is thy faithfulness" (v. 23).

Most people know that hymn, a beautiful hymn. It still gives consolation and renewed hope to millions of people. When an individual turns to God in the most trying of times, when all looks very dark, that person, through faith, can turn on a light not visible to the physical eye. Through eyes of faith, one can be assured of God's faithfulness.

Conclusion

So, what does one learn from this material?

Surely one must first conclude that both the praise and the lament are integral to the believer's life. One must learn to praise God always, taking one's self-identity from relationship with God who is the author and the creator of all things: "We are thy people and sheep of thy pasture" (Psalm 79:13).

One must learn to enjoy God by reflecting on who He is and what He has done for His people in a personal sense: "Be thankful unto him, and bless his name" (Psalm 100:4).

In the lament, one learns that to be human is to experience pain. There is no way to avoid it. Job says, "Man is born unto trouble, as the sparks fly upward" (5:7). But in the times of trouble and despondency, believers must bring their sorrows to Him. God will give peace that passes all understanding.

God's peace truly does pass all understanding. The author of Lamentations had no visible reason for hope. The situation was bleak. It was bad. There was no light on. But God turned sorrow into joy. He showed a way of hope through faith in His unfailing faithfulness.

18

Wisdom Literature— Proverbs

By Hannah Harrington, Ph.D.

The prime example of wisdom literature from the Old Testament is the Book of Proverbs. Wisdom literature is not limited to Israel, however. It is a phenomenon throughout the ancient world. For example, in ancient Egypt, one would be introduced to wisdom literature. In ancient Babylon, one would find proverbs and wise sayings.

Wisdom Literature in General

How does one define wisdom literature? James Crenshaw gives a good working definition: "Wisdom is a particular attitude towards reality. It tells us what we can accomplish by practical wisdom, by common sense." In the vernacular, that means "using our heads." The sage accepts the facts of life in a community where there is good and evil, where there will be some rich and some poor. The sage would try to help the individual live in society, making better rather than worse choices.

The ancient sage would admonish the student, "Keep your eyes and your ears open. Use discretion. Be disciplined and develop character." Often one will find in this literature information about the environment, animals, plants, and human behavior. The idea is that one studies his surroundings, studies the universe, asks questions about it, and tries to live in harmony with it. This is true throughout wisdom literature as well.

Human beings are the point of orientation in wisdom literature. It focuses on human experience. The same is true in Biblical wisdom literature. One does not wait for divine revelation to answer every single question. God has given to each one already the gift of a working brain, and He fully expects each individual to use it. In other words, wisdom literature accepts the reality that answers to every single human question are not going to come drifting down from heaven. Some things God expects people to chew on, to think about, to work out, to deal with on their own.

In Biblical wisdom literature, again one will find the same source of themes as those found throughout the ancient world—emphasis on obedience to parents, the danger of adultery, the danger of rash words, the danger of strong drink, and an emphasis on the hard questions in life such as undeserved suffering. One will also find emphases on family relationships, rearing children, friendships, issues of death, and inequities in society.

Again, it is not surprising that in all segments of the ancient world, human beings would devote time to these kinds of instructions and issues. Crenshaw continues his definition by saying, "Wisdom is the reasoned search for specific ways to ensure well-being and the implementation of these discoveries in daily existence." The idea is basically a reasoned search for how to live a good life.

One should note this truth: Never think that faith is opposed to reason. Faith is not opposed to reason. Faith goes beyond reason. Many times faith transcends reason. Faith often provides assurance in areas where it cannot produce hard evidence. But faith in and of itself is a reasonable choice.

Faith in Christ, for example, is the result of a reasoned decision, a reasonable choice. There are very good reasons for accepting Christ's work of salvation. So, the point made here is that an emphasis on faith—and, as all have noticed, many of these chapters have stressed the importance of faith—should never be thought to downplay the value of reason. God gives individuals brains in order to weigh choices and evaluate decisions.

Proverbs

The Book of Proverbs is all about making wise choices. The original purpose of the book was to instruct the young on how to achieve a good life. It was for decision making in the process of daily life, and also for responsible leadership. Many different forms and structures are utilized in the Book of Proverbs. Some of these are characteristic of most all wisdom literature, such as special vocabulary and structures. In those structures, for instance, one can find a debate, a proverb, a riddle, or just poetry. One might also find a hymn, or an allegory, or even a disputation, all common to wisdom literature.

Consider the use of imagery, for example. Imagery and eloquent vocabulary help to elevate particular truths, making them memorable and really quite beautiful. Here is an example. Rather than saying, "Do not commit adultery," Proverbs says, "Can a man carry live coals in his vest pocket without burning his clothes?" (6:27). That is a strong, vivid analogy. Here is another, "Can a man walk on live coals without scorching his feet?" (6:28). These illustrate the kind of dialogue found in wisdom literature. The writer is trying to get the individual to think about the consequences of what he does.

The man seduced by the married woman of Proverbs 7 is described as "a bird rushing into a trap, not realizing his very life is at stake" (v. 23). Just the way the sayings are put together almost demands that a person think about his decisions. One should think the matter all the way through, considering the consequences.

One of the favorite analogies in the Book of Proverbs is that of the two paths. The right way leads to blessing; the wrong way leads to dire consequences, perhaps even death. The analogy also establishes the important principle that a person cannot walk on both paths at the same time. Either one walks toward blessings—toward that which is good, toward life—or one walks in another direction entirely— toward pain, suffering and death. There is no middle lane down which to walk. One is either going north or south. There can be no going both ways at the same time with each way leading to a separate destiny. Proverbs 4:27 insists, "Do not swerve to the right or to the left; keep your foot from evil" (*NIV*). Proverbs thus models this major value.

The book also models the value of eloquence, saying it is a good thing, a value—"A word fitly spoken is like apples of gold in pitchers of silver" (25:7).

An example of exquisite form or literary artistry is found in Chapter 31, speaking about the ideal woman. The description starts in verse 10 and continues to the end of the chapter. Verses 10 through 31 make up what is called an acrostic, similar to what was found in Lamentations. Each verse begins with the next letter of the Hebrew alphabet.

Probably the most obvious literary element in wisdom literature is the parallelism of the poetry. This is throughout all wisdom literature and also found in some nonwisdom literature, in other words, just plain poetry. For example, as one finds with many of the psalms, two lines make the same point. Sometimes these lines are synonymous—"Wisdom will place upon your head a fair garland. She will bestow on you a beautiful crown" (4:9). The second line says the same thing as the first, only with a few poetic differences. This is called parallelism—"she" is parallel to "wisdom;" "will bestow on you" is parallel to "your head." In the other line, "crown" is parallel to "garland" in the previous line.

Here is another example: "Say to wisdom, 'You are my sister,' and call insight your intimate friend" (7:4, *RSV*). Written out, the parallelism is even more obvious:

"Say to wisdom, 'You are my sister,'
And call insight your intimate friend."

The words "say" and "call" are parallel. The same is true of "wisdom" and "insight." They are talking about the same thing. "You are my sister" parallels "your intimate friend." In English they have the same rhythm and cadence. It is a poetic device, and very artistic. It is also a good teaching tool—making the same point, but saying it in different ways—especially for children who seem naturally to relate to rhythm. Teachers often use such devices.

Sometimes, in wisdom literature, the two lines are antithetical. In other words, they *do not* say the same thing. They say opposite things, but they are at the same time saying the same thing. Here is an example: "The memory of the righteous is blessed, but the name of the wicked will rot" (10:7, *NKJV*). The writer is saying two opposite things but those two things are making the same point.

Here is another antithetical statement, one more well-known. "Trust in the Lord with all your heart and lean not on your own understanding" (3:5, *NKJV*). "Trust in the Lord with all your heart" parallels "your own understanding" in the next line.

Biblical Wisdom Literature

Most of what has been said to this point applies equally to all wisdom literature throughout the ancient world. Biblical wisdom literature includes a common-sense approach to life. It talks about timeless truths. It is not relegated to any particular space or any particular time in history. Its truths are universal. They are eternal. They are just as appropriate today as they were thousands of years ago. Yet because of their timelessness, those truths link together the past and the present. All individuals are part of that stream of humanity which can be guided by the truths of this literature. Nevertheless, Biblical wisdom is unique because it always takes God seriously. It says from the start, "The fear of the Lord is the beginning of knowledge" (1:7).

Now, that is different. One would never find that concept in the Egyptian wisdom literature. One would not find it in Hittite or Babylonian text either. This is something uniquely Biblical. All these other instructions are very important and they are gone over in detail, but they are in and of themselves totally inadequate when it comes to the major human problem. The starting point of true wisdom must be "the fear of the Lord."

The inherent question raised here is, "How can humankind please God?" That is why the rest of the instruction is important. Not just because it is the common-sense way of living, but because it is the way to please God more than anything else in the world. God is the one who is Creator of the universe. He has set it in order. He is the one who has laid out the rules of nature. Certainly, one is to live in harmony with nature, but it is even better for one to learn about the Creator, to get acquainted, and to establish fellowship with Him. One will understand the creation much better, if he knows the Creator.

In the final analysis, wisdom is a gift of God. It is something that the righteous person must pray for and pursue with all of his heart. The wise know God, because they walk with Him in daily life. They tap into the divine source of wisdom in order to cope with life's problems. They seek God in the common, everyday ritual of life. God promises, "Discretion will preserve you; understanding will keep you" (2:11, *NKJV*). Thus, the righteous person combines reason with the pursuit of God's wisdom. Reason and God's wisdom are not antithetical. They are not opposed to each other. Both are needed. An individual must use his brain to full capacity and, at the same time, always pursue God's wisdom.

217

Wisdom must be sought by every individual. It is not something limited to a prophet or to a special apostle. Wisdom is something everyone needs. And all must search for it diligently. One might come to a clearer understanding of this by comparing the sage to the prophet of God. The prophet is like God's hit man. He is equipped with special power, and he is going to use that power in a particular situation. The Spirit of God comes upon the prophet with power and, in some cases, the prophet has been known to lead people in battle right next to the general. God has revealed much about Himself through the mouth of the prophet. The prophet speaks and God's Word comes forth to the people. This kind of prophecy, of course, is not an ordinary or daily affair. The Spirit rushed on the prophets for specific messages to the nation during a particular crisis.

But wisdom, as described by Proverbs, is an individual matter, incumbent on each and every person. It is a matter of making the best choices in daily life on a regular basis.

One more curiosity in this study of wisdom literature is that, both in the Bible and outside of it, wisdom is often personified as a woman. Some texts call her Lady Wisdom or the Wisdom Woman. Here are a few samples.

1. "She is more precious than rubies: and all the things thou canst desire are not to be compared unto her. Length of days is in her right hand; and in her left hand riches and honour. Her ways are ways of pleasantness, and all her paths are peace. She is a tree of life to them that lay hold upon her: and happy is every one that retaineth her" (3:15-18).

2. "By me kings reign and rulers make laws that are just" (8:15, *NIV*).
3. "Wisdom pours out her spirit on her followers and reveals her words to those who seek her" (see 1:23).

Wisdom requires commitment. Those who obtain her must be committed to her, and if they are, they will be more than satisfied.

The question is, Why is wisdom personified as a woman? The word wisdom in Hebrew is a feminine noun. In Hebrew, one can tell when nouns are feminine by the ending of the word. The "ah" on the end of a noun is feminine. Biblical feminine names often end this way, for example, Sarah and Hannah. This is not true of the name Ruth, but then Ruth was a Moabite. What about the name of the first women, Eve? In Hebrew, Eve is Evah. This is a very common name in Israel today, and it ends with the feminine "ah." Such are the arguments of the grammarians.

However, there may be something else going on here, because one cannot always tell from the gender of a noun anything particular about its meaning. Every noun in Hebrew is either masculine or feminine—for example, table, right, chair—but it does not necessarily mean one or the other has masculine or feminine characteristics. For this reason, the grammatical argument may not be valid. Nevertheless, it seems very purposeful that wisdom is personified as a woman in the Book of Proverbs. Proverbs was probably originally written for the classroom. Even if written as a one-on-one tutorial, it is still a book of instruction for young people. In the ancient world, of course, girls did not go to school, so in this case, the class is composed of boys. And one of the most critical choices every young man must make has to do with women.

Every young man, sooner or later, is going to be very concerned about women—the choice of the right woman. In the normal course of events, both the right woman and the wrong woman are going to be attractive. There are reasons for choosing what may be considered the right woman, and there are reasons for choosing the wrong woman. Sometimes young men cannot tell which is the right woman and which is the wrong woman. Understandably, this is going to be a very critical choice. The young man must make use of all his intellect and his will. He must pursue God's wisdom to make the right choice.

As noted earlier, this business of right choices is an underlying theme throughout wisdom literature, whether it is in the matter of marriage or something else. One must use the brain to make right choices. One must also pursue God's will and wisdom. Just as it is sometimes difficult for a young man to choose the right woman, so it is sometimes hard for him to choose wisdom. Both wisdom and folly have their attractions. If wisdom were the only thing attractive, then everybody would go the right way. But folly also has its attractions. The Biblical writer insists that one choose God's wisdom, illustrated by Lady Wisdom as opposed to Dame Folly.

Lady Wisdom represents the good choice. Dame Folly speaks of one's wrongful choice, often based on temporal, sensual pleasures, selfishness, greed, and sometimes just plain laziness. God, as the source of wisdom, actively seeks to attract the young man to His ways. God reproves, pleads, turns away, indites, reaches out to help the person on his quest for wisdom and a meaningful life. God is an active being, blessing and protecting the one who chooses Him.

Finding true wisdom requires the same type of commitment that is required of the young man trying to find the right girl. It is going to take everything in his power to figure it out, but he knows the reward is priceless. So it is with true wisdom. It is going to take everything for the individual to make wise choices. One must keep using his head every day, with every decision, and one must keep pursuing God's will. Here again, the reward is absolutely priceless.

Scripture says all earthly goods cannot equal her (wisdom), and whoever holds onto her is happy (see Proverbs 8:11). To find wisdom is more than worth all the effort.

Conclusion

In this study, one should have learned that in the Bible, as well as throughout the ancient Near East, wisdom is considered a quality every human seeks in order to live the best possible life. In the Bible, wisdom is disciplined, human achievement under the umbrella of God's will. The good life is the godly life.

What does this mean?

First, it means the individual behaves within the framework of God's laws. That is the structure of his life. The Mosaic law code is assumed and reinforced over and over.

Second, an individual must make maximum use of his power of reason and discipline in order to be truly wise. The Mosaic law does not tell one everything he needs to know for every single situation in life. So, one must fill in those blanks the best he can and make wise choices, evaluate the consequences, and weigh the benefits.

Finally, the wise person will acknowledge that, despite his greatest efforts to be wise, true wisdom still rests with God alone. He is the author of wisdom. The wise person will go beyond his own human efforts—intelligence and discipline—and he will actively seek out the will of God. He recognizes that an individual cannot be truly wise without constant reference to, and guidance from, God.

Two verses quite appropriately bring this study to a close.

"The fear of the Lord is the beginning of knowledge" (Proverbs 1:7; see also 9:10).

"In all thy ways, acknowledge him, and he shall direct thy paths" (Proverbs 3:6).

19

Job and Ecclesiastes

By Hannah Harrington, Ph.D.

Both books in this study—Job and Ecclesiastes—help with the question, "What happens when good behavior does not appear to be rewarded?" Another way to phrase it: "Where is the justice of God when the righteous suffer, sometimes at the hand of the wicked?"

It is very nice to read the Book of Proverbs which basically tells one how to live, along with certain guidelines and principles. If one lives godly, good things happen; if one lives wickedly, bad things happen. Each knows, of course, that even with the most godly of people, trouble is a part of human living. Job and Ecclesiastes are writings that provide a balance to the optimistic attitude of Proverbs. They speak to a side of life which everybody experiences at one time or another—death, suffering, and discouragement are all part of life's underside.

In this study, the writer of Ecclesiastes first makes observations on life and then shares his view of God. Then Job gives a particular story, portraying a specific man who is very upright and godly, but who yet experienced disaster after disaster.

The Book of Ecclesiastes

The opening verses of this book are famous: "Vanity of vanities, saith the Preacher, vanity of vanities; all is vanity" (1:2). All is utter futility, totally meaningless. The Hebrew word used here is *hevel,* referring to a vapor. Surely the writer must have been at an all-time low to come up with this conclusion. But he continues with, "What does man gain from all his labor at which he toils under the sun?" (v. 3, *NIV*). In other words, what does it amount to? "Generations come and generations go, but the earth remains forever" (1:4, *NIV*). In other words, life is cyclical. Nothing really changes. No progress is really made. Life just tracks around over the same ground. Babies are born; the elderly die. There is nothing new under the sun.

He continues, "All things are wearisome" (1:8, *NIV*). Everything is a bore. Longings of the human heart are never really fulfilled. They are never really satisfied. These are his words, "The eye never has enough of seeing, nor the ear its fill of hearing" (1:8, *NIV*). Life is like chasing the wind. It is a twisted thing, and it cannot be made straight (see 1:14, 15). Even the pursuit of wisdom, which was discussed in the last chapter, is like "chasing the wind" (see 1:17). For as wisdom grows, taxation grows. "To increase learning is to increase heartache" (see 1:18). One might conclude this man goes along with the common phrase, "Ignorance is bliss." He even says "Much study is a weariness of the flesh" (12:12).

Nevertheless, those are strange words for a wisdom writer. Ecclesiastes is considered wisdom

224

literature. But the author goes on to say that having fun is a waste of time, too. Merriment and fun is all futile, meaningless (see 2:3). It too is vapor. There is nothing good in it. He admits to being the wealthiest man in Jerusalem, but he knows riches do not make a person happy. The writer says he became so wealthy that he owned many homes, gardens, orchards, water pools, slaves, animals, silver, gold. He had coffers of luxuries. He denied himself nothing. He used that money. He bought this and that, whatever he desired. Then he looked at his possessions and realized they had no real value. In fact, he concluded real value did not exist under the sun (see 2:4-11).

In a yet further depressing point, the writer says that whatever one accomplishes, whatever he does, whatever he gains, he is going to leave it to someone else. That person may squander the whole nest egg. He might turn out to be an utter fool (see 2:13-19). But whether one is wise or foolish, he is going to die just the same. He has no control over it, and he is going to be forgotten. No one is going to care that he ever lived (see 2:16).

In addition to all this, there is actually no real justice in the world. Sometimes a wicked man lives a long life and a good man dies early (see 7:15). What is the use? Sometimes, an upright man is rewarded according to the conduct of a scoundrel. Sometimes a scoundrel is rewarded according to the conduct of the upright (see 8:14). Here are some of his words:

> I returned and saw under the sun that the race is not to the swift, nor the battle to the strong, nor bread to the wise, nor riches

to men of understanding, nor favor to men
of skill; but time and chance happen to
them all. For man also does not know his
time: Like fish taken in a cruel net, like
birds caught in a snare, so the sons of men
are snared in an evil time, when it falls
suddenly upon them " (9:11, 12, *NKJV*).

So what is the use? One fate comes to everybody. That is death. Nobody has a chance against
it. One yearns to master life, but one day each is
going to just ram against the wall.

And finally, he gives one more discouraging fact:

I said in mine heart concerning the estate
of the sons of men, that God might manifest them, and that they might see that they
themselves are beasts. For that which
befalleth the sons of men befalleth beasts;
even one thing befalleth them: as the one
dieth, so dieth the other; yea, they have all
one breath; so that a man hath no preemi-
nence above a beast: for all *is* vanity. All
go unto one place; all are of the dust, and
all turn to dust again. Who knoweth the
spirit of man that goeth upward, and the
spirit of the beast that goeth downward to
the earth? (Ecclesiastes 3:18-21).

What is the use? Both man and beast return to
dust. Who knows if a man's life breath rises upward
and an animal's sinks downward? The writer is
saying he sees no difference between what happens
to humans and what happens to animals. It seems
to him like both turn into dust. Who knows what
happens after that?

A bit of advice: If one is feeling depressed, do not spend time in the Book of Ecclesiastes. Read the Psalms. Ecclesiastes represents a man who sees no true value anywhere.

However, the book itself brings up some interesting questions. First, How did such a book as this get into the Bible? Second, What keeps this writer from just cracking up in total despair? He is obviously a man of Israel. He is in the community of faith. What keeps him from just cursing God, giving up, and putting an end to it all?

Deeper than the despair is an underlying reverence for God and faith in His control of the universe. A view of God becomes evident when he writes, "God is eternal. Everything comes from him" (see 3:11). We have a similar idea in the New Testament when told, "He is the author and finisher of our faith" (Hebrews 12:2). The writer of Ecclesiastes does believe God is in control. He has set times for things. He knows what He is doing. Men may not understand what He is doing, but He knows. He set "A time to be born, and a time to die; a time to plant, and a time to pluck up . . . a time to kill, and a time to heal. . . . A time to weep, and a time to laugh. . . . A time of war, and a time of peace" (3:2-8). Moreover, the writer says, God's works are good. "He hath made every thing beautiful" (2:11).

Another thing he said, "God will judge, even though it doesn't always look like it" (11:9).

"Not to worry," he tells the young man, "Just follow the desires of your heart, and the glances of your eyes, but know full well that God will call you to account for all such things" (see 11:9).

When all is said and done, the writer concludes, the sum of the matter is to "Fear God and keep His commandments, for this is the whole duty of man" (12:13, *NIV*). These concluding words seem a little contradictory in terms of what was said earlier, but one must understand the depressing observations were made with the natural eye. Underlying what one sees with the human eye is a consciousness of God that undergirds and keeps one from committing suicide. Somehow the writer does believe. Faith pops up through the soil of despair here, and one sees that the writer does have faith in God. His concluding advice to the young reveals that faith. He says wisdom is a good thing, though it may not seem like it. It may seem like a lot of work and a lot of toil and a lot of weariness. He gives some further good advice. God gives wisdom and knowledge and joy to those who please Him. Keep an understanding of God. Take Him seriously. Take His vows seriously. Do not be rash and vow to do things and not do them. Such will bring one into disfavor with God. If one gets into God's disfavor, he is going to be sorry. Those are the negatives.

On the positive side, he says, do good. Whatever good one can do, do it. Do it now, because when one gets into the grave, he has no further chance to do it. He says to enjoy life. And, whenever one does eat and drink and find enjoyment, consider it a gift of God. So, one certainly can say in conclusion to Ecclesiastes that the individual with faith is much better off than the one without it. The writer's fear of God keeps him from discarding Proverbs and throwing it into the wastecan. He may have found much inequity around him, but he nonetheless was not going to throw Proverbs into the

228

wastecan. His fear of God keeps him from toppling. The principles he was raised on keep him from cursing God and arrogantly rejecting the law of Moses. He has a strong belief in God and that balances him. It keeps him from going right over the edge when he hits life's frustrations.

The Book of Job

Job is a wonderful book because it gives a personal example of a man who experienced terrible disaster and remained true to God. It is an example of one whose life was above reproach, to whom trouble came in barrels. Yet, through all of his problems, Job's faith remained unshakable. In fact, Job was able even to challenge God from a position of spiritual confidence. He knew he loved God, and that is where his confidence rested. In his time of trouble, Job drew nearer to God, rather than running away as a hypocrite. The minute he comes into trouble, the hypocrite throws up his hands and quits. But the true believer keeps bringing his trouble to God.

Job wanted to understand. He wanted God to explain. If there was sin in his life, he wanted to confess and get rid of it. But he could not figure it out. What had he done that had so apparently displeased God?

It is an unusual story. God and Satan had a discussion about Job. God was very pleased with his servant Job and let Satan know it. Satan thought Job only served God because God had made him rich. He said to God, "Job would be a fool not to serve you. You have made him a very wealthy man. However, if You would allow trouble to come upon Job, he would turn his back on You" (see 1:9-11).

Satan's logic corresponds to the human. Who would want to serve a God who would bring trouble? But God was sure of Job's commitment. He was sure Job was loyal and he was going to remain faithful. Again, remember, God never places on anyone more than he can handle. He is not going to permit the troubles of Job on a weaker believer unable to handle it.

God allowed Satan to bring one disaster after the next upon Job, just so long as he did not take his life.

Job was considered one of the three most righteous men in the Old Testament. His life was exemplary. He was a prayerful man and one who worshiped properly through sacrifices before God. As noted in an earlier study, Job not only offered sacrifices for himself, but for each and every member of his family. He offered sacrifices just in case a member of the family might have sinned. His was a wonderful example for parents of any generation. Job prayed for himself and he prayed for all of his children.

Nevertheless, one day disaster struck. His oxen were plowing in the field and his donkeys were grazing when the Sabeans attacked, killing all the workers, and stealing all the animals. While Job was still trying to digest that bit of bad news, another disaster hit. Fire fell from heaven and burned up his sheep and the shepherds watching over them. On the heels of this news came word that the Chaldeans had come, three bands of them, taking all his camels and slaying his servants. Worst of all, while his sons and daughters gathered for a feast at the elder brother's house, a terrible wind blew upon the house, killing everyone.

How does one respond to such news as that?

Job's response was truly amazingly. He said, "Naked came I out of my mother's womb, and naked shall I return thither: the Lord gave, and the Lord hath taken away; blessed be the name of the Lord" (1:21).

How many Christians of today could respond like that?

Satan was not finished. He asked permission to attack Job's health, saying, "Skin for skin, yea, all that a man hath will he give for his life. But put forth thine hand now, and touch his bone and his flesh, and he will curse thee to thy face" (2:4, 5).

God granted His permission. Satan could inflict disease upon Job, but he could not take his life. That is how Job came to have severe inflammations, awful sores, from head to foot over his entire body. He was in terrible shape, and in great pain. His wife looked at him and said, "Do you still retain your integrity, Job? Just curse God and die" (see 2:9). Job was appalled at this suggestion. He found it incomprehensible that one would accept good from God and not accept the bad.

Three so-called friends came to comfort Job. Even though their so-called comfort turned out to be the kind one could do without, they make for an interesting and revealing story. They sat with Job and reproached him for his sins. To their way of thinking, Job had to have sinned for such calamity to have fallen. Day after day, they urged Job to repent. Job's reaction proved a faith far deeper than that of his friends. Job knew in his heart that he loved God. He asked God to show him where he had sinned.

Job did not understand God's actions, but he knew God and he witnessed, "[God] knoweth the way that I take: when he hath tried me, I shall come forth as gold" (23:10). Job was emaciated, covered with sores, physically near death, but yet he knew every human life is in the hands of the Almighty. He expressed this faith even more explicitly in the words, "I know that my redeemer liveth, and that he shall stand at the latter day upon this earth: And though after my skin worms destroy this body, yet in my flesh shall I see God" (19:25). One may well wonder how Job knew this, but there is no mistaking his faith. Inspiration came to him in some manner. Faith found root, with determination and confidence that permitted him to declare, "Though he slay me, yet will I trust in him" (13:15).

In the end, God did finally reveal Himself to Job. God also had some words for Job's so-called friends. He chastened the friends, and He gave Job a new family. The book ends by saying, "The Lord blessed the latter end of Job more than his beginning" (42:12).

Conclusion

What, then, is one to say or do when God does not seem fair?

First, in reference to Ecclesiastes and the Book of Job, one should keep in mind that these writers did not have the help that is available today. They had very little of the Old Testament and none of the New Testament as aids to faith and revelation of the full story of God's love for mankind. They may have had the Mosaic law, which would have been most of the Pentateuch; but for the most part, they wrote from life experience and human conscience. They saw only "life under the sun," as Ecclesiastes puts it. Believers today have a wonderful source in the New Testament. Jesus tells about heaven. Paul tells about theology. John the Revelator tells about hope in the future—there is a life after this one; there is reward and punishment. God *is* fair and *just* and, in the final outcome, He will have the last word.

The writer of Ecclesiastes did not know all these wonderful truths. He could not even figure out the difference between a man and an animal at death. Neither did these writers have the presence and comfort of the Holy Spirit in the Pentecostal sense. They lived on the other side of Pentecost. Nevertheless, both the writer of Ecclesiastes and the Book of Job are striking examples of honesty and faith for believers tried by life's contradictions and frustrations. These books speak of faithful individuals— men who knew God and who maintained faith in Him even in the midst of trouble.

One hardly wishes to hear another speak of God being present during times of trouble when that speaker has had little experience with hard times. The men studied in this chapter had been there. They knew of trouble and injustice and of how the human reaction to such really can and does put faith to the test. The writer Samuel Terrien says of them, "They maintained a sense of God's presence within the signs of His absence."

We also learn from these books that the life of faith is not a simple cause and effect principle. Every good deed does not bring an immediate reward, nor does every bad deed result in immediate punishment. Life is more complex than that. God is a person; He is not just a blind responder to a principle. God desires a relationship with each individual. He treats each in terms of that relationship and of His sovereign will and purpose. Life is anything but a push-button affair. God is not interested in a bargain-table arrangement. He seeks full devotion and total commitment, and He designs the steps of the believer's life to best cultivate that type of relationship.

Even in matters such as those which occurred in the life of Job, God is testing and trying man's faith. Satan's accusation is real. Some only serve God for what they can get out of it. But the true believers, the saints, do so out of love and reverence. They are the triumphant ones.

It seems a quirk of human nature that one seldom says to God, "Why are you so good to me?" but quite often wants to ask, "Why are things so bad?" Job reminds the believer that faith accepts both the good and the bad, bowing to God's sovereignty. If one understood all that God does, then He would not really be God. His ways are beyond human understanding so one should certainly not expect to comprehend it all.

Job never does discover the whole story. Today, each believer knows far more about it than Job, but he did hang on to his faith and he did submit to the sovereign, righteous judgment of God. His story reinforces the principle—only God is sovereign. Human beings cannot put Him on trial or bring His wisdom into question. He still remains the Author of wisdom and the Creator of the universe. The believer's lot is simply to "Fear God, and keep his commandments." Such is "the whole duty of man" (Ecclesiastes 12:13).

20 Prophets and Prophecy: Part 1

By Rickie Moore, Ph.D.

This chapter is the beginning of a study which covers the destruction of Israel as a kingdom. The chapter of Israel's history that moves from the division of the kingdom after the death of Solomon in 922 B.C. to the destruction of Jerusalem in 586 B.C. is a piece of history that is told essentially from a prophetic perspective. Therefore, a study of the prophets and prophecies of the Old Testament is in order.

Books of the Prophets

The books of the Old Testament that are often referred to as the historical books—Joshua, Judges, Samuel, and Kings—were categorized by the Hebrews when they gathered their materials to make their canon of Scripture as prophetic materials. They called these books, which today are called historical books, the former prophets. Then, the latter prophets, often referred to as the writing prophets, are subdivided into the major prophets—Isaiah,

Jeremiah, Ezekiel, Daniel—and the minor prophets, which are the remaining 12 books. These 12 prophets were gathered together into a single scroll by the Hebrews, who first gathered and arranged the prophetic material.

The division of the kingdom of Israel was a division between the Northern and the Southern kingdoms. Where there is division, there is a death of vision. However, God revealed His vision to the prophets. The prophets gave an account of Israel's history that really represented God's version of the history, or as some have called it, His story. The prophets were raised up to give God's version of the story. Therefore, this chapter will give an overview of the prophets and prophecy as a whole.

Communicating Prophecy to the People

Prophecy, the prophetic tradition in Israel, began with Moses. Deuteronomy 18 contains a section of Scripture that makes it very clear that Moses is regarded in the Old Testament as the beginning of the prophetic tradition. Deuteronomy 18:15-22 records the following:

> "The Lord your God will raise up for you a Prophet like me from your midst, from your brethren. Him you shall hear, according to all you desired of the Lord your God at Horeb in the day of the assembly, saying, 'Let me not hear again the voice of the Lord my God, nor let me see this great fire anymore, lest I die.' And the Lord said to me: 'What they have spoken is good. I will raise up for them a Prophet like you from among their brethren, and will put My words in

236

His mouth, and He shall speak to them all
that I command him'" (*NKJV*).

Moses was recounting that moment at the
mountain called Horeb, also called Sinai, where God
met His people and sought to reveal to them His
Word. He revealed His Word to the people in written form, writing the Ten Commandments with His
own finger. Not only did God give His people His
Word in written form, but he also intended to give
His people His Word in another form—the spoken
Word. The people were afraid that they were going
to die. There is a long tradition in the Old Testament that if people encounter God face-to-face, His
holiness and glory will be too much for humans to
bear, and it will cause their death. On this occasion, the people were experiencing this firsthand,
and they shrank back and asked Moses to mediate
for them. They said to Moses: "You go near and let
us move back lest we die" (see Exodus 20:19). On
that occasion, God heard and granted their request,
calling Moses to come near to Him. Thus, Moses
became His prophet, and the prophetic tradition
came to Israel at the same time of the beginning of
the written Word of God. Moses would not be the
last person to draw near to God, to hear His voice,
and to speak what God has said to the people.
Rather, he was the first of a tradition of people who
would come after him.

After Moses, came the prophet Samuel, located
in the second major division of Hebrew Scripture—
the historical books or, what the Hebrews called,
the former prophets. The account of how God called
Samuel is found in 1 Samuel 3: "Now the boy Samuel

ministered to the Lord before Eli. And the word of the Lord was rare in those days; there was no [open vision]" (v. 1, *NKJV*). That statement indicates that the Word of the Lord, was rare in those days. Obviously, Israel had the written Torah that Moses delivered from Mt. Sinai; however, it must be understood that this passage is not talking about the written Word. The written Word had been given and established and was available at that time. Consequently, there was something else being referred to that was not present in Israel at that time. Even though it is called the Word of the Lord here, it is obviously pointing to the prophetic word which is reinforced by another term called *vision*. His Word is not confined to what is written down, but it comes by different means, including hearing the voice of God and speaking it. Another media included seeing God's manifestations, such as Israel saw once again at Sinai, and then revealing those to the people of God. Vision, the Word of God in this prophetic sense, was rare in the time of Samuel. Therefore, God was calling a prophet once again like Moses, just as Deuteronomy 18 had predicted.

Israel's departure from faithfulness to the law of God happened time and time again. When this happened, they were moving from the presence and availability of God's revelation. Because of God's love for His people, He would raise up a prophet again and again. Even though Samuel was a little boy at this time, he was being called to fill the role of a prophet in Israel. Eli was the keeper of the Torah, given by Moses, but there was still a scarcity of God's Word. Therefore, God provided a prophet in the form of Samuel.

Eli, representing the religious leadership, was at first not helpful to Samuel in what God was doing in his life. Samuel encountered God at night; in fact, he heard a voice in the night calling his name. The young boy went to Eli, the priest, his elder and spiritual leader, and described to him what he heard. But Eli, according to the text, was dim of sight. Not only was his sight failing in a physical sense, but it would also seem that his condition represented the dimness of his spiritual sensitivities as well, because he was not able to discern that Samuel was hearing from the Lord. So, Eli sent Samuel back to bed. This happened again with the same results. In a sense, what was happening, was that God was raising Samuel up, but this spiritual leader was putting Samuel down. This seems to be a paradigm of what happened so often in Israel's history. God's Word was being suppressed, even by the religious leadership, but God raised up a new generation—a generation that was not hardened or set in their ways or calloused to the voice of the Lord. Finally, a turning point in the story took place when the old man, Eli, told the young boy to return, and if he heard this voice calling his name again, he should say, "Here I am. Your servant is listening" (see 3:9). This was the beginning of an important moment in Israel's history—God's calling of Samuel. By the end of Chapter 3, Samuel is established as a prophet in Israel.

ETYMOLOGY OF THE WORD *PROPHET*

The English word *prophet* was taken from the Greek word *prophetes*. The word *prophetes* is formed from two different parts: a verb which has to do with calling and a prefix which has more than one meaning.

The prefix *pro* can mean "before"; therefore, the prophet is someone who calls something before it happens. In other words, the prophet is someone who predicts the future.

But the prophet of the Old Testament was much more than a predictor. The prefix *pro* can point to the idea of "forth," as well as "before." Therefore, the prophet is a person who "calls forth," who "speaks out." When one considers the bulk of material that makes up the prophetic books of the Old Testament, he will find that much of that material is not a prediction of future events, rather it is a message from the prophet that addresses the present situation. Thus, the prophet speaks forth. In other words, it is God bringing His revelation to bear on the present moment, talking about issues and addressing issues and problems of the present moment. The prophet then is not just a foreteller, but a "forthteller."

The third meaning of the prefix *pro* points to the idea of "for." In other words, the prophet is a person who speaks on behalf of someone else. In fact, this third use of the prefix *pro* is also the third nuance of *prophetes*. The Hebrew term *nabiy* (pronounced "naw-bee"), which is being translated from the Hebrew, also focuses on the same verb having to do with calling. Thus, a prophet is someone whom the Lord calls.

The Call of the Prophet

At the beginning of many of the prophetic books is a story about how the prophet was called. Such is the case in 1 Samuel 3, a story showing how God called the prophet Samuel. The call of the prophet is given a lot of priority in the Old Testament. A prophet did not come to his role by way of heredity or appointment by any human system, rather he became a prophet because he was called by God to be a spokesperson for Him.

The Role of the Prophet

The prophet was more than just a predictor, more than just a "forthteller," the prophet was a messenger. In the ancient world, the role of a messenger was not a menial, insignificant, or unimportant role. That was obvious from the way that communication, especially international communication, was carried on. It was a time that did not have telephones, telegraphs, video cameras, or such. Messages between nations had to be exchanged through messengers. The messenger would go into the court of the king and receive the message, perhaps in written form, but he would also receive instructions from the king and then go represent that word in the court of another kingdom. The messenger of the ancient world could be considered equivalent to the ambassador of today. Thus, the role of a prophet was a very important role in the ancient world.

THE PROPHET AS MESSENGER

Prophets are very diverse in terms of their personality, their style, and in the very flavor of their material and messages. But they are messengers, nonetheless. The importance of the role of the messenger can be seen in a common phrase in the prophetic materials in the Old Testament. It is the phrase, "Thus says the Lord." It parallels what kings used in the ancient world. Archaeologists have found

241

tablets where international messages from one kingdom to the other have been found, and that same phrase is used to introduce royal messages between kingdoms. Thus, the messenger role indeed is the key way of understanding how the prophet functioned.

Isaiah 6 gives an example of the prophet moving and functioning in the role of a messenger. In the year that King Uzziah died, Isaiah saw the Lord sitting on a throne, high and lifted up, and his train filled the Temple (v. 1). This verse makes reference to the human kingship of Uzziah, and also the divine kingship of God. The human king is passing away, but God's kingship is being pictured as abiding and remaining. Isaiah, who is in the Temple on this occasion, gets lifted up into the heavenly court through visionary experience. Isaiah hears the voice of God speaking and responds by saying, "Here am I! Send me" (v. 8, *NKJV*). Isaiah, in other words, was just simply saying he recognized that the divine king had a message and he was volunteering his services. He was responding to the implication that he was being called upon to bear that message and to be a messenger.

THE PROPHET AS POET

The second aspect of the prophet's role moves in an unexpected direction. Even though the prophet was a messenger, he was also a minstrel or a poet. We wouldn't expect a court messenger to carry a message to another king or another kingdom or people in the form of poetry. Messengers normally spoke in technical prose—very precise language— because when passing international messages, he did not want to be misunderstood; therefore, he spoke in very plain language, not in language that was artistic, symbolic, or suggestive of multiple meanings. However, that was the primary way that God's messengers, the prophets, spoke and wrote—in poetic form.

God's messenger was aiming to speak to more than just the mind of the human audience, he was aiming to speak to the heart, and poetry is the language of the heart. Poetry does not just inform; poetic language moves and evokes deeper aspects of the human faculty. Like music, poetry moves the entire being, and that is what God is all about. Prophets were not messengers that reinforced the establishment; messengers brought about change. God was on the move, and He was moving the prophet to bear a message—a poetic message—that would move the people of Israel at very deep levels. These people had established themselves and had reached an arrangement that they did not want to see changed. They were heavily invested in the way things were, but God raised up a prophet precisely because He wanted to change the way things were. Therefore, He used poetic language that fit the purpose of moving people, not merely informing them, but transforming them. That is the language of prophecy.

The prophets used poetry that was drawn from two directions: the past and the present. The poets drew from ancient traditions, things in Israel's past, promises that had been forgotten, the covenant of God, and the Torah which had largely been buried underneath the traditions of people. The prophets again and again reached back to ancient traditions that were so old that when the prophets brought them forth again, they were like brand new. God inspired their poetry to take on new forms, to lift up images and pictures of God's future such as never had been seen or thought about before. Thus, the prophets were poets of the old and the new. They drew from old materials, but they also opened up brand new visions of God's message for the present time. These messages very often judged the present, but gave promises about Israel's future; thus, they exhibited the combination of judgment and hope. So, the poetry of the prophets then combined the old and the new, and they combined hope and judgment.

21 Prophets and Prophecy: Part 2

By Rickie Moore, Ph.D.

A study of the prophetic role is continued in this chapter. As was seen in the previous chapter, the prophet filled the role of messenger and poet. Other terms were also used to describe his ministry.

The Prophet As a Madman

A motif that runs throughout the prophetic materials of the Old Testament illustrates that quite often the prophet was someone whom people regarded as a person who had lost his mind. Scripture confirms this. Consider these words in Hosea 9:7: "The prophet is a fool, the spiritual man is insane" (*NKJV*). Apparently, Hosea is quoting what people are saying about prophets. Elisha is referred to as a madman in 2 Kings 9:11. Jeremiah has this to say about himself: "I am like a drunken man . . . like a man whom wine has overcome, because of the Lord, and because of His holy words" (Jeremiah 23:9, *NKJV*). Apparently Jeremiah is quoting popular opinion about prophets and prophecy when he records this characterization of prophets: "Every man who is demented and considers himself a prophet" (Jeremiah 29:26, *NKJV*). In 1 Samuel, there are a couple of statements in which the people are asking if Saul is also among the prophets (see 19:24). Saul's madness, his mental imbalance is well known. He called young David to his court to play the harp, to soothe feelings and to help him with his mental difficulties. It seems the people were associating Saul with the prophets because of his mental instability.

So, this motif offers evidence that the prophet was very often seen by the popular crowds as a mad person. It is like an Old Testament precedence for what happened in Acts 2, where God's prophetic Spirit was poured out upon His people just as the prophet Joel in the Old Testament had predicted. When the people began to prophesy, onlookers were amazed and wondered if they were out of their right mind. They even concluded that they might be "full of new wine"(Acts 2:13). The apostle Peter clarifies the situation with these words: "These are not drunk, as you suppose . . . this is what was spoken by the prophet Joel" (Acts 2:15, 16, *NKJV*). So, there seems to be a precedent for the present-day Pentecostal heritage in the Old Testament prophetic tradition.

A HOLY ENCOUNTER

When a prophet is given a message from God, it comes out of a holy encounter. Moses had such an encounter at Sinai when he saw the fire of God burning and heard the voice of God speaking from the fire, and he came near to that holy place. When a prophet has an encounter with God, he enters into God's "sanity," which most people consider "insanity." The common perception that most people have most of the time is insanity. Humanity inhabits times and cultures that really are crazy, but they become so normal to man's way of thinking that they are called normal, and God's way of seeing things is called crazy. When a prophet enters into the sanity of God, he sees things as they really are. He sees the uncleanness, the brokenness, the division among people, and the abnormalities that common perception treats as the norm. He sees all of that and is never the same.

That is what happened to Isaiah. The sixth chapter of Isaiah illustrates the messenger role of the prophet, but it also illustrates the other roles of poet and madman. When Isaiah sees God and receives the message that God has for him to share, he is given the message in poetic form. But it is a message that people will not understand. Most sermons and lessons on Isaiah 6 end with "Here am I! Send me" (v. 8). But God continues to speak to Isaiah, and this is what He says:

> "Go, and tell this people: 'Keep on hearing, but do not understand; keep on seeing, but do not perceive.' Make the heart of this people dull, and their ears heavy, and shut their eyes; lest they see with their eyes, and hear with their ears, and understand with their heart, and return and be healed" (Isaiah 6:9, 10, *NKJV*).

That is what God said to Isaiah. He gave Isaiah a very provocative message in the form of poetry. It was not a message that was easy for the people to receive. The people wanted to respond to the prophet, and they wanted him to speak in terms they could understand. But the whole purpose of God speaking through the prophet was to confront the people for having had life and reality on their own terms. God did not raise up the prophet to accommodate this way of thinking. Rather, He sent the prophet to confront and counter the terms by which people had understood their reality and grasped their world. The prophet contradicted the terms of the status quo and of the present worldview.

ISAIAH'S PERSONAL EXPERIENCE

Isaiah's worldview and Isaiah's reality were shattered when he saw the holiness of God. That is why he said, "Woe is me, for I am undone! Because I am a man of unclean lips, and I dwell in the midst of a people of unclean lips" (Isaiah 6:5, *NKJV*). This focus on the uncleanness of the lips suggests uncleanness of the very language that is used to grab hold of one's reality and to name one's world. The very way things are named and defined are polluted, and men are unaware of it. It is normal to them. But when Isaiah saw God's holiness, he realized that the problem in the world went much deeper than he had imagined; that his own sinfulness went much deeper; that the impurity and pollution even of his language was unclean; and so he was ruined. His whole way of seeing the world was shattered. In fact, he found out that the way he had seen the world was crazy, now that he had seen God's sanity. Isaiah now had the role of carrying that vision back to a people who did not want to be confronted. They would rather that he had reinforced them in their ways. Thus, in their eyes, the prophet became a madman.

ISAIAH IN THE NEW TESTAMENT

It is interesting that Jesus quotes from Isaiah 6 several times in the Gospels. Paul quotes from Isaiah 6 at the end of the Book of Acts. Although the New Testament quotes Isaiah 6 several times, there are no instances where the first part of this chapter is ever quoted. But the message God gave to the prophet is quoted repeatedly even by Jesus. When does He quote it? He quotes it when people ask Him why He spoke in parables. In Sunday school students are taught that Jesus used parables so that people could understand what He said. But Jesus, quoting Isaiah, said the exact opposite. He said that, like Isaiah, He used parables so that people would not understand. The reason for this approach was that the people wanted Him to give them a revelation. Their attitude was, *we will consider God's revelation if it is in our terms*, but Jesus, came to show the world that human terms were crazy, and were under the judgment of God. So Jesus, just as the Old Testament prophets who came before Him and whose ministry He fulfilled, was considered a crazy person in the same way they were.

The prophet is a messenger, a poet, and a madman. However, to understand the role of the Old Testament prophet, there is a final term to consider.

The Prophet As a Martyr

It is as if martyrdom is part of the prophet's job description. Most of the prophets of the Old Testament were literally killed. The world could not tolerate their poetry, their insanity, which was actually God's sanity. But what needs to be understood

249

is that the martyrdom of the prophets did not just take place at the end of their lives. It took place when they were called. It took place when they saw God because, as the Hebrews knew, if a person saw God's face, he could not survive. So in this sense, in the year that King Uzziah died, Isaiah died. Why? Because he saw God. And he died, and he knew he died. He knew it the moment that it happened. And he said words that really point to his own martyrdom. He said, "Woe is me." That expression is not used in modern English, but it is a term that points in the direction of death. The next thing Isaiah said even more explicitly pointed to his own death. He said, "I am undone." Some have translated that *I am ruined.* One person even translated it this way: *I am wasted. It's over for me. I'm a dead man.* Isaiah knew he was dead because he had seen God in His holiness and His glory. The very moment that a person sees God's face, death occurs, but it is a living death—a living out of the death experience.

What would happen to a minister today if God met him and gave him a message that collided with public opinion the way that Isaiah's message did? He would be called upon to live out a death experience.

ENTERING INTO THE DEATH EXPERIENCE

Isaiah's message through the rest of Chapter 6, deals with God's sending a death upon His people. He is sending a judgment, an ending of the world as they knew it, an exile. Yet the messenger that has to bear the news about that death enters into the death before anyone else does. It is the death of his reputation and of public approval. It is a message that is so heavy and so hard that it will not be accepted. God knew that from the outset. Therefore, He chose a prophet not only to come and announce the death, but also to enter into the death experience.

GRIEF: THE PROPHET'S PRIMARY PASSION

Many people have the idea that prophets were troublers of the status quo—that they were attackers of the establishment—and that is true. They were often called to carry out assignments that put them into strong conflict with kings and rulers and keepers of the establishment. But it needs to be understood that prophets were not just merely angry critics. Anger was not the primary passion of the prophets; it was grief. They went beyond being angry at the way things were to being pushed into the grief of God. In fact, they bore that grief. Anger is blaming, but grief reaches the point where one really does not know who to blame. He just knows that it hurts; he cries out in desperation. That is what the prophets come to in their ministry and in their role of being a messenger and a poet and a madman. They came into the grief of God—God's grief over the very judgment that He is having to send upon His people for His name's sake, for His holiness' sake.

Conclusion

To summarize what has been said, the prophets, especially the pre-exilic prophets, bore the message of the destruction of Israel as a kingdom. They bore a message about a death—the death of Israel, the exile of Israel. But the first person to go into the Exile, to enter into the death experience, was the prophet himself, as was seen in the case of

251

Isaiah. But while the prophet is the first one to enter into the death, he is also the first one to enter into the life beyond the death.

The final words of Isaiah 6 give a glimpse of that life beyond the death. The people were not ready for that life, because they did not want to go through the death experience to get to it. They did not want to go through the radical repentance and the radical change that finding that life requires. But Isaiah says, "Here I am! Send me. Send me into that exile. Send me into that death." But then he recoiled at the awful reality of it.

> Then I said, "Lord, how long?" And He answered: "Until the cities are laid waste and without inhabitant, the houses are without a man, the land is utterly desolate, the Lord has removed men far away, and the forsaken places are many in the midst of the land. But yet a tenth will be in it, and will return and be for consuming, as a terebinth tree or as an oak, whose stump remains when it is cut down. So the holy seed shall be its stump" (Isaiah 6:11-13, *NKJV*).

To paraphrase this passage, Isaiah asked, "How long, O Lord. How long, O Lord?" And the Lord said, "It is going to get worse before it gets better. There is going to be a tenth remaining, but then I am going to burn that until there is nothing left but a stump." But then comes that final word of hope, that life beyond the death, the holy seed is in the stump. Isaiah was the first to go into the Exile, but he was the first to enter into the new life beyond the death.

22

A History of the Northern Kingdom

By Rickie Moore, Ph.D.

Drawn from the Books of Kings, this chapter covers the history of the Northern Kingdom. The Books of Kings are placed within a collection of books that the Hebrews called the former prophets. It is interesting that the history of the Northern Kingdom is placed in a collection called prophets. This indicates that the historical perspective is a prophetic perspective. The prophets are telling God's version of Israel's history.

David, anointed by God to be the king of Israel, united the kingdom. How he accomplished that unification of the tribes of Israel is recorded in the Books of Samuel. Much tension existed between the tribes of Israel from the earliest days of the nation, and these tensions continued between the northern and southern tribes. This was one of the challenges David faced when he assumed the throne. God led David and showed him ways that he could help bring all of the tribes into strong unity. One of the means by which this was accomplished was through the conquest and the establishment of the city of Jerusalem as the place where the ark would be brought and where God would cause His name to dwell. Bringing Israel into unity and overcoming some of the north/south tribal differences were among David's greatest accomplishments.

Solomon's Reign

Solomon, who followed David, built upon that unity and his key contribution was to build up the kingdom of Israel. But as he built it up, he also sowed seeds of division within the kingdom.

SOLOMON'S FOREIGN AFFAIRS POLICY

Solomon sowed seeds of division within the kingdom in two different ways. First, he did so because of his foreign affairs policy. Solomon was a man who reached out to other nations through trade and commerce. He recruited people from these nations to participate in his building efforts, including the building of the Temple in Jerusalem. However, these contacts with foreign lands brought foreign influences which began to infiltrate into Israel.

The people first asked for a king during the time of the Judges and the prophet Samuel. They cried out in their struggle with all of the challenges of their time, and they asked God if they could have a king like the kings of other nations. God responded with some resistance and told them that what they were doing was essentially opposing His own kingship in some respects. But He allowed them to have a king whom Samuel anointed. The king in Israel, however, was different from the kings of other nations, because he stood under the sanction and authority of the Word of God.

Contrary to God's intention in allowing Israel to have a king, Solomon began more and more to model after the royal courts of these other kingdoms. With trade, commerce and other contacts with foreign nations, there came an increased affiliation with the culture, the customs and the conventions of these other societies. As a result, God's kingdom in Israel lost its distinction more and more.

Solomon's foreign affairs policy also led him to sexual liaisons. His affiliations with foreign kingdoms involved his taking many women from other nations into his royal harem. As he took these women in, he also brought into the court of Israel all of their attachments to their religious rituals and beliefs. Solomon's conduct began to have a negative impact on Israel as the beliefs, idolatries and pagan religious practices of his many wives and concubines began to infiltrate the nation.

SOLOMON'S DOMESTIC AFFAIRS POLICY

There is another major way in which the seeds of division began to be sown in Solomon's kingship, and it may be called domestic oppression. Solomon was a builder whose building efforts in Israel are covered in the first 11 chapters of Kings. These projects could be termed a building bonanza, because not only did he build the Temple, but he also built up the royal palace. This required the construction of many buildings which, in turn, required a huge amount of both human and financial resources. In order to accomplish his dream, Solomon taxed the people of his kingdom in a very oppressive way.

Rehoboam's Reign

After Solomon's death, the impact and injustice of this heavy taxation began to reveal itself. Although Solomon built up the kingdom, he also sowed seeds of division through his foreign and domestic affairs policies. When his son, Rehoboam, succeeded to the throne, the people were still chaffing under the impact of King Solomon's rule. As Rehoboam began to plan for his own rule, he consulted with the elders and the young men (see 1 Kings 12) about how to manage the economic and political affairs of his kingdom. The elders and the young men gave very different advice to the new king. The elders called for Rehoboam to lighten the load and to lift the heavy levels of oppression and taxation off the people of Israel. The young men, eager to push still further in the direction of building up the kingdom, called for Rehoboam to tax and oppress the people in an even greater way. Under this kind of pressure—this division between the elders and the young men over the oppressive policies of Solomon's kingship—the cracks of division in Israel's kingdom grew larger and larger. At this point, God sent His prophet to bring words of judgment about how God would break apart the kingdom and put part of the kingdom into the hands of another successor—Jeroboam.

Jeroboam's Reign

Jeroboam owed his reign to the division brought about by the things done during King Solomon's reign. Division causes vision to die. As Jeroboam began his rule in the northern half of the now divided kingdom, the deterioration of the vision that God had for His people in the beginning became more and more evident.

Jeroboam established two very consequential changes in his kingdom. There was an obvious problem with both kingdoms still observing one central place of worship in Jerusalem. In order to avoid this problem, Jeroboam established new places of worship so his subjects would not have an attachment to the city of Jerusalem. He set up alternative worship sites in two of his towns: Dan in the northern part of the region and Bethel in the southern region of his kingdom. He also set up golden calves in these places which was a blatant violation of God's covenant that had been established in the wilderness at Mt. Sinai. In the wilderness, the people fell into the worship of a golden calf and came under divine judgment.

It is not all together clear that Jeroboam saw the obvious link between what the people of Israel had done in the wilderness and what he was now doing in Dan and Bethel. There is speculation that he saw these golden calves not as objects of worship, but rather as representative of the seat upon which the divine presence would rest. It is not clear, then, that Jeroboam saw what he was doing as an outright violation of his belief in the one God. However, because this was not done by the Lord's command, it was, in spite perhaps of Jeroboam's good intentions, condemned as one of the most notorious sins that was ever committed in the history of Israel. As Jeroboam is succeeded by other kings, he is looked upon as the one responsible for establishing idolatry in Israel, and other kings are accused of following in the ways of Jeroboam. This accusation was a strong word of condemnation and an infamous way to remember Jeroboam.

Jeroboam also established non-Levitical priests to serve at Dan and Bethel. This was another step in the continuing deterioration of God's vision for covenant among His people. Jeroboam set the tone for what followed in the Northern Kingdom in the years ahead, that is, the continuation of the idolatry that he established in the cities of Dan and Bethel.

Northern Kingdom Dynasties

Since there was not a single dominant dynasty in the Northern Kingdom, several dynasties followed the reign of Jeroboam. The Northern Kingdom was known for its political intrigue and conflict, resulting in assassinations and coups. Thus, kings did not continue in the same line, but the kingdom was passed from one family to another with much more inconsistency than in the Southern Kingdom.

THE HOUSE OF OMRI

Two of the dynasties that emerged in the Northern Kingdom are most interesting. The house of Omri was established as the third dynasty of the Northern Kingdom in about 1885 B.C. and remained in power for a full generation. Omri was a very strong leader and was perhaps best known because of his son, Ahab. Ahab married a Phoenician princess named Jezebel who came in and played a role in the setting up of a special capital in Jezreel in the Northern Valley of Israel. Jezebel was an avid Baal worshiper and very aggressively promoted Canaanite pagan worship throughout the land of Israel. Ahab and Jezebel were known as perhaps the most evil and threatening rulers that ever reigned in Israel because they attempted to nullify the covenant with Israel's one God and impose Baal worship throughout the land. God raised up the prophets Elijah and Elisha to confront this evil and to save Israel from Ahab and Jezebel's agenda.

THE HOUSE OF JEHU

The dynasty of Omri came to an end when God raised up a man named Jehu who was anointed by the prophet Elisha to bring God's judgment against the house of Ahab and Jezebel. He was a zealous leader who took an aggressive stance against idolatry. According to 2 Kings 9, 10, Jehu began to swing the sword of God's judgment that resulted in the slaughter of many people in the house of Ahab and Jezebel, including associates and sympathizers. It was actually a very bloody encounter that seemed to take on a life of its own. Jehu's zeal seemed to exceed spiritual bounds so that he appeared to enjoy carrying out this violent judgment. In later days, the blood bath that Jehu brought against the house of Omri was looked upon in a very negative way. Since his actions were carried out in a very judgmental way, they were later condemned by the prophet Hosea.

One thing is clear, something was not right in Jehu's heart. As violently, vigorously and aggressively as he fought against the idolatry of Jezebel, he still let the worship centers stand that Jeroboam had established in Dan and Bethel. Despite his zealous political actions, Israel was not turned around, and the slide towards destruction in the Northern Kingdom was not stopped. After Jehu's reign, the same things that existed before his reign continued: more dynasties, more political intrigue, more assassinations and more division. God raised up a remnant through the prophets Elijah and Elisha, but the majority of the inhabitants of the Northern Kingdom did not turn away from evil, and so the possibilities of its outright destruction continued to hang over the northern dynasties.

Conclusion

If modern secular historians were giving the account of the history of the Northern Kingdom, they would talk about the kingdom's inevitable destruction because of the rise of Assyria, the super power in this Mesopotamian region north of Palestine. But there is a different perspective that is Biblical and prophetic. From that perspective, the destruction of the Northern Kingdom did not come about because of the political agenda of the Assyrian Empire, but because of their unfaithfulness, their sin, and their departure from God's covenant. The coming of Assyria to destroy the Northern Kingdom, which took place in 722 B.C., came about as judgment from God, predicted by His prophets. The Assyrians were very ruthless conquerors, and God's judgment was very severe.

The Assyrians had a practice of scattering the people they had conquered by carrying them into exile and not keeping them together as a single people. (The Babylonians treated the people of Judah differently when they conquered them. They carried the people of Judah away when Judah fell and kept them intact in a ghetto in Babylon.) The nation of Assyria had a much more devastating form of captivity. They scattered exiles over the empire and brought in other people from other places to intermix with them resulting in an ethnically impure people. This is what produced those who came to be known as the Samaritans. Samaria was the main political capital of the Northern Kingdom and the main area left after the destruction wrought by the Assyrian army. When the people came back from Babylonian exile, there was a conflict that developed once again between the northern and the southern populations; that is, between the mixed remnant around Samaria and those who had come back from Babylonian captivity to rebuild the city of Jerusalem. The destruction of the Northern Kingdom left circumstances that continued to cause division throughout the history of God's people.

The next chapter deals with the prophetic ministries of Elijah and Elisha, which were important in the midst of the Northern Kingdom. They established a remnant whose faithfulness became the grounds for any hope for the future of God's people.

23

Elijah and Elisha

By Rickie Moore, Ph.D.

As noted earlier, this major topic, "The Destruction of Israel as a Kingdom," is presented in the Books of 1, 2 Kings. The Books of Kings were grouped by the Hebrews in a collection they called the *Former Prophets*, thus giving two designations: *Kings*—the name for the books—and *Former Prophets*—the name for the collection.

Kings and Prophets

These two terms, *kings* and *prophets*, are important because they represent the tension one finds in this portion of Israel's history. This chapter features a series of clashes between the kings of Israel and the prophets of Israel. A classic example, of course, is when Elijah the prophet squares off against Ahab the king. God's prophet was raised up to stand against the Baal worship that was being promoted by King Ahab and Queen Jezebel.

Overall, the history of the kingship of Israel is one of failure. Thus, the storyline of the two Books of Kings is one of the failure of human kingship. On the other hand, the story shows how prophecy was fulfilled and how God's Word and revelation through the prophets was fulfilled. This contrast between failure of kingship and fulfillment of prophecy is glaringly obvious, even though not every king failed and not every prophet carried out his calling. A few of the kings in this study performed well, and some of the prophets failed miserably. Overall, however, it is a story of failed human kingship and fulfillment of prophecy.

Royal Reports and Prophetic Stories

The Books of 1, 2 Kings are composed, basically, of two kinds of literature, royal reports and prophetic stories. The royal reports focus upon the kings of Israel and Judah, and they all have a very familiar structure. Certain phrases are repeated. Most Bible students will easily recognize the formula and the ring of these reports. They start with an opening statement of when and how that individual began to reign, followed by some basic facts regarding the age and the length of reign for that particular king. Very often there is a comment about the queen mother. Then will come an evaluation of the reign of the king of Israel or of the king of Judah, with likely mention of David or Jeroboam. David is lifted up as a model of faithfulness, whereas Jeroboam, the first king of the northern tribes, is lifted up as a notorious kingship failure. Individual kings are evaluated in terms of how they compared to either the ways of David or the ways of Jeroboam.

Following this, the royal reports feature recollections and records of events that marked the reigns of the kings. This may go on for several chapters or it may be covered in a few verses. The length of the record of events varies greatly, but eventually the reports come back to a reference of further information available in other sources. Then will follow a concluding statement about the king's death. This is the recurring pattern of these royal reports.

At the same time, another type of literary material streams through 1, 2 Kings that is known as the story or the testimony. Rather than always focusing upon the kings of Israel and Judah, these stories very often are focused on common people, especially the prophets. One can always find this contrast—royal reports or prophetic stories.

The prophetic stories are not given in a predictable pattern. They are very lively and often full of surprises. Unlike the royal reports, the reader never really knows how the story is going to unfold. Therefore, matching the central conflict between kings and prophets, there is something of a literary tension between the types of materials. Ultimately, as one follows the story of 1, 2 Kings, the prophetic stories tend to gain the upper hand.

Royal reports feature the agenda, the plan, and the power of the monarch, but the stories feature the power of God—God working through common people, God working through prophets. Not always taking place at headquarters, or in the center of human power, the stories carry the reader into the backwaters of Israel. They show a prophet living by a brook, or visiting the home of a nobody, or some widow in a remote region of the kingdom. The implied point is that God is not restricted to what is going on at the royal court. He is at work in other places as well, in humble places, not always tied, as one commentator puts it, to the political headlines.

God may be at work in places where nobody is noticing, but that is where God's kingdom is being revealed. That is where God's future is unfolding. Gradually, the things people tend to take so seriously in the political realm are passing away, while God's kingdom in the world is being established in a humble, but lasting manner.

The Structure of 1, 2 Kings

In the structure of the Books of Kings, one finds further illustrations of these points. All of this helps one to see where the prophets—Elijah and Elisha, in particular—fit into this period of Israel's history.

PART ONE

The first 11 chapters of 1 Kings features the kingdom of Solomon. This is before the kingdom divided. It essentially highlights all the buildings that Solomon had a hand in building—the Temple, his palaces, other royal residences. Solomon was the builder of Israel's kingdom, but that building effort came at quite a cost.

PART TWO

In the second portion of the structure of 1, 2 Kings, the kingdom of Israel divided after the death of Solomon. Much of the pressure which produced this division may be attributed to Solomon's tax policies and his heavy hand of oppression on the people to expedite his massive building program. But the kingdom split as part of God's judgment upon the sins of Solomon. This account constitutes a great bulk of the material of 1, 2 Kings—1 Kings 12–2 Kings 17.

The storyline relates to both kingdoms, moving back and forth between Israel in the North and Judah in the South, though it eventually ends with the very tragic account of how the Northern Kingdom falls before the expanding Assyrian Empire. The Assyrian Empire conquered many of Israel's neighbors before finally coming to Samaria and laying it waste, thus effectively ending the Northern Kingdom.

PART THREE

The rest of the Kings material, 2 Kings 18–25, focuses strictly on the remaining kingdom of Judah. So far, this structure has covered the one kingdom of Solomon, the divided kingdoms, and then the Kingdom of Judah.

PART FOUR

It is important to note, however, that most of this material—in fact, the central bulk of this material, 1 Kings 17—2 Kings 13—centers on the prophets Elijah and Elisha, not the kings of Israel at all. Roughly one-third of all the material of 1, 2 Kings focuses on Elijah and Elisha. Even while the royal reports frame the two books, the writer's central attention moves from the Kings to the prophets of God. This is an important point to keep in mind. It helps the reader understand how the kings of Israel are falling away from the covenant with God; but how, at the same time, God sends His royal messengers, the prophets, to represent His kingdom over and against the failed human kingship.

God's Requirements for Kings

Years earlier, the first prophet, Moses, had given Israel a message in the Book of Deuteronomy, anticipating what would happen when Israel moved into the Promised Land, asked for a king, and failed to keep God's statutes. Moses had laid down a law of kingship, found in Deuteronomy 17. Here is a portion of what he wrote, which reinforces the point of how God's covenant increasingly stands in tension and conflict with the human kingship of Israel and Judah.

> When thou art come unto the land which the Lord thy God giveth thee, and shalt possess it, and shalt dwell therein, and shalt say, I will set a king over me, like as all the nations that are about me; thou shalt in any wise set him king over thee, whom the Lord thy God shall choose: one from among thy brethren shalt thou set king over thee: thou mayest not set a stranger over thee, which is not thy brother. But he shall not multiply horses to himself, nor cause the people to return to Egypt, to the end that he should multiply horses: forasmuch as the Lord hath said unto you, Ye shall henceforth return no more that way. Neither shall he multiply wives to himself, that his heart turn not away: neither shall he greatly multiply to himself silver and gold. And it shall be, when he sitteth upon the throne of his kingdom, that he shall write him a copy of this law in a book out of that which is before the priests the Levites: and it shall be with him, and he shall read therein all the days of his life: that he may

> learn to fear the Lord his God, to keep all
> the words of this law and these statutes, to
> do them: that his heart be not lifted up
> above his brethren, and that he turn not
> aside from the commandment, to the right
> hand, or to the left: to the end that he may
> prolong his days in his kingdom, he, and
> his children, in the midst of Israel
> (Deuteronomy 17:14-20).

Moses anticipated the people were going to look to the nations around them and want a king. They were going to get their eyes off God and His desire for Israel to be different. God even indicated here that He was going to allow kingship, but then He gave some laws that were to turn Israel's kingship away from that of other nations. For one thing, they were to choose a king from among themselves and never a foreigner. The king God would approve was supposed to be one who would write for himself in a book, a copy of the law—a book he was to read all the days of his life. He was to fear the Lord his God by keeping all the words of this Torah and turn neither to the right nor to the left.

Israel's kings were to be *subject* kings, not *divine* kings. They were to be subject to the revelation of God as mediated through the written Scripture, and through the revelation of God's prophets. The king was not to be lifted up socially or economically. He was to be a brother, not a Lord over the people. Unfortunately, so many of the things the king was *not supposed to do* actually became characteristic of Solomon's reign.

So, even as one hears the story of Solomon and all his greatness, he hears echoes of Moses' prophecy and sees that prophecy fulfilled, as Solomon moves away from God's expectations of kingship. This contrast has even caused one commentator to ask if maybe the Books of Kings should not be written with a question mark. In other words: Kings? Are these kings? God raised up His prophets to press that question. Thus, a full one-third of the material of 1, 2 Kings is devoted to those prophets whom God raised up to question the legitimacy of their kingship.

Mission and Purpose of the Prophets

The two names, Elijah and Elisha, give some understanding of the mission and major purpose of these two most illustrious prophets of the 9th century B.C. The name *Elijah* means "Yahweh is God." The last part of Elijah's name is an abbreviation for Yahweh. The phrase "Yahweh is God," of course, perfectly fits the mission of Elijah. He was raised up primarily to confront the threat of idol worship as represented by Baal. So many people in that day were, in a sense, saying, "Baal is god." They were ascribing divinity to Baal rather than Yahweh, or perhaps, they ascribed divinity to Baal in addition to Yahweh, sort of mixing the two. "Halting between two opinions" was the popular phrase Elijah came to ascribe to the people.

Thus, Elijah confronted one of the two major threats to the faith of Israel in the 9th century B.C.— loss of true, faithful worship of Yahweh in light of a turn toward Baal. Baal worship was largely promoted by Queen Jezebel, the Phoenician queen married to Ahab. Elijah championed a message which declared

Yahweh, not Baal, to be God. He challenged Baal even at the beginning of his prophetic ministry when he, through the unction of the Holy Spirit, declared, "I have a message from the true God, and there will be no rain" (see 1 Kings 17:1). Those words were glaringly significant when one realizes Baal was associated with rain. He was the god of Canaanite faith, credited with bringing storms, rain, and fertility to the land.

"Only Yahweh, the God of Israel, has power to withhold and to grant rain," Elijah declared to King Ahab (1 Kings 17:1). His statement included the phrase, "neither dew nor rain," and it was a direct affront to Jezebel and everything she represented in terms of religion.

Even as Elijah declared, there was no rain in the land. The people became miserable from the drought, and this set the stage for Elijah's confrontation with the 450 prophets of Baal on Mount Carmel (1 Kings 18). One could call this the "showdown" on Mount Carmel. It is a familiar story, packed with drama and suspense. First, Elijah challenged: "Bring the prophets of Baal to Mount Carmel." This unknown prophet of a few years ago, this man who suddenly appeared out of nowhere to declare there would be no more rain, is now a voice to be reckoned with. King Ahab could no longer afford to overlook or ignore him.

So, there was a gathering of all the people of Israel on Mount Carmel, plus 450 prophets of Baal, and one prophet of Jehovah. Elijah was totally in charge. He set the rules of the contest, summed up in, "The God that answereth by fire, let him be God" (1 Kings 18:24). Baal's prophets tried hard. They tried all day. They engaged in the rituals of their religion, even while Elijah mocked them. No fire. Then came Elijah's turn. He wanted none to doubt the power of Jehovah, so he had the sacrifices soaked with water three times. Then he prayed a simple prayer:

> Lord God of Abraham, Isaac, and of Israel, let it be known this day that thou art God in Israel, and that I am thy servant, and that I have done all these things at thy word. Hear me, O Lord, hear me, that this people may know that thou art the Lord God, and that thou hast turned their heart back again (1 Kings 18:36, 37).

As all know, the fire fell. It consumed the sacrifice, the wood, the stones, and licked up the water in the trench built around the altar. Thus, the prophet Elijah carried out his mission with flare and drama.

Nevertheless, Scripture gives a reminder that not even Elijah was perfect in all that. He proved himself to be very human and capable of weakness; in fact, this happened soon after Carmel, when Elijah, in fear, runs from Queen Jezebel's threat on his life. The reader sees his humanness once again when he is brought back into line by the tender voice of God on Mt. Horab.

The name *Elisha* means "God saves." His name also appropriately fits his mission. This successor to Elijah, this son in the faith, so to speak, was raised up to combat the second major threat to the faith of Israel in the 9th century B.C.—the threat of militarism.

The Northern Kingdom was threatened at this time by their neighbor, Assyria, also called Aram. This was not the superpower Assyria, but what is known today as Syria. This small city state caused all kinds of problems with their border raids and constant military incursions into the Northern Kingdom during the 9th century B.C. It was the kind of situation that prompted the northern kings to look towards military resources in order to survive, trusting more and more in the arm of the flesh rather than the power of God for their security and salvation.

Elisha was raised up to say that one should not trust in the arm of the flesh, because it is God who saves. God's people, God's kings, should trust Him only. Elisha fulfilled his mission through many stories, such as when God used him to blind the Syrian army that had him and his servants surrounded. Although Israel seemed greatly outnumbered, Elisha told his servant not to be afraid. He then prayed for God to open the eyes of his servant, and he saw God's angelic hosts surrounding them in numbers far greater than the enemy.

Elisha also showed Israel the way to God's salvation when the capital city of Samaria was under siege by the Syrian army. The city was starving, and the king was ready to give up, tearing his garments in despair. Elisha gave a prophecy, saying that on the very next day God would bring total deliverance to the city. Next morning, God used four humble lepers, stuck outside the city walls, dying of starvation, to go over to the Syrian camp and bring back word of God's deliverance.

In these and in other ways, God raised up Elijah and Elisha to show the way and to preserve the faith of Israel. The faith of Israel that says, "Yahweh is God, not Baal;" and to say "God saves, not the arm of flesh," represented by armies.

Theme of This Time Period

Another story of note, and one less familiar than those already mentioned, relates to the sons of the prophets, 2 Kings 6. Here, the reader is introduced to a theme that will come up again in the study of other prophets. This is the story:

> And the sons of the prophets said unto Elisha, Behold now, the place where we dwell with thee is too strait for us. Let us go, we pray thee, unto Jordan, and take thence every man a beam, and let us make us a place there, where we may dwell. And he answered, Go ye. And one said, Be content, I pray thee, and go with thy servants. And he answered, I will go. So he went with them. And when they came to Jordan, they cut down wood. But as one was felling a beam, the ax head fell into the water: and he cried, and said, Alas, master! for it was borrowed. And the man of God said, Where fell it? And he showed him the place. And he cut down a stick, and cast it in thither; and the iron did swim. Therefore said he, Take it up to thee. And he put out his hand, and took it. (2 Kings 6:1-7).

It is a delightful little story, though odd, because it seems the point is all about a house being built for the sons of the prophets. Yet, the story ends without revealing whether the house gets built. The story is important, however, because it shows something about the house God is trying to build. This whole period of kingship is marked by the desire to build houses. For example, Solomon wanted to build God's house, and God was pleased. But Solomon's building ambitions seem tainted before the story ends as he begins to reach out greedily to exploit every resource in order to keep on building. Others followed Solomon's success, building and building, but they were seeking to build houses of royal success rather than the house of God. All kinds of treacheries followed. The kingdom was split and God's house, at least in the spiritual sense, fell down. With the prophets, on the other hand, one sees God trying to build another kind of house—a house referring to family and children.

Earlier scriptures had referred to the house of David. In fact, even before the period of the kingship now being studied, when David said he wanted to build God a house, God said he could not; but, at the same time, God said he was going to build David's house. This referred to David's family, his lineage through which would come the Messiah. The real house God is building is family, human descendants, the seed of Abraham, which has been God's desire from the very beginning. That is what was happening in this little story about the school of the prophets. It was about an elder, Elisha, and about his children who were saying they wanted to build a physical house. But even more important than building that physical house—which may or may not have been completed—was the building of a holy bond between sons of the prophets and their spiritual father.

275

Note the delicacy of the story. The children came. They had this desire stirring in them to build. The elder blessed them. Sometimes it is so hard for elders to bless the efforts of the young and what is stirring inside them, because they are too wrapped up with their own projects. But here, the elder blessed the proposal of the children—the sons of the prophets. And then one sees the grace of God at work in the children, too. Once they got the permission of the elder, they said, "Come with us. Come and help us build" (see 2 Kings 6:3).

We see how God honors that turning of the hearts of the elder to the children, and the turning of the hearts of the children to the elder. Very quickly one sees how powerfully God honors that, as revealed through the miracle of the ax head that swam.

God's grace was at work in that story, because Elisha, the old man, was once a young man and he surely remembered asking the elder Elijah to give him a blessing. In fact, he asked for a double portion. Elijah finally told him, "I cannot give that except you stay with me" (see 2 Kings 2:10). Elisha proved he would do anything to stay with the elder. Now, the heart of the elder is turning towards the younger ones, and the hearts of the young are turning towards the elder once again.

The occasion in 2 Kings 2, where Elisha refused to be separated from the elder Elijah and saw him translated in a chariot of fire, just about marks the dead center of 1, 2 Kings when considered as one work. It seems apparent that the central position of the story represents the central point God is trying to make—the building of God's spiritual house. When the heart of the father is turned toward the son, and the heart of the son toward the father—that is the house God is building. All those other houses have received much attention, but it is the spiritual house that God's miracle sanctions.

Summary

In 1, 2 Kings, the reader sees a sad story of the failure of human kingship, one that plays out precisely as the first prophet Moses had foretold. Yet, in the very center of the book, one sees how God is preserving the central truth, the central revelation, that is going to preserve His house forever. God's house is the center of the message being set forth in the Kings, a house which is spiritual, represented through miraculous events in the lives of both Elijah and Elisha, and also represented by God's willingness to preserve, even miraculously, His house, represented by the drawing of the hearts of the elders toward the young and the young toward the elders.

The heart of the message set forth in the lives of Elijah and Elisha is simple—God is always going to preserve His house.

Jonah and
Amos

By Rickie Moore, Ph.D.

Even though Elijah and Elisha are the only prophets given lengthy treatment in 1, 2 Kings, a number of other prophets had vital ministries during the same period of Israel's history. Some of these are only barely mentioned in Kings and others not mentioned at all. In fact, they are not mentioned in the entire collection of the historical books or in what the Hebrews called the Former Prophets.

Bible scholars know about these other prophets because books named after them have been preserved elsewhere, namely in the collection of Biblical writings the Hebrews called the Latter Prophets. The Latter Prophets are made up essentially of four books—Isaiah, Jeremiah, Ezekiel, Daniel, as well as the Book of the Twelve. In the present canon of Scripture, Christians break those apart into 12 other books; for the ancient Hebrews, however, they were all placed on one scroll called the Book of the Twelve.

This study looks at two of the three prophets from the Book of the Twelve who had ministries in the Northern Kingdom. The Book of Hosea will be taken up in the next chapter, and that will complete the subsection on the history of the Northern Kingdom. The three prophets who had ministries in the Northern Kingdom were Jonah, Amos, and Hosea, often referred to as three of the 12 minor prophets. They are called minor because of the size of their books, not because their ministries are insignificant. Upon completion of these three minor prophets of the Northern Kingdom, focus will shift to prophets of the Southern Kingdom, or Judah.

The Prophet Jonah

The prophet Jonah is named in only one verse of the Kings and that is 2 Kings 14:25. The ministry of Jonah took place during the time of Jeroboam II who reigned in the Northern Kingdom during the first half of the 8th century B.C. One finds in 2 Kings 14:25 that Jonah, "the son of Amittai, the prophet, which was of Gathhepher" accurately prophesied of Jeroboam's recovery of some lost territory, though the specific details of what happened are not given. Thus, most all of what one knows about Jonah is found in the Book of Jonah itself.

This book is characterized by at least two rather odd features. First, no other minor prophet or no other prophet in the Book of the Twelve is presented to the reader totally in terms of a story. Most of the minor prophets, as readers will note, feature messages. In the Book of Amos, one reads mostly the messages of Amos, and in the Book of Hosea, the messages of Hosea. But in the Book of Jonah, one reads a story *about* the prophet, rather than messages *from* the prophet.

Second, the story one reads about Jonah, this prophet of the Northern Kingdom, does not focus upon the Northern Kingdom at all. It is the story of how God calls Jonah to go preach to a foreign nation, specifically the city of Nineveh, capital of the mighty Assyrian Empire.

God's call for Jonah to go to Nineveh is the action of the story, yet the book does not focus as much on the external history of this event as upon the internal response of Jonah to his divine assignment. The external event itself is told very quickly, and the reader does not get many details about varying aspects of Jonah's going to Nineveh. The fast-moving story tends to leave the reader with lots of questions unanswered. Again, the sustained focus of the story seems to be on how Jonah is reacting, what Jonah is thinking, and what Jonah is saying as he takes this journey.

Nineveh was the capital city of the Assyrian Empire. It was a grand city for its day, built on the oppression of other peoples, on subjugation, and on taxation. That is what an empire is all about— the conquering of other nations and the use of their people and resources. Thus was Nineveh built, and its reputation was well-known by people throughout the region, including the Israelites.

At the time of Jonah and king Jeroboam—first half of the 8th century B.C.—Assyria had not as yet conducted any major campaigns down into the Palestinian region. They were still fighting off others, with main attention turned elsewhere, but they had already begun to exert pressure on Israel, demanding certain resources and taxes. The people of the Northern Kingdom were already beginning to fear Assyria, and one can easily imagine the uncertainty with which they viewed the future.

Eventually Assyria would be the power that would bring an end to Jonah's country, the Northern Kingdom of Israel. Thus, one can understand how Nineveh represented to Jonah not only a foreign city full of strange people, but also a very threatening enemy city. This explains Jonah's resistance to God's call and why he would run away when God told him to go preach to Nineveh. It also helps give background and explain why Jonah would react so angrily when God relented His judgment after the people of Nineveh repented.

Jonah resisted the call to go to Nineveh, ran away, and then finally reacted angrily to his prophetic assignment. As the story unfolds, the culminating, entire final Chapter 4 of the book is all about how God probes into the prophet's reaction. Rather than spending a great deal of time going over a very familiar story, one might find it more profitable to focus on some of the striking lessons and revelations the book offers.

1. *How God struggles with and against those whom He calls to the prophetic task.* Something of this was revealed in the story of the prophet Elijah— how God wrestled with Elijah after he ran away from his prophetic call. God does not just leave it at that. Scriptures indicate how God returns to His called prophets and struggles with them even when they

have failed. God assigns to prophets very difficult tasks, but God also nurtures and develops the prophet. He corrects the prophet until he comes into fulfillment of his calling.

The prophetic assignment entails some growing. God struggles *with* and sometimes even *against* those people whom He calls to the prophetic task. For example, God wrestled with Elijah under the juniper tree. This goes along with something very fundamental to the faith of Israel. Jacob was renamed Israel following a night when God wrestled with him. But as God wrestled with Jacob and blessed Jacob through that encounter, He really defined who Jacob was. Jacob was Israel, meaning "one who wrestles with God."

That is saying something not only about Israel the person, but it is also saying something about Israel the people, for the people were in the loins of Jacob and also the object of God's promise. Thus, the people of Israel are the ones with whom God wrestles.

As God deals with Jonah, He is showing the reader something about how He deals with His entire people. One can look at the entire Book of Jonah as a kind of symbolic representation of how God deals with His people—sending them into exile, just like He swallowed up Jonah in the fish, and then bringing them out of exile to begin fulfilling their mission to all nations of the earth.

2. *How God's message of judgment is always set within the larger context of His mercy.* God has mercy and forgives even the people of Nineveh—those ruthless, conquering people filled with violence and

murderous acts against weaker neighbors. Within the human context, it is hard to love that kind of people. In the Book of Jonah, God picks one of the worst nations, one of the worst cities one could imagine, and shows the extent of His mercy and grace even for them.

As it always is, God's wrath and judgment against Nineveh is set within a larger context of His mercy. As the Bible so often says, "God's wrath is but for a moment, but his mercy endures forever" (see Psalm 136:1). God judges, but God is not judgment. God is love. And so His judgment is set within the context of His love and His grace and His mercy.

Thus, in the final chapter, God comes against His prophet who carries the message of judgment. He comes against this messenger of judgment so that he will not have a judgmental attitude. One sees here that God is very much a God of passions, and He confronts Jonah in order to perfect his attitude. He is calling for His prophet to bear His message with the same kind of heart and the same kind of attitude that represents the heart of God.

3. *How the God of Israel cannot be restricted to always take sides with Israel.* The God of Israel is sovereign, and certainly not restricted to the side of Israel alone. This God is so radical and so daring that He can be found taking sides even with Israel's enemies against His own prophet and His own people. Of course, that understanding prepares one for how God takes the side of Israel's enemies in judging His people as He will do for the Northern Kingdom and also for the Southern Kingdom later on. There are many more lessons in the Book of Jonah, but these three are especially worth noting.

The Book of Amos

The name *Amos* comes from a word meaning "to carry." Possibly, it represents the idea of being carried by God. God carried Amos, one might say— called him and carried him from the South to the North. That is one of the distinctions of the prophet Amos. He was called from a southern city of Tekoa, about five miles south of Jerusalem, to go to the Northern Kingdom and prophesy.

Like Jonah, Amos prophesied during the time of Jeroboam II. The purpose of the book is to warn the people of the Northern Kingdom that they faced devastating judgment for their sins. This prophecy came during a time period that was only about a generation away from the complete destruction of the Northern Kingdom. Thus, God raised up Amos at a strategic time. The day was getting late, and Amos was given a crucial warning about the coming judgment.

The judgment Amos declared was not just a slap on the wrist. Amos understood that God was "roaring from Zion; He was coming like a lion" (see 1:2). The judgment He had in view was a very devastating one, involving destruction of the entire kingdom and the complete taking away captive of the population.

Some of the famous statements in the Book of Amos that bring attention to the severity of God's judgment are . . .

"The virgin of Israel is fallen; she shall no more rise" (5:2).

"The end has come upon my people of Israel" (8:2).

Amos was given a vision of a basket of summer fruit. Through this vision, God was warning His people that the end—the harvest, the final culmination of His work—was drawing near, and the absolute end was threatening to come upon Israel (see Chapter 8).

Why was God judging His people? There are basically two dimensions of Israel's sins that are discussed throughout the Book of Amos—social injustice and religious compromise. Often, people of a liberal political persuasion are concerned about social sins, while those of a more conservative orientation tend to be concerned about sins thought to relate to religious or spiritual matters of personal morality. God's prophets do not differentiate between social sins and personal religious sins. Rather, they hammer away about God's concerns with both these violations of His covenant.

The social injustice Amos prophesied against comes through in a number of statements. He talked about how Israel was selling "the needy for a pair of shoes" (8:6). He spoke against the "cows of Bashan," his reference to the wealthy women who were encouraging their husbands to exploit so that they could live an excessive and materialistic lifestyle: "the cows of Bashan . . . on the mountain of Samaria, who oppress the poor, who crush the needy" (4:1, *NIV*).

Social injustice was a very important matter to Amos. He was helping Israel to see once again that God's covenant is all about taking care of the weak and the poor and the needy of society. As the Book of Deuteronomy sets forth the covenant of Israel, and repeats so often: Israel is called to care for the widow, the orphan, the sojourner, those who are weak and need the help of others. Amos emphasizes that covenant concern with social care and with social justice.

He also was concerned with religious compromise (syncretism) and hypocrisy. Several elements seemed to be involved in Israel's religious compromise at this time. There was the mixing of Israel's faith with pagan practices. This was not the outright rejection of the worship of Yahweh, but just as in the time of Elijah, it was the importing of pagan influences and pagan practices. Amos mocked their worship. Apparently, it was a time when a great deal of worship was going on—much church attendance, so to speak—but Amos mocked the shallowness and the insincerity and the compromise of all the worship and the sacrifice that was going on.

When he said such things as, "Come to Bethel and transgress; at Gilgal and multiply transgression" (4:4), he was mocking their worship. It was a call to worship with a shocking twist, for he also said later, speaking for Jehovah, "I hate your religious feasts" (5:21). Amos the prophet was delivering the Word of God here: "I despise your feasts, and I take no delight in your solemn assemblies" (5:21, *RSV*).

Immediately after that, he said, "Let justice run down like water, and righteousness like a mighty stream" (5:24, *NKJV*). Amos was showing the people that they could not have faithful religion if they had social injustice. The two do not go together.

When God's people come to God's house, they are expected to come with clean hands and a pure heart (see Psalm 24:3, 4), as people who have practiced justice throughout the week. They are not to be people who simply lift their hands to worship God and lay sacrifices on the altar without meaning. True worship influences daily life.

The first verse of the Book of Amos introduces this book as "The words of Amos . . . which he saw." There are two terms—*words* and *visions*—that really point to the two major sections of the book. The first six chapters state essentially the words of Amos' message—words of judgment concerning Israel's sins of social injustice and religious compromise. The second portion of the book has a series of visions, thus picking up on the words given in the introductory verse—"the words and the visions of Amos." His were indeed words of judgment and visions of destruction.

The Book of Amos is a rather dark book in terms of the heavy emphasis on judgment and destruction, but the hour is late and one knows from the message that there is an element of mercy in judgment. When judgment is not the final judgment, it is always merciful. It is merciful to be warned that judgment is coming. This means there is an alternative. Judgment could be coming without one being aware of it. God calls prophets—messengers of judgment—to serve His mercy in warning people. For as Amos said at one point, "Perhaps the Lord . . . will have mercy" (5:15, *NIV*). The very point of all this harsh judgment, this shock treatment, is to try to turn the people around.

Highlights of Amos' Message

Three highlights of Amos' message stand out—one in the beginning of the book, one in the middle of the book, and one at the end.

BEGINNING

Amos begins by pronouncing judgment, not first of all against Israel, but against Israel's neighbors.

288

He gives a series of very short messages of judgment—oracles, as prophetic messages are sometimes called—against foreign nations and the city states that surround the Northern Kingdom of Israel. These war oracles are essentially oracles of judgment because of war crimes the nations have committed. It shows that God, even while He is dealing primarily with Israel, is also dealing with all nations, because ultimately His purposes are for all nations. It is perhaps a way to get Israel's attention, because it is easy for one to hear judgment against the neighbors. After Amos gets the people's ear with these oracles of judgment, however, he brings the judgment home to the Northern Kingdom. That is the opening highlight of the book.

MIDDLE

In the middle of the book, Chapter 7, there is a dramatic encounter between Amos and Jeroboam's priest, Amaziah. This takes place at the city of Bethel—a religious center established by Jeroboam, the first king of the northern tribes, and now Jeroboam II is ruling. Jeroboam has his priest, Amaziah, conducting religious affairs in Bethel. *Bethel* means "house of God." However, Amaziah the priest confronts Amos the prophet and says to him, "Go home. Don't prophesy here. This is the house of the king" (see 7:13). Notice the point. Bethel means "the house of God." Although Bethel has been made a place of worship, it is a place of false and idolatrous worship. A downward progress has been made from Bethel, "the house of God," to "the house of the king." God's house is being pushed out of the picture.

ENDING

The final highlight in the Book of Amos comes in the last chapter of the book, Chapter 9. The chapter begins with a picture of the pillars that surround the altar of God. Apparently the pillars of God's house—the Temple—are being knocked down. This was the final vision Amos saw, a vision of destruction upon nothing less than God's own Temple. God was willing to destroy not only the kingdom of Israel, but His own house as well, because of Israel's unfaithfulness.

However, at the very end, there is a single oracle of hope over and against judgment and destruction. The final verses point to a glorious promise of hope beyond the judgment. It is not a promise of hope that provides any way to avoid the judgment, but it is a word of hope that looks beyond the judgment (Amos 9:11-15).

This is the promise, Amos says, of the raising up of the fallen tabernacle of David and the restoration of the ruined land (see v.11). This connects with what was said earlier about the ministries of Elijah and Elisha. One sees once again God's concern about His own house. He is willing to suffer the destruction of His own house, the Temple and the nation of Israel, in order to save His spiritual house, to ultimately raise up His fallen tabernacle, the house of David, through which He intends to reign forever.

25

Hosea

By Rickie Moore, Ph.D.

The name *Hosea* means "salvation" or "Yahweh saves." It is a great deal like the name of Elisha, except it uses an abbreviation for the word *Yahweh* instead of the word for God, *el*. Hosea, like Amos and Jonah, prophesied during the days of Jeroboam II, with a ministry that focused like theirs on the Northern Kingdom. However, Hosea's ministry seems to have extended a bit later than theirs. So, Hosea can be seen as the prophet of the last generation of the Northern Kingdom—the last messenger of judgment before destruction came. And perhaps, he is also the clearest messenger of the mercy of God.

Hosea's Call

The Book of Hosea shows how God called him, not just to carry His Word, but also to bear and reveal His passions. God probed into the passions of Jonah, but in the case of the prophet Hosea, it is as if the Lord called Hosea to enter into an experience

291

that would inevitably force Hosea to feel the very feelings of God. It is important to recognize that the prophetic books and the different prophets are very diverse. It is as if God has different aspects of Himself that He seeks to reveal through the prophets, and there is no end to all that He wants to reveal. It is important to understand that it is not just His Words, not just information and messages that God is trying to reveal, but it is His very heart.

In Hosea 1:2, the writer says, "When the Lord first spoke through Hosea, the Lord said to Hosea" (*RSV*). That is a really important combination. When the Lord began to speak *through* Hosea, he spoke *to* Hosea. Many times a prophet will appear with an announcement from God: "Thus says the Lord." But what people, many times, do not realize is that long before the message of the prophet is delivered publicly, there have already been some other revelations of God going on that have been direct and personal to the prophet. Therefore, the Book of Hosea says that before God spoke *through* Hosea, God spoke *to* him. The structure of the book itself even reflects those two dimensions. In the first three chapters, God's Word to Hosea is all about God's calling Hosea to enter into a marriage. The rest of the book, Chapters 4 through 14, record the Word of God through the prophet Hosea—messages, oracles—that springs forth from this experience. God sent Hosea through an ordeal in order for him to be ready to bear the message that corresponded with that experience.

Hosea's Marriage Experience

Hosea's call is perhaps one of the most shocking calls and one of the most shocking commands in all of Scripture. He says to him, "Go marry a woman of harlotries, and have children of harlotries" (see 1:2). How could God ask somebody to do something that violates His own standard? The covenant God had with Israel is stained, marred, and flawed by Israel's disobedience; simple pronouncements do not seem to get through. God will go to further lengths to get the attention of His people. He will even do things that are shocking. He will even do things that cause friction with His own standards of righteousness and holiness. This was true with other prophets also, such as Ezekiel whom God asked to have contact with unclean things—to eat unclean foods. That was very difficult for a priest to do. But God went to that length to try to awaken His people. God had already been trying through other prophets—Elijah, Elisha, and Amos—to get the attention of the Northern Kingdom. But now God, in the case of Hosea, speaks to him in a shocking way in order to get the attention of His people.

God consumes Hosea's entire life into the message. Hosea's message is not going to be just words; it is going to be actions. This is another aspect of the poetry of the prophets: the prophetic message is artistically rendered. It was given even in dramatic ways, ways that are acted out even in the very real experiences of human life, in this case, marriage to a woman of harlotry. His children will be the children of a harlot. There is no way to make that nice. Translators and interpreters of Scripture tend to recoil at the words of God to Hosea. In fact, interpreters debate as to whether or not Gomer was a harlot at the beginning, before Hosea married her. Their own sensibilities and their own conservative instincts lead them to debate whether or not she could have been a harlot at that moment. Maybe she was just predisposed toward becoming a harlot later, is the way some explanations are given. There is no way to be conclusive about that. Maybe Hosea himself did not know, because God speaks in ways that cause one to struggle and wonder about the exact meaning. When God called Hosea to marry this woman, perhaps His words left Hosea to wonder if she was chaste or not. Likewise, in the New Testament, Joseph was also disturbed about Mary. But in this case, God was pushing Hosea into something without much reassurance, and the amazing thing is that Hosea was willing to do something very difficult. An encounter with the Lord is so overwhelming that it will enable an individual to do things that are almost humanly impossible. Thus, Hosea took a step that surely brought scorn and stigmatization in his own society.

Hosea took the step of marrying Gomer, and then the reader learns that she bore him a son. God's instructions were not finished with just the daring command to marry a harlot, then He followed that with a command that Hosea named the child Jezreel. That name once had a very positive meaning; in fact, the Hebrew word *Jezreel* means "God sows, God plants." God conceives seed, one might say. But no longer was Jezreel a positive name because of what happened after Jezebel made the city of Jezreel her capital, generations earlier. God finally raised up Jehu to come against Baal worship and against the house of Ahab and Jezebel. King Jehu carried out the judgment of God, but it resulted in a blood bath. In fact, the blood flowed in such great measure that the name Jezreel, which had originally been a very positive name, had now taken on a very stained connotation. When people heard the name Jezreel, probably the first thing they thought of was bloodshed. It was as if God were telling Hosea to name his firstborn son Bloodshed. In today's time, it would be like naming a child Auschwitz. Regardless of what the word had meant, because of the awful tragic acts that had happened in that place, the name now had a very negative connotation. Jezreel pointed not only to the bloodshed that had been there with the massacre of Jehu against the house of Ahab and Jezebel, but it also predicted the bloodshed that would occur with God's judgment against the house of Jehu for what he did in that place. Thus, Hosea's act of marriage and his act of having and naming a child—acts that are supposed to be holy in human life—are now being taken over by God to bear a very hard and harsh message of judgment.

Two more children came into the marriage of Hosea. A daughter was born next, but unlike the case of Jezreel, the text does not specify that Gomer bore the second child of Hosea. God told Hosea what to name the child, and the very name of the child reflected that the child was not Hosea's child. The daughter was named *Lo-ruhamah,* which means in Hebrew "not cared for." This is the kind of response that a father might feel towards a child born of his wife, but fathered by another man. And then another child, a son, was born. And God once again specifies what the name is to be. The name of the third child was *Lo-ammi,* which means in the Hebrew language "not my people." Being given a name like that, the child was almost certainly not of the lineage of the prophet Hosea. He was "not my people." Thus, Hosea was sent into what surely could be described as an awkward situation.

Before Hosea even knew the word that was going to come *through* him, this was the hard word *to* him. And Hosea obeyed. But no sooner did he obey than he was pointed toward a prospect, that in some ways, might even seem harder. Because after the marriage to this woman, after the children—the second two of which were most likely illegitimate—a divorce happens between Hosea and Gomer. God then came to Hosea (see Chapter 3) and said to him: "Go again, love a woman who is beloved of a lover and is an adulteress," even as the Lord loves the people of Israel. God is beginning to reveal His Word through Hosea with that statement. He is beginning to indicate why it is that He has asked Hosea to do this. As Hosea obeyed, he was acting out what God himself was experiencing. Hosea was called not only to act out what had transpired in the violation of the covenant, but he was also being called to act out what God was promising would happen because of the great love of His own heart, as far as the restoration of a violated marriage. God said to Hosea, "Go love a woman who has betrayed you, who has done you wrong, and is still even in the midst of that betrayal" (see 3:1).

Beginning in verse 2, Hosea begins to tell the actions that he takes, actions that seem almost mechanical. They do not seem to be filled with love, but at least Hosea is moving in the direction of paying the price for Gomer. Her harlotries have put her into such debt that she is no longer a free woman. So Hosea, in order to redeem the marriage, has to redeem Gomer out of slavery. Hosea takes those steps out of obedience to the Lord.

Lawsuit Imagery

In the rest of the book, Hosea presents a lawsuit. In fact, that is how Chapter 4 introduces the message that will unfold in the rest of the book: "Hear the word of the Lord, O people of Israel! The Lord has filed a lawsuit against you" (4:1, *NLT*). God has a case, and He is pressing it against His own people, because His people have violated the marriage. This is a divorce court, and God is the violated, betrayed husband. He is the wronged party in the marriage, and He is pressing a lawsuit. Just like in the case of Gomer, there has been unfaithfulness to the marriage. There has been an adulterating of the marriage. Hosea paints the picture of God's judgment. Even though he is often referred to as the prophet of love, he paints the picture of God's judgment even more harshly and more severely and more radically than Amos. Israel has played the part of the harlot, and that is what begins to unfold in all of these passages of the lawsuit.

God is a king who is unlike the kings of the nations. God presses lawsuits, but not like any of the lawsuits that are in the world's courts today. God's lawsuit ultimately presses, not toward final prosecution, but toward a surprising and amazing promise—a promise to restore the marriage. Just as He calls Hosea to act out the restoration of his marriage, God says, "I will take back My people" (see Chapter 14). It is not a grace and a hope that avoids the judgment, but it is a grace and a hope that reaches even beyond the bankruptcy of the judgment against the Northern Kingdom that is coming. God through Hosea acts out how He intends to reach beyond that divorce—that judgment—and amazingly take back the unclean woman.

Chapter 2 anticipates the passages in the lawsuit, including the very final paragraph of Chapter 14, which points the way to restoration. Even early in the Book of Hosea, God is revealing that the broken and restored marriage of Hosea is being applied to the broken, violated marriage, and the promise of restoration, that God is now offering through this prophet and through this prophetic book. How does God turn things around? The first part of Chapter 2 gives a graphic picture of the utter devastation of the unfaithful woman who represents God's people. She is utterly bankrupt and forsaken by everybody.

Finally in verse 14, there is a surprising turn around which says, "Therefore, behold." Given what precedes the "therefore" of verse 14, one would think that God was about to say, "Therefore, I am going to give even more judgment." However, at that point comes the surprising "therefore" of grace: "Therefore, behold, I will allure her, and bring her into the wilderness, and speak [tenderly] to her. And I will give her her vineyards . . . and the valley of Achor for a door of hope" (vv. 14, 15). In other words, God is going to turn the very place of trouble into the doorway which opens up into hope. "And she shall sing there, as in the days of her youth, and as in the day when she came up out of the land of Egypt" (v. 15). What God, the husband, intends to do is a grace that is so great that it registers belief in what the woman is going to do. As everyone knows, it is hard to restore that trust and that belief in the betraying spouse. But God not only registers faith in what He is going to do, but He also assures an even greater measure of grace.

Immediately God begins to describe a wedding—a wedding just like the original wedding. That wedding day when groom and bride believed in each other.

> "In that coming day," says the Lord, "you will call me 'my husband' instead of 'my master'" (v. 16, *NLT*).

God is envisioning a second wedding and He is witnessing the wife saying "I do."

> "I will take away the names of Baalim out of her mouth, and they shall no more be remembered by their name. And in that day will I make a covenant for them" (vv. 17, 18, *NLT*).

It will be a big wedding, and God, through Hosea, describes how the beasts of the field will be there, the birds of the air, and the creeping things of the ground. All of creation is being called to attend this wedding.

But how is the Lord speaking tenderly to the woman? The word in Hebrew means "speaking with the heart." Verse 19 begins to tell how it is that God is going to speak tenderly when He says, "I will betroth thee unto me for ever . . . I will betroth thee unto me in righteousness, and in judgment, and in lovingkindness, and in mercies. I will even betroth thee unto me in faithfulness: and thou shalt know the Lord" (vv. 19, 20). There is the faith that the woman will not only say the words "I do," but will actually enter into the covenant, into intimacy and will be faithful to it. "Thou shalt know the Lord" (v. 20), God promises the woman. But how will God speak tenderly? That is disclosed in the remaining verses of Chapter 2: "'In that day,' says the Lord, 'I will answer the heavens'" (v. 21). God is answering the heavens. God is speaking. Is he speaking tenderly to the woman? The woman who is so downcast, so completely forsaken and abandoned that she may not be able to hear a direct word from the husband who is now willing to take her back. Perhaps that is the point. God is speaking indirectly. That is the only way that His tenderness can reach the woman. He answers the heavens, and the heavens answer the earth. And the earth shall answer the grain, the wine, and the oil, and they shall answer Jezreel (see v. 22). Jezreel is the son who has been separated from the father, even as the mother has been separated from the father, the husband. That is what happens when a marriage breaks apart. The children get separated from their father. They grow up having been the seed of a father, but they do not know who that father is.

However, in these verses, God is promising to speak. The Father is reaching through all of creation to get back to that son, that hungry son, because there is no marriage and there is no income and there is no grain, wine, or oil. The woman has forgotten who gives the grain, wine, and oil, according to an earlier verse in Chapter 2. But God has not forgotten the child who needs the grain, wine, and oil; therefore, God speaks through all of creation to reach the cry of that child, the cry of Jezreel who does not even realize that his cry is ascending all the way to heaven. Accordingly, God is answering that cry and He is coming to that firstborn son to redeem the name—as if to say, "I have sown you." This son is not illegitimate. As He embraces Jezreel, God's mercy is getting to the heart of this woman who is so shamed and is so low that grace can scarcely reach her. That is how God speaks tenderly.

He redeems the name of Jezreel and He owns the child that bears His name. But He goes even further, because not only does God reach out and embrace Jezreel, the Son of His seed, but He reaches to embrace Not Pitied ("not cared for"), and He says, "I will say to Not Pitied, I will have pity." He redeems Jezreel's name, but He changes Lo-ruhama's name from Not Cared For to Cared For. And He changes the youngest son's name, Lo-ammi—He says, "You will no longer be Not My People, for you are My People" (see 2:23). God's grace even reaches to the point that He owns not only the seed of His own loins, but He owns those children who were born illegitimately.

The Northern Kingdom was destroyed, and the Assyrians brought in other peoples that mixed with them to produce a people considered to be half-breeds—the Samaritans. But God is pointing to a restoration of the covenant, even beyond all of the violation and illegitimacy. God's plans are not revealed how He intends to make that restoration, but Jesus reached out to the Samaritans during His time on earth. The same God today is reaching out to the children who have lost their names. God is calling mankind back into a relationship with Him, but not a relationship of shallow worship. Hosea blasts that in his lawsuit, showing how God's people come to the places of worship and sacrifice, but nothing is ever conceived. Children are not being born. God is calling mankind to a relationship of knowing Him—a relationship that will conceive children, whose names are known.

26 A History of the Southern Kingdom of Judah

By Rickie Moore, Ph.D.

The history of the Southern Kingdom of Judah covered a time period from the division of the Kingdom after Solomon's death in 931 B.C. to the destruction of Jerusalem in 586 B.C. The Southern Kingdom lasted 135 years longer than the Northern Kingdom, which perished in 721 B.C. at the hands of the Assyrian Empire. It consisted of only two of the 12 tribes of Israel—Judah and Benjamin—and took its name from the tribe of Judah which was the more dominant of the two tribes. These tribes remained with Solomon's son, Rehoboam, upon the passing of King Solomon, when the other 10 tribes seceded and followed Jeroboam.

The Stability of the Southern Kingdom

For several reasons, the Southern Kingdom, though smaller in number of tribes, was more stable than its northern counterpart. The most important reason for this was that Jerusalem, with its God-ordained inheritance as the Hebrew center of worship

303

and the place where the Temple was established, remained with the Southern Kingdom and had a very stabilizing effect on it.

A second factor that contributed to the stability of the Southern Kingdom was the Levitical priesthood. When Jeroboam, in the Northern Kingdom, resorted to setting up alternative places of worship, he also set up alternative keepers of the worship service. He established a priesthood that did not have the inheritance or the lineage of the Levite priests.

A third factor that helped the Southern Kingdom remain stable was the singular dynasty that was maintained throughout all its years. In the Northern Kingdom, through treachery and assassinations, various families gained power and controlled the throne. But in the Southern Kingdom, the house of David maintained control and the kingship was passed from father to son. At times, there were coregencies that overlapped between father and son. This contributed to a continuity in the Southern Kingdom that was not experienced in the Northern Kingdom.

Another factor that helped the Southern Kingdom to survive longer and to maintain greater stability was that there were several periods of revival. At least five periods of significant covenant renewal took place among the Southern tribes, but nothing on this scale happened in the Northern Kingdom. In fact, there was no thoroughgoing national revival at all in the Northern Kingdom.

A final factor that aided the Southern Kingdom in maintaining its stability was that eight of its kings did what was right in the eyes of the Lord. This was not the case in the Northern Kingdom where the kings were not as faithful in following after the ways of David. These righteous kings pursued a path that led God's people back to the covenant. They were not all perfect; they had flaws, but they followed after the ways of the Lord and this helped Judah to survive.

Despite this positive report, there were more wicked kings than righteous kings in the Southern Kingdom. Although the good kings had a stabilizing effect and represented faithfulness to the Hebrew's covenant with God, these factors were not enough for the Southern Kingdom to avoid the same outcome as the Northern Kingdom. They lasted almost a century and a half longer, but they still faced the same outcome. They came under divine judgment because of the sins of covenant unfaithfulness, which fell into two major categories: sins of social injustice and sins of religious apostasy—the constant turning away from God to other gods. In a religious sense, this entailed idolatry, the worship of idols and, in a political sense, it meant turning away from trust in God to trust in human alliances, very often human military alliances, which could be called the arm of the flesh.

The Kings of the Southern Kingdom

Over a period of three and a half centuries, almost 30 kings reigned in the Southern Kingdom. This study covers only the major players and sketches the highlights of the kingdom of Judah by looking at some of the kings of Judah and also by considering some of the prophets who ministered in Judah.

REHOBOAM

Rehoboam was the first king of the Southern Kingdom. He inherited the throne from his father,

Solomon, and faced the civil strife that Solomon's oppressive policies had produced. Rehoboam continued the oppressive ways of his father which increased tension throughout the kingdom and resulted in its splitting. Shortly thereafter, Egypt, the superpower in the South, came with force and spoiled cities and seized the Temple treasures. It is an example of living by the sword, and dying by the sword. It is also a picture of experiencing the kind of judgment that God brings when men depend on things rather than on Him. Rehoboam is also known for bringing in idol worship alongside temple worship like his father, Solomon. In this, he resembled his father Solomon and carried the sins of Solomon into his part of the divided kingdom.

ASA

Asa was the first of the kings of the Southern Kingdom who followed in the ways of David, and did what was right in the eyes of the Lord. He led a reform to abolish the idolatry that had been established during the time of Solomon and Rehoboam and got rid of most of the idol worship. His kingdom also was attacked by the Egyptian Empire, but in this case, Egypt was defeated.

Although Asa was known for his devotion to the Lord, that devotion waned in his later years. He imprisoned a prophet who was raised up to rebuke him. Ill health plagued him during this time and it caused him to turn his authority over to his son, Jehosaphat, who reigned for a short time as a coregent.

JEHOSAPHAT

Jehosaphat reigned from 873 B.C. to 848 B.C. and is known as the second king of Judah who did what was right in the eyes of the Lord and followed in the ways of David. He is known for a rather extensive campaign to abolish idolatry in the land which had crept back into Judah during the latter years of King Asa. Jehosaphat not only destroyed false worship, but He also offered important initiatives in a constructive vain. He sent Levites throughout the land to teach the Torah, the law of Moses. And furthermore he appointed judges for the towns, much like Moses had appointed judges to help him administer the covenant polity of Israel. Jehosaphat also fortified cities and had a very positive, pragmatic role in building up his country. He strengthened the military, but he never quit trusting in God as the strength of the nation. A good example is when a coalition of neighboring states, including Moab, Amman, and Edom, rose up with armies against his kingdom. Jehosaphat turned to the Lord in fasting and prayer and looked to the Lord as his strength. When the battle came, he followed God's unusual instructions to place Levitical singers in front of the army to go into battle praising God, and God gave him victory.

There was one major failure in the reign of Jehosaphat. He formed a political alliance with the Northern Kingdom, which involved a marriage between his son, Jehoram, and Athaliah, the daughter of Ahab and Jezebel. Athaliah was very much like her mother. She resorted to treachery and murder to establish and extend her power. For a short time, she was queen of the Southern Kingdom and killed as many legal heirs to the throne as she could find. She brought idolatry back into Judah, and she did so with an aggressiveness that resembled the policies of her mother.

307

JOASH

Joash, the boy king, figured prominently in the story of Athaliah. While Athalia was trying to kill all of the heirs to the throne, Joash was hidden in the Temple by Jehoiada, the priest. When Joash was 6 years old, Jehoiada brought him out and had him crowned king, thus ending Athaliah's reign and ultimately leading to her death.

JEHOIADA

Jehoiada was the real power during the early years of Joash's reign. He instituted many significant reforms abolishing the idolatry encouraged by Athaliah and restoring the Temple and temple worship that had fallen into disrepair. After Jehoiada's death, Joash became soft on idolatry, and it reemerged in the Southern Kingdom. Some military defeats were suffered during the latter years of his reign, and finally Joash was assassinated.

UZZIAH

King Uzziah is probably best remembered as being the king during the time when Isaiah the prophet was first called. He was the sixth king of the Southern Kingdom who did what was right in the eyes of the Lord and followed in the ways of David. He enlarged the territory of the Southern Kingdom to its greatest expanse, even dominating the regions of Edom and Philistia, which gave him the greatest domain of any of the southern kings. He opposed idolatry, but not as zealously as some of the other kings of Judah, because he left some of the high places. His was a rather lengthy reign. He was stricken with leprosy in his latter years, at which time his son reigned with him as coregent.

AHAZ

King Ahaz was a wicked king who favored and actively promoted idolatry. He was impressed with an altar he had seen in Damascus, the capital city of Assyria, and had a pagan-style altar constructed at the Temple in Jerusalem. At one point during his reign, he had the temple doors locked. He was so involved in Baal worship that at one point he had one of his own sons sacrificed.

Ahaz faced a very significant political and military crisis during his reign. A coalition of the neighboring countries, including the Northern Kingdom, formed an alliance and tried to get the Southern Kingdom to join them. The alliance was formed in rebellion against the Assyrian Empire because of the high tribute the Assyrians were demanding that they pay. King Ahaz did not want to join this coalition, so he appealed to Assyria for help. As a result of this action, the Southern Kingdom was drawn into the orbit of the Assyrian Empire as a subjugated vassal. Ahaz escaped the threat of this northern coalition by sacrificing the freedom of the Southern Kingdom.

HEZEKIAH

The king of the next generation in Judah was Hezekiah who was considered to be the seventh king who followed what was righteous in the eyes of the Lord and followed the ways of David. He turned back the policies of his father, Ahaz, by reopening the Temple, by purging the land of idolatry, by destroying the high places and by reinstituting the Passover. Hezekiah led the nation in a very significant revival, a renewal of the covenant with God.

He not only instituted these religious reforms, but he also brought about very significant political reform as well. He broke ties with Assyria and repealed many of the associations with Assyria that had come during the time of his father.

Like Ahaz before him, Hezekiah faced his own political and military crisis. Assyria responded to this breaking off of ties by invading and destroying many of the cities and besieging Jerusalem. This is one of the most significant historical events in all of Judah's history. In fact, the story of this invasion is told three times in Scripture: in the Books of Kings, in the Books of Chronicles, and also in the Book of Isaiah. Perhaps this is the only event in Hebrew history that is covered synoptically three times. Unlike his father, Hezekiah turned to God in prayer during this crisis and God delivered him.

Even though Hezekiah brought the Southern Kingdom back to God and presided over one of the most dramatic, divine deliverances in the history of God's people, there is still a sad footnote to his life. Late in his reign, Hezekiah courted the Babylonians as they were beginning to rise to power, brought them into his royal court, and showed them all of the treasures of the Temple. God was very displeased and announced to him, through the prophet Isaiah, that judgment would come to the kingdom because of his actions. He was told that the Babylonians would come once again to his kingdom and carry off many of the treasures that he had shown them.

MANASSEH

Manasseh holds the distinction for being the most wicked king in the history of Judah. He did all he could to reverse the reforms of his father, Hezekiah, and to kill the prophets. He closed the Temple, burned all the copies of the Scripture that he could find and reestablished Baal worship. He even sacrificed one of his sons to Baal Molech. Manasseh ruled for 55 years, more than half a century, and so his evil policies had a chance to be established very deeply in the life of the Southern Kingdom. He led the kingdom of Judah so far down the road away from covenant faithfulness to God that by the time his reign was over, the writers of the Books of Kings considered the kingdom to be beyond recovery, even though the king who followed him made some efforts to turn the people back to God. Literally, Manasseh led the kingdom of Judah pass the point of no return. Very close to his death, he experienced a conversion, but there was to be no hope that the Southern Kingdom could avoid exile.

JOSIAH

Remarkably, Josiah, the son of Manasseh, was one of the best kings of Judah. He was the eighth and the last king of Judah who did what was right in the eyes of the Lord and followed in the ways of David. He was another boy king, like Joash, beginning his reign when he was only 8 years old. The goodness of Josiah came from within, as well as from the counselors who led him in his early days. He turned to the Lord even as a young boy and by the time he was 20 years old, he led the nation of Judah in a national revival that was perhaps more dramatic in some ways than the revival that happened during the time of Hezekiah. The reform efforts led by Hezekiah and Josiah respectively were the two

311

most significant revivals that happened in all the years of the Southern Kingdom. Josiah destroyed paganism in virtually every place, destroyed all of the high places, and centralized worship once again in Jerusalem. He orchestrated a national covenant renewal that culminated in a fervent celebration of the Passover. His reform was dramatic and striking on every level.

Midway through the cleaning up of the Temple, a great discovery was made: a copy of the book of the law of Moses. Finding this law book had a great impact on Josiah and he reacted with a deep spiritual response. He ripped his clothes and wept, and he followed the commands of the book of the law. He responded by going even further in his reform efforts by enacting the things that were written in this ancient scroll of Moses. It was an amazing thing that the copy of the law of Moses had been lost within the very walls of the Temple. But Josiah's people found it, and Josiah followed its instructions. The result was a time of peace and prosperity, a time relatively free from any kind of major foreign military intrusion. Josiah's reign, consequently, turned out to be the lull before the storm. Perhaps it was God's last attempt to get as many people as possible to turn back to the covenant, back to doing what was right in the eyes of the Lord.

Josiah, as good as he was, came to a very tragic end. It is one of the most stunning deaths of a king in all of Scripture. Because of Josiah's faithfulness, one would have expected him to have lived a long life and to have come to a very satisfying end, but he was killed in what turned out to be a relatively meaningless battle. The Egyptian army was moving through the coastal region of Palestine on its way to Nineveh to help the Assyrians fend off an invasion by the Babylonian Empire. The Egyptians were not really interested all that much in the Hebrews, but Josiah, who seemed to be more afraid of Assyria than of them and did not want anybody to help the Assyrians survive, went with his armies to the plains of Megiddo and was killed in that battle. It seemed a very unnecessary death, and it brought to an end the reign of one of Judah's best kings. What followed that tragic death was the beginning of the end for the entire kingdom of Judah.

JEHOIAKIM

The last two kings to serve in Judah were Jehoiakim and Zedekiah. Jehoiakim came to the throne just in time to face the intrusion of the Babylonian Empire. The Assyrian Empire, that caused so much trouble for the Palestinian kingdoms, gave way to the Babylonian Empire. The Babylonians caused just as much devastation for the Southern Kingdom as the Assyrians had for the Northern Kingdom. The Babylonians first invaded Palestine soon after Jehoiakim took the throne. In 606 B.C. to 605 B.C., they exacted heavy taxation on the kingdom and even deported some of the young men of Judah, some of the best and the brightest, including Daniel and the three Hebrew children.

The prophet Jeremiah was very active during the reign of Jehoiakim and met with opposition from the king who feared the direction the prophet called for him to take. In 597 B.C., Jehoiakim rebelled against the prophesies of Jeremiah, which included a warning that God would use the Babylonians against the kingdom of Judah. This action by the Babylonians was God judging His people, and God was calling for His people to submit to that judgment, but Jehoiakim would have no part of it and rejected the prophecy of Jeremiah. The Babylonian invasion came with great force as Jerusalem was completely subjugated and a massive number of people were deported. This was considered the first massive deportation of exiles. Still, the nation of Judah survived for 10 more years.

ZEDEKIAH

The Babylonians placed on the throne the final king of the Southern Kingdom, Zedekiah, who ruled the kingdom's last decade. He was a very weak vassal, a puppet of the Babylonian Empire. As the Babylonians were busy in other parts of their empire, several officials around Zedekiah pressured him to withhold tribute and pursue outright rebellion against the Babylonian Empire. Zedekiah was so weak that he was controlled by whomever he was near. He feared Jeremiah who called for him to submit to the Babylonians because it was submission to the judgment that God had already decreed. He also feared the persecutors of Jeremiah who were opposed to paying tribute to Babylonia, and eventually he had the prophet imprisoned. Zedekiah vacillated then back and forth for this final decade of the Southern Kingdom, and in 588 B.C. led a rebellion against Babylonia. This brought on the Babylonian's final invasion in which they came with great force to deal with the disloyalty of the Southern Kingdom. They killed thousands, destroyed the land, sacked all of the outlying cities around Jerusalem, and finally laid siege to Jerusalem itself. Zedekiah and some of his people attempted to flee from Jerusalem, but they were captured. He was forced to see the killing of his own sons before the Babylonians put out his eyes, making this the last thing he saw and emblazoning this picture in his memory.

Conclusion

The Temple was destroyed and the city made uninhabitable. There was only a handful of people that remained and this included Jeremiah. They remained at a nearby village called Mizpah, and the rest of the Jerusalem population was taken captive to Babylon. This was the fulfillment of the judgment predicted by a long line of prophets and brought about by the violation of God's covenant. So, this threat of divine judgment for disobedient Israel, which started with Moses, finally came to pass.

27

Isaiah: Part 1

By Rickie Moore, Ph.D.

Isaiah was the major prophet of the 8th century B.C. For more than a generation, Isaiah prophesied in Jerusalem. The most likely time parameters for his work would be 740 B.C. to 701 B.C. It may be that he actually prophesied a bit beyond 701 B.C., but due to his involvement in the Assyrian crisis of King Hezekiah in 701 B.C., scholars know these dates for certain. Among many things special to Isaiah, one fact stands out preeminently—he was used of God to speak to two generations in his own lifetime: the generation of King Ahaz and the generation of King Hezekiah.

Divisions of the Book of Isaiah

The Book of Isaiah can be outlined in a number of ways. The one used here was chosen to especially highlight Isaiah's ministry to two generations, along with a message that even has relevance far beyond his own day and time. Many of the prophets of Israel were raised up for a certain period of time and, in some cases, they prophesied for their own generations, but Isaiah is unique in the way he spans his own generation, extending even to the next. This fact is very much related to what God was doing through Isaiah—showing how He works from generation to generation, in spite of the many forces of evil that seek to hinder His plan.

Literary Structure of the Book of Isaiah

1.   God Holds Court, Chapters 1–5
2.   Isaiah in Supreme Court, Chapter 6
3.   Isaiah and Ahaz—Refusing Generations, Chapter 7
4.   Book for New Generations, Chapters 8–35
5.   Isaiah and Hezekiah, Remnant Generation, Chapters 36–39
6.   Book for Renewed Generations—Holy Generation, Chapters 40–66.

The Lawsuit

The very first verse of Isaiah introduces the book as "the vision of Isaiah." "The vision of Isaiah the son of Amoz, which he saw concerning Judah and Jerusalem in the days of Uzziah, Jotham, Ahaz, and Hezekiah, kings of Judah" (1:1). When one thinks of Isaiah's vision, it usually relates to Chapter 6. Of course, this great vision plays a significant role in Isaiah's ministry, but one needs to keep in mind that Isaiah's entire ministry—all his many years of receiving words and messages from the Lord—are summed up in the opening verse as a vision. In other words, all of his messages come together to constitute a single vision.

Isaiah's vision unfolds in terms of the analogy of a covenant lawsuit. Since God has a covenant with His people, it follows that God has covenant terms, a law which He expects His people to obey. When they obey, they receive God's blessings; when they disobey, they come under God's curse. God calls His prophets as prosecuting attorneys, so to speak, to execute His indictments when His people have violated the covenant. That is how Isaiah begins— as God's prosecuting attorney: "Hear, O heavens, and give ear, O earth: for the Lord hath spoken, I have nourished and brought up children, and they have rebelled against me" (1:2).

God is calling court through His prophet Isaiah. It is a court so large all the heavens and the earth are called as witnesses to the case. Immediately, God proceeds to give, through His prophet, the charge against His people: "I have nourished and brought up children, but they have rebelled against me. The ox knoweth his owner and the ass his master's crib: but Israel doth not know, my people doth not consider" (1:2, 3).

God's charge is laid out in very general terms at first—a charge of "forsaking the Lord"—but the message becomes more specific as the reader proceeds through to the end of Chapter 5. Even as God lays out the case against Israel through his prophet Isaiah, God also interrupts His own case, just as very often happens in court cases today. For example, God interrupts His own case in Chapter 1 with this very famous passage: "Come now, and let us reason together, saith the Lord: though your sins be as scarlet, they shall be as white as snow; though they be red like crimson, they shall be as wool" (v. 18).

God calls for an interruption here. It is like a sidebar in a case where the judge calls litigants to the bench. He indicates here His willingness to entertain a pardon. Even at this late stage in Israel's sinfulness and in their repeated violations of the covenant, God is willing to entertain a pardon if Israel will turn from sin. After this, the case resumes and God's indictment is laid out in more specific terms.

Two specific charges are highlighted in this first chapter: First, is the sin of false worship or, one might say, phony worship. God's people come to the Temple in Jerusalem and they go through the act of worship, but the text here says, "your hands are full of blood" (v. 15). Second, the people of Israel are committing sins against their neighbors. They are exploiting, as it were, murdering their neighbors in their social dealings. Theirs is a combination of religious sins and social sins, something mentioned before through the mouths of the prophets.

The case is interrupted again. As God lays out His charges with more incriminating detail, He also mentions more wondrous prospects and possibilities if His people will listen. One finds this promise at the beginning of the second chapter:

> And it shall come to pass in the last days, that the mountain of the Lord's house shall be established in the top of the mountains, and shall be exalted above the hills; and all nations shall flow unto it. And many people shall go and say, Come ye, and let us go up to the mountain of the Lord, to the house of the God of Jacob; and he will teach us of his ways, and we will walk in his paths: for out of Zion shall go forth the law, and the word of the Lord from Jerusalem (2:2, 3).

Note the contrast: In Chapter 1, Israel is summoned into court with the heavens and the earth called as witnesses—a dark moment of judgment for God's people. Then in Chapter 2, the Judge of creation reveals in a far distant future God's purpose in all of this—not judgment as an end in itself, but God's intent and goal of leading His people to a glorious future. Beyond the trials of the present, beyond this court case, beyond this indictment and even the sentence of this present moment in history, God's ultimate goal is for Jerusalem to be raised up. God's judgment is designed to bring about a much greater salvation. This message, of course, parallels the very meaning of the name *Isaiah,* "the Lord saves." God's ultimate purpose, even in judgment, is salvation, not only for His people but for all nations.

These periodic interruptions within the court trial show both sides of God's work. God is active through Isaiah to judge, but this is part of a more ultimate effort on God's part to bring salvation through His people to others. That is how prophetic vision is. It often breaks open into the larger dimensions of God's work.

In some ways, one might note, Isaiah has the largest and the broadest vision of all the prophets. He sees up close the immediate future of Israel, but he also sees the distant future, a fact revealed repeatedly throughout the book.

Chapters 3 and 4 give more detailed indictments. However, once again, interruptions to the court case take place, which look forward to more ultimate works of God's salvation.

Chapter 5 sums up the first section of Isaiah: actually, a summing up of the trial and covenant lawsuit.

An oddity of this chapter is that it begins with a song—a love song concerning God's vineyard. One does not normally associate songs with court cases. Lawyers may not use poetry, but prophets do. In this case, Isaiah uses even lyrical language to lay out the case. God seeks to get the attention of His people, so He sings a love song through His prophet.

The love song tells the story—a summary of the entire history of Israel. God had showered His love on His people Israel, but they had betrayed His love. The imagery is that of a vineyard into which God put great effort and cultivation and to which Israel responded by producing wild grapes and going their own way. It is a sad love song—a song of love gone awry. God is going to be forced to destroy His vineyard.

Following this song of the vineyard, comes a listing of six woes, consequences which stem from the sentencing of the people of Israel. These six woes bring Chapter 5 to a close on a very dark and heavy note.

The Supreme Court

In Chapter 6, something rather remarkable happens. Isaiah himself is ushered into an even higher court of God, one might call it the Supreme Court. The scene shifts from that of God coming to earth to hold court to one in which Isaiah sees God on His throne and is ushered into that court. This Supreme Court reveals the holiness, the majesty and the glory of God. God is surrounded by angels crying "Holy, holy, holy, is the Lord of hosts: the whole earth is full of his glory" (6:3).

This is perhaps the most familiar text in all of prophetic literature, often commented on and preached about. The overwhelming force of this vision on the prophet Isaiah is well known. Isaiah had just spoken six woes in Chapter 5; but now, when Isaiah personally sees the glory of God, he can only pronounce a woe upon himself. Isaiah realizes he is not just standing above the judgment, and he is not just the prosecutor who is pressing the judgment of God; he is also standing among the people for the glory of God, and he is also the accused, along with all of his people. He is able to respond only with, "Woe is me" (v. 5). He saw himself as a man of unclean lips, living among a people of unclean lips.

The implication of the Hebrew term used here is "I'm unclean. I'm sinful. I'm lost, I'm wasted. I'm dead. I'm a goner." And thus, upon realizing he is judged, and openly confessing that fact, Isaiah comes to a turning point.

God lifts a coal from off the altar and cleanses Isaiah, taking away his sin so he can become a messenger for God. It was a painful experience. One can imagine having lips burned, deformed lips as it were. Submitting to the judgment of God is always a painful, deforming ordeal. However, as Isaiah entered into the experience of judgment, as he yielded to it rather than resisting it, God transformed Isaiah just as He wanted to transform the people of Israel. If they too would yield to God's judgment, they would also be raised up and transformed.

What happens in the remaining verses of Chapter 6 is a preview for the rest of the book, especially where it makes reference to three generations.

Again, note how Isaiah's ministry addresses two generations in his own lifetime and one generation beyond. These three generations can be described as (1) a refusing generation, (2) a remnant generation, and (3) a holy generation.

In response to Isaiah's, "Here I am. Send me," God says:

> Go, and tell this people, Hear ye indeed, but understand not; and see ye indeed, but perceive not. Make the heart of this people fat, and make their ears heavy, and shut their eyes; lest they see with their eyes, and hear with their ears, and understand with their heart, and convert, and be healed" (6:9, 10).

This is, one must admit, a rather amazing statement. It essentially indicates that Isaiah is being called to speak a message the people will not hear, will not see, will not understand, and will not receive. His message will be refused by the generation to whom he is being sent.

This is one of the most quoted verses in the gospels of the New Testament. Jesus quoted this statement by Isaiah repeatedly. The gospels seem to make no reference to the vision of Isaiah, but on numerous occasions point to this passage. When asked why He spoke in parables, Jesus quoted this verse from Isaiah. He claimed to speak in parables, not to make the kingdom easier to understand but more difficult, so that "seeing, they would not see." In other words, both Isaiah and Jesus were bringing a message on God's terms, and that is always difficult and frustrating for those being judged. God's prophetic message of judgment is not given on terms the people would choose, because He is already judging *their terms.* God is not merely judging the people; He is judging the very terms by which they would be willing to receive a message. That is the very nature of God's judgment.

Isaiah's task was most difficult—taking a message to a people who would refuse to hear. He recoiled from it, asking, "Lord, how long?" (see v. 11). How long was he going to have to carry this unheeded message of judgment? God told him:

> Until the cities be wasted without inhabitant, and the houses without man, and the land be utterly desolate, and the Lord have removed men far away, and there be a great forsaking in the midst of the land (vv. 11, 12).

Even though this refusing generation will be one that experiences the consequences of its refusal, a significant new promise of a remnant emerges:

> But yet in it shall be a tenth, and it shall return, and shall be eaten: as a teil tree, and as an oak, whose substance is in them, when they cast their leaves: so the holy seed shall be the substance thereof (v. 13).

Isaiah is being alerted from the very first day of this visionary experience that beyond the refusing generation will be a remnant. There *will be* a remnant generation, but the remnant generation will be burned again. God is going to judge the refusing generation and he is going to spare a remnant, but that remnant will pass through the fire. All this reminds one of the fire that burned Isaiah's lips. No one can avoid the fire. The refusing generation is going to be destroyed by it, the remnant generation is also going to be burned, but the holy seed will be preserved in the stump. The very last words of Chapter 6 indicate the remnant generation will be a remnant of the remnant, which will be a holy generation or a holy seed.

King Ahaz

Chapter 7 of Isaiah begins a record of the time of King Ahaz and introduces what might be called the Syria/Ephraim crisis—a coalition of northern neighbors who are coming against King Ahaz. Ahaz is worried. In verse 3, Isaiah is instructed to go meet Ahaz.

Significantly, in Chapter 6, God had told Isaiah to say something to this people. In Chapter 7, one sees the first specific event marking fulfillment of that lifetime call to speak. God instructs Isaiah to go immediately, on this particular day, and meet Ahaz. He is to go with his son, *Shear-Jashub*, a name meaning, "remnant shall return." God is very specific as to where the meeting is to take place—"at the end of the conduit of the upper pool in the highway of the fuller's field" (v. 3). This location was just outside the city wall, a most strategic water source for the city of Jerusalem, especially if under siege by an invading army.

Under imminent threat of attack and siege from Syria and Eprhaim, it is understandable that Ahaz would be checking out defenses and especially the water which is going to be so very critical. That is where God told Isaiah to go meet Ahaz.

Isaiah has a word from the Lord, a simple message: "Take heed, and be quiet; fear not . . . for the two tails of these smoking firebrands" (v. 4). God told Ahaz that the evil these men planned would not stand. Within 65 years, Ephraim would be broken into pieces and no longer be a people. The head of Ephraim, of course, was Samaria. What God was saying to Ahaz through His prophet was "Do not be afraid of these powers. They may seem mighty in your eyes, but they are nothing to me." Now, "If you do not believe this word," God is saying to Ahaz, "if you respond in fear rather than in faith, then you will not stand."

Again the Lord spoke to Ahaz and said, "Ask . . . a sign of the Lord thy God" (v. 11). Isaiah has given Ahaz one message about fear and faith, but now, as if God realizes it is a hard thing for a king to trust in a word from God when armies are coming, He offers Ahaz a sign. Ahaz can name the sign, as if God were giving him a blank check. "I will give you any sign you ask," God says, "Let it be as high as heaven or as deep as hell" (see v. 11).

There is no other place in Scripture where God says anything quite so radical, allowing someone to pick a sign. But Ahaz says, "I will not ask, neither will I tempt the Lord" (v. 12). King Ahaz is in effect saying, "I don't want to weary the Lord by asking for a sign." Isaiah's immediate response is, "Don't you know you're wearying him by what you're doing now, by not asking for a sign. God is getting tired of you" (see v. 13). "Therefore, the Lord himself will give you a sign: 'Behold, a virgin shall conceive, and bear a son, and shall call his name Immanuel'" (v. 14). *Immanuel* means, "God with us."

Isaiah goes on to talk about this child. The thrust of the sign is that God is saying, whether you believe the word or not, it is true. Whether you ask for a sign or not, I am going to give you one that will confirm the word I am now giving.

The name Immanuel signals grace and salvation. That, of course, goes along with the truth of the Word. God's Word is a word of grace. God's sign to King Ahaz continues to unfold. There are other parts to it. God is going to bring upon Ahaz, upon his people and his father's house such days as have not come since the day Ephraim departed from Judah, namely the King of Assyria. The message starts out as a very positive word sign—a child is going to be born, one in whose honor mothers will name their children—but the sign continues to unfold, to foretell the coming of the king of Assyria.

Ahaz is not nervous at this point, because he is depending on Assyria to be the way this crisis will be averted. God continues:

> And it shall come to pass in that day, that the Lord shall hiss for the fly that is in the uttermost part of the rivers of Egypt, and for the bee that is in the land of Assyria. And they shall come, and shall rest all of them in the desolate valleys, and in the holes of the rocks, and upon all thorns, and upon all bushes. In the same day shall the Lord shave with a razor that is hired, namely, by them beyond the river, by the king of Assyria, the head, and the hair of the feet: and it shall also consume the beard. And it shall come to pass in that day, that a man shall nourish a young cow,

and two sheep; and it shall come to pass,
for the abundance of milk that they shall
give he shall eat butter: for butter and
honey shall every one eat that is left in the
land. And it shall come to pass in that day,
that every place shall be, where there were
a thousand vines at a thousand silverlings,
it shall even be for briers and thorns. With
arrows and with bows shall men come
thither; because all the land shall become
briers and thorns. And on all hills that shall
be digged with the mattock, there shall not
come thither the fear of briers and thorns:
but it shall be for the sending forth of oxen,
and for the treading of lesser cattle (vv. 18-
25).

That closing passage is a lengthy piece of poetry,
full of graphic images that start off very positive but
end up not quite so clear. The passage is a little bit
ambiguous, surely enough to make Ahaz wonder
what the prophet is implying. The king of Assyria is
coming . . . and he is going to settle in all these
different places . . . places that are now fertile like a
garden . . . and they are going to be reduced to wild
places where briers and thorns grow. Perhaps Ahaz
wondered, "Has this totally positive sign now turned
sour on me?"

Ahaz is never really told the full scope of the
sign he is given. Then comes Chapter 8. The rest of
this entire section must be seen as flowing out of
how Ahaz responds to this crisis, to this Word of the
Lord. In Chapter 8, God speaks to Isaiah, not in an
ambiguous way as He had spoken to Ahaz, but in a
very clear way.

Here is a summary of God's message to Isaiah: God told him to take a large tablet and write on it in common characters that he has reliable witnesses—Uriah the priest and Zechariah the son of Jeberechiah. Isaiah is being given another son and told what to name him. The name of his first son carried a message of grace. Isaiah continues: "And I went unto the prophetess; and she conceived, and bare a son" (8:3). This reference is to the fact that Isaiah is being given a son, and Isaiah, like Hosea before him, is being told what the name of that son is to be. His other son, was named *Shear-Jashub*, meaning "a remnant shall return." This second son will bear a message, not of grace, but of judgment. His name is to be *Maher-Shalal-Hash-Baz*, meaning "plunder and spoil"—the kind of things that take place when a foreign army comes to invade.

The Lord spoke to Isaiah again:

> Forasmuch as this people refuseth the waters of Shiloah that go softly, and rejoice in Rezin and Remaliah's son; now therefore, behold, the Lord bringeth up upon them the waters of the river, strong and many, even the king of Assyria, and all his glory: and he shall come up over all his channels, and go over all his banks: and he shall pass through Judah; he shall overflow and go over, he shall reach even to the neck; and the stretching out of his wings shall fill the breadth of thy land, O Immanuel (vv. 5-8).

Conclusion

Through Isaiah, God gave Ahaz a sign of how He was going to deal with this Syria/Eprhaim crisis, followed by an ambiguous word. Then Isaiah was given an unambiguous word—a very clear word that helped interpret what the original sign to Ahaz meant. It meant not merely grace for the moment, but that, on the heels of the subsiding crisis, there would come a greater crisis. Why? Isaiah was told directly. This people had refused the waters of Shiloh, a poetic way of saying they refused the gentle word of grace. Ahaz was out at the water course, wanting to make sure there would be water; but the water God was trying to give was the gentle flowing waters of His word.

Because God's Word was refused by King Ahaz, God was going to allow the waters that took care of this present crisis to create a much larger one when the armies of Assyria would come. The Assyrians were going to keep coming, passing into the land of Judah, and all the way up to Judah's neck.

"God is with us" means God is going to take care of this crisis, if His children will trust Him. However, it also means judgment follows when salvation is rejected. "God is with us" to judge His people.

28

Isaiah: Part 2

By Rickie Moore, Ph.D.

The last chapter concluded with Chapter 8, where Isaiah was being shown what God's word is in the aftermath of his encounter with Ahaz. God had given Ahaz a word and a sign relative to the present crisis, but Ahaz rejected it. As a result, God turned the sign toward an additional unfolding of events that would lead to judgment for him and his generation. In Chapter 8, Isaiah is being shown very clearly what Ahaz was only shown indirectly—the unfolding sign of Immanuel, which will eventually bring judgment on the land of Judah.

This chapter continues from that point, with a warning from the Lord to Isaiah: "For the Lord spake thus to me with a strong hand, and instructed me that I should not walk in the way of this people" (8:11). Isaiah is acknowledging that God told him all of these things in order to make it clear that the sign was going to keep unfolding in the direction of judgment upon Judah. Isaiah is being called to move in a different direction from Ahaz. He is to depend on God's Word rather than trust in the arm of flesh.

God also tells Isaiah not to fear what the people of Israel fear: "Neither fear ye their fear, nor be afraid. Sanctify the Lord of hosts himself; and let him be your fear, and let him be your dread" (vv. 12, 13). If it is God one dreads, then He becomes a sanctuary rather than "a stone of stumbling and . . . a rock of offence" (v. 14), as He became to the inhabitants of Jerusalem.

God is warning that judgment is coming against Jerusalem, for He is setting a trap. Those not trusting in the Word of the Lord are going to stumble. They will be snared, broken, and judged. But God is giving Isaiah another path to walk—a path, not just for Isaiah alone, but for His children and the disciples whom He shall recruit. In other words, God is giving Isaiah a twofold message for the new generation. His promise is to Isaiah's children *Shear-Jashub*, which means "a remnant shall return"; and to *Maher-Shalal-Hash-Baz*, which means "spoil and plunder come quickly." It is a message of salvation and a message of judgment. God is going to judge the old generation, but Isaiah is to gather the disciples and the children of a new generation around him to seal up the teaching, as it were, in a book of what is going to come in a future day.

The New Generation

The new generation, a remnant generation, that Isaiah is gathering around himself will be prepared for that coming crisis. These words are to be bound up in a book. All this helps the reader to understand the chapters that come next—they are the book. They are, in fact, the teaching that Isaiah is being given in order to prepare the future generation to face the larger crisis that is coming.

What God tells Isaiah in Chapter 8 is reinforcement of what Isaiah had been told in Chapter 6—a severe judgment is coming, one that will devastate the land; but a remnant will heed God's Word and remain. It is all beginning to unfold. This is the book now, the book for a new generation. Many things are in the book to help the new generation face the coming crisis.

In Chapter 10, Isaiah is given an oracle about how God will raise up Assyria, and bring Assyria to Jerusalem. Then, God will judge Assyria at that very point. God will use Assyria as His instrument of judgment to bring great devastation upon Judah, then suddenly, God is going to cut the Assyrians down. This new generation is being told God will provide a way of salvation out of the judgment. They are not to fear:

> Therefore thus saith the Lord God of hosts, O my people that dwellest in Zion, be not afraid of the Assyrian: he shall smite thee with a rod, and shall lift up his staff against thee, after the manner of Egypt. For yet a very little while, and the indignation shall cease, and mine anger in their destruction. And the Lord of hosts shall stir up a scourge for him according to the slaughter of Midian at the rock of Oreb: and as his rod was upon the sea, so shall he lift it up after the manner of Egypt. And it shall come to pass in that day, that his burden shall be taken away from off thy shoulder, and his yoke from off thy neck (10:24-27).

In this book, Isaiah is attempting to teach the new generation not to make the same mistake Ahaz made. When the enemy came, Ahaz feared. He did not believe the Word of God. This new generation is being asked to fear God alone, not the Assyrians. God will break the Assyrian burden from off Judah's neck.

In Chapters 13 through 27, Isaiah gives a long section of oracles against foreign nations. God shows in these oracles that He is judge of all nations. The inevitable question is, Why should Judah depend upon powers who are themselves already marked for God's judgment? Judah should trust in God alone.

Many other teachings are found in these chapters, but they all have to do with preparing the new generation to face the coming crisis.

King Hezekiah, Representing the New Generation

Finally the crisis comes, recorded in Isaiah 36 and especially 37. Hezekiah was a child during the early days of Isaiah's prophecy, but now this child of the new generation has become leader of the nation. Hezekiah, according to some scholars, represents the remnant generation. He certainly represents the remnant generation as Judah passes through this crisis, because the crisis threatens to bring an end to the entire nation.

Hezekiah responds to this crisis in a manner different from his predecessor Ahaz. Because he responds with faith in God, He remains after the crisis is over, thus representing the remnant generation Isaiah spoke about earlier in Chapter 6.

There are significant parallels between the crisis of Ahaz and that of Hezekiah. Both were involved in a military invasion, though one must note that

Hezekiah's generation faced a far bigger threat from Assyria than did Ahaz from Syria. The Assyrian armies marched into Judah, destroyed their cities, and put a stranglehold on the city of Jerusalem itself. The crisis focused similarly for both Ahaz and Hezekiah. Isaiah met Ahaz at the conduit of the upper pool by the road of the fuller's field. Hezekiah's story shapes up in the very same place. God once again brings an army, the Assyrian army this time, to the very same place at the conduit of the upper pool by the road of the fuller's field (see 36:2).

Hezekiah, just like Ahaz, is called upon to make a choice between faith and fear. The book Isaiah has been given to record for a new generation emphasizes Israel's choice of faith in the Word of the Lord. This story differs from that of Ahaz, because Hezekiah does not turn away. He does not seek deliverance through foreign political alliances.

Hezekiah's Personal Crisis

Hezekiah went into the Temple and turned his face toward God. He took the threatening letter from the Assyrian army officials, spread it out before the altar, and cried out to God. Hezekiah knew that if God did not deliver him, then it would simply be the end for him, for Jerusalem, and for the nation of Judah.

Because Hezekiah cried out to the Lord, the prophet Isaiah was called upon to deliver God's Word to the king. Isaiah's message this time was a word of complete salvation, matching the meaning of Isaiah's name. His mission was to carry a word of salvation, and in Isaiah 36 and 37, there is revealed one of the most dramatic stories of God's salvation in all of Scripture. In a single night, God destroyed the Assyrian army and saved Jerusalem and the Southern Kingdom. Note the drama of these verses:

> And this shall be a sign unto thee, ye shall eat this year such as groweth of itself; and the second year that which springeth of the same: and in the third year sow ye, and reap, and plant vineyards, and eat the fruit thereof. And the remnant that is escaped of the house of Judah shall again take root downward, and bear fruit upward: For out of Jerusalem shall go forth a remnant, and they that escape out of mount Zion: the zeal of the Lord of hosts shall do this (37:30-32)

This message, obviously, was not for Hezekiah alone. Nor was it simply for Hezekiah's own generation, but it was set within the unfolding of many generations, thus representing the promise of salvation for all. The remnant generation would take root downward and bear fruit upward. God was working from generation to generation. Degeneration occurs when kings like Ahaz refuse to follow the Lord. Death enters into Israel's genes, one might say. But God will redeem, restore, revive and turn all that around. The salvation God brought to Hezekiah's generation was also for many generations to come. That was the meaning of Isaiah's vision.

Hezekiah was a child of the new generation who found God's salvation rather than his judgment through this Assyrian crisis. However, that is not the end of the story for Hezekiah. In Chapter 38, when Hezekiah fell ill, he cried out to the Lord just as he had done for his nation. God delivered him from personal crisis just as he had delivered him from the national crisis.

Hezekiah's personal deliverance results in a dramatic 15-year-extension of his life. Then comes Chapter 39, one final, significant episode in Hezekiah's life. The story reveals much about Hezekiah and the remnant generation he represents. The entire chapter is very strategic.

> At that time Merodachbaladan, the son of Baladan, king of Babylon, sent letters and a present to Hezekiah: for he had heard that he had been sick, and was recovered. And Hezekiah was glad of them, and showed them the house of his precious things, the silver, and the gold, and the spices, and the precious ointment, and all the house of his armour, and all that was found in his treasures: there was nothing in his house, nor in all his dominion, that Hezekiah showed them not. Then came Isaiah the prophet unto king Hezekiah, and said unto him, What said these men? and from whence came they unto thee? And Hezekiah said, They are come from a far country unto me, even from Babylon. Then said he, What have they seen in thine house? And Hezekiah answered, all that is in mine house have they seen: there is nothing among my treasures that I have not showed them. Then said Isaiah to Hezekiah, Hear the word of the Lord of hosts: Behold, the days come, that all that is in thine house, and that which thy fathers have laid up in store until this day, shall be carried

to Babylon: nothing shall be left, saith the Lord. And of thy sons that shall issue from thee, which thou shalt beget, shall they take away; and they shall be eunuchs in the palace of the king of Babylon. Then said Hezekiah to Isaiah, good is the word of the Lord which thou hast spoken. He said moreover, for there shall be peace and truth in my days (39:1-8).

Judgment Upon the Remnant Generation

Hezekiah represented the remnant generation, the generation that had been saved, and yet a flaw is revealed in this short chapter. Hezekiah revealed himself as being more concerned with showing off his treasures to the Babylonians than with protecting his kingdom. The greatest treasure of all, of course, was the treasure represented by the seed of Abraham. Hezekiah showed he really did not care about God's salvation for future generations. He was simply glad to have "peace and security in his own day."

Isaiah, however, understood God to say judgment was coming on the remnant generation. The remnant that remained was itself going to be burned, and Hezekiah showed why. Even though the people of the remnant generation were faithful enough to experience salvation for themselves, they still did not care for the thing God cared for most—the holy generation that was to come.

The last words of Chapter 6, focused upon the holy seed that was to come out of the stump. That is what God determined to preserve. The remnant generation represented by Hezekiah, one that cared only about itself, could never produce the holy seed. Thus, there had to be a purifying, a burning, a judgment of the remnant; even the remnant faithful enough to turn to God's Word, but not enough to give themselves up for the next generation. All of which points to a further burning and a further crisis. In the rest of the Book of Isaiah, one finds something of another book designed to prepare a still further generation for a still further crisis, the Babylonians.

Isaiah lived through the crisis of the Ahaz generation and the Hezekiah generation, but this still further crisis looks to yet another time, 100 years beyond the lifetime of Isaiah. Just as God had entrusted Isaiah with a message for two generations, He entrusted to him, through the book, a message that would prepare the remnant generation for that ultimate crisis of purification, which would in reality be the Babylonian exile.

Moving from Chapter 39 to Chapter 40, the reader finds himself in a completely different setting—one that points ahead to the Babylonian crisis. The writing is even addressed to an audience that seems to be living within Babylonian exile. At this point, the Book of Isaiah is no longer addressing the generations of his own lifetime. It becomes a book that has been sealed up, as it were, for another generation in the future which will face the ultimate crisis of the Babylonian exile. The book is designed to prepare that future generation and, in a sense, all future generations for the ultimate crisis—one that threatens not only their lives but also to bring an end to their history and the world as they know it.

This is why the Book of Isaiah speaks all the way to our own present time. It speaks to all generations that will face ultimate tests that bring them to the point of death. One might even use the expression "through the death," because that is what this part of the Book of Isaiah is saying. After the worst possible scenario, after the nation was completely destroyed, there was still a word of salvation and hope. It is a message of hope even for a future generation going through a test that means loss of homeland, loss of the nation, loss of the world as they know it.

With Chapter 40 come these consoling words, "Comfort ye, comfort ye my people, saith your God. Speak ye comfortably to Jerusalem, and cry unto her, that her warfare is accomplished, that her iniquity is pardoned: for she hath received of the Lord's hand double for all her sins" (vv. 1, 2). The fight has caused them to lose their nation. They are in exile, as many verses that follow will indicate. But yet they are being given a word of grace that calls them out of exile, that calls them, in effect, out of death.

Just as Isaiah saw in his initial vision in Chapter 6, a burning of the remnant, a complete cutting off will come. This was fulfilled through the complete cutting off of the Southern Kingdom. Nevertheless, even as the stump is cut down to the very roots, there is a holy seed that sprouts and begins to emerge. This is the message found in Isaiah 40 through 46.

Isaiah is a book of messages calling Israel back from the dead, back from the death of exile. The sprout coming out of the stump of exile is a word of hope that brings Israel back to life. It is a word of life given to those who have fully embraced the burning, even as Isaiah did.

Isaiah's lips were burned. He entered into the judgment—the first to enter into the death experience of going into exile. Isaiah submitted to the burning of his own lips and now God's remnant, God's people, are to be similarly burned so that new life can spring forth. That is the message of the latter part of Isaiah.

The Suffering Servant

For those who have fully entered into death, comes word of new life. Nowhere is that message more clearly set forth than in the songs of the servant one finds in the latter part of Isaiah, culminating in one of the most famous passages of the book—Chapter 53. In this chapter is the Suffering Servant, a person who resembles Isaiah, giving His life for the next generation. This passage, of course, is totally fulfilled in the Suffering Servant who is to come, the Messiah, Jesus Christ. It is Jesus Christ who suffers completely, who fully enters into the exile and who fully faces and embraces the judgment of God. Our Lord's full entry into judgment, into death, causes life to spring forth. Through Isaiah the prophet, God is here depicting the way of the Suffering Servant to all of the remnant generation, showing how the holy seed is to be produced: "Yet it pleased the Lord to bruise him; he hath put him to grief: when thou shalt make his soul an offering for sin, he shall see his seed, he shall prolong his days, and the pleasure of the Lord shall prosper in his hand" (53:10). Hezekiah's days were miraculously prolonged, but he did not live to see his offspring.

The next verse says, "He shall see of the travail of his soul, and shall be satisfied" (v. 11). Hezekiah and the generation that would come from him were going to die. Hezekiah was satisfied with that. But it is only the remnant that passes through the fire and produces a holy seed that satisfies the Suffering Servant. They shall not die. Thus, He sees the fruit of the travail and His soul and is satisfied.

Conclusion

That is what the Exile is intended to bring about. It is a judgment, a burning that will bring Israel to nothing in order for the holy seed to come from the stump.

Today, God asks His children to follow in the steps of the Suffering Servant, to take up their crosses, to lay down their lives, to see their travail as bringing forth a holy seed in a new generation. That is what Isaiah did and how he lived his life. He laid down his life for the next generation. Thus, he was able to bear the revelation of the coming One who would do that like no other.

The Messiah accomplished His work perfectly. Now, He calls His disciples to do the same and follow Him. Just as God called Isaiah, He now calls His people to lay down their lives in order to bear the holy seed.

Such is the vision, the wonderful message, brought in the 8th century B.C. by the prophet Isaiah.

29

Micah

By Rickie Moore, Ph.D.

The name *Micah* means "who is like the Lord."
Micah is one of the minor prophets of major scope.
Unlike several of the minor prophets, whose prophetic ministry is of a single message or of a single
event, Micah's ministry spans many years. He is
introduced in relation to the reigns of three kings—
Jotham, who reigned from 742 B.C. to 735 B.C;
Ahaz, of the Northern Kingdom; and Hezekiah, who
reigned from around 715 B.C to 687 B.C. This time
span gives a sense of where Micah fits into the Old
Testament chronologically.

Micah was a contemporary of Isaiah. His ministry also focused on Jerusalem, even though, oddly,
Micah came from a small southern town near the
territory of the Philistines. The book opens with
these words: "The word of the Lord that came to
Micah the Morasthite in the days of Jotham, Ahaz,
and Hezekiah, kings of Judah, which he saw concerning Samaria and Jerusalem" (1:1). These words
give a great deal of quick information about the prophet.

Micah's message, the Word of the Lord which refers to the entire book, represents a single word from the Lord concerning Samaria and Jerusalem. These two cities were the capitals of the Northern Kingdom and the Southern Kingdom.

Micah's word from the Lord is primarily a word of judgment and the entire book is dominated once again by the form and imagery of a lawsuit, just as has been the case with some of the other prophets.

The Lawsuit

Although the lawsuit imagery is prominent throughout the prophets, it dominates the Book of Micah from beginning to end. The book divides into four literary parts, all concerned with the lawsuit:

- Introduction: Summons, charges, and response (Chapter 1)
- Development: Specifics of the crimes, leaders, and the sentence (Chapters 2 and 3)
- Interruption: Recess of the trial, oracle of promise, and hope (Chapters 4 and 5)
- Summation: Causes, charges, punishment, and response (Chapters 6 and 7).

The Case Itself

Micah introduces his lawsuit in the second verse: "Hear, all ye people; hearken, O earth, and all that therein is: and let the Lord God be witness against you, the Lord from his holy temple" (v. 2). This is the legal language of a courtroom. It is like the summons a bailiff gives for all present to take heed: "Hear ye, hear ye." Although the lawsuit is introduced in these opening verses in very general terms, there will be more of the language as one moves through the book.

Micah is addressing all the people of the earth, a rather audacious summons for a man from a small village in a small nation. He boldly claims to have a message all the world needs to hear. When one thinks about that message a little further, then the appropriate nature of Micah's claim becomes even more obvious and amazing. It is indeed the case that the message Micah received from the Lord has echoed and reverberated around the world many times over. In fact, Micah's message is being read and studied by multiplied thousands of people around the world this very day. The key reason for this, of course, lies in the fact that this obviously was not just Micah's own message, but a revealed word from the Lord.

Immediately after Micah's lawsuit summons was addressed to all the earth, Micah announced the coming of the Judge: "Behold, the Lord cometh forth out of his place, and will come down, and tread upon the high places of the earth. And the mountains shall be molten under him, and the valleys shall be cleft, as wax before the fire, and as the waters that are poured down a steep place" (vv. 3, 4). Micah's courtroom is as big as the earth. The Judge's advent is rather overwhelming and striking.

One must understand, though, that Micah is not merely predicting some future event. He has had a word from the Lord. Micah has been there. He is bearing witness to what he himself has seen—the advent of the Judge—and he is trying to make all of the earth aware of coming judgment.

Laying out the lawsuit even further, though still in general terms, Micah states the charges: "For the transgression of Jacob is all this, and for the sins of the house of Israel. What is the transgression of Jacob? Is it not Samaria? And what are the high places of Judah? Are they not Jerusalem?" (v. 5). Micah is not naming the nature of the sins at this point, just simply saying, it is obvious. In other words, if one wants to see the sins of the Northern Kingdom, just look at Samaria. If one wants to see the sins of the Southern Kingdom, just look at Jerusalem. The wickedness of those cities was plain to see.

Following this general statement of the charges, Micah also hints in general terms of the sentence against both the Northern and the Southern Kingdoms. More specific charges will come in later chapters of the book. Pronouncement of the sentence is made first against Samaria:

> Therefore I will make Samaria as an heap of the field, and as plantings of a vineyard: and I will pour down the stones thereof into the valley, and I will discover the foundations thereof. And all the graven images thereof shall be beaten to pieces, and all the hires thereof shall be burned with the fire, and all the idols thereof will I lay desolate: for she gathered it of the hire of an harlot, and they shall return to the hire of an harlot (vv. 6, 7).

These words are so graphic they elicit a response. Using courtroom description, one might call this a reaction from the gallery, but more precisely, these words seem to be a response from the prophet Micah himself—a lawyer's response to his own case:

> Therefore I will wail and howl, I will go stripped and naked: I will make a wailing

like the dragons, and mourning as the owls.
For her wound is incurable; for it is come
unto Judah; he is come unto the gate of
my people, even to Jerusalem (vv. 8, 9).

Micah is laying out the case of the Lord, the charges and the summation, but even before he gets to the point of turning specifically to what God is going to do to Jerusalem, he understands the prosecution against Samaria is coming eventually upon his own land of Judah. Micah reveals himself suddenly as a lawyer forced to prosecute a family member, and he becomes so emotional that he cries out in lamentation. The rest of Chapter 1 becomes a plea for others to join him in the lament.

Development of the Case

Micah develops the case during Chapters 2 and 3. This study will center on three things which represent how Micah develops God's lawsuit against his people.

1. *He specifies the crimes.* No real details of the crimes were listed in the first chapter, but one comes quickly to some specifics in Chapter 2: "They covet fields, and take them by violence; and houses, and take them away: so they oppress a man and his house, even a man and his heritage" (2:2). Elsewhere there are allusions to how God is going to destroy the idols of Samaria. Thus, religious sins are part of God's lawsuit against His people—sins that take place in the context of wrong worship. However, Micah shows God's concern not only for religious sins but also sins that are social, national, political, and even economic in nature. The very

breadth of these sins seems to be a major focus in the development of Micah's lawsuit.

2. *Micah specifies the guilty parties.* Many other examples are given as one reads through the verses of Chapters 2 and 3, but economic exploitation and social oppression especially occupy Micah. Not only does he specify crimes, but he also mentions the criminals, certain specific groups of people within the entire population that the Lord's lawsuit singles out. Note his specific mention of leaders: "And I said, Hear, I pray you, O heads of Jacob, and ye princes of the house of Israel; Is it not for you to know judgment? Who hate the good, and love the evil" (3:1, 2). Micah's clear implication here is that the leaders have a special responsibility to carry out justice, to make sure justice is served, to protect justice in God's land among God's people; but the very ones who have been given responsibility are they who have violated justice. It has been the leaders who have presided over and perpetrated these social and economic sins that have oppressed the people.

Another verse is pertinent: "The heads thereof judge for reward, and the priests thereof teach for hire, and the prophets thereof divine for money: yet will they lean upon the Lord, and say, Is not the Lord among us? None evil can come upon us" (v. 11). The verse is relevant to the sinful leaders of ancient Judah, but it seems to be relevant to today as well. Leaders today practice their professions for their own gain. With the responsibility of serving the people, they end up exploiting them instead for their own economic gain. So, Micah specifies the crimes and the criminals who happen to be the leaders, the heads, the rulers of the houses of both the Northern and the Southern Kingdoms.

3. *Micah specifies the sentence.* Note the last verse of the chapter where Micah introduces the sentence with a lawyer's "therefore": "Therefore shall Zion for your sake be plowed as a field, and Jerusalem shall become heaps, and the mountain of the house as the high places of the forest" (v. 12). Micah speaks in no uncertain terms, even more directly than one hears from the prophet Isaiah, declaring that the holy city of Jerusalem is going to be destroyed. The proud city shall become a heap of ruins. This was a most daring statement for a small-town prophet in 700 B.C. Jerusalem was still very much prominent, still a very strong city, known internationally for its political and economic stability.

Interruption of the Case

Present-day lawsuits are often interrupted or even recessed for a time. Chapters 4 and 5 of Micah's prophecy seem like something of a recess. He backs away from his vigorous pressing of God's case and God's judgment against His people and inserts an oracle of promise and hope for Jerusalem and Zion. The first three verses are strikingly dramatic:

> But in the last days it shall come to pass, that the mountain of the house of the Lord shall be established in the top of the mountains, and it shall be exalted above the hills; and people shall flow unto it. And many nations shall come, and say, Come, and let us go up to the mountain of the Lord, and to the house of the God of Jacob; and he

> will teach us of his ways, and we will walk
> in his paths: for the law shall go forth of
> Zion, and the word of the Lord from Jerusa-
> lem. And he shall judge among many
> people, and rebuke strong nations afar off;
> and they shall beat their swords into plow-
> shares, and their spears into pruninghooks:
> nation shall not lift up a sword against
> nation, neither shall they learn war any
> more (4:1-3).

These are well-recognized words of promise and hope that turn away from Micah's lawsuit of judgment to a much more ultimate assembly where God will set up court once again. In this future court, people will come to learn of the Lord. God's mountain of Zion will be raised up to become the highest place in all the earth.

So well known is this oracle that one can read virtually the same words in the second chapter of Isaiah. Scholars debate whether Isaiah quoted Micah or the other way around, but the more fundamental truth is that both prophets took up this vision from a revelation of the Lord. No matter how terrible the judgment upon Jerusalem and Zion, there is a future hope. There is no hint of avoiding the present judgment, only a hope on the other side of judgment. Micah makes this clear:

> Be in pain, and labour to bring forth, O
> daughter of Zion, like a woman in travail:
> for now shalt thou go forth out of the city,
> and thou shalt dwell in the field, and thou
> shalt go even to Babylon; there shalt thou
> be delivered; there the Lord shall redeem
> thee from the hand of thine enemies (4:10).

God's judgment of exile to Babylon is still going to happen, but there is hope beyond that. One must remember, specifically, that the hope that arises is not merely from Zion. God raises up hope from another source, even an unlikely source, couched in terms of a prophecy about another small town: "But thou, Bethlehem Ephratah, though thou be little among the thousands of Judah, yet out of thee shall he come forth unto me that is to be ruler in Israel; whose goings forth have been from of old, from everlasting" (5:2). Earlier Micah prophesied of judgments against the leaders, but in this passage there is promise of a leader who will be raised up in a distant time in a humble place called Bethlehem. This leader will bring hope for all mankind.

Summation of the Case

In most all lawsuits there comes a time for summing up, a time when the session of the court is reconvened. That is exactly what seems to take place at the beginning of Chapter 6.

> Hear ye now what the Lord saith; Arise, contend thou before the mountains, and let the hills hear thy voice. Hear ye, O mountains, the Lord's controversy, and ye strong foundations of the earth: for the Lord hath a controversy with his people, and he will plead with Israel (vv. 1, 2).

Micah calls the court to order with an introduction similar to what he used in Chapter 1. Then comes the summary of God's argument against His people. This summary argument is pertinent not only to Micah but also for all of God's prophets. In a way, these words sum up the entire revelation God has given through all His prophets across the many generations during which He raised them up: "He hath showed thee, O man, what is good; and what doth the Lord require of thee, but to do justly, and to love mercy, and to walk humbly with thy God?" (6:8).

Those words not only summarize God's lawsuit and the heart of the message of all His prophets, but they are also a response from Micah himself. Micah responds to all this by doing three things.

1. *Micah laments judgment.* He laments just as it is recorded in Chapter 1. This lament is phrased as follows: "Woe is me! for I am as when they have gathered the summer fruits, as the grape gleanings of the vintage: there is no cluster to eat: my soul desired the firstripe fruit. The good man is perished out of the earth: and there is none upright among men" (7:1, 2).

Noteworthy here is the fact that the prophets do not stand over the judgments they deliver. Although they are prosecutors who execute God's message of judgment, they are also the objects of that message. They, too, stand under the judgment of the Lord. This is a very pertinent truth about prophetic revelation and prophetic ministry.

2. *Micah submits to judgment.* "Therefore I will look unto the Lord; I will wait for the God of my salvation: my God will hear me" (7:7). Although Micah is prosecuted along with everyone else—and he laments over that fact—nevertheless, he knows that submission to judgment brings the possibility of appeal. Hope is possible even within the judgment. Pardon and restoration are of God's grace.

Micah states his own determination to wait for the salvation of the Lord.

3. *Micah sees hope of restoration.* What opens up the Book of Micah to readers of all the ages is a final thing in this summation of the lawsuit. Micah sees hope not just for himself, but promise of restoration for all his people. The concluding passage of the book expresses it as follows:

> Who is a God like unto thee, that pardoneth iniquity, and passeth by the transgression of the remnant of his heritage? He retaineth not his anger for ever, because he delighteth in mercy. He will turn again, he will have compassion upon us; he will subdue our iniquities; and thou wilt cast all their sins into the depths of the sea. Thou wilt perform the truth to Jacob, and the mercy to Abraham, which thou hast sworn unto our fathers from the days of old (7:18-20).

That concludes the lawsuit of Micah—a judgment from the Lord, a judgment that is inescapable and has to be faced. Nevertheless, in facing it, Micah opens up the hope that lies beyond judgment, not only for himself but for all the people of God.

30

Nahum,
Habakkuk,
Zephaniah

By Rickie Moore, Ph.D.

Nahum, Habakkuk, and Zephaniah are three books of the Old Testament which consist of three chapters each. They are similar in another respect—all of their prophetic messages are related to the same general time period: the last part of the 600s B.C. God was raising up His messengers during this significant time, because it was the final decades before the fulfillment of the prophecy about the fall of Jerusalem and the exile of His people.

The Book of Nahum

Nahum, first of all, is probably the most obscure prophet in many ways. He comes from a town called Elkosh, but no one knows where it is. Bible scholars assume that it was a small southern town, as was the case of Amos and Micah who also came from small southern towns. However, no one knows for sure. An interesting tradition says Capernaum could have received its name from the prophet Nahum, for it is a fact that the name *Capernaum* literally means "town of Nahum." But that is not established conclusively.

In the first verse of the Book of Nahum, the reader is told that Nahum has a burden (Hebrew, *mas-saw*) from the Lord and that it concerns Nineveh, the capital of the superpower, Assyria. During this time period, Assyria was a major power that built a grand empire and did so by subjugating many peoples, including, at times, God's people in the land of Israel. Nahum was called by God, about a century after the prophet Jonah, to announce the downfall of that wicked city. This is the same city that turned around and repented after Jonah preached to them. Now, a century down the road, they are being judged for the great iniquities that they have piled up and the cruelty that they have perpetrated on God's people and many other nations in the course of their empire building. Nineveh fell in 612 B.C. This date gives what little indication is available about the time period when Nahum delivered his message. It was obviously some time before 612 B.C.

The name *Nahum* comes from a root word meaning "compassionate." It is ironic that someone who bears the name of compassion would be asked to deliver a message of vengeance. On the other hand, perhaps it is completely appropriate. It does make sense that someone named "compassion" deliver a message of judgment to those who are about to be the recipients of that judgment. Jonah's problem was that he did not have compassion. He had a message of judgment, but he did not have the right passion in his heart to deliver it. He delivered a message of judgment in a judgmental way, not having pity like God had for the city that He was judging. Therefore, Nahum was the appropriate person to deliver this message of judgment to Nineveh the second time around.

Nahum begins his message, first of all, by giving a revelation of God's nature. "The Lord is a jealous and avenging God" (1:2, *NIV*). These words set the stage and the tone of Nahum's prophecy, and it will be followed throughout. This is a strong, harsh book. It is a book that is filled with the vengeance of God against the perpetrators of evil. "The Lord is a jealous and avenging God . . . the Lord takes vengeance on his foes and maintains his wrath against his enemies" (v. 2, *NIV*). Terms are piled up in this second verse of the book, underscoring, underlying, highlighting the point that God is coming for the purpose of vengeance. "The Lord is slow to anger and of great might, and the Lord will by no means clear the guilty" (v. 3, *RSV*). There is reference here for God's being slow to anger, which is first revealed to Moses when he asked to see the glory of the Lord. God passed by Moses and revealed to him His name. This is a very famous moment in the revelation of the Old Testament, where God reveals that His nature is love, compassion, and being slow to anger. Perhaps, Nahum is remembering that revelation to Moses; nonetheless, he is putting the accent, not on the compassion and the mercy of God and his steadfast love, but on the vengeance of the Lord, even though that wrath is slow in developing. Nevertheless, it cannot be presumed upon, for it finally comes.

Another Hebrew word which should be underscored is the very first adjective that is used for the

Lord—"jealous." Actually, the word in Hebrew is *kan-no*. Perhaps the more accurate translation is "the Lord is a passionate God," as some translations, particularly Jewish translations, render that verse. It comes from a root idea that means "to be hot." He is not like the God that theological systems so often portray as a God that is just immutable, unchanging, completely indifferent, and unaffected. The God of the Old Testament is a passionate God. One side of that passion is that He is a jealous husband. He is very jealous about His relationship with His people, like a husband who embraces his partner with intense feeling. In fact, this very word is used in the Song of Songs in that way in the very last chapter. It says, "love is strong as death; jealousy (*kan-no*) is cruel as the grave" (8:6). The passion of God is not only a vengeful passion, but it is also a compassion just like in the meaning of the name *Nahum*.

The Book of Nahum reveals the passion of God, primarily in terms of vengeance. Most of the book is a preview of Nineveh's destruction. It is developed very graphically in Chapters 2 and 3. God is reeking havoc on the city of Nineveh, which had reeked havoc on so many other cities and so many other peoples. God finally reached the point where His wrath was poured out against the perpetrators of evil. But even in the midst of this vengeance and this destruction of Nineveh, there is still a pocket of compassion for those who submit to the Lord and do not resist His attempts to draw them back. Previously, Nineveh had responded to God's offer of mercy through Jonah, but then obviously went on about their own evil ways. This element of compassion within judgment can be seen in Nahum 1:7. "The Lord is good," it says there. The opening of the book says the Lord is *kan-no*, but verse 7 says that *kan-no* includes the goodness of God: "The Lord is good, a strong hold in the day of trouble; and he knoweth them that trust in him."

Why is this book in the Bible? Perhaps, it is included for the following two reasons. First, it is in the Bible as a promise to God's people that evildoers will not get away with their crimes. If one has ever experienced brutalization by someone powerful, it is a blessed promise to know that evil will not go on forever and evildoers will not get away with the evil that they have done. The vindication of that promise is recorded through the actual historical fall of Nineveh in 612 B.C. Second, the Book of Nahum is in the Bible as a warning to God's people that evildoers will not get away with their crimes, because God's judgment will fall on them as well, if they do not repent. This is a very important truth for Jerusalem and Judah to realize in this late period of Judah's life. It is a warning to God's people, as well as a promise that evildoers will not get away with their evil actions.

The Book of Habakkuk

The name *Habakkuk* comes from a root word meaning "to embrace." The Book of Habakkuk is introduced with the phrase, "The burden (Hebrew, *mas-saw*) of the Lord." Habakkuk is a prophetic book that reveals something about the experience of being a prophet. This book is not simply God's message through a prophet to another, rather it is a book that relates the struggle that goes on between

361

Habakkuk and God as God is giving him a *mas-saw*. The Hebrew term *mas-saw* is sometimes translated "oracle," which draws attention to the pronounced message. However, it is sometimes translated "burden," which draws attention to the heaviness with which the message is carried.

The book begins: "The oracle that Habakkuk the prophet received" (1:1, *NIV*). But immediately following that, Habakkuk cries out to God, trying to get His attention, concerning a burden that he is feeling about his land. In Chapter 1, Habakkuk sees violence being done in his land. He sees evil being perpetrated, and he cries out, "How long, O Lord, must I call for help, but you do not listen?" (v. 2, *NIV*). Obviously, Habakkuk has a burden that he is trying to convey to the Lord, but the prior verse has already stated that Habakkuk has a burden that is from the Lord. And that is the way it is with the prophetic experience: God begins to stir in the heart of a person even before that person realizes that it is God stirring his heart. The burden of the Lord can begin as a burden within one's heart, stirring and throbbing. Many times, the individual will not even realize that it is God at work, giving, cultivating, and deepening that burden within his heart. God does that very thing within Habakkuk.

Habakkuk, in essence, says, "O Lord, aren't You going to do something about what's going on in this land?" God responds to him in verse 5 and says: "Look at the nations and watch—and be utterly amazed. For I am going to so something in your days that you would not believe, even if you were told" (*NIV*). The Lord is saying in response to Habakkuk's cry, "I am doing something and you would not believe what all I am doing and what I am about to do.

You would not be able to fathom it if I were to tell you and I am just about to tell you, Habakkuk." What does God tell Habakkuk? He tells him that He is raising up an ancient nation to come against this land where Habakkuk sees all of this intolerable wickedness going on. God is going to do something very dramatic, very momentous. He is going to raise up this great nation—Babylon—to come against His land. It is very striking how Habakkuk's response to the Lord changes in tone. It is as if Habakkuk says, "How long, O Lord?" And God says, "Here I come, Habakkuk." Habakkuk then responds, "Wait a minute." In essence, Habakkuk is saying, "Surely You wouldn't perpetrate such a plan against Your own people." And so Habakkuk presses a complaint.

In earlier prophets and prophecies, one remembers how the prophets would often press a case for God against the people. But it is as if here Habakkuk is pressing a case back to God. At the beginning of Chapter 2, he says, "I will stand at my watch and station myself on the ramparts; I will look to see what he will say to me, and what answer I am to give to this complaint" (2:1, *NIV*). Habakkuk is going to wait for an answer from the Lord. God soon answers and says, "Write the vision, and make it plain upon tables, that he may run that readeth it" (2:2). The reader is not told at this point what the vision is. Habakkuk has been given the vision, and along with the vision, he has been given a word to write down. The very act of writing it down would almost indicate that it needs to be preserved. The fact that it needs to be preserved indicates that there is a waiting that has to take place. Habakkuk has waited for the vision, but now that he has the vision,

God says, wait for it to come to pass. It will not delay. It will hasten. The fulfillment of this vision will not be slow. It will be quick. The statement that follows is not clear as to who is making it—God or Habakkuk. Nevertheless, Chapter 2, verse 4 says, "Behold, he whose soul is not upright in him shall fail, but the righteous shall live by his faith" (paraphrase). It may be that God is talking to Habakkuk, reinforcing His exhortation to wait: "Live by faith, Habakkuk. Don't live by sight." In other words, the wicked people run after what satisfies, but God is calling Habakkuk to live by his faith. If one has faith, he will wait for the fulfillment of the vision. Habakkuk has found something to help him to wait upon the Lord. This is a new way to live rather than the way he had been living. Earlier he had asked, "How long?" but now he says, "Behold, the righteous, the people who wait upon the Lord and get a vision from the Lord, can wait upon the Lord." They can live in a different way; they can live by faith.

In the beginning, it is very clear that Habakkuk has a burden, but he is not aware that it is a burden from the Lord. However, God is placing His burden into the prophet; in fact, He deepens it. He makes it worse, so Habakkuk calls out all the more. But that is what prepares him for a further revelation—a vision from the Lord that is worth waiting for. However, the rest of Chapter 2, does not reveal what the vision is. The reader must wait before he can find out exactly what Habakkuk has been shown. Nevertheless, in the rest of that chapter, the prophet is speaking as if the fulfillment of that vision is a foregone conclusion. That is what happens when a person lives by faith and not by sight. In fact, Habakkuk is showing through the woes that he pronounces that he recognizes that the fulfillment of that vision—the destruction of the Babylonian Empire—is a foregone conclusion. He culminates the second portion of that message with these words: "But the Lord is in his holy temple; let all the earth be silent before him" (2:20, *NIV*). Habakkuk, in the beginning, was crying out, but when he finally saw the full vision of what God wanted to reveal to him, he fell silent. This is similar to what happens in the Book of Job. When Job finally gets a vision of God, it brings him to put his hand over his mouth. So, a very similar struggle is displayed in the Book of Job that is seen here in a shorter version in the Book of Habakkuk.

The last chapter is called "A prayer of Habakkuk the prophet" (3:1, *NIV*). This prayer becomes a song; as a matter of fact, at the very end of Habakkuk, there is a reference that this message is to the choir master with stringed instruments. It is a musical notation that reveals to the reader that it is not just a prayer, but it is a prayer song. At the beginning of this chapter, Habakkuk says, "Lord, I have heard of your fame; I stand in awe of your deeds, O Lord. Renew them in our day, in our time make them known; in wrath remember mercy" (3:2, *NIV*). After one gets a vision of the Lord, it changes the way he prays. In the beginning, Habakkuk was praying, "Lord, let me see justice." When he found out just what God's justice really entailed, he realized he was not ready for God's plan of justice. Now that he has seen a vision, his prayer in the last chapter is different. He is not saying, "Lord, let me see vengeance"; he is saying, "in the midst of wrath, remember mercy." Habakkuk was praying that way in the end because of the vision.

The rest of Chapter 3 finally reveals what has already been revealed to Habakkuk—the content of that vision. It is nothing less than a vision of God himself. "God came" (3:3). Habakkuk, like every single one of the prophets, saw God. That is what the prophetic revelation is all about. The prophets saw God in different ways; because God is so vast— there is no end to the ways that He can reveal Himself. But still it is the same, because He is God.

Habakkuk has to resort to song, because mere narration, prose, and report are not sufficient to capture and to express the glory of the vision of the Lord. He is bearing witness, though, in this chapter to the coming of the Lord. Here again, he is not just simply predicting that God is going to come, but he is bearing witness because he has already experienced it. He has already seen it, and he is bearing witness to it. When one sees the coming of God into his life, in the forceful, revelational way that the prophets did, then he is seeing a preview of the ultimate coming of the Lord. And that is what Habakkuk saw.

In verse 16, Habakkuk says, "I heard and my heart pounded, my lips quivered at the sound; decay crept into my bones, and my legs trembled" (NIV). He is saying this is what seeing the vision has caused to happen in him. And that is what this vision of God will cause to happen in anybody who sees it. For example, it happened to Isaiah; it happened to Job; and it is the same thing that happened again and again to prophets all the way through the Bible. Even in the Book of Revelation, when John saw a vision of God in the form of Jesus Christ, he fell at His feet as dead. Habakkuk is giving an example of how God places His revelation into man, and the vision of Himself before man in ways that will change his life.

Habakkuk realizes that God's people are going to be judged. Habakkuk himself is judged by the coming of the Lord. But because he embraces that judgment, he is able to say, "I will wait patiently for the day of calamity to come on the nation invading us" (v. 16, *NIV*). In light of God's vision of Himself, Habakkuk says, "I can wait." And then a marvelous conclusion:

> Though the fig tree does not bud and there are no grapes on the vines, though the olive crop fails and the fields produce no food, though there are no sheep in the pen and no cattle in the stalls, yet I will rejoice in the Lord, I will be joyful in God my Savior. The Sovereign Lord is my strength; he makes my feet like the feet of a deer, he enables me to go on the heights (3:17-19, *NIV*).

Habakkuk says that he may not see all of the fruits of justice with his eyes, but as the song says, "I have seen the glory of the coming of the Lord." And because he has seen God, all of his prayers are answered, and he can sing God's song.

The Book of Zephaniah

Zephaniah, is the third prophet in this triad of Nahum, Habakkuk, and Zephaniah, who was called in the last half of the 600s B.C. as Judah was approaching its end. The name *Zephaniah* very clearly means "the Lord has hidden." Zephaniah not only has a name that is very easy to decipher, but the Book of Zephaniah also traces his genealogy back three generations to someone named Hezekiah. It is very likely that he is the great, great grandson of King Hezekiah of Jerusalem. The first verse says that he is given a word of the Lord in the days of Josiah. King Josiah came to the throne as a young man in the 620s B.C., and he is remembered for his reforms and for leading his nation back to serving Jehovah. Since Zephaniah was called during Josiah's time period, his message would naturally relate to Josiah's reforms. He, in fact, may have had some influence, along with other prophets who prophesied in that general period of time, to these events in Judah.

The thrust of Zephaniah's three-chapter message is the coming of the Day of the Lord, which other prophets mention as well. However, for no other prophet does it dominate the book as much as it does for Zephaniah. These prophets are not just simply predicting something, they are not just relaying some information, but they are sharing something that they, in a sense, have glimpsed for themselves.

Two emphases—judgment and mercy—dominate the Book of Zephaniah. The overriding emphasis of Zephaniah's message, however, is judgment. God is serious about His righteousness and about His holiness, which encompasses His vengeance against evil and evildoers. That is the dominating message in the last days in the life of Judah. Here again, God is raising up messengers with warnings of judgment in order to turn His people around. Even the message of judgment is merciful.

Zephaniah paints a picture of God's judgment on the entire earth; thus the Day of the Lord is not just a concern for a limited group of people, but rather the entire earth. God cannot come without shaking everything. And He intends to shake everything when He comes. The Day of the Lord envelopes the entire earth, but it also envelopes Judah—God's people. God, in fact, will use other nations to judge His people. But yet, within that, God intends ultimately to judge those nations as well.

The two themes of judgment and mercy are very clearly expressed in the second verse. "I will sweep away everything from the face of the earth, declares the Lord" (*NIV*). The coming of the Lord does not leave anything unmoved or, consequently, anything of the earth unshaken. Everything is shaken that can be shaken. And in that respect, everything is judged. However, Zephaniah says this: "Seek the Lord, all you humble of the land, you who do what he commands. Seek righteousness, seek humility; perhaps you will be sheltered on the day of the Lord's anger" (2:3, *NIV*). That is the heart of Zephaniah's message about the Day of the Lord's coming to judge the earth, to judge Judah, and to judge all nations. The heart of the message is "Seek the Lord . . . seek humility . . . perhaps, you may be hidden" (see v. 3). That is the very heart of Zephaniah's own identity. He is bearing a message that goes right to the heart of his own name. "Perhaps, the Lord will hide us on the day of His coming wrath." That is the message of the book, together with the final verses, which develop God's promise of mercy. It is not developed very much in respect to all nations, but there seems to be a hint of this in 3:9. There is mercy, not just for Judah, but mercy that will be offered to all of the nations. Zephaniah 3:9 says, "Then will I purify the lips of the peoples, that all of them may call on the name of the Lord" (*NIV*). Notice the plural in the word *peoples*. That could be translated "nations," because it is the same word in Hebrew. "I will change the speech of the nations to pure speech that all of them may call on the name of the Lord and serve him with one accord." Those who read this can see foreshadowing in three places:

1. "All nations" referred to in Acts 2 on the Day of Pentecost.
2. "A pure speech," represented by "cloven tongues like as of fire" in Acts 2.
3. To serve the Lord in "one accord," which is a glimpse of Pentecost in the breaking forth of God's promise from the nation of Judah and Jerusalem unto the entire earth.

The rest of the Book of Zephaniah, verses 10-20, detail and draw specific reference to God's hope and God's promise to Judah. "At that time, I will gather you; at that time I will bring you home." This is the promise of homecoming beyond the Exile. "At that time, I will bring you home. I will give you honor and praise among all the peoples of the earth when I restore your fortunes before your very eyes, says the Lord" (v. 20, *NIV*). This is the burden, the word, the message, the revelation of God through the prophet Zephaniah.

31 Jeremiah: Part 1

By Rickie Moore, Ph.D.

The study of the destruction of Israel culminates with Jeremiah, the prophet. Jeremiah prophesied during the same time (600s B.C.) as the last three minor prophets that were studied. However, his ministry extended further than theirs—all the way to the point of carrying Judah into the actual event of the Babylonian invasion and exile and the physical destruction of Jerusalem. And for that reason, Jeremiah had an extremely important role to play among the prophets. Other prophets saw the destruction coming, but it was Jeremiah who actually went into that experience with his people.

Jeremiah's Background

The name *Jeremiah* means "the Lord throws." It is interesting that someone with the name "the Lord throws," was actually thrown into the midst of the most wrenching historical event in the history of Israel and of the Old Testament. Two events towered over all the others in the importance that they played in the Old Testament: the Exodus from Egypt, which dominates the Pentateuch, and the Exile, which took place in the fall of the Northern Kingdom and the fall of the Southern Kingdom. Since those two events were the greatest two events in the Old Testament, Jeremiah's role was indeed very significant.

Overview of the Book of Jeremiah

The Book of Jeremiah can be divided into the following eight sections:

Chapter 1:	The Call
Chapters 2-6:	Judah's judgment (lawsuit imagery)
Chapters 7-10:	Phony Religion
Chapters 11-20:	Real Faith (raw prayer)
Chapters 21-28:	Opposition Against Jeremiah
Chapters 29-33	Book of Hope
Chapters 34-44:	Jeremiah's Journey to the End
Chapters 45-52:	The End of the Nations and Jerusalem

Jeremiah's call is introduced as "The words of Jeremiah, the son of Hilkiah, of the priests that were in Anathoth" (1:1). Jeremiah had a priestly heritage from the town of Anathoth, where possibly his family could have descended from the priests who were exiled when the kingdom split. There were certain priests who were exiled from Jerusalem, according to the narrative of the Book of 2 Kings which says that these priests went to a town called Anathoth (see 2:26). And so for Jeremiah to be from a family of priests of Anathoth makes a connection that could go as far back as those banished priests during and after the division of the kingdom. If this is the case, it would explain how that Jeremiah could grow up so close to Jerusalem and yet be an outsider to Jerusalem, because these priests represented a northern priestly family which was banished to the South. The ancestry of Jeremiah very likely experienced an exile. Thus, God called Jeremiah from a family who had experienced an exile, to bring Israel into that experience of exile, with special focus on Jerusalem.

Time of Jeremiah's Ministry

The Book of Jeremiah says:

> The word of the Lord came [to Jeremiah] in the days of Josiah, the son of Amon king of Judah, in the thirteenth year of his reign. It came also in the days of Jehoiakim, the son of Josiah king of Judah, unto the end of the eleventh year of Zedekiah, the son of Josiah king of Judah, unto the carrying away of Jerusalem captive in the fifth month (1: 2, 3).

It seems as though that rather long introduction is emphasizing Jeremiah's ministry during the reign of Josiah, the one who is so famous for his reforms, but even more so to emphasize Jeremiah's context in relation to the captivity of Jerusalem. That is the end point of Jeremiah's ministry.

Jeremiah's Call

Jeremiah's call aims toward the fall of Jerusalem. Chapter 1 continues:

> The word of the Lord came to me, saying, "Before I formed you in the womb I knew you, before you were born I set you apart; I appointed you a prophet to the nations." "Ah, Sovereign Lord," I said, "I do not know how to speak; I am only a child." But the Lord said to me, "Do not say,'I am only a child.' You must go to everyone I send you to and say whatever I command you" (vv. 4-7, *NIV*).

This dialogue is a very intimate exchange between the Lord and a young man. He is clearly a young man, because he is afraid that he is too young to do what God has asked him to do.

Both Jeremiah and Isaiah were called by God to deliver a message of judgment. However, Jeremiah's call focuses on God's intimacy, but in comparison, Isaiah's call focused on God's majesty. Isaiah had a vision of God's throne that was high and lifted up. The royalty and the majesty, the transcendence of God are all emphasized in his call. On the other hand, Jeremiah's call emphasizes the intimacy and the nearness of God. The conversation uses imagery and language that is very intimate; in fact, it is as intimate as the womb of a woman: "Before I formed you in the womb I knew you" (v. 5, *NIV*). The same God; the same general message of judgment leading into the Exile, yet God had a fresh way of presenting His revelation to His prophet.

In the next verses, God says:

> "Do not be afraid of them, for I am with you and will rescue you" . . . Then the Lord reached out his hand and touched my

mouth and said to me, "Now, I have put my words in your mouth. See, today I appoint you over nations and kingdoms to uproot and tear down, to destroy and overthrow, to build and to plant" (vv. 8, 9, *NIV*).

In those words are echoes of language from the Book of Deuteronomy. As Moses is about to die, he announces that God will raise up a prophet like him. He says God will put His words in the mouth of the prophet. There are echoes of Deuteronomy 18:15 which show up in Jeremiah 1:9. He was a prophet like Moses, and just like Moses, his mouth was touched: he was given a word for a time. Moses was given a word at the difficult moment that is referred to as the Exodus. Jeremiah was given a very difficult word in a similar way, at a very difficult time called the Exile.

JEREMIAH'S MESSAGE

Four verbs sum up the thrust of Jeremiah's message and ministry: pluck up, tear down, destroy, overthrow. These are four words of judgment. But then there are two words of hope given—build and plant (see v. 10). It is as if God is going to give the power to bring those events about through the tongue of Jeremiah: out of his mouth is going to flow power to accomplish this destruction of judgment and this planting and rebuilding of hope.

Another thing that is indicated in Chapter 1 is that Jeremiah's message will be an unwelcome message. However, God says, "Be not afraid of them" (v. 8, *NIV*). The reader is not even told who "they" are yet, but simply "be not afraid of them." It goes without saying that this message that Jeremiah carries is going to be powerful, and also powerfully opposed. Therefore, God is giving Jeremiah reassurance that He will be with him.

JEREMIAH'S VISIONS

Along with the words that God spoke to Jeremiah in his call, God also gave him two visions. The first one seemed to be more hopeful, because it was a vision of an almond tree budding. A budding tree is always a signal of spring, and God explained that this picture of spring meant that He was watching over His Word to perform it. Jeremiah's second vision was a sinister one. He saw a boiling pot, with contents boiling and the pot tilting toward spilling its contents all over the land of Judah. God interpreted this vision to Jeremiah by saying that He had a foe coming from the North who was coming against the land. God continued by saying that He was going to bring nations against Jerusalem, and they were going to come and surround the city. However, God's words implied even more than that to Jeremiah. They implied that he too was going to be besieged, but by his own people. Then God transferred all of the promises of Zion to Jeremiah. He told Jeremiah that He was going to make him like a fortified city with fortified walls and iron pillars (see vv. 18, 19). However, God admonished Jeremiah not to be afraid even though they were going to fight against him. There was no ambiguity; there was no uncertainty about that in Jeremiah's call. He was being called in a way that very clearly entailed opposition. He knew it from the outset, but God promised to deliver him. That set the stage for everything that followed.

Judah's Judgment—Lawsuit Imagery

Jeremiah was the final messenger of judgment until the downfall of Jerusalem. The judgment against Judah is laid out once again in Chapters 2-6, where Jeremiah uses as a primary form in presenting his message, the covenant lawsuit that has been used time and time again. He used the legal language of controversy, complaint, trial, sentencing, and judgment; however, there is something fresh and different about Jeremiah's presentation of God's case against Judah.

Just like Jeremiah's call that had very intimate language, the message of judgment against Judah employed a similar style, using intimate language, even sexual symbols and phrases. God told His marriage partner, Judah, that they had been unfaithful to Him. And because they had violated their marital covenant—their intimacy—He was going to expose all of their wickedness. Jeremiah portrays all of this in language that is very shocking and, in some cases, people would even call it earthy. For example, the second chapter says: "How can you say 'I am not defiled; I have not gone after the Baals?'" (v. 23, *NIV*). "Gone after the Baals" is a sexual phrase that is used in this passage. God continues, "See how you behaved in the valley; consider what you have done. You are a swift she-camel running here and there, a wild donkey accustomed to the desert, sniffing the wind in her craving—in her heat who can restrain her?" (vv. 23, 24, *NIV*). Earlier in that chapter, God said, "Long ago you broke off your yoke and tore off your bonds; you said, 'I will not serve you!' Indeed, on every high hill and under every spreading tree you lay down as a prostitute" (v. 20, *NIV*). God resorted, through Jeremiah, to shocking language in order to get Judah to wake up and turn to Him before it was too late.

Phony Religion

The next segment of the Book of Jeremiah has been labeled "Phony Religion." The emphasis of this division is Chapter 7. This chapter tells a story, and it is a story about how Jeremiah was sent to the Temple of the Lord. He was told to go stand in the gate of the Lord's house and proclaim his message. The word that Jeremiah was called to deliver at the gates of the Temple was a word of judgment against the Temple and against all the worship that was taking place there. The sins of Judah—the social sins and the sins of economic exploitation—which Micah and Amos exposed were still there. The religious sins of worshiping pagan idols were there as well. But it went beyond that—even worship of the Lord that took place in the Temple was polluted and phony. The people went to the Temple and even had chants and songs, but their worship was polluted.

The people kept emphasizing that God had given them the Temple. God had promised His covenant through David to be forever. Indeed, God's promise to David lived on in Solomon, who built the house of the Lord. God's covenant called them to obedience, but in their minds, God's promises would override any serious concern about living faithfully to the law of God. That was the popular theology that was going on during Jeremiah's time. The people were wrapping themselves in theology—in religious ritual—believing that somehow if they just simply went to the

Temple that everything was going to be fine. But God called Jeremiah and sent him to that very place and told him to stand in the gates of that place and proclaim His message. It was a very difficult assignment, to say the least.

Jeremiah thundered a message against the people at that point and said to them in effect, "God chose Shiloh, just like He chose Jerusalem. Did God judge Shiloh? Did he judge the priesthood that was there at Shiloh? Did he judge that religious establishment? Yes, he did and he will judge this religious establishment as well" (see 7:12-15). It was a dramatic collision with the conventional wisdom. Everybody assumed that as long as the Temple stood there, everything would be all right. Nothing could threaten as long as the Temple was there. But against that massive perception that was prevailing at that time, Jeremiah was bearing witness to the truth that no one could fathom. God was going to destroy the Temple that he had brought forth by His promise and by His Word because of covenant unfaithfulness.

God continued speaking through Jeremiah by saying in essence, "Amend your ways and your doings and I will let you dwell in this place. If you truly amend your ways and your doings, if you truly execute justice one with another, if you do not oppress the alien, the fatherless, or the widow or shed innocent blood in this place, and if you do not go after other gods to your own hurt. . . ." However, verse 24 says, "But they did not listen or pay attention" (*NIV*). As a matter of fact, another version of that same story is told later on in Chapter 26. Some additional information is given in Chapter 26 that is not included in Chapter 7. It tells about this event, because the people, after Jeremiah finished, tried to kill him. Therefore, God's message very quickly brought immediate reaction and began to fulfill His predictions that people would fight against Jeremiah and oppose him.

Real Faith

The next section of Jeremiah, in some ways, is the most striking part of the book because it gives an insight to the extent that no other prophet has given. After focusing upon Israel's and Judah's phony religion, the faith that was taking place within the life and within the heart of Jeremiah comes into focus. In Chapters 11-20, a series of passages occur which are not messages of God through Jeremiah; they are prayers of Jeremiah to God. Jeremiah is speaking back to God, similar to Habakkuk's prayer at the beginning of his book—a contention with God. Jeremiah has been given a very difficult task, and because of that difficulty, Jeremiah is resisting and struggling. The Book of Jeremiah records evidences of Jeremiah's inner struggle—his intimate times of prayer with God. It is like having pages from Jeremiah's prayer journal; in fact, it is a little bit like what is found in the Book of Jonah. However, Jeremiah goes further. These prayers reveal authentic faith as opposed to the phony faith that was prominent and popular in Judah during this time. What does Jeremiah do in these prayers? He complains; he laments; he cries; he pours out his grief. These are the characteristics that caused Jeremiah to be called the weeping prophet.

There are possibly two reasons for these prayers being in the Bible. One, they demonstrate real faith or raw prayer—the kind that would wrestle with God and against God like Jacob did by the Jabbok River. God's people do not like to struggle; instead, they like to build little systems and little kingdoms where they can escape from any kind of suffering. They like to convince themselves that they can live any way they please just as long as they do their little rituals, then everything will be all right. But God has not put His people into the world just to have a complacent and comfortable life; He has put His people into the world to be a witness of His truth, His kingdom, and of His passion in the world. However, God's people drift away from that until God raises up a Jeremiah who will wrestle with Him all over again. And out of that wrestling match, there is real faith and there is raw prayer to God. Jeremiah prays those kinds of prayers in Chapters 11-20.

In Chapter 15, Jeremiah says to God, "Why have You done this to me? Why have You been unfaithful to me, like an unfaithful brook? Why have You given me Your Word to eat, and it was sweet when I ate it, but now my experience is bitter? I've prophesied what You're going to do, and yet You haven't done it. The wicked are prospering and I am being persecuted. God, why? Why are You doing this to me?" (paraphrase of vv. 15-18). He turns the lawsuit of God around on Him, and in Chapter 12; for instance, he says, "Righteous are You, O Lord, when I plead with You; yet let me talk with You" (v. 1, *NKJV*). The translator refrains from really saying what the Hebrew language says. The Hebrew has that same phrase later on when Nebuchadnezzar captured King Zedekiah when he was destroying Jerusalem.

Nebuchadnezzer brought Zedekiah into his presence and brought charges against him. That is the very same phrase Jeremiah is using against God. Just like Nebuchadnezzar put Zedekiah on trial; Jeremiah, the prophet, is daring to put God on trial. He says, "I know You are the judge, but nevertheless I am going to plead my case against you." That is the clear wording of the Hebrew text. Such raw prayer is distasteful; in fact, translators do not like it. That is why they water it down even in the translation. But Jeremiah pours out his complaint to the Lord to show the kind of real prayer and raw faith that it takes to get through these terribly difficult times and seasons in God's history.

A second reason for including these prayers in the Bible is to show God's own passions. As Jeremiah is crying, and pouring out his passions, even that is reflecting the presence of the Word of the Lord or the burden of the Lord in him. Jeremiah is weeping over his nation and for himself. God is weeping. Behind all of Jeremiah's tears and his lamentations, there is the revelation of struggle going on in the very heart of God. In other words, that is what the raw prayers and passions and laments of Jeremiah reveal. In Jeremiah 9, there is a famous verse that says, "Oh, that my head were waters, and my eyes a fountain of tears, that I might weep day and night for the slain of the daughter of my people" (v. 1, NKJV). Everyone attributes that to Jeremiah, but a little further down at the end of verse 3, it is designated as something that the Lord is saying. The Lord is weeping through His prophet Jeremiah, and it is a great struggle that brings that weeping about. Such is the real faith and the raw prayer of Jeremiah.

32 Jeremiah: Part 2

By Rickie Moore, Ph.D.

This chapter begins with the fifth section of the Book of Jeremiah and deals with opposition against him.

Opposition Against Jeremiah

In Chapter 21 and beyond, Jeremiah delivered oracles against leadership, especially against kings and shepherds, and in Chapter 23, he gave a lengthy oracle against prophets. The prophets represented a group of people with whom Jeremiah had lots of trouble. At the beginning of his tenure, during the good times, before anybody could even imagine that Babylon would rise and threaten Judah, Jeremiah's opposition seemed to have come primarily from the priesthood, and later from the kings of Judah. Now, in this fifth section, he was opposed by prophets.

It is quite likely that there were not many prophets around during the good times, but when things started looking more threatening, when the storm clouds began to gather, there was a rise in prophetic interest. There were many people who came forth to propose what the future held for Judah, and many of these were prophets who preached out of their own imagination. Jeremiah delivered some scorching oracles against these prophets who were prophesying hope. There was a good market for that kind of preaching. Every generation has to take care to avoid this same temptation. The market is seductive and can encourage people to say the things that the people want to hear, because that makes everybody feel good and it makes a great deal of money for the speaker. He sells many more books that way. But the message of Jeremiah was an all together different message. He had sought the counsel of the Lord and learned that the true word of the Lord was a hard word. The word that everybody wanted to hear and believe was a word of optimism, but Jeremiah began to deliver prophetic judgment against the prophets of hope.

In Chapter 27, God told Jeremiah to wear a wooden ox yoke and thereby represent the last decade of Judah, during the reign of Zedekiah. This yoke represented the bondage God would put Judah under by means of the nation of Babylon. God had warned that this day was coming through many prophets, but now He had Jeremiah say it with an object lesson.

Chapter 28 features a dramatic confrontation between Jeremiah and the prophet Hannaniah. Commentators say Hannaniah was a false prophet, but the text just called him a prophet. He looked like a prophet; he spoke like a prophet; he said "Thus says the Lord" just like a prophet. He told the people what they wanted to hear and even backed it up with a dramatic visual to match Jeremiah's. He took the ox yoke off Jeremiah's neck while all the people were watching and said, "This is how God is going to smash the yoke of Babylon." To the onlookers, this action probably felt like the anointing; they probably thought it was the anointing. It probably had a tremendous reinforcing effect on what they believed. But it was a lie. Jeremiah went home that day without having the last word. It is amazing how God will allow His instruments to serve Him in weakness. Only after Jeremiah went home did he get a word from the Lord about Hannaniah's judgment. Why did God not give it to him while all the people were watching? Then when they saw Jeremiah's prophecy fulfilled, they would have had reason to pause and say, "Well, maybe, Jeremiah is the true prophet after all." But God did not choose to do that.

God kept the vindication of Jeremiah hidden. This is what He does when He is judging a people. The people would say, "We would believe this if somebody could make it clear to us." They said that to Jesus. They said to Him, "Do not speak in parables. Make it clear. Make it plain. Why do you speak in parables?" Jesus said, "I speak in parables so that people will not understand and will not hear" and then He quoted Isaiah. The very form in which God delivered the message was already judging the tastes and the appetites of the people who were being judged. God keeps His judgment hidden from those who seek for it on their own terms, not on God's terms.

Jeremiah was opposed, but God was opposing the people through Jeremiah. Even as they seemed to be winning against Jeremiah, God was fulfilling His judgment against them. When Jesus was brought accused before the court of this world, He stood there like Jeremiah in complete weakness. When God's people judge the true messenger, it verifies their sin and brings God to the culminating point of His judgment.

Book of Hope

The sixth section of the Book of Jeremiah may be termed the book of hope. In the Book of Isaiah, by contrast, the message of hope can be found throughout the book. But for Jeremiah, it was not that way, most of his messages of hope are concentrated in this single section: Chapters 29-33. Some scholars call this section the book of consolation. It hangs together under the theme of restoration and picks up on the terms of planting and building that were given to Jeremiah in his call experience. In this book of hope, Jeremiah unfolded the message of building and planting. The shape of this book is a message in poetry that is surrounded by stories. The hope offered in this section is hope for those who embrace God's judgment. It is not hope based on avoiding judgment. The people can find a refuge in God if they will submit to His judgment.

In Chapter 29, Jeremiah wrote a letter to people who had already been exiled and told them to build houses and plant vineyards. These people who had already been deported to Babylon resisted the idea that they were going to have to stay very long. But Jeremiah said to them in effect, if you go ahead and settle down and face the fact that God has delivered this judgment, then He will begin to give you peace. It will be the peace of Babylon; but it will be peace that will sustain you until God brings you home. At the end of this book of hope, there is a story about the Babylonian army coming and laying siege to the city of Jerusalem. In the midst of that event, God told Jeremiah to go buy a piece of land for a family inheritance. He told him to get witnesses, pay for the land and make it official. It was one of the most incredible things God asked Jeremiah to do. But right in the middle of a war-time siege when property would not have been worth anything, Jeremiah demonstrated his belief in God's future by redeeming family property.

Between these stories, in the middle section of the book of hope, there are poetic messages that are dominated by the theme of building and planting, but also they show that the way of hope is the way of crying and embracing the pain. Jeremiah painted a picture of God identifying with the tears of Rachel who was weeping for her children because they do not exist. The cry of Rachel, though, became the cry of God himself, when He says His heart turns within Him in compassion. The word *compassion* is a word closely associated with womb, a word God used when He called Jeremiah. One commentator says it is as if God's insides, His very womb was turning in compassion and in grief and in longing for His people. Because of God's passions, there opens up in this section one of the most famous messages of hope.

> "Behold, the days are coming," says the Lord, "when I will make a new covenant with the house of Israel and with the house of Judah—not according to the covenant that I made with their fathers in the day that I took them by the hand to bring them

out of the land of Egypt, My covenant which they broke, though I was a husband to them," says the Lord. "But this is the covenant that I will make with the house of Israel: After those days, says the Lord, I will put My law in their minds, and write it on their hearts; and I will be their God, and they shall be My people. No more shall every man teach his neighbor, and every man his brother, saying, 'Know the Lord,' for they all shall know Me, from the least of them to the greatest of them," says the Lord. "For I will forgive their iniquity, and their sin I will remember no more" (Jeremiah 31:31-34, *NKJV*).

Jeremiah saw a new covenant. Everything seemed to be in the process of being destroyed, including Jerusalem and the Temple. For those whose lives revolved around the Temple, its destruction meant the destruction of everything. The impact of its destruction is seen even today. People still come to the wailing wall in Jerusalem and weep and wail, because they are still devastated over the very magnitude of this event that Jeremiah talked about here.

In the midst of the destruction of everything, God said He was going to do something brand new— He was going to make a new covenant. This new covenant would carry forward the old covenant because it was based on the Torah, but this time it was going to be inscribed on the heart, not on tablets of stone.

This was a glorious vision of a heart work that God was going to do. This was what made Jeremiah so special. He lived through an event that broke his heart and that represented the broken heart of God. Then he revealed that God's real purpose was to reach the hearts of His people. God's objective was to change the heart of His people, not just change their behavior, or the external circumstances, but to change the heart. Maybe the reason Jeremiah was chosen to deliver the message of the new covenant was because of his own heart brokenness that enabled him to see the need for God's heart work.

Jeremiah's Journey to the End

Jeremiah's journey to the end was not a journey towards some happy ending. He did not live happily ever after. Rather, he faced persecution and imprisonment. A king came to listen to him prophesy and then rejected the prophecy. Too fearful to follow out Jeremiah's instructions, he persecuted and imprisoned the prophet. Finally, when Jerusalem fell, Jeremiah ended up being taken against his will to Egypt. The last account given of Jeremiah was a couple of years later as he was giving prophecies in Egypt against the idolatry of the remnant who had gone as refugees to Egypt. But he is rejected to the very end, and the curtain closes on Jeremiah's life.

To say that Jeremiah was rejected to the very end is to say that he was faithful to the very end. That is still how ministers will be evaluated. Not on the basis of all those results that are so much talked about, but on the basis of their faithfulness. Jeremiah had a hard message which he faithfully delivered, and he also faithfully endured the consequences that delivering it brought.

End of the Nations and Jerusalem

Because of Jeremiah's faithfulness, God could be faithful in fulfilling his prediction of the end of Jerusalem. Jerusalem could not claim that it had had no warning. They were so fully informed of the consequences of their ways, that they were without excuse in God's courtroom. God brings an end to Jerusalem.

There is a long section that prefaces the actual story of Jerusalem's fall. It is a collection of materials against foreign nations. God is going to use the nations to judge Jerusalem, but make no mistake about it, the nations too are going to face their judgment in the end. God wants that to be clear.

Conclusion

In Chapter 52, there is a brief account of the fall of Jerusalem. It is not the last thing in the Book of Jeremiah chronologically, but theologically it is. It is a fitting conclusion, a conclusion that was anticipated from the very first verse of the book. Jeremiah's life was not vindicated in his own lifetime. But in retrospect, readers can look back upon the entire book and the entire period of Jeremiah, and they can say that he was right. Jerusalem fell. Everybody else said it would not; Jeremiah said that it would, and it did.

33

The Babylonian Exile

By David C. Cooper, D.Min.

New Testament believers need to understand the riches of the Old Testament in order to understand the foundations of their faith. They must come to see the Old and New Testaments as one book; in fact, the Bible itself is one story of God's love for His creation. The central theme of the entire Bible is redemption—God redeeming the creation that He loves. In the Old Testament, redemption is anticipated in the coming of the Messiah, and that redemption is typified and foreshadowed in Sabbath regulations, the sacrificial system, the worship style of Israel, and in the Old Testament economy. In the gospels, redemption is accomplished by the death, burial, resurrection, and ascension of Jesus Christ. In the Book of Acts, the message of redemption is proclaimed to the whole world. In the apostolic letters, redemption is applied to every form of life as believers learn to live out what it means to be the redeemed people of God. And then in the Book of Revelation, redemption is consummated in the fulfilled promise of the new heaven and a new earth.

Many think that the Old Testament is in the past and not relevant for believers today. However, believers must remember that the Old Testament is reserved for their learning and discipleship in the New Testament era. The Bible says in 1 Corinthians 10:6, that everything that happened to Israel in the Old Testament serves as an example for New Testament believers. If 2 Timothy 3:16 is to be taken seriously, that "All Scripture is given by the inspiration of God and is useful for teaching and instruction," then believers must learn that there is much in the Old Testament for their learning. Romans 15:4 says, "For everything that was written in the past was written to teach us, so that through endurance and the encouragement of the Scriptures we might have hope" (*NIV*). The Old Testament as it presents the story of God's love for creation and His redemption of humanity, does so while focusing on Israel as a nation. Israel came through the line of Abraham beginning about 2000 B.C. According to Genesis 12:3, Abraham was given the promise that the Messiah would come and that all nations would be blessed through him. Therefore, what God would do through Israel was not for Israel exclusively, but it was for all nations. Israel was redeemed and emancipated from Egypt in about 1450 B.C. under the leadership of Moses. When they came out of Egypt, they went into the wilderness and arrived at the base of Mt. Sinai where they received the Law and all of the directions that started the formation of Israel as a nation. To look at Israel, one must also look into the workings of God's redemption, thereby gaining lessons about what it really means to live as the church—as the covenant people of God—because

Israel and the church are united together under one head, even Jesus Christ.

In this fourth section of the journey through the Old Testament, the theme of the restoration of Israel as a nation will be the central focus. This period of Israeli history is known as the postexilic period. It is a period of history that began with the Babylonian invasion and exile of Israel into the land of Babylon. It began in 605 B.C. and it lasted until about 400 B.C. before the period that is called the intertestamental period from Malachi to Matthew. This chapter will begin the journey into the restoration of Israel as a nation and an understanding of what happened to Israel as they were exiled to Babylon. It is important to take a glimpse of the whole Babylonian invasion and captivity, in order to answer these questions: What happened to the Jews? Why did this invasion happen? What was life like in Babylon? And by what means did God take them out of Babylon and bring them back into Jerusalem and reestablish Israel as a nation?

The Exile Foretold

The prophet Jeremiah foretold the Babylonian exile. After Solomon's death, his son Rehoboam became king. Civil war broke out in the nation about 930 B.C. The 10 nations to the north became known from that point as Israel. They were under the leadership of Jeroboam, the rebel king. The Northern Kingdom continued until the time that they returned home and the Temple of the Lord was rebuilt in 516 B.C. or 515 B.C. The Book of Lamentations is a series of Jeremiah's crying and weeping before the Lord in intercession as he laments the fall and the destruction of Jerusalem.

Three Phases of the Exile

There were three deportations of Jews out of Jerusalem and out of the land of Judah who were carried into Babylon. The first exile took place in the year 605 B.C. Daniel and his friends and others of the nobility of Jerusalem were exiled by King Nebuchadnezzar in this first deportation. Then in the year 597 B.C., there was another much larger deportation. Ezekiel, who became a prophet of God in Babylon was exiled in the second deportation and a group of about 10,000 Jews were exiled in this second deportation. Then came the final deportation which was the most expansive and was really the catalyst or the culmination of the deportation and exile of Jews into Babylon. This came between the years 588 B.C. and 586 B.C. Babylon, under the leadership of Nebuchadnezzar, surrounded Jerusalem in a military conflict and laid siege to the city in 588 B.C. It took two years for the Babylonians to conquer Jerusalem. Finally, the city fell in 586 B.C. And then followed a massive deportation of Jews to Babylon. Zedekiah was the last Judean king and a descendant of David. He, himself, was exiled to Babylon. His eyes were gouged out. He was led to Babylon in shackles of iron. So, the Exile happened over a period of years in three deportations, 605 B.C. with Daniel and others, 597 B.C. Ezekiel and 10,000 Jews, and finally the destruction of Jerusalem and the Temple in 586 B.C. and the major deportation.

Reasons for the Exile

The following question needs to be considered: If Israel was the chosen people of God and God's hand was upon them as His nation of grace, how and why did God allow the Exile to happen? There are two main reasons. The first reason is because of Israel's idolatry, immorality, and disobedience to God. The chronicler records in 2 Chronicles 36:11-21, that the reason they went into captivity was because of their rebellion against God. Leviticus 26:33 is a warning given by Moses at the very beginning of this nation that if they persisted in rebellion and idolatry, the ultimate punishment and discipline would be that they would be scattered among the nations. Thus, there was a spiritual reason, first of all, for this exile to Babylon.

But there was a second reason that is more practical or down-to-earth that can be understood historically: A political alliance was formed by Zedekiah against Babylon. Now, at the time of King Zedekiah, Judah was already under the domination of Babylon from 605 B.C. and following. Babylon dominated Israel as a vassal state, allowing the Judean kings to continue to reign. They allowed the Jews to practice their worship in the Temple and they maintained their standard of life. They required only that Israel, Judah and Jerusalem, the capital city, be in submission to Babylon and that they pay taxes to Babylon. However, Zedekiah formed a military alliance with Egypt, although he had been warned by the prophets not to do so. Even Isaiah had warned the kings about going down to Egypt and relying on them for help. Zedekiah, the Bible says in 2 Kings 24:20, rebelled against the king of Babylon. Had he never done that, they would have never gone into exile. He was also warned by the prophet Jeremiah not to rebel against Babylon. Nevertheless, he formed a political alliance with Egypt, seeking to gain independence from Babylon, and that is what brought the invasion of the Babylonian army in the year 588 B.C. It is not as though God just got angry in heaven and decided to disperse the Israelites; all of these actions, although they were orchestrated by God and under the sovereignty of God, were played out in the drama of human actions. It was the military, political rebellion against Babylon that angered and infuriated Nebuchadnezzar and brought the invasion that finally led to their exile into the land of Babylon.

There they were, the covenant people of God, out of their homeland—the Land of Promise given to Abraham—without the capital city of Jerusalem, now in Babylon without the great Temple of the Lord. Nebuchadnezzar destroyed the great Temple of Solomon, that magnificent structure. In fact, he leveled it to the ground and carried off the holy articles— the ark of the covenant, the altar of incense, and all the holy articles that were used in sacred worship. All of that was taken into Babylon as well. The Jewish people now found themselves in a pagan land, exiled from their homeland. They felt hopeless; they were in despair; they wondered if they would ever be restored as the people of God.

It is important to understand the psychology of the Jews in Babylon and to understand the writings of the prophets in this postexilic period. What they needed more than anything else was hope. And that becomes the theme of these next chapters. When the reader tries to make sense out of what the prophets were saying to the Jews in captivity, he must hear this ongoing theme of hope that God's hand has not left them, God's promise has not been abandoned, that God is going to bring them out, and God is going to restore them.

Learning to Live in Captivity

Several questions come to mind when one considers the implications of living in exile: How were they to live? How were they to conduct themselves? How were they to live now under the secular influence of the Babylonian Empire? The psalmist addressed that in Psalm 137. It was there that he shared how they really felt emotionally in the land of Babylon. He says, "By the rivers of Babylon, there we sat down, yea, we wept when we remembered Zion. We hung our harps upon the willows . . . those who carried us away captive required of us a song . . . saying, 'sing us one of the songs of Zion.' How can we sing the Lord's song while in a foreign land?" (vv. 1-4, *NKJV*). And that question really summarizes the psychology and the emotions of the people of God in Babylon. "How can we sing the songs of the Lord? How can we have faith? How can we have hope here in the land of Babylon?"

Jeremiah, the prophet, was not carried off into captivity. In fact, after the exile, he lived in Egypt. But Jeremiah sent a letter to the elders and the priests who were in Babylon and he gave them instructions as to how they should teach the people to live in the land of Babylon. This letter, found in Jeremiah 29:4-7, is very insightful:

> This is what the Lord Almighty, the God of Israel, says to all those I carried into exile from Jerusalem to Babylon: "Build houses and settle down; plant gardens and eat what

> they produce. Marry and have sons and daughters; find wives for your sons and give your daughters in marriage, so that they too may have sons and daughters. Increase in number there; do not decrease. Also, seek the peace and prosperity of the city to which I have carried you into exile. Pray to the Lord for it, because if it prospers, you too will prosper" (*NIV*).

This passage is very fascinating. Jeremiah is telling them to go on with life. In other words, Babylon is only a parentheses—a temporary time. They are there because of the poor leadership of those Judean kings who rebelled against God. But the instructions contain an element of hope. He tells them to marry, to have children, to have grand-children. Do not decrease, but increase. Continue to grow; continue to expand; continue to mature. It was a word of hope letting them know that God's hand was still on them. He also told them to build houses, to settle down, and to even pray for the city of Babylon itself.

What a parallel to today's times where believers can feel and sense the invasion of secularism. Is the church supposed to withdraw? The instructions are very appropriate for these times. He says that if "Babylon prospers, [they] will prosper." The same is true for the church in America today or all over the world. If the city, the nation, where the church is located, prospers, then the church is the recipient of the blessing.

So, Israel was given a message of hope. They were told to go on with life, to prosper, to increase, and to pray for the prosperity and the blessings of God even in the land where they were. Then Israel was called upon by God to be a witness of His grace and His glory and His love to the people of Babylon. Those exiled Jews were to turn that experience into a missionary endeavor and be the salt of the earth and the light of the world even in the land of Babylon until God called them home. And Jeremiah goes on in that letter to give them the promise of deliverance. He reawakens in them the sense of hope that they are not going to stay in Babylon. Jeremiah says:

> This is what the Lord says: "When seventy years are completed for Babylon, I will come to you and fulfill my gracious promise to bring you back to this place. For I know the plans I have for you," declares the Lord, "plans to prosper you and not to harm you, plans to give you hope and a future" (29:10, 11, *NIV*).

That verse has become very popular in the church in recent years. It is a verse that many believers are familiar with. That deliverance came to pass because the great empire of Babylon did not last. In fact, Daniel the prophet saw a vision and interpreted the dream of Nebuchadnezzar that there would come a series of Gentile world powers.

PROMISES FULFILLED

The promise to bring the Jews out of Babylon came to pass historically when the armies of the Medes and the Persians conquered the Babylonians. This was foretold in Daniel 5, which records the incident of the hand writing on the wall. Belshazzar, a descendant of Nebuchadnezzar, was king of Babylon at that time. The handwriting on the wall said that he was "weighed in the balances and found wanting" (v. 27). That very night the army of the Medes and the Persians invaded Babylon through the great aqueduct system. And the Persian Empire conquered Babylon. The result of that was that Cyrus, the Persian king, was moved by the Spirit of God to allow the Jews in Babylon to return home. The army of the Medes and the Persians conquered Babylon on October 12, 539 B.C., and God raised up Cyrus. The Book of Isaiah calls him "my anointed servant" (see 45:1). And God raised up Cyrus of Persia and allowed the Jews through his leadership to return home. Furthermore, it was the Persian government that actually funded the project financially to rebuild the city of Jerusalem, to rebuild the wall around the city, and to rebuild the Temple of God in Jerusalem. This points out once again that God is sovereign. God even anointed and used Cyrus, the Persian king, to bring this promise to fulfillment.

Now, this is how the Books of the Chronicles end. They end with this great promise being fulfilled of bringing the Jews back home. It is interesting to note that Ezra picks up in the very same place that Chronicles end.

> In the first year of Cyrus King of Persia, in order to fulfill the word of the Lord spoken by Jeremiah, the Lord moved the heart of Cyrus King of Persia to make a proclamation throughout his realm and to put it in writing: "This is what Cyrus king of Persia says: 'The Lord, the God of heaven, has given me all the kingdoms of the earth and

he has appointed me to build a temple for
him at Jerusalem in Judah. Anyone of his
people among you—may the Lord his God be
with him, and let him go up'" (2 Chronicles
36:22, 23, *NIV*).

That proclamation is fascinating. Cyrus, a Persian king is saying the reason that he is king is because of God's sovereignty in his life. He says that the Lord God has moved upon his heart to build a temple for Jerusalem, and he invites any Jew now living in this region of Babylon, now under the Persian rule, to go back home if he wants to. Many took him up on his offer. However, not all the Jews returned. Many actually lived out their lives in the land of Babylon under the rule of the Persians. But that began this process of the return of the Jews back to their homeland.

Shift in Worship

Something happened to these Jews living in Jerusalem that gives insight into some things in the New Testament. There was a shift in their worship from the Temple of God to the Torah or the law of God. When they went into exile, they obviously lost the Temple. Up to that point, the Temple had been the central point of their worship, their celebration, and their sense of God's presence with them. But once in Babylon, they did not have the Temple. What were they to conclude? That God had left them? That God had abandoned them? How were they to know that God was with them even in Babylon? Consequently, there came a shift from the Temple worship to the centrality of the Torah, which is the law of Moses, the Pentateuch, the written Word of God. The Jews in Babylon, under the leadership of the priests, began to gather in small groups for worship in their communities where they gathered around the Torah. So, wherever they had the Torah, the written Word of God, there they gathered. They heard the Word read and expounded, and they prayed and sang praises to God. Now, that created a shift in the way that the Jews perceived worship. And, it was these perceptions that they carried back with them when they went home to Jerusalem. Even though the Temple was rebuilt by Zerubbabel and finished in 516 B.C., and even though there was the Temple enlarged by King Herod when Jesus came, one reads about synagogues. There is no mention of a synagogue in the Old Testament. Where did the synagogues come from? The Jews brought the idea of the synagogue back to Israel that they had learned about in Babylon. The synagogues were like local churches. They were in every town, in every village in Israel, even though there was a Temple. The people would go to the synagogue on the Sabbath, they would worship, and the focal point of synagogue worship was the Torah, the law of God, the written Word of the Lord. It is the same model found in New Testament ministry. Today when believers gather for worship on the Lord's day, it is the preaching and the reading of the Scripture that is the central point of their worship. When the Israelites gathered around the Word, they had the sense that God was with them. God was not simply contained or confined to the Temple and the Holy of Holies. Wherever the people of God came together and they read and shared the Word, they had the sense of the living presence of God with them. They learned that principle of the centrality of the Word while in Babylonian captivity. So, there was a shift then from the Temple to the Torah that set up the synagogue worship style that is seen in the New Testament.

That Temple was very important to the Jewish people. It was important to them for three reasons. One, it built enthusiasm. They had the sense that God was among them in power. Two, it restrained their idolatry, because it was there that they worshiped, and they worshiped according to the Levitical order. They worshiped the Lord God, and their sacrifices taught them of the grace of God and the atonement for sins. Third, the Temple was important because it unified the people around a central place of worship. When they came back from exile, they still had the Temple that they had rebuilt. But, they also had the synagogue worship which had taught them the importance of the Word of God.

Timeless Truths

When one goes back and reflects upon these Jews in exile for 70 years, and the sovereignty of God who brought them back as He moved upon the heart of Cyrus, king of Persia, there are timeless truths that one can learn about the Exile. There are three truths coming from this period of history.

1. *God's faithfulness is independent of human response.* Even though the Jews were unfaithful, God remained faithful to them to preserve them, to fulfill the covenant given to Abraham, and to bring them back home. That is an encouragement to all believers. The Bible says in 2 Timothy 2:13, "If we are faithless, he will remain faithful" (*NIV*). They learned that truth even though they were faithless

and broke the covenant. God would never break His covenant and God's faithfulness would never change.

2. *The sovereignty of God rules over human history.* Even though there was war, chaos, exile, and dispersion, God reigned over all. God moved even on the heart of a Persian king and put it in his heart to let the Jews go back home, and even to fund the project to rebuild the Temple of the Lord. Even a Persian king said that the Lord Almighty had put that in his heart. No wonder Proverbs says, "The king's heart is in the hand of the Lord; he directs it like a watercourse wherever he pleases" (21:1, *NIV*). So, even though there is chaos in world conditions, believers can lift their eyes beyond the earthly realm and see that God reigns over all.

3. *National preservation is dependent on spiritual faithfulness.* The Jews lost their nation for awhile. They suffered dispersion and invasion, because they sinned against God. There is a national consequence to sin. There is judgment and there is discipline, but what one must see is that God's purpose and goal in His disciplinary action is to redeem them and restore them, not to destroy them. That is the most important lesson to be learned.

The discipline of the Lord comes as an expression of His love. Even though God disciplines His people because of immorality and willful sin, God still gives 21st-century believers the same promise that He gave to them: "'I know the plans I have for you,' declares the Lord, 'plans to prosper you and not to harm you, plans to give you hope and a future'" (Jeremiah 29:11, *NIV*).

34 Ezekiel and Obadiah

By David C. Cooper, D.Min.

Life is not determined so much by the surrounding conditions as it is the conditions of one's heart. Ezekiel, the prophet of God, taught the Israelites how to live out their faith even in the midst of the paganism of Babylon. Ezekiel is called the strangest of the Old Testament prophets. When one reads the Book of Ezekiel and looks at his life, he sees that this man was an eccentric personality, to say the least. Not only is he regarded the strangest of the prophets because of his use of imagery, symbolism, and parables of apocalyptic signs, but he is also called the prophet of personal responsibility. Ezekiel stressed to the people of God that faith is a matter of the heart, and it is a matter of an individual's relationship with God. Now, this is a very, very important point that is built upon by the rest of the prophets. It can be seen in John the Baptist, because in his preaching in Matthew 3, he told all of Israel, "Do not say . . . to yourselves 'we have Abraham as our father.' I tell you that out of these stones God can raise up children for Abraham" (v. 9, *NIV*). "Repent, for the kingdom of heaven is near" (v. 2, *NIV*). So, John the Baptist was echoing the same theme as Ezekiel and other prophets: The people of Israel could not hide behind this mass of corporate religion; they had to come to know God personally in their hearts. Each person had to believe in God. Each person had to be a worshiper of Yahweh. Each individual was responsible to God for his or her own spiritual walk.

Theme of Ezekiel:
Personal Responsibility

The theme of personal responsibility can be found throughout the Book of Ezekiel. Ezekiel 18 shows the prophet Ezekiel beginning to confront the problem of people hiding behind corporate religion, even blaming the conditions of the present on the sins of the past as he calls them to assume responsibility for their lives in the here and the now. "The word of the Lord came to me: 'What do you people mean by quoting this proverb about the land of Israel: The fathers eat sour grapes and the children's teeth are set on edge'?" (18:1, 2, *NIV*). He goes on to say "the soul who sins is the one who will die" (v. 4, *NIV*). While they were in Babylon in captivity, the proverb—"the fathers eat grapes and the children's teeth are set on edge"—was quite popular. In other words, they were saying the reason they found themselves in this condition was because of the sins of the past. It seems that from the very beginning of time, people have blamed others: they have blamed environmental conditions and parental upbringing for their present conditions. Today's society can be called the age of victimization. In fact, this proverb would fit in very well today. It is always somebody else's fault. And that is the meaning of that proverb. But when God said "the soul that sins will die," He was saying that each individual is responsible for his own problems. God is also saying through the prophet that if one assumes responsibility for his own life, then God will bring His blessing into that individual's life. Do not blame the past, and do not blame what other people did before. Assuming responsibility for one's own life is really the central theme of Ezekiel's ministry as he assumed the role of the prophet of personal responsibility.

Ezekiel, the Man

Ezekiel was carried off into exile by the Babylonians in the second deportation in the year 597 B.C. At that time, he was a young priest in Jerusalem, according to Ezekiel 1:3. When he went into Babylon, he was there as a priest and had to minister to his people. In the fifth year of being in Babylon, God's hand came upon him in an unusual way and ordained and called him to be a prophet. So, not only was he a prophet of God, but Ezekiel was also a priest of the Lord, schooled in the Levitical order. God brought a prophetic call on him to be a preacher, to be an encourager, and to help the people of God to live out their lives of faith even in the land of Babylon. His ministry spans a period of 22 years as a prophet in exile. When one reads the Book of Ezekiel, it is important to understand that he is a man of God preaching to his people, but not in Jerusalem. All of his ministry takes place in Babylon—the land of captivity.

THREE QUALITIES

Each prophet was an individual with a personality of his own. Ezekiel had three fundamental or paramount qualities in his life that give insight into the kind of person he was.

1. *Ezekiel had a flaming zeal for God.* This quality was evident in his efforts to vindicate God and uphold His cause. Here was a man that had a great deal of passion about his ministry and about what he was doing. He wanted to see the people of God live out their lives of faith in Babylon, because he knew the promise of going home was going to be fulfilled.

2. *Ezekiel was a dogmatic man.* He was dogmatic about his beliefs. He was also dogmatic about his convictions, which were reflected in his preaching.

3. *He used apocalyptic and prophetic symbols to explain what God was doing in the world.* This alone made him something of a unique figure. There were 12 symbolic acts by this prophet recorded in Scripture. There were even times when he actually acted out in a dramatic form the message that God had placed in his heart. He may be one of the forerunners of the modern ministry by the means of drama. Five of the messages that he delivered are in his book and come in the form of parables—stories that people could relate to now as an earthly story with a heavenly meaning.

TWOFOLD THEME

Ezekiel had a twofold theme: judgment and hope. In the midst of the judgment they were under, because of the consequences of their own sins, God was giving them a message of hope to know that they were coming out of captivity. And as one reads the Book of Ezekiel, it is important to keep these two themes in mind. Ezekiel talks about the judgment that has happened and he also talks about that final destruction of Jerusalem that is going to come later in 586 B.C. But in the midst of that, of knowing that destruction is going to come, he still preaches a message of hope to the people of God. Other apocalyptic prophets—Daniel, in particular, and Zechariah, and in the New Testament, the Book of Revelation—have hope as their theme. The undergirding principle or message that all apocalyptic literature in both Old and New Testaments has is an awakening of hope for the people of God. The purpose of this literature is to encourage people in the midst of very chaotic times that God is sovereign, that God's hand is upon them, and that God will preserve His people. Before the fall of Jerusalem in 586 B.C., Ezekiel talked about that devastation as the judgment of God because of Judah's sin. After the fall of Jerusalem, Ezekiel's message then took the form of hope. Ezekiel became something of a pastor to these exiles in Israel. He went from house to house and public meeting to public meeting, and in the small gatherings, he proclaimed the message of hope to the people of God. Like Jeremiah, he also first saw a very important day—the day of the new covenant. It is central in the Book of Ezekiel and appears in two passages: Ezekiel 11:18-20 and 36:24-28. It can also be found in Jeremiah 31:31-34 where he prophesied about the new covenant. Jesus also used this terminology at the Last Supper when He broke the bread and gave the cup of the

Passover, and He said: "This cup is the new covenant in my blood, which is poured out for many for the forgiveness of sins" (see Matthew 26:28). That terminology is taken by Jesus from the writings and the language of Jeremiah the prophet and also Ezekiel. So, Ezekiel and Jeremiah actually talk about the new spiritual covenant—the transformation of the heart. Ezekiel puts it this way:

> For I will take you out of the nations; I will gather you from all the countries and bring you back into your own land. I will sprinkle clean water on you, and you will be clean; I will cleanse you from all your impurities and from all your idols. I will give you a new heart and put a new spirit in you; I will remove from you your heart of stone and give you a heart of flesh. And I will put my Spirit in you and move you to follow my decrees, and be careful to keep my laws. You will live in the land I gave your forefathers; you will be my people, and I will be your God. (36:24-28, *NIV*).

Ezekiel then announced a new covenant where God was actually going to transform the human heart, take out the heart of stone, and give a new heart, and a new spirit. And He would even put the Holy Spirit within. That was fulfilled, after the resurrection of Jesus, when the Spirit came on the Day of Pentecost, and now New Testament believers have the indwelling presence of the Holy Spirit. Ezekiel talked about how that day would come with the coming of the Messiah.

Organization of the Book of Ezekiel

Understanding the organization of the Book of Ezekiel is important because it is a lengthy book with a great deal of content. The book itself can be divided into three simple sections. One, Chapters 1–3 contain Ezekiel's call and commission into the ministry. Two, Chapters 4–24 talk about the coming judgment, the fall of Jerusalem, and the final deportation in the year 586 B.C. Three, Chapters 25–48 contain Ezekiel's ministry after the fall of Jerusalem as he talks about their deliverance out of Babylon and God's promise in their lives. He also gives them a vision of hope for the future.

KEEPING HOPE ALIVE

The whole thrust of Ezekiel's ministry was to keep hope alive within his people. That was the point of his preaching; that was the point of every parable he gave; that was the meaning of the symbolic acts; and that was the interpretation of the apocalyptic messages of the kingdom of God and of the Messiah. His whole purpose was to keep their hope alive so they would not grow in despair in Babylon. How did he do that? What was it that he taught them? He taught them three very important truths:

1. *He taught them that God was with them even in Babylon.* Before, they perceived God to be in the Temple. God was relegated to the Holy of Holies. The Shekinah glory of God was there. But in Babylon, God was also with them. The same way in Genesis, when Adam and Eve sinned and left the Garden of Eden: it is a story of grace, not merely of judgment, because God went with Adam and Eve out of the Garden. That is the whole point of Genesis 4, when God gave them their son and the first words from Eve's

411

mouth in Genesis 4:1 and following were "the Lord has given me a son." She declared the goodness of the Lord. They realized that even though they had sinned in Eden, even though they had forfeited the blessing, God was still with them. God was going to bless them and prosper them. And that is a message that everyone needs to know: Even when believers stumble and fall, God is still with them. And that was what those Jews in Babylon needed to know—that God was with them in Babylon. They needed to know that whenever they gathered together to worship and read the Word of God and pray, that the presence of the Lord that had been in that Holy of Holies was still very much with them.

2. *He taught them the meaning of being the chosen people of God.* Many people today still do not understand what it means for Israel to be the chosen people of God. They think that God chose Israel and rejected everybody else. That is not true. God does not have an exclusive love for Israel. God is no respecter of persons (see James 2:3-9). God chose Israel in the sense that He chose them for a purpose. He chose them to be the nation to whom the Messiah would come. But the Messiah was not for the Jews only. The Messiah was for the whole world. The blessing of Abraham was a blessing for all nations. Before Abraham was a Hebrew, he was a Gentile, a pagan—he came from Ur of the Chaldees. To be a Hebrew meant "to be a wanderer or a pilgrim." They were not called Jews until the time of this Exilic period. They were followers of Judaism; thus, they were Jews. So the blessing of Abraham and Israel to be chosen was not an exclusion of other nations. It meant that God chose them for a purpose, and that

purpose was to be the nation to whom the Messiah would come. They had a responsibility to witness to all the world of the one true God—"to be His witnesses"—Isaiah said. The same commission was placed upon the church—"to be My witnesses"—Jesus said. So, he enlarged their concept of what it meant to be chosen. It did not mean that they were special; it did not mean that they were better than anybody else; it meant that they had a sacred responsibility now in the land of Babylon. They were to live out their faith, be a witness for God in the land of their captivity, and minister to the Babylonians. He kept their hope alive, because He gave them a missionary purpose even in the land of Babylon.

3. *He transformed their whole idea of corporate religion to a personal relationship with God.* Ezekiel told them that they had to assume personal responsibility for their own walk with God. He was the prophet of personal responsibility. Now, the point of all of that is to say that their time in Babylon was not wasted time. The Babylonian exile helped shape and mature Israel in their religion, their worship and their life of faith. They learned that God was bigger than the Temple, that God was with them wherever they were because they could walk with God as Enoch walked with God, and they learned that being chosen did not mean that they were exclusive. It meant that they were to be inclusive and they were to be a witness to all nations—they had a missionary calling. And it also moved them to a point of maturity—to understand that they could not hide behind the faith of their fathers. They could not even blame the sins of their fathers for their

413

present condition. Life is today what one chooses to make it. One can believe God, repent, obey, and walk with God, because religion is a matter of personal responsibility.

Four Great Visions

All the material in the Book of Ezekiel, and these 48 chapters, focus on four great visions that were given to him by God. It is important to understand these visions, because they are the essence of everything that he preached and taught.

1. *The vision of the sovereign God (Chapters 1–3).* This is a very bizarre vision. Ezekiel sees the glory of God; he sees angelic messengers; he sees a wheel in the middle of the wheels; and he sees the cherubim. It was an awe-inspiring vision. All of the details of that vision showed Ezekiel the greatness in the power of God. He realized that God was bigger than the fall of Jerusalem and their exile in Babylon, that God was still in control, that God reigned over all, and that God was going to fulfill His promise. In capsule form, that was the vision of the sovereign God.

2. *The vision of God's glory departing from the Temple (Chapters 8-11).* This is the most dismal of all the visions, because the glory of God is departing from the Temple. What Ezekiel sees in advance is that invasion of Nebuchadnezzar in 586 B.C. when he destroyed the city of Jerusalem, leveled the Temple to the ground, and destroyed Jerusalem. In this vision, Ezekiel talked about the glory of God departing from the Temple because there was corruption in the priesthood and idolatry in the land.

3. *The vision of the valley of dry bones (Chapter 37)*. Most people who know anything about the Bible know about this vision. Although Israel had been destroyed by Babylon, Ezekiel saw that Israel was going to live again. The principle of resurrection is taught here. There are some who say the whole concept of life after death is not taught in the Old Testament. That is not true; it is taught here—particularly in this passage. Rabbis have always used this passage to talk about the fact that God is a God of resurrection. In his vision, Ezekiel saw the valley, and God asked him: "Son of man, can these bones live?" (v. 3, *NIV*). The dry bones were a symbol of the devastation of Israel after the Babylonian invasion in 586 B.C. when the whole city was destroyed. And he said, "Lord, you alone know" (v. 3, *NIV*). "You are sovereign," in other words. "Prophesy to the wind" (see v. 9). In other words, "As you preach My word, the wind will come." The word *wind* in Hebrew is *ruach*. It is the same word that is translated Spirit for the Holy Spirit or the Spirit of God in the Old Testament. The wind, the breath, the Spirit of God are all the same word in Hebrew—*ruach*. "Prophesy to the wind." In other words, the Spirit of God will come and He will give life again to the nations. Ezekiel saw that incredible happening as the bones came together: the sinew, the muscle structure, the skin, and finally they stood on their feet—a vast army—when the Spirit of God entered into them. This was a vision confirming that God was going to put the nation back together and breathe new life upon them spiritually. The Spirit was going to come into them, and God would revive the nation. One often sees in this very vision a correlation of spiritual revival as God still comes by the

power of His Word and the power of His wind—the Spirit—and revives the church. It was a vision of resurrection and new life.

4. *The vision of the new Temple and the glory of God returning (Chapters 40-48)*. This is a vision that has a little bit of controversy about it as people dialogue and debate about what this particular vision means. First of all, when the Jews came back home from that Babylonian exile, they rebuilt the Temple. It was rebuilt under the leadership of a man named Zerubbabel, who was appointed governor by the Persian government. Zerubbabel himself was a descendent of David and was the last person of a Davidic lineage that actually occupied a political position in Jerusalem. They rebuilt the Temple and, of course, the glory of God came to that Temple. But there is something prophetic about this vision, because it also seems to be, as many scholars believe, a vision of the Temple in the last days, in the millennial kingdom of the Lord Jesus Christ. Some see in this vision the millennial Temple of the last days. But there is something spiritual as well about this vision, because the people of God really are the temple. The temple is greater than a building. Jesus said of Himself in John 2, that He was the temple of God. If He destroyed it in three days, He would raise it up again (see John 2:19). When the church came on the Day of Pentecost and the Spirit entered the hearts of the believers, the Bible says, in 1 Corinthians 6:19, that "your body is a temple of the Holy Spirit" (*NIV*). In Ephesians 2:19-21, the church is the temple of God, and then in the Book of Revelation, Chapter 21, the new temple in eternity, really in that Holy City, is a portrait of the people

of God. When one reads about the fourth vision of the temple of God, he is actually reading about something spiritual. He is reading about God putting His people back together as a holy priesthood and as a spiritual temple. Spiritual analogies can be drawn out of that vision and what it means even today to live as the church, as the spiritual temple of God, and the dwelling place of God in this life.

Obadiah

Ministering with Ezekiel was another prophet named Obadiah. He has a very short book that can be dated to the writings of the prophet Ezekiel. He was also a prophet in exile. Obadiah is the shortest of all the prophetic books that are written. Not much is known about the author or about his background. His name means "a servant or worshiper of the Lord." While there is some debate about when exactly he prophesied, it can, with some certainty, be placed with the writings and messages of Ezekiel.

Obadiah's Message

He had one simple message. He foretold the destruction of the nation of Edom. Edom was located in the desert south of Israel. Today, one can visit the ancient city of Petra, the beautiful red rock city. Petra was a stronghold in the ancient area of Edom. Today, the city of Petra is located in modern-day Jordan. When Moses and the Israelites came out of Egypt, Edom would not allow them to pass through their land on the way to the Land of Promise. Malachi himself, the last of all prophets, talks about the fall of Edom of which Obadiah prophesies. The Edomites were the descendants of Esau. There was an ancient hostility, Ezekiel says, between the descendants of Esau and the people of Israel. This ancient hostility was played out when Israel fell to the Babylonians. The Scripture says that the Edomites rejoiced at their destruction, even though they actually were their brothers through Abraham. They gloated over the destruction of Jerusalem. Psalm 137 says, "By the rivers of Babylon we sat and wept" (v. 1, *NIV*). That was a song of lament of the Jews in Babylon. At the very end of that Psalm, they talk about how the Edomites gloated over the fall of Jerusalem (see vv. 7-9). Obadiah talked about the fact that Edom itself would eventually fall into obscurity. It is interesting to note that Ezekiel also talked about the fall of Edom. In fact, in Ezekiel 35:5, he talks about the fact that Edom harbored an ancient hostility. This age-old conflict still exists in the world today between the Jews and the Arabs. These descendants, even though they have the same origin, have incredible conflict toward each other. That same tension existed between Israel and the Edomites. So, Obadiah proclaimed the fact that Edom itself would fall into obscurity. In Obadiah 15, he makes this statement about Edom: "The day of the Lord is near for all nations. As you have done, it will be done to you; your deeds will return upon your own head" (*NIV*).

Obadiah ends his short letter with a great messianic promise, a message of hope. He says in verse 21: "Deliverers will go up on Mt. Zion to govern the mountains of Esau. And the kingdom will be the Lord's" (*NIV*). Now, that may be the most important statement in Obadiah. "The kingdom will be the Lord's." Again, he is saying that God is sovereign;

that God rules over all; and that the kingdom of the Lord, in the final analysis of human history, will be ruled by God. Christ will reign as king. Messiah will reign as king over all nations.

Conclusion

Ezekiel and Obadiah were prophets in exile. What was the point of their ministry? Their messages gave the people in exile a hope—a hope of the God of resurrection, a God that would bring new life out of captivity.

> I saw this illustrated last fall when my wife and I took a tour group to Israel. We went to Masada which was built by Herod. He always feared an invasion, and he built several places where he could flee to and protect himself if his throne were ever threatened. Anyone can visit the great stronghold of Masada today, built on a mountain peak, a virtual fortress.
>
> After the time of Jesus, the Romans invaded Jerusalem, destroyed the city, and tried to bring an end to Israel. There were 900 plus Jews who escaped into Masada. The Roman armies surrounded Masada, and it took them months to build a siege ramp to get the Jews out of Masada. To this day, Masada is a symbolic representation of the Jewish resolve to never be defeated and to never allow itself to be subjugated under the tyranny of another world empire.
>
> "Masada shall never fall" is a declaration made by all those who join the Jewish and Israeli army today. In fact, Israeli soldiers

are taken on a tour of Masada. There, they are given a Bible and brought back to an understanding of Masada and the resolve of those 900 plus Jews who withstood the entire Roman army for several months before eventually falling.

As the Roman army came into Masada, most of those Jews, except for a few women and children, actually committed suicide rather than to be taken by the hands of the Romans. They would not even allow the Romans the joy of conquering them at Masada.

While at Masada on our last trip, we saw something that we had not seen before. There was a new archaeological find. In one of the synagogues there, they had just found a new set of scrolls. When they opened the container that held these ancient scrolls, there on the top of this pile of scrolls was the scroll of Ezekiel, and it was opened to Ezekiel 37—the vision of the dry bones. Evidently, the last passage of Scripture they read, before they actually committed suicide rather than die at the hands of the Romans, was the vision of the valley of dry bones. They believed that even though Rome was invading them that God would raise them up once again.

The entire message of Ezekiel and Obadiah is a message of hope. God is sovereign. What He starts, He will finish.

35

Daniel

By David C. Cooper, D.Min.

This chapter takes a look at the time of the end from the perspective of the prophet Daniel. It has been said that the farther back one looks, the farther forward one is likely to see. A look back in history to the ancient prophecies of the Bible, gives insight into things to come in the future. Everyone is interested in the future. Today, there is a resurgence of interest in psychic phenomenon, prediction. Everyone wants to know what will happen in the days to come. Perhaps, the reason the prophecies of Daniel have always been so important and interesting to people is that he wrote of things to come, of the time of the end.

Daniel, the Man

Daniel was taken out of Judah in the first Babylonian deportation in the year 605 B.C. He grew up in the land of Babylon. More importantly, he grew up in the court of Nebuchadnezzar, the king. He, along with other companions from the nobility of Israel, were taken from Israel to be trained and then to serve Nebuchadnezzar in his court. The Book of Daniel provides more historical information about the Babylonian captivity than any other book of the Bible. His material is considered both historical, because it covered the times in which he lived, and prophetic, because God unveiled future events to His prophet.

Daniel's life parallels that of Joseph. They both were taken captive. They both remained faithful to God, and the result of their faithfulness was that God gave them favor. Both of these men were elevated to high positions in the government in which they served. The name *Daniel* means "God is my judge." When he got to Babylon, his name was changed to *Belteshazzar*, which means "prince of Baal," the god of the Babylonians. It also could be translated "Baal protects his life."

Even though, the Babylonians changed his name, Daniel always referred to himself by his Hebrew name, Daniel. In fact, he refers to himself 75 times as Daniel in his book. The changing of his name, along with that of the three Hebrew children to Babylonian names, Shadrach, Meshach and Abednego, was an effort on the part of the Babylonians to change their identity and to somehow get them to blend into the culture of the Babylonians. Daniel never did; he lived out his name: "God is my judge; God is in control of my life; God is Lord of my life." He was faithful to the Lord, his God, in the land of Babylon.

Theme and Literary Divisions

The theme of Daniel is very simple: God is sovereign; God rules over all; God is in ultimate control of what happens historically in this world. This is what is meant by the sovereignty of God. The Book of Daniel can be outlined in three simple sections. The first section is Chapter 1, which gives the historical context by showing how Daniel and his friends were carried into Babylon. There, they were being trained in the court of the king, but at the same time, they maintained faithfulness to their Hebrew diet and God gave them favor in Babylon. Chapters 2-7 form the second section which pictures God's dealings with the Gentile nations and Gentile world powers. What is interesting about this section of Daniel is that it was written in the Aramaic language, which was the common language of the Near Eastern world at that time. As he deals with the Gentile nations, he actually writes in the Aramaic language. He reveals the coming of these world empires and how God will deal with them.

In Chapters 8 through12, the third section, Daniel goes back to telling of the destiny of Israel, that is, God's purpose and plan for Israel as it unfolds in times to come even until the time of the end.

Four Great Truths

When the Book of Daniel is considered in its entirety, four great truths emerge from his life and prophecies.

1. *God rules over the nations.* Daniel interpreted a dream for Nebuchadnezzar and also had a series of dreams and visions himself. He saw an unfolding of history that is unparalleled, including the Babylonian Empire and its fall to the Medes and Persians. He also saw that after Persia there would come a swift empire, conquering with great power—this empire was Greece under Alexander the Great. Further, he

saw that after the fall of this great leader, his empire would be divided into four subsections, which it was. He saw that one of those subsections, Syria, would persecute Israel, which happened under Antiochus Epiphanes. He saw the coming of Rome, where Rome dominated the Syro-Palestinian Era, in 63 B.C., and then he even talked about the Antichrist. It is really amazing to think about what Daniel saw in his dreams and visions from God, that is, the unfolding of human history. These descriptions were amazingly accurate, even years in advance of these coming empires. The bottom line to what he saw was that God rules over the nations. Great empires—like the Babylonian, the Medo-Persian, the Greek, and the Roman—came and went, demonstrating that God rules over the history of the world. He is ultimately in control of what every nation does.

This was made clear in Eastern Europe. Communism dominated the landscape of Eastern Europe during the 20th century. Millions of people were slaughtered in that region at the hands of the Nazis and the Communists. Such mass murders took place in both Russia and Nazi Germany. But in one fell swoop, the hand of God came, communism fell, the Iron Curtain fell, the Berlin wall came down, and now Christianity is thriving in Eastern Europe because God reigns over the nations; He is sovereign.

Daniel related how God revealed a mystery to him in the night and that mystery was of these coming nations. And he praised the God of heaven, saying:

> Praise be to the name of God for ever and ever; wisdom and power are his. He changes times and seasons; he sets up kings and deposes them. He gives wisdom

424

to the wise and knowledge to the discerning. He reveals deep and hidden things; he knows what lies in darkness, and light dwells with him. I thank and praise you, O God of my fathers: You have given me wisdom and power, you have made known to me what we ask of you, you have made known to us the dream of the king (Daniel 2:20-23, *NIV*).

Immediately afterward, Daniel interpreted Nebuchadnezzar's dream. But he gave God praise, because he realized it was the Lord who raised up kings and deposed others. So, Daniel knew that God ruled over the nations.

2. *Spiritual conflict underlies world conditions.* This second great lesson learned from Daniel is somewhat mystical. In Chapter 10, Daniel prayed and fasted, and then an angel came to him. The angel told Daniel that the "prince of the Persian kingdom resisted me for twenty-one days" (v. 13, *NIV*). The angel told Daniel that there was an actual conflict between the angelic messenger and demonic powers. He refers to the demonic power as the prince of Persia. There were demonic powers that were influencing what went on at a national level. It is important to understand that behind the scenes of wars and conflicts there are spiritual forces at work in this world, and Daniel gave a glimpse into that. Paul referred to the same thing in Ephesians 6:12: "We wrestle not against flesh and blood, but against principalities, against powers, against the rulers of darkness of this world, against spiritual wickedness in high places." So, he gave a glimpse of the spiritual world.

3. *God will judge sin in the end times.* Daniel saw, with the coming of these empires, horrible oppression. This was true in Medo-Persia, Babylon, and Greece, where horrible atrocities took place under those empires. Rome itself, during the time of Christ and the first century, had 60 million slaves. In fact, the Roman Empire was built on the backs of slaves. Even in today's world, there are oppressive governments. But what Daniel says is that these empires will not claim the final day of battle. The last and final of all of these empires will be Antichrist's kingdom in the last days during the Tribulation period. However, the Antichrist's kingdom will not thrive, because in the end, God will send His Son from heaven, and Jesus will rule as Lord over all. It is important to remember the promise that God will judge sin, and righteousness will rule in the person of Jesus. In Daniel 2, he describes this event as he interprets the dream of Nebuchadnezzar. In fact, he describes the second coming of Jesus:

> "You looked, O King, and there before you stood a large statue—an enormous, daz-zling statue, awesome in appearance. The head of the statue was made of pure gold (Babylon), its chest and arms of silver (Medo-Persia), its belly and thighs of bronze (Greece), its legs of iron (Rome), its feet partly of iron and partly of baked clay (the revived Roman Empire under the Antichrist's kingdom in the last days). While you were watching, a rock was cut out, but not by human hands (Jesus, who is not of human origin). It struck the statue on its feet of

iron and clay and smashed them. Then
the iron, the clay, the bronze, the silver and
the gold were broken to pieces at the same
time and became like chaff on a threshing
floor in summer. The wind swept them away
without leaving a trace (2:31-35, *NIV*).

In other words, the remnants of all of these
empires, of what Greece did when it conquered the
world, of what Rome did in dominating the world, of
what Hitler did in Nazi Germany, and even what is
going on around the world today—will be swept away
never to be remembered again. "But the rock (Jesus,
the Messiah) that struck the statue (the second coming) became a huge mountain and filled the whole
earth" (v. 35, *NIV*). That is the kingdom of Christ in
the Millennium. The coming of Christ will bring forth
a kingdom that will fill the whole earth. And Isaiah
said the knowledge of the Lord will cover the earth
as the waters cover the sea (see 11:9). Daniel goes
on in Chapter 2 to talk about the end-time judgment: "In the time of those kings, the God of heaven
will set up a kingdom that will never be destroyed,
nor will it be left to another people. It will crush all
those kingdoms and bring them to an end, but it
will itself endure forever" (v. 44, *NIV*). The same
truth can be found in Revelation 11:15: "The kingdom of the world has become the kingdom of our
Lord and of his Christ, and he will reign for ever
and ever" (*NIV*). So, this is the third great truth of
Daniel: God will judge sin in the last days. These
kingdoms of oppression culminated to the Antichrist
who will be destroyed, and the kingdom of Christ
will endure forever.

4. *God is in control of history.* That does not mean that God causes everything to happen in history, but it does means that God is moving history toward a rendezvous with Himself. God is ultimately in control of what happens historically in the world. Nebuchadnezzar found out this truth the hard way. He lived in pride and exaltation, and as a result, he went through a period of insanity. When he came to himself, he recognized that he was not God, but that the God of heaven ruled over all. After his encounter with God, he made the following proclamation:

> At the end of that time, I, Nebuchadnezzar, raised my eyes toward heaven, and my sanity was restored. Then I praised the Most High; I honored and glorified him who lives forever. His dominion is an eternal dominion; his kingdom endures from generation to generation. All the peoples of the earth are regarded as nothing. He does as he pleases with the powers of heaven and the peoples of the earth. No one can hold back his hand or say to him: "What have you done?" . . . Now I, Nebuchadnezzar, praise and exalt and glorify the king of heaven, because everything he does is right and all his ways are just. And those who walk in pride he is able to humble (Daniel 4:34-37, *NIV*).

Nebuchadnezzar issued that decree in writing to all the inhabitants of the entire Babylonian Empire. What an incredible witness. What an incredible testimony that happened in his time. The influence of Daniel had prevailed in his life. Daniel was a minister to the Babylonian king, so much so that Nebuchadnezzar recognized the one true God and praised Him, because Nebuchadnezzar said: "I'm not in control; God is in control; I'm not king; God really is king over all." The Bible refutes dualism. Dualism says that God is in one corner, and the devil is in the other, and they are in conflict. That is not a Biblical notion. God is sovereign over all. Lucifer is a fallen angel. With demonic powers, he influences affairs in this world, but there is no war between the devil and God. God rules over all. He transcends everything. The conflict is with the devil and humanity. Thus, God is in control of history.

Daniel, the Apocalypse of the Old Testament

The prophetic side of Daniel is astounding. The Book of Daniel is a companion book to the Book of Revelation. In fact, to really understand the symbolism and language of Revelation, one needs to go back and learn that same symbolism and language in the apocalyptic writings of the Old Testament, in particular writers like Daniel, Isaiah and Zechariah. The language of Revelation is actually taken from the language of the Old Testament; consequently, without that understanding, it would be difficult to make sense out of the symbols of the Book of Revelation. They are all the same throughout these apocalyptic writings, both Old and New Testaments alike. The word *apocalyptic* comes from the Greek word *apokalyptein*, and it simply means "to take the cover off something; to unveil that which was hidden; to now make it known." So, Daniel is going to take the veil off the future and let the reader see what is going to happen in the time to come.

Many of the prophecies that Daniel gave have already been fulfilled before the time of Christ, but some of them are yet to take place. They concern what the angel tells him is the time of the end. It is important to remember that all apocalyptic litera-ture, in particular Daniel and Revelation, were given to the people of God during times of difficulty and persecution to give them a vision of hope. The Book of Revelation is especially meaningful to believers of today's church who are persecuted around the world, because it tells them that even though they are per-secuted by an oppressive world power, Jesus is Lord and God will reign in the end. So, the message of the apocalyptic writers is hope for the people of God even when they are going through persecution.

The apocalyptic and prophetic messages of Daniel are a series of dreams and interpretations. There is, first of all, the dream of Nebuchadnezzar in Daniel Chapter 2, when he saw that great statue. The statue was a way of illustrating these coming world Gentile powers. Then there were four private dreams and visions that were given to Daniel in Chapters 7 through 12. When one looks at all those dreams and visions and interpretations, there are some very important lessons to be learned when looking at them in their entirety.

1. *The succession of four world empires.* These four empires would dominate Israel until the time of Christ: Babylon, Medo-Persia, Greece, under Alexander the Great, and then Rome. He sees the com-ing of these four Gentile world powers in succession.

2. *The rise of Antiochus Epiphanes IV.* Daniel saw an empire that came out of the fall of Greece. Greece again was divided and ruled by four of Alexander the

Great's generals. And one of these nations, Syria, located just north of Israel, dominated Israel. The rule of Antiochus Epiphanes IV sought to exterminate the Jews. He is, for want of a better term, an ancient Hitler. What Hitler tried to do in the Holocaust is exactly what Antiochus Epiphanes tried to do to the Jews before the time of Christ. Antiochus ruled Syria from 175 B.C. to 164 B.C. This took place about 174 years before the time of Christ. He invaded Jerusalem; he desecrated the Temple; he sacrificed a pig on the altar. Then he built an altar to Zeus next to the altar of God, and he closed down the Temple. During the tyranny of Antiochus, the Jews were not permitted to worship God in the Temple.

A group of insurrectionists arose who were called the Maccabeans. One can read about this historical revolt in the Book of the Maccabees and the Apocrypha where their military exploits are recorded. During a period of three years, they fought against the armies of Antiochus and the Syrian army using gorilla warfare. The hand of God was upon them, and they were able to overthrow and drive out the Syrian army from Israel. They rededicated the Temple, consecrating it back to God. It is one of the most sacred celebrations of the Jewish people today. The rededication of the Temple took place on December 25, 165 B.C. That celebration is known as Hanukkah, or Feast of Dedication, or sometimes it is called the Festival of Lights. Even Jesus himself went to the Feast of Dedication (see John 10:22). The Jews were celebrating God's deliverance from the hand of Antiochus. That is important because Antiochus is also a type of the Antichrist to come.

431

When one reads in Daniel about this invasion by Antiochus and Syria, he knows that part of it has happened historically, but it is an example or type of the kind of man the Antichrist will be in the end times.

3. *Daniel's seventy weeks.* Some consider Daniel's seventy weeks as the most fascinating part of the Book of Daniel. In Chapter 9, Daniel sees a period of 70 weeks—one prophetic week is seven years—a period of 490 years that God is going to do something special in the nation of Israel.

> Seventy "sevens" (490 years) are decreed for your people (the Jews) and your holy city to finish transgression, to put an end to sin, to atone for wickedness . . . to seal up vision and prophecy and to anoint the most holy (the Messiah). Know and understand this: From the issuing of the decree to restore and rebuild Jerusalem until the Anointed One (Jesus), the ruler comes, there will be seven "sevens" and sixty-two "sevens" (vv. 24, 25, *NIV*).

So, there are 69 "sevens," or 483 years, from the time the Temple was rebuilt until the time of Messiah. He states exactly when the Messiah will come into the world, and his dating is precise. So, 69 of these 70 "sevens" have already taken place, referring to the coming of the Messiah. Then, he tells about this time of the 69 "sevens" and the coming of the ruler.

> It (the city) will be rebuilt with streets and a trench, but in times of trouble (v. 25).

> (When they rebuilt Jerusalem and the Temple, there was much opposition. This is recorded in the Book of Ezra and the Book of Nehemiah.) After the sixty-two "sevens," the Anointed One will be cut off (the crucifixion of the Messiah) and will have nothing. The people of the ruler who will come will destroy the city and the sanctuary. (He is talking now about the Antichrist who will come and destroy Jerusalem and the Temple.) The end will come like a flood: War will continue until the end, and desolations have been decreed (v. 26, *NIV*).

When people today talk about war and achieving world peace, they need to understand that it will never happen. Wars and desolations will continue until the end. It is wonderful to negotiate peace, but in fact, the evil in human hearts will fulfill this prophecy. "He (the Antichrist) will confirm a covenant with many for one "seven" (v. 27, *NIV*). So, Daniel saw a vision of seventy times seven—490 years or 70 weeks. Sixty-nine of these weeks have already been fulfilled from the time the Temple was rebuilt in Jerusalem until the time of the Messiah's crucifixion and His resurrection. But something will happen in one "seven." It is as though one seven-year period has been left. This is the period that is referred to as the Great Tribulation. This is the only place in the Bible which gives any indication that the Tribulation will last seven years. In fact, it is the only passage that gives a time period for the Great Tribulation period. So during the Tribulation, the Antichrist, will make a covenant with Israel. But "in the middle of the 'seven,' he will put an end to sacrifice and offering" (v. 27, *NIV*). (The same way that Antiochus Epiphanes did.) He will put an end to worship. He will desecrate the Temple. "And on a wing of the temple, he will set up an abomination that causes desolation, until the end that is decreed is poured out on him" (v. 28, *NIV*). The abomination of desolation will finally occur in the time of the Antichrist. It occurred with Antiochus Epiphanes when he desecrated the Temple; it happened in Rome when they invaded Jerusalem in A.D. 70 and destroyed the Temple; but the final abomination of desolation about which Jesus also spoke in Matthew 24:15, will happen in the Great Tribulation period. The Antichrist will make a peace treaty with Israel, violate his covenant, and he again will desecrate the Temple of God and persecute the people. But his end has been determined; he will be destroyed as the prophet said.

4. *The second coming of Christ.* Jesus will come again in the last days as a rock from heaven, crushing the oppressive empire of the Antichrist and the other nations of the world. His kingdom will rule over all (Daniel 2:34, 44).

5. *The last days.* The fifth element that is seen in these dreams and visions of Nebuchadnezzar and Daniel is the fact that the rule of the Antichrist will be ended at the return of Jesus Christ. Considering all of this, one can certainly conclude that this is a fascinating book, to say the least. Daniel was a man who saw not only the end of Babylon, the Medes and the Persians, Greece and Rome, but he also saw into the times that go even beyond today's times. He literally saw the time of the end.

A Preview of Eternity

The Book of Daniel ends with a preview of eternity. Some people say that the immortality of the soul and life after death are not taught in the Old Testament. That is simply not true. The principles of resurrection and the immortality of the soul are taught throughout the Old Testament. Daniel gives a glimpse of that in Chapter 12. In fact, this is the last message that Daniel receives from the angel of God. He ends with an eternal hope—a glimpse of what will happen. The angel Michael, who was the great protector of Israel, speaks to Daniel about the end times: "Multitudes who sleep in the dust of the earth will awake: some to everlasting life, others to shame and everlasting contempt. Those who are wise (the people of God) will shine like the brightness of the heavens and those who lead many to righteousness, like stars for ever and ever" (12:2, 3, *NIV*). In John 5:28, 29, Jesus makes the very same statement that the multitudes who are in the dust of the earth shall arise—some to life everlasting, and some to everlasting contempt. It as though Jesus is quoting the prophet Daniel. Christ said, "Do not be amazed at this, for a time is coming when all who are in their graves will hear his voice and come out— those who have done good will rise to live, and those who have done evil will rise to be condemned" (*NIV*). Throughout the Old Testament, mankind is shown that God is a God of everlasting life. When Jesus reflected back on the burning-bush experience, He talked about resurrection and life after death. He said God is the God of the living; He is the God of Abraham, Isaac, and Jacob; He is the God of the living, not the dead, implying that those patriarchs are not really dead. They are in heaven with God (see Matthew 22: 31, 32). Job, in the midst of his calamity, talked about eternal life and resurrection. In Job 19:25, he said, "I know that my redeemer lives, and that in the end, he will stand upon the earth. And after my skin has been destroyed, yet in my flesh I will see God" (*NIV*). Job proclaimed life after death. After David and Bathsheba fell into their sin and had a child who was very ill, David fasted and prayed. But the child died. David then got up from his place of mourning and went to the Temple of God and worshiped. His servants did not understand, but David talked about life after death concerning the death of his son. "But now that he is dead, why should I fast? Can I bring him back again? I will go to him, but he will not return to me" (2 Samuel 12:23, *NIV*). Fascinating. David knew that when he died, he would actually meet that child on the other side. In fact, David said in Psalm 16:10, 11, speaking of the Messiah, "You will not abandon me to the grave, nor will you let your Holy One see decay" (v. 10, *NIV*). "In thy presence is fulness of joy; at thy right hand there are pleasures for evermore" (v. 11, KJV). Thus, the last great message is that God is a God who gives eternal life.

This is how the book closes, and the last message the angel told Daniel was, "As for you, go your way till the end. You will rest, and then at the end of the days, you will rise to receive your allotted inheritance" (12:13, *NIV*). He told Daniel that he would live forever. Then, he was told to go his way, "because the words are closed up and sealed until the time of the end" (12:9, *NIV*). In the same way today, there are "date setters" who want to predict when Jesus will come again. But no one knows the day nor the hour that the Son of Man will come, according to Matthew 24:36. But believers must go their way, trust God with the future, and remember the words of Jesus: Be ready, be watchful, and be faithful for in an hour that is unexpected, the Son of Man will come.

36 The Restoration of Israel and Ezra

By David C. Cooper, D.Min.

The word *exodus* brings to mind the deliverance of Israel out of the land of Egypt. However, the nation of Israel had a second exodus, when they came home from Babylon. The Books of Ezra, Nehemiah, and Esther must be seen together because they tell the story of the Jews coming out of Babylon, going back to their homeland of Israel.

Going Home

The Jews went into captivity under the Babylonians during the invasion of Nebuchadnezzar, and they were there for 70 years. Babylon was defeated by the armies of the Medes and the Persians in the year 539 B.C. Cyrus, the Persian King, was moved by the Holy Spirit to give the decree that the Jews could return home to Jerusalem to rebuild the city and to inhabit their land once again as the people of God. The Book of Ezra, in particular, tells the beginning of their return. Nehemiah, then, gives the final story as the exiles begin to make their way back home.

The Jews received a fresh start, and that is the heart and the soul that is seen in the postexilic period.

THE GOD OF NEW BEGINNINGS

Spiritually, when one looks at this period of history and the Books of Ezra, Nehemiah, and Esther, one can see a portrait of the God of new beginnings. Before the Israelites went into captivity, Isaiah prophesied about their return. He gave them a message of hope, letting them know that God would bring them back, and he gave them a picture of a God of new beginnings. In Isaiah 43, he said to them: "Forget the former things; do not dwell on the past. See, I am doing a new thing! Now it springs up; do you not perceive it? I am making a way in the desert and streams in the wasteland" (vv. 18, 19, *NIV*). When one hears those words, he hears something of the kind of message that the Jews received; the kind of hope that they had; and the fact that now God was giving them a new beginning—a time to start over. The promise found in Jeremiah 29:11 was now being fulfilled: "I know the plans I have for you," declares the Lord, 'plans to prosper you and not to harm you, plans to give you hope and a future'" (*NIV*). The hope and the future of which he spoke was their ability to leave Babylon and come back home.

ORDER OF THE RETURN

The exiles did not all come back at once; in fact, not all the Jews returned home. Many of them continued to live out their lives in Babylon, now under the rule of the Persian Empire. There were three main groups that returned, and it is important to understand this chronologically in order to understand the Books of Ezra, Nehemiah, and Esther. The first group that returned came back in the year 537 B.C. That happened just two years after the Persians conquered Babylon and Cyrus issued a decree that the Jews could return home. This first group consisted of 50,000 plus Jews, and they came back under the direction of a man named Zerubbabel. Zerubbabel, a descendant of David, was appointed to be the governor of Judah and Jerusalem under the order of the Persian government. All the Davidic kings reigned in Jerusalem, and God had promised David, in 2 Samuel 7, that he would never fail to have a descendant to reign upon the throne. Even though Zerubbabel was not a king, the Persian government did appoint him as the governor. He then became the political leader as this first group of 50,000 plus Jews began to make their way home. Spiritually, he was accompanied by a man named Yeshua, who was the high priest. Thus, Zerubbabel, the political leader, and Yeshua, the high priest, together led the first group of exiles back home.

The second group came a number of years later in the year 458 B.C. This group was led by Ezra (see Ezra 7, 8). He was a scribe and a priest of God. He came to bring spiritual reforms, and there is a book in the Old Testament that bears his name—the Book of Ezra. In the Apocrypha, he is called by the name of Esdras, but he is the same person.

The third group came in the year 445 B.C. with Nehemiah who was the cupbearer to King Artaxerxes. He had a sense of destiny about his own people. Jerusalem was still in ruins and they were not doing very well. Nehemiah led the project to rebuild the wall around the city. Thus, it is important to understand that the return of the Jews out of Babylon took place over a period of many years, gradually coming home at different times and different stages. The three main groupings were as follows: First, Zerubbabel and Yeshua, the high priest led a group; second, Ezra led a group; and finally Nehemiah came to rebuild the walls of the city, leading a group.

THE PERSIAN KINGS

The Medes and the Persians overthrew Babylon in 539 B.C. There were four Persian kings mentioned in the Books of Ezra, Nehemiah, and Esther. The first was Cyrus who reigned from 559 B.C. to 530 B.C. Cyrus gave the order for the Jews to return home, gave the order for the Temple to be rebuilt, and then helped to fund that project. After Cyrus came Darius I. He reigned over Persia from 522 B.C. to 486 B.C. The names Cyrus and Darius were used as titles similar to Caesar; thus, many of the rulers actually used the title Darius. In fact, in the Book of Daniel, one can read about Darius, the Mede, who also used this title, but was under the authority of the Persian king. Cyrus was the first Persian king, then Darius I, then Xerxes was the third Persian king. He reigned from 486 B.C. to 465 B.C. Esther became queen about the year 520 B.C. The events of Esther's life take place in the time period between Chapters 6 and 7 of Ezra. She became the queen to Xerxes, after he deposed Vashti as his queen when she fell out of favor with him. So, Esther was queen along with this third Persian king, Xerxes. Then there was Artaxerxes I who reigned from 465 B.C. to 424 B.C. Nehemiah served as a cupbearer to King Artaxerxes. He was the king in power when both Ezra and Nehemiah made their pilgrimage and journey back to the Holy Land. Thus, when reading the Books of Ezra, Nehemiah, and Esther, the importance of the chronology of the kings is realized.

The Book of Ezra

The Book of Ezra consists of two simple sections. The first section consists of Chapters 1 through 6. In this section, Ezra records the story of the first group that came back to Israel. Even though he was not with them, he records the account of Zerubbabel and the 50,000 Jews and how they began to rebuild the Temple. He also tells how they went through a period of discouragement, but finally they completed the Temple. Then he tells how he made his personal journey back to Jerusalem as a spiritual leader, because he would become the catalyst of spiritual revival and spiritual reforms.

The second section of Ezra consists of Chapters 7 through 10. This section tells about his return and his ministry in the nation of Israel. The theme of Ezra is restoring the nation. Israel had been exiled not only to Babylon, but also dispersed to Assyria during the time of the Northern Kingdom. The Assyrian Empire to the north of Israel was now under the Persian government. So, not only did Jews return from Babylon, but also many of the Jews from Assyria returned as well. Thus, the spiritual theme of restoring the nation was fulfilled when the city of Jerusalem—the capital city—was rebuilt, the great Temple of God—the centerpiece of Jewish worship—was reconstructed, and spiritual reforms took place. They needed to be brought back to an understanding of what it meant to live as the covenant people of God. So, the Book of Ezra focuses on two main events: one, the rebuilding of the Temple, and two, the restoring of the city of Jerusalem, which led to the spiritual revivals that followed.

Restoring the Nation

The restoring of the nation was about rebuilding the Temple and then rebuilding the city of Jerusalem itself. The Temple, originally built by Solomon, was totally destroyed by Nebuchadnezzar. Cyrus received a message from God and gave orders for this Temple to be rebuilt. He also returned all the sacred articles that had been in the original Temple that Nebuchadnezzar had carried away into Babylon (see Ezra 1:7-11). The new Temple, which is called the Zerubbabel Temple, was rebuilt and finished on March 12, 516 B.C., almost 70 years after it was destroyed by Nebuchadnezzar.

REBUILDING THE TEMPLE

The process by which they rebuilt the Temple was quite impressive. First of all, they built the altar of God. This is very significant. They did not build the Holy of Holies first; they did not build the actual structure of the Temple first; they first built the ark—the altar of God. As soon as they raised the altar, they began to sacrifice burnt offerings, and then they reinstituted the daily offerings. So, they began first with the altar, then the sacrifice, and then the worship. The altar teaches two vital lessons. First, God saves by a sacrificial offering. Every offering on that altar was a type of Jesus who would die for man's sins. God saves by His grace through the innocent who bears the sins of the guilty. God has always been a God of grace, as shown from Genesis to Revelation.

Second, the offerings also represented the worshiper, dedicating himself to the Lord, as Romans 12:1 instructs: "Offer your bodies as living sacrifices" (*NIV*). Thus, the sacrifices of the Jews taught that God saves by an act of His grace and that believers should offer themselves as living sacrifices.

The altar of burnt offering was set up, and Yeshua, the high priest, and his fellow priests served at the altar. At this time, the Jews now celebrated the great Feast of Tabernacles. They were beginning to recapture the worship that they had before the Babylonian exile. For example, there were three great annual Jewish festivals where all the Jewish males were required by law to go to Jerusalem. In the spring, they celebrated the Passover, 50 days later they celebrated Pentecost, and then later in the fall, the Feast of Tabernacles. So when they were rebuilding the Temple, the first order of business was to set up the altar and reinstitute the sacrifices and worship.

Second, they laid the foundation for the Temple itself under the leadership of Zerubbabel. This story can be found in Ezra 3:10. When they laid the foundation, they had a great celebration and worship service. The priests and the Levites were there. The musicians were there, and it was a tremendous worship time, perhaps even singing one of the great psalms of the Old Testament. "Give thanks to the Lord, for he is good. His love endures forever" (Psalm 136:1, *NIV*). When Solomon dedicated the Temple, they sang this same song and praised God. His love had indeed endured forever. There were some there, however, who saw the foundation and realized that this new Temple was not going to be as massive or

445

glorious or attractive as the great Temple of Solomon had been. They wept when they realized that somehow this new Temple would not even compare in its physical structure to the Temple of Solomon.

After they laid the foundation, when it seemed that everything was going well, there was opposition that arose from some of the people who lived around Israel. They intimidated them, put fear in them, and soon the people became discouraged. The construction on the Temple came to a grinding halt. In fact, they did not work on that Temple for the next 14 years. The only thing that they had was the foundation and the altar of God. The construction stopped completely. Zerubbabel himself was very discouraged, even feeling like a failure because he could not complete what God had called him to do. At this point, God sent two prophets, or two preachers, and they had one task—to encourage Zerubbabel, the priest, and the people to go back to work on the Temple. They urged the people to finish their task, and they reminded them that God was with them and that God was raising up their nation again. Those two prophets were named Haggai and Zechariah. Haggai told them that the glory of this house would be greater than the former house, which is an incredible statement to make, and it was Zechariah who told them, in the fourth chapter, that this Temple was going to be rebuilt "not by might, nor by power, but by my Spirit saith the Lord" (4:6). This well-known verse came in the context of Zerubbabel being encouraged by Zechariah that he should go back to work on the Temple. He assured him that God would do what He had promised He would do, and that God would give him strength by the Spirit to fulfill the task.

THE TEMPLE COMPLETED

They resumed work in the year 520 B.C. and worked on it for another four years. It was finished in 516 B.C. during the reign of Darius. When the Temple was finally completed, they had a great dedication service with celebration to the Lord, and they again observed the Feast of the Passover. They dedicated that Temple to God. It is interesting that the Hebrew word for *dedication* actually came from the Aramaic word Hanukkah. They now had their new Temple, and they celebrated the fact that God's glory was with them. They also commemorated the Feast of the Passover.

Thus, the two great events in Ezra and Nehemiah are one, the rebuilding of the Temple and two, the rebuilding and restoration of the city of Jerusalem itself which came under the leadership of Nehemiah. With Nehemiah, also came the ministry of the prophets Malachi and Joel. These two prophets helped the people learn what it meant to live once again as the covenant people of God. So, Ezra writes in Chapters 1 through 6 about how this Temple was rebuilt, how the people got discouraged, and finally how they completed the project and began to have a sense of identity.

Reviving the People

Now that the Temple was rebuilt, Ezra came with the second group of exiles in the year 458 B.C. Ezra's mission was to bring spiritual revival.

EZRA, THE MAN

Who was this man Ezra? His Jewish name means "helper," and he came to help rebuild and restore and revive God's Word in the midst of His people. He came to Jerusalem some 60 years after the Temple had been rebuilt. He was a Levite and a descendant of Aaron. Thus, he was also a priest of God. He served as a scribe and as a secretary for Hebrew affairs in the Persian court. So, he too, like Nehemiah, was involved in the political situation of Persia. Ezra was a man of many talents. First, he had a rich spiritual background; second, he was a Levitical priest. He understood the Law, and he had a heart for God. Third, he was a scribe, and fourth, he was a literary man—learned and educated, not only in Hebrew history, but also in the affairs of the Persian government itself. God used him during this time as a minister of the Word. When he led this group back to Israel, they numbered about 1,800 people who traveled over 900 miles back to their homeland. Ezra carried with him a treasure in the amount of about $3,000,000 in modern-day currency. This came from the Persian government, under Artaxerxes, to help minister to the people and to help provide what they needed in Jerusalem.

When Ezra got back to Jerusalem, he was very concerned with the moral laxity of the people and with their spiritual complacency. He noticed that many of them had intermarried with pagans and had violated the law of God in doing so. Now, there was the real threat of idolatry coming into the land. Ezra was moved to speak the Word of God to them. He was also moved to fasting and praying. As a result, God began to use him as a catalyst of spiritual revival.

THE MINISTRY OF REVIVAL

The word *revival* means "to come back to life again." It is a word that refers to a spiritual awakening of people turning their hearts back to God, of being sensitive to the Lord, and of seeking God with all their hearts. Three important components of revival come into focus as one studies Ezra's life and ministry.

1. *The preaching of the Word of God.* Ezra 7:10 is really the key verse of the Book of Ezra. It gives information about Ezra and about his ministry. "For Ezra had devoted himself to the study and observance of the Law of the Lord, and to teaching its decrees and laws in Israel" (*NIV*). Now, the law of the Lord is the written Word of God. He had the scriptures—the law of Moses, the Psalms and the prophets. So, Ezra had devoted his whole life to studying the written Word, and now he was teaching the law of God in Israel. He taught what it meant to obey the Word and to have the blessings of obeying the Word of God.

When one looks at revival throughout history, he finds that in all revivals, in both Old and New Testament times and in the history of the church, that there has never been a revival that was not brought about by the preaching of the written Word of the living God. Scripture is the very heart of all revival, because God anoints His Word and confirms His Word with signs following. So, Israel was not only enjoying the rebuilding of the Temple and the actual rebuilding of the city and of the nation, but their hearts also needed to be rebuilt. The family structure needed to be rebuilt—the way they lived in relation to God and each other. That was what really needed to be rebuilt. Ezra was the man who preached and taught the Word of the Lord, as well as the other Levites who joined him in that ministry. And it was that preaching of the Word that brought about the real revival and reforms that they needed.

2. *Prayers of the people.* Prayers of confession, prayers of repentance, prayers where the people were honest with God, that is what repentance means. It means "to be honest with God, to be willing to turn away from everything wrong, and to turn to God." Repentance is a turning around—it is making an about-face in life; it is a change of mind, literally; it is a change of heart; and eventually, a change in the direction of the way one lives. The people began to pray as they heard the Word of God preached through Ezra. They began to talk to God. They began to be honest about what they had done with their lives and the way that they were living. They made confessions. They were honest with God in their prayers, and they repented. They told the Lord they wanted to change. "While Ezra was praying and confessing, weeping and throwing himself down before the house of God, a large crowd of Israelites—men, women, and children— gathered around him. They too wept bitterly" (Ezra 10:1, *NIV*). So, they followed his leadership. He did not tell them to pray. He prayed, and as he prayed, they followed him. Leaders do not simply stand before people and tell them what to do. Real leaders do what God expects. Ezra himself was praying. He was confessing his own sins. He was having a heart-to-heart talk with God himself and praying for his own people, and they were moved by his communion and his confession to God. Suddenly, a great revival of prayer broke out as people began to take an honest look at where they were in their walk with God.

So, there was the preaching of the Word, and that brought conviction. Then, there were the prayers of

Ezra and the people of God, the confession, and the repentance. But there is another element of revival that is often overlooked. If all people talk about is confession and repentance, then they have not seen the full measure of revival. So, there was a third element.

3. *The prospects of hope in spite of past failures.* When God's Word comes, it always comes with a message of hope. God's Word is always positive. God does indeed call men to confess and to repent, but the reason that He does is to bless and restore people so that they can enter into the abundant life that He wants to give.

Ezra's final message to the Israelites was a message of hope. They had sinned and some of them had gotten involved in intermarriage, and their children had grown up not even able to speak Hebrew. That's how far they were from their history and from their faith. They had violated the laws of God by intermarrying with the Canaanites. Now, it was not a violation of the law for Jews to intermarry, but certain intermarriages were prohibited. It was prohibited for the benefit of the nation. Ezra and the others leaders had to deal with those types of issues. Many decided to correct their marriages and to rectify what they had done.

The people got honest with God, and they began to look at how they really had not obeyed or followed God. Their city was being rebuilt, and now they had a Temple. But God is not a God of the Temple; God is a God of the heart, and they were learning that now under the ministry of Ezra. And before they became too discouraged about all the failures they had made, Ezra told them that there was hope. He told them it did not matter what they had done in the past; it did not matter how many mistakes they had made; it did not matter how many sins they had committed: God is a God of new beginnings. That is the message of Ezra. Ezra 10:2 makes one simple, powerful statement: "But in spite of [their sins], there is still hope for Israel" (*NIV*).

Hope is the message of Ezra to everyone today. As leaders, ministers, and lay persons, that is the message that God wants to give to sinners today. Believers are to proclaim the Word, be honest with God, confess, and repent. But be sure to tell people that, in spite of everything that has happened, there is always hope—for God is the God of new beginnings.

37

Nehemiah

By David C. Cooper, D.Min.

The word *leadership* means "influence." Leaders guide others to the degree that they influence them either positively or negatively. Sociologists say that every person has at least eight people under his or her direct sphere of influence. For those who find themselves in leadership positions, especially in the church, know that sphere of leadership is much larger. If one is looking for a model of effective leadership, the Book of Nehemiah is a perfect example. Nehemiah serves as one of the great examples of leadership found in the Word of God.

Nehemiah, the Man

Nehemiah grew up as a Jew in Persia. His ancestors, like those of Ezra's, decided not to go back to Israel. When the decree was given by Cyrus, they chose to remain. They had made their homes there since the Exile. They had maintained their way of life and had learned how to carve out their own way of Judaism, even in the midst of captivity. Nehemiah was exalted by God in the court of the Persian king Artaxerxes. In fact, he served as cupbearer to the king at the beginning of his story in the Book of Nehemiah. A cupbearer was more than an errand boy; a cupbearer was more than someone who just did certain kinds of secretarial functions for the king; the cupbearer was a close confidant of the king. He was a person whom the king trusted implicitly because of his integrity and because of his character. So, Nehemiah was a man much like Joseph and Daniel, finding himself elevated to a position of prominence in the court of a pagan empire.

Life was going along smoothly, when suddenly he went through a major transition in his life and career. The Holy Spirit moved in his heart and burdened him about the condition of his own people back in Jerusalem. Nehemiah himself describes how the call of God came on his life to go back to Jerusalem and help with the rebuilding process and the restoration of the nation and the city.

> The words of Nehemiah son of Hacliah: . . .
> They said to me, "those who survived the exile and are back in the province are in great trouble and disgrace. The wall of Jerusalem is broken down, and its gates have been burned with fire." When I heard these things, I sat down and wept. For some days I mourned and fasted and prayed before the God of heaven (1:1, 3, 4, *NIV*).

Then, he records the prayer that he had when he called out to God on behalf of his people and what God would have him do. And the Lord placed it in his heart that he was to go back to Jerusalem and that he, as a leader, was to organize the effort to coordinate the work and to lead the construction project to rebuild the wall around the city. All ancient cities were surrounded by a wall. It was that wall that protected them from an enemy invasion. So, at this point, Jerusalem, although the people were back there, was still not a protected city at all. It is an interesting fact that in Jerusalem today, one can actually see remains of part of the wall that was rebuilt during the time of Nehemiah. So, rebuilding the wall was very important, as well as the whole restoration process of the city of Jerusalem.

One wonders how Nehemiah could undertake this project; after all, he worked for the Persian king. There was no way that he could leave, so he prayed that God would give him favor and that God would move on the heart of Artaxerxes, allowing him to return home. That is exactly what happened. When Artaxerxes noticed that Nehemiah was somewhat troubled, he asked him about it. Nehemiah told him what was going on in Jerusalem and how he was burdened. Artaxerxes then allowed Nehemiah to go back and to help in the reconstruction of Jerusalem. Throughout the Book of Nehemiah, he grows in prominence and in leadership. In Nehemiah 1:11, he is a cupbearer to King Artaxerxes; in 2:12, he is a builder of the great Jerusalem wall; but then in 8:9, he is the governor. The Persian government actually appointed him to be the new governor—the leader over Jerusalem and Judah at that time.

Literary Divisions

The Book of Nehemiah is divided into two sections. Section one is the rebuilding of the wall. This account is found in Chapters 1 through 7. The reader learns how Nehemiah organized the work, motivated the leaders, fought off opposition, and how they finished the whole project in only 52 days. The second division of the book is the renewal of the covenant, which is found in Chapters 8 through 13. In this portion, the reader learns how Ezra joins with Nehemiah in bringing spiritual influence to the people. This is the account of the continuation of revival that was started under the leadership of Ezra. Thus, the Book of Nehemiah is divided into two simple sections: the rebuilding of the wall (Chapters 1 through 7) and the renewal of the covenant (Chapters 8 through 13).

Rebuilding the Wall

While reviewing the history of rebuilding the wall, one can learn something about leadership. In fact, there are some valuable lessons to be learned about what it means to serve as a leader. Nehemiah exhibited the following 13 principles of leadership.

1. *Concern for others (1:3).* The first principle of leadership is concern about other people. When Nehemiah heard that the exiles back in Jerusalem were in disgrace and that they were not doing what God had called them to, he himself was moved with compassion. He was concerned. So, there is an emotional element to leadership: one should actually be concerned about the people he is trying to influence and lead.

2. *Personal involvement in solving problems (1:4; 2:11).* Nehemiah did not stand aloof and just give orders; he personally got involved in the process. The first thing he did was pray, and then he asked

God what he needed to do in the process. In obedience to the urging of God, he actually went to Jerusalem to be part of the solution (see 2:11). Artaxerxes gave him the permission, and then he tells what happened: "I went to Jerusalem, and after staying there three days I set out during the night with a few men" (2:11, 12, *NIV*). That is when he began to make an inspection of the wall. Thus, he got involved personally. One cannot stand aloof as a leader and just give out orders for everybody else to do the work. Real leaders get involved, roll up their sleeves, and become a part of the solution.

3. *A vision from God (2:12).* A vision is simply a sense mentally of what God wants a person to do. As Nehemiah and his men went out at night and surveyed the wall, he said: "I had not told anyone what . . . God had put in my heart to do for Jerusalem" (2:12, *NIV*). So, he says that this whole plan to rebuild the wall was not something that he came up with; it was something that God had put into his heart to do. And that is how leaders are motivated.

4. *Realistic planning (2:13).* Nehemiah was a man who planned. There are many people who have a dream and a vision, but they do not have any concrete or realistic plans to make it come to pass. They simply become dreamers, and they never accomplish their goals. Nehemiah tells how he began: "By night I went out through the Valley Gate toward the Jackal Well and the Dung Gate, examining the walls of Jerusalem, which had been broken down, and its gates, which had been destroyed by fire" (2:13, *NIV*). He went to all the different gates and made a full inspection, and then he declared that it was time to rebuild the wall of Jerusalem so that it would no

longer be a disgrace: "I also told them about the gracious hand of my God upon me and what the king had said to me" (v. 18, *NIV*). Nehemiah made an inspection, and he began to plan what the construction project would be like, what it would take, and how they would organize their efforts.

5. *Ability to motivate others (2:17,18).* There was no way that Nehemiah by himself could do this. So, he tells the people, "The gracious hand of my God [was] upon me. . . . Let us rebuild the wall of Jerusalem" (2:17, 18, *NIV*). The word *us* is the most important word a leader can use. Nehemiah enlisted the participation of the people. He said this was a project that God not only had led him to do, but had also put it in his heart to share with others. Thus, he motivated others to get involved in the project.

6. *Willingness to share the credit for success (4:6).* In Chapter 4, the people go through opposition, but they were willing to fight through it. "So we rebuilt the wall till all of it reached half its height, for the people worked with all their heart" (4:6, *NIV*). He does not say that he worked with all of *his* heart; he does not talk about himself; he tells about the group—the team effort. Nehemiah was a man who believed in team leadership, and he was willing to share the credit. He said "the people worked with all their heart."

7. *Ability to maintain poise under pressure (4:14, 22).* There is no leader who is not going to receive opposition at some point for something that he or she wants to do. There will always be some kind of opposition. Chapter 4 tells all about the opposition that they received from the people who lived around that area that did not want to see the wall completed.

They wanted to see Jerusalem remain in the crippled state in which it was left after the invasion, and there were even some who threatened to invade and attack them. The people in Jerusalem became terrified; they did not have a protective wall; they did not have much of an army; and so they were terrified. In order for Nehemiah to keep them motivated and to finish this project, he had to find a way to help them not give in to fear and to maintain their courage. So he himself, as a leader, kept his poise. "After I looked things over, I stood up and said to the nobles, the officials and the rest of the people, 'Don't be afraid of them. Remember the Lord, who is great and awesome, and fight for your brothers, your sons and your daughters, your wives and your homes'" (4:14, *NIV*). He told them to fight for what was important to them. And he motivated them with that kind of mind-set. "At that time I also said to the people, 'Have every man and his helper stay inside of Jerusalem at night, so they can serve us as guards by night and workmen by day'" (4:22, *NIV*). They went on to put a tool in one hand and a weapon in the other as they learned to build and battle for the glory of God. Thus, Nehemiah kept his poise under pressure.

8. *Fairness for the underprivileged (5:9-11).* There were those in Jerusalem who were underprivileged; there were those who were poor; there were those who were hurting financially. Nehemiah made sure that their needs were met. He showed fairness and justice for the underprivileged. This is a constant theme of the prophets—making sure that the poor and the underprivileged are cared for. Nehemiah displayed this same characteristic.

9. *Devotion to his work (5:16).* He said, I did not act like some of these nobles who try to exert authority over people. He said, "Instead, I devoted myself to the work on this wall" (v. 16, *NIV*). He did not try to lord over people; he did not try to intimidate people or dominate them. That is not leadership. As a leader, he devoted himself to what God had given him to do, and other people followed that example.

10. *Dependence on divine strength (6:9).* As a leader, Nehemiah leaned on God. He needed divine strength. He knew that he could not do this project by himself. There was a great deal of pressure; in fact, there was even opposition that came at times. Nehemiah found that he had to battle all of that emotionally. He says, "They were all trying to frighten us, thinking, 'Their hands will get too weak for the work, and it will not be completed.' But I prayed, "now strengthen my hands'" (6:9, *NIV*). Now, that is a prayer that every leader can pray, whether he is an ordained minister or a lay person of the church. At times when one feels opposition and things are not going right, he can pray "Lord, strengthen my hands." Nehemiah leaned on God for strength to do what God had called him to do.

11. *Persistence to complete a task (6:15).* The following statement might have been the most important statement that Nehemiah made in these writings: "So the wall was completed on the twenty-fifth of Elul, in fifty-two days" (v. 15, *NIV*). He completed the work. That is a great sense of satisfaction when God has put something in one's heart to do and he finally finishes it. Jesus also talked about the problem of those who start a project, but they do not count the cost and they do not finish it. He talked about

how embarrassing that can be when one launches a project or a vision, but he has not really thought through what it is going to take to finish it (see Luke 14). What an important lesson for every leader. One might have a good dream, a wonderful vision, but he must make sure he has organized it and planned it and structured it, so that he can actually finish the project. It is only when one finishes what God calls him to do that one can really celebrate and rejoice.

12. *Good judgment of character in selecting qualified leaders (7:2).* Nehemiah had good judgment when it came to selecting qualified leaders. He put in charge of Jerusalem, his brother Hanania. Along with Hanania, the commander of the citadel, because he was a man of integrity and he feared God more than most men do. The people whom he selected were men of integrity. He was a good judge of character when it came to selecting other people to serve with him in leadership.

13. *Encourage people in their spiritual walk (8:9, 10).* Nehemiah was a politician; he was a builder; he was having to lead the city like a governor in a construction project; but he was also a spiritual man. When revival came, he was also there encouraging the people. He said to them "The joy of the Lord is your strength" (v. 10, *NIV*).

That is the first half of Nehemiah: they rebuilt the wall! While scrutinizing Nehemiah, one learns a great deal about what it means to be in leadership, to bring a team together, to give them a vision, to motivate them, to encourage them, and to fight through the opposition until one can finish what God has called him to do.

461

Renewing the Covenant

In the second half of Nehemiah, one reads about Jerusalem rising out of the ash pile. The people have been home for many years; the Temple has been rebuilt; the sacrifice has been reinstituted; ardent worship has been reestablished, and Ezra has brought spiritual reforms. Now, Nehemiah has come back; they have rebuilt the protective wall; houses are being rebuilt; the city is being reinhabited; and God has brought them a continued sense of His presence in a spiritual awakening. This is an overview of what is contained in Nehemiah Chapters 8 through 10.

To read Chapter 8 of Nehemiah, is to read one of the most exciting chapters in the entire Old Testament. When one reads this chapter, he can even visualize the people as they gather together in the square at the Water Gate. There, they have built a podium, and they had a pulpit where Ezra, the scribe, took the law of God and began to read it. As he read, the people began to rejoice. The Bible said the people celebrated and said, "Amen! Amen!" (v. 5, *NIV*). They confirmed what God was saying. When one reads the eighth chapter of Nehemiah, it is like reading about a modern-day revival service. The Bible said that Ezra praised God. The people lifted their hands and they shouted "Amen." They bowed down and worshiped the Lord. As Ezra read the Word, their hearts were stirred and challenged. Sometimes, they did not understand all that was read, so the Levites would then meet with the people in small groups and they would take time to teach them. They would let the people ask questions, so that the people could understand the details of the Word. This exemplifies the ministries of both preaching and teaching.

In preaching, there is a proclamation; in teaching, one takes time to break the Word down and to give people the understanding. The Scripture says in this eighth chapter of Nehemiah that the Levites gave the people an understanding, and the people became sorrowful. Some had conviction of their sins and they began to weep, and then the word came, "Do not . . . weep . . . for this day is sacred to our Lord. Do not grieve, for the joy of the Lord is your strength" (8:9, 10, *NIV*). God never wants the end product of the ministering of His Word to be a discouragement to the human heart. Indeed, they were challenged and some were convicted, but God wanted them to know that they were forgiven and cleansed. They were His people, and the strength they had for living was the joy of the Lord—the joy that comes from knowing the grace of God and the love of God and the blessing of God. So, there was an incredible revival and a time of renewing the covenant.

FEAST OF THE TABERNACLES

During this time, they also celebrated the great Feast of Tabernacles as they acknowledged God as the source of all their blessings. It is important to understand the purpose of that feast. It was a harvest festival, celebrating God's blessings and prosperity. The Feast of Tabernacles was instituted when the Jews came out of Egypt into the wilderness. It was a festival that also commemorated God's redemption. Thus, the Feast of Tabernacles served a three-fold purpose. It is important to know this, because that is what worship today is all about.

The Feast of Tabernacles was first, a recollection of the past—the people lived in booths. If one goes to

Israel today during the Feast of Tabernacles, he can see people living in the booths once again. The Orthodox Jews will actually live in these booths, temporary dwelling places, because it commemorates the time that they were in the wilderness and they lived in a temporary dwelling place before they inherited the Land of Promise. So, the Feast of Tabernacles helps them to remember the past, the bondage in Egypt, and how God brought them out of Egypt through the parting of the Red Sea. And they remember how God fed them in the wilderness with manna, how God gave them the pillar of fire by night, the cloud by day, and how the protective hand of God was upon them. So, in celebrating the Feast of Tabernacles, they went back and remembered the whole Egyptian experience, the wilderness experience, and the deliverance of God.

Not only was it a recollection of the past, but second, it was also an anticipation of the future. Because as they were in the wilderness, they thought about the Land of Promise, the land flowing with milk and honey.

Third, it was a celebration of the present blessings of God. That is what worship today is all about. Worship means that God's people remember the past—that they think about what God has done for them in Christ, on the Cross, and in the Resurrection, which is their real deliverance. Believers anticipate in worship the future blessings of God—that there is a real heaven, and there is a new earth. But they also celebrate the present blessings of God that they have today. Paul put it this way in Ephesians 1:3: "Praise be to the God and Father of our Lord Jesus Christ, who has blessed us in the heavenly realms with every spiritual blessing in Christ" (*NIV*). When the church comes together, it should remember what God has done in the past with Christ, what God is going to do in the future, and give God praise for who He is and what He is doing today. Thus, Ezra read the Word, the Levites gave them the understanding, and they said, "The joy of the Lord is [our] strength." They celebrated the Feast of Tabernacles, and it was a time of wonderful spiritual blessing.

THE COVENANT RENEWAL SERVICE

The word *covenant* is one of the most important words in the entire Bible, especially in the Old Testament. It expresses the nature of God. God has demonstrated, in the Old Testament in Hebrew, His love. It means His covenant love, His loyal love, His steadfast love. Covenant love means that God has made a covenant with mankind to redeem him and that God is faithful to the covenant. It does not matter what one does, he can never change God's faithfulness to the covenant. On the other hand, man can be unfaithful to the covenant. The Israelites had been unfaithful, and that is why they had been in Babylonian exile. So, it is fitting now that they would renew the covenant, which meant that they were going to pledge their faithfulness again to the covenant. It did not mean that the covenant was broken—the covenant can never be broken. The new covenant that believers have in Christ, which is the fulfillment of everything in the Old Testament, can never be broken. God is always faithful to the covenant. God is always faithful to man; however, at times, man is not faithful to God.

465

So, the Israelites had a covenant renewal service; they pledged themselves to be faithful to the covenant that God had given to them. Moses received the covenant as they became a nation, as they received the Law, as they became a nation of priests (see Exodus 19:6). After the wilderness experience of rebellion and they came into the Land of Promise under Joshua, the last act of Joshua's ministry (see Joshua 24) was to renew the covenant at Shechem. It is there that he said, "If God is God, then serve him . . . as for me and my house, we will serve the Lord. Choose you this day whom you will serve" (v. 15). The people and the leaders promised that they would serve the Lord. They were pledging themselves to be faithful again to God. They were renewing the covenant.

In the ministry of King Josiah, king of Judah, they found the Law of God in the Temple. The law of God had been lost and forgotten. That is how far they had fallen from God spiritually. And the Law was brought by Hilkiah, the priest, to Josiah. When he read the Law, he wept, and the Law was then proclaimed in all of Israel. The Bible says in 2 Chronicles 34:31, that Josiah called the elders of Jerusalem together, and they "renewed the covenant in the presence of the Lord," which meant they were pledging themselves to be faithful to the Word of God. That is exactly what Nehemiah did. It really was kind of a culmination of the ministry of Ezra and Nehemiah. Now, they are back in their land. They have their Temple. The wall has been rebuilt. They are out of Babylon. They have gone home. They have a new beginning. But all of that means nothing unless they are really committed in their hearts to the Lord.

So they renewed the covenant and they pledged themselves to be faithful to God.

CONFRONTING THE ISSUES

The Book of Nehemiah ends with the last portion of his ministry. After the wall was completed, after that great time of spiritual renewal, Nehemiah went back to Persia, after being in Jerusalem for 12 years. And then he came back to Jerusalem for a second time. He was appointed the governor of Jerusalem, and he brought some final spiritual reforms that are found in Nehemiah 13. They address the Sabbath issue. The Sabbath had been violated; it was just another day for commerce. Nehemiah had to deal with the Sabbath issue. He also had to deal with the fact that the people had not been faithful with their tithing and their giving in the support of the priesthood and the ministry. And he also confronted the problem of intermarriage with pagans. The Law did not forbid all types of intermarriage, but there were some that were forbidden because they were pagan and they would cause the people to lose their faith. Thus, Nehemiah dealt with those three issues: tithing, honoring the Sabbath day, and what it really means to have a home that glorifies and honors God.

Of all that Nehemiah teaches, this book instills in its readers what it really means to lead others, to bring a team together, to motivate them, to share what is in each other's hearts, to help people press through during times of discouragement, and then to finish what God has called them to do. However, the most important lesson to be learned from Nehemiah and Ezra is that people can build all the

walls they want to build, all the temples, all the structures, all the things that are material—as wonderful as they may seem—but the greatest rebuilding
that happens is the rebuilding of the heart. Believers need to love the Lord with all their hearts, all
their minds, all their soul, and all their strength,
but the most important thing they need to do in
times of unfaithfulness is what Israel learned to do
in the postexilic period, they learned how to renew
the covenant and again live in the blessings of the
Lord.

38

Esther

By David C. Cooper, D.Min.

The name of God has always been held in sacred honor by the Jewish people. In the Ten Commandments, one can read the commandment, "You shall not take the name of the Lord your God in vain" (see Exodus 20:7). In the Hebrew language of the Old Testament, there are several recorded names for God. God is *El-Olam*, which means "the everlasting God." God is *Elohim*, which means "God is creator." God is *El-Shaddai*, "the nourisher and provider for His people." He is the Almighty God. God is *Adonai*, which means "He is Lord, ruler and master of all." But the most important and sacred name of God in the Old Testament is the name *Yahweh*, or Jehovah. It appears some 6,800 times and means "the eternal One who reveals Himself and makes Himself known." *Yahweh*, or Jehovah, is the covenant name of God.

As sacred and as important as the name of God is, it is interesting to know that there is a book in the Bible where the name of God is never mentioned.

469

That is the Book of Esther. Even though the name of God is never mentioned in the Book of Esther, God certainly reveals Himself in the course of the actions that unfold in the drama of this book. And this is very significant. The author intentionally omits the name of God to reflect something about how the people felt in the time of Esther. During this time, the people of Israel had gone into captivity. First, they went into the Assyrian captivity in 722 B.C., and they were dispersed all over the known world. Then, in 586 B.C. and the final overthrow of Jerusalem, the remainder of the Jews living in the South and around Jerusalem were exiled to the land of Babylon. For many years, they had lived without their homeland, without their Temple, and without the city of Jerusalem. They felt as though God had forgotten them. They felt as though God were silent. But even when man thinks God is silent and uninvolved in his life, God is very much at work. This is the lesson found in the Book of Esther.

Background of the Book of Esther

Looking into the Old and New Testaments, one finds a very unique feature—God's anointing and use of women. Even though culturally and historically, women have had to fight at times for their recognition and place in society, God has never shown favoritism between men and women. Such an example is found in the Book of Esther. Esther, a young Jewish girl, was raised to a place of prominence in the Persian government and used as an instrument of God to save His people.

Several highlights stand out in the overview of this marvelous book. The author of the book is unknown.

He was probably a Jew who lived in Persia, because he was well versed in the Jewish religion and also in Jewish nationalism. The author's knowledge of Persian customs, his familiarity with the capital city of Susa, and the absence of any reference to the land of Judah or the city of Jerusalem suggests that he was a resident of Persia. The earliest date for the authorship of this book has been suggested shortly after the events in Esther occurred, which would have been around 460 B.C. This was before Ezra's return to Jerusalem. Evidence suggests that this book was probably written before Persia fell to the Greeks in 331 B.C. The author's purpose is to show that when God is silent, He really is not silent at all. When one thinks God is not at work in his life, He really is at work behind the scenes. Nevertheless, there is also a historical purpose to the book as well. This book records the institution of the Jewish festival known as Purim, which is a two-day festival, celebrating God's deliverance of His people during the time of the Persians. This feast today is celebrated every year in the Jewish religion somewhere between February and March. So, the purpose of the Book of Esther, then, is to teach that when God seems to be silent, He really is not silent; He is very much at work in the believer's life. And historically, it records the institution of the Festival of Purim, so that the Jews will always remember God's act of deliverance.

The Unfolding Drama

This book reads much like a Shakespearean play. It unfolds from scene to scene as the reader observes God at work in saving His people.

THE SETTING

The setting of this book takes place between the events recorded in Ezra 6 and 7. The first remnant of Jews had returned from Babylon, and this was before Ezra led the second group back. The events of Esther take place in the city of Susa, which was the royal throne and capital of the Persian Empire. It was the winter palace for the kings. In fact, one of Daniel's visions occurred in the city of Susa, and Nehemiah also served here while he was cupbearer to King Artaxerxes.

THE MAIN CHARACTERS

The first character is King Xerxes, the Persian king. The next person is Esther, who is a young Jewish girl in the royal harem. Her Hebrew name is Hadassah; her Persian name is Esther, probably meaning "star." The third person in this drama is Mordecai. He is Esther's cousin. Some translations say uncle, but the Hebrew word means that he was a close relative. He took care of her because her parents died when she was young. The fourth personality is a man named Haman. Haman was the highest royal official that served with the king in the Persian government.

THE BANQUET

The story begins with a great banquet held by King Xerxes. Esther 1:1-3 gives the setting:

> This is what happened in the time of Xerxes, the Xerxes who ruled over 127 provinces stretching from India to Cush. (Cush is located in the upper Nile region.) At that time King Xerxes reigned from his royal throne in the citadel of Susa, and in the

third year of his reign he gave a banquet
for all of his nobles and officials. The military leaders of Persia and Media, the
princes, and the nobles of the provinces
were present (*NIV*).

For 180 days, he displayed all the wealth and
power of the Persian Empire, and then he had a
special banquet—a feast for seven days. During that
time, there was a great party spirit and a lot of fes-
tivities. Toward the end of that banquet, Xerxes, who
had drunk too much wine, invited Queen Vashti to
wear the royal crown and to come before all of his
leaders, so that he could display her beauty. Now,
Vashti was having a banquet of her own for the ladies
at the same time that King Xerxes was holding his
banquet. She refused to come and parade her beauty
before his leaders. Xerxes was stunned. What was
he to do with a queen who would not obey the king's
request? He called all of his wise men together, those
who were his closest counselors, and asked what
should be done. And they said, "if word of this gets
out, then none of our wives will respect us." So,
they counseled him to pass a decree that Vashti be
banned from the presence of the king and deposed
from her position. And that is exactly what happened.

THE SEARCH FOR A NEW QUEEN

Vashti vacated the position, and the search for
a new queen was about to begin. The time came
when the king's anger subsided, and a search was
made through the royal harem to find a queen for
him. Esther was prepared, as many of the young
girls were, to come and meet the king. As soon as
Xerxes met her, she won his heart, and he selected

473

her to be the next queen of Persia. This is an example of the favor of God. God gave her divine favor and put her in that position for a special purpose. It seems to be just a coincidence that this young Jewish girl would now be the queen of the Persian Empire, but the hand of God was very much at work behind the scenes. Again, this is the underlying spiritual theme of this book.

THE CONSPIRACY

During this time, now that Esther had become queen, her cousin, Mordecai, overheard two men talking about a plot to kill the king. He uncovered this plot and made it known to the royal officials who saved Xerxes' life. The two officials who conspired against the king were hanged, and the events were recorded in the books of the annals of the king. But nothing was ever done for Mordecai to honor him or to recognize him for his intervention to save the king's life.

THE PLOT

The next main event and issue that was raised in the Book of Esther, as this drama unfolds, is Haman's plot to destroy the Jews. Mordecai was a thorn in the flesh of Haman. Haman was a man full of pride and arrogance, a man who envied position. And Mordecai never gave Haman his "due" respect. Mordecai knew the kind of man that Haman was—he had evil in his heart. Because Mordecai never would give him public recognition or honor, Haman hated him. As a result, Haman generalized his hatred towards all the Jews and began to work on a conspiracy to destroy and exterminate all the Jewish people in Persia. This was a holocaust in the making. Haman went to the king and was able to persuade the king to believe that the Jews would somehow be a threat to his kingdom; consequently, the king signed a decree giving Haman permission to exterminate the Jewish people. The king signed the decree with his signet ring, so that the decree could never be changed. It is at this point that the reader begins to see why God placed Esther in her position as queen of Persia.

Mordecai learned about Haman's plot to destroy the Jewish people and went to Esther. He appealed to her that she needed to go to the king and intercede on the behalf of her people. In Esther 4:12-16, an interesting conversation takes place between Mordecai and Esther. He appeals to her to go and intercede for her people before the king. She, however, was reluctant to do this. It had been 30 days since the king had even asked to see Esther, and the queen was not allowed to go and seek an audience with the king. She could go to the king only if he invited her. If someone asked to see the king of Persia, and got into his presence, the king would either extend the royal scepter, which meant that the person was welcome in his presence, or he could withhold the scepter. If he withheld the scepter from a person who came into his presence, that person would be taken out and executed, because they had defiled the presence of the king. This same rule applied even to the queen. So, the queen never went and sought an audience with the king on her own. She always waited for the king to call for her. But he had not called for her in 30 days, so Esther was very reluctant to seek an audience with the king.

> When Esther's words were reported to
> Mordecai, he sent back this answer: "Do
> not think that because you are in the king's
> house you alone of all the Jews will escape.
> For if you remain silent at this time, relief
> and deliverance for the Jews will arise from
> another place, but you and your father's
> family will perish. And who knows but that
> you have come to royal position for such a
> time as this?" (4:12-14, NIV).

This is a marvelous insight on the behalf of
Mordecai. In actuality, it is a challenging message
for everyone. God puts His people in various positions in life to fulfill His will and His purpose. This
message touched Esther's heart. It brought faith in
her heart, and Esther sent this reply to Mordecai:

> "Go, gather together all the Jews who are
> in Susa, and fast for me. Do not eat or
> drink for three days, night or day. I and
> my maids will fast as you do. When this is
> done, I will go to the king, even though it is
> against the law. And if I perish, I perish.'"
> So Mordecai went away and carried out all
> of Esther's instructions (4:15-17, NIV).

She put her life on the line on behalf of her
people. Her words are challenging: "If I perish, I perish." She realized that God had exalted her to that
position to save her people.

THE INTERVENTION

How would Esther make intervention for her
people? Her wisdom was displayed as she entered
the king's chamber that day. He extended the royal

scepter and asked, "What do you want, Esther?" He was willing to give her anything. He loved her. But she had only one request. She said, "I want you and Haman to attend a banquet that I will have for you." Obviously, his curiosity was peaked, but she did not tell him anything about what was in her heart. He agreed to come to this special banquet. Two important events happened. First, there was one banquet, and Esther took care to provide a wonderful meal and hospitality for the king and for Haman, but she never talked about anything that was weighing on her heart for her people. Second, she invited the king and Haman for a second banquet.

Before the second banquet occurred, two important events took place. First, Haman had a gallows built 75 feet high on which he planned to hang Mordecai. Second, the night before the second banquet, the king could not sleep. He had the book of the annals of the kings brought in and read to him. As the reading was going on that night, he heard the story of how Mordecai had uncovered a plot to assassinate the king, and how Mordecai had saved his life. The king asked what had been done for Mordecai, and he learned that nothing had ever been done to honor the man. Naturally, the king wanted to honor Mordecai.

The next morning, he brought Haman into his council and presented him with the scenario. The king asked Haman, What should be done for a man who gave his life to save the king? What should be done to honor the man that the king loves? Haman thought that King Xerxes was talking about him, so he said that this person should be given the royal robe and put on public parade throughout the city of Susa. Consequently, all the people would honor this man as he was paraded around on the king's horse. Haman fully believed that the king was going to exalt and honor him. Haman was stunned when the king said, "I want you to do this for Mordecai." Haman could not believe what he was hearing from the king. So, Haman, then, had to do that very act of honor for Mordecai. He was dressed in the royal robe, with the royal seal, placed on the king's horse, and taken through the city. Mordecai was honored among all the people. This, of course, infuriated Haman and made him more intent to carry out his conspiracy to exterminate the Jewish people.

THE DELIVERANCE

The second banquet was held. This was the moment of confrontation. That day Esther told the king of the plot to exterminate her people. She told King Xerxes that it was Haman who wanted her and all the Jews killed. The king did not know what to do, because he had signed and sealed a royal decree. So, for a moment he stepped out of the room. Haman was terrified, and he begged Esther to intercede for his life. She was reclining on the couch, and Haman fell down next to her, pleading with her to intercede for him. At that same moment, the king walked back into the room and saw Haman next to his wife, the queen. He thought Haman was trying to seduce her, and that infuriated the king even more. Haman's head was covered with a bag, and the royal officials led him out. A man named Harbona, one of the king's eunuchs, told the king about the gallows, and the king gave the order for Haman to be hanged. Haman was then executed on the very gallows he had built for Mordecai.

THE BLESSING

Now came the blessing. The king ordered that the entire estate of Haman be given to Esther and her family. Mordecai was exalted by King Xerxes to take the place of Haman in the king's court. The king then wrote a new order, allowing the Jews to defend themselves against their enemies.

THE CELEBRATION

Of course, one can only imagine the incredible celebration that took place among the Jewish people when they learned that God indeed was not silent, even though they were in a place of exile far from their homeland. God was still with them; His hand was still upon them. So, they instituted a celebration known as the Feast of Purim. The Feast of Purim celebrates God's act of delivering the Jews during the time of the Persians. The word *Purim* is from the word pure, meaning "lot," because Haman cast lots to decide on which day the Holocaust would take place. Queen Esther wrote a royal decree of her own for all the Jews in Persia, designating two days of celebration. Today, the Book of Esther is read by the Orthodox Jews during the Feast of Purim.

Conclusion

The triumphant theme of the Book of Esther is God's providential care for His people. When God seems silent, He really is not. God is always speaking to believers and working in their lives, even when they do not see Him at work. The absence of the name of God reflects the feeling of the people that God was absent from their lives. But God really was very much at work all the time. Even as Christ said, "His eye is on the sparrow," God is always watching over His people. This is what is meant by the providence of God. There is a great theological and practical truth taught as one studies the lives of Mordecai, Esther, and Haman. Jesus said, "Those who humble themselves will be exalted, and those who exalt themselves will be humbled" (see Luke 18:14). Mordecai and Esther were humble servants of God, and God exalted them to positions of great prominence. Haman, on the other hand, exalted himself, and he eventually was humbled, bringing an ultimate end to his life.

For the Jews who lived in Persia, the Book of Esther then became very important. It helped them to hold onto their unique faith as the people of God, even though they lived in a foreign land. God is always at work even when believers do not see Him. God is always speaking, even though He may seem silent.

One final point about the Book of Esther. When Jesus was born in Bethlehem, according to Matthew 2:1, and following, that there were wise men, or Magi, from the East who came to Bethlehem. They saw His star—an astrological phenomenon that was a sign that the messianic prophesies were fulfilled. Who were those wise men? How did they know that a Messiah would be born in Israel? These wise men were from Persia. The Jews who lived in Persia taught the Word of God, and it was there that even the wise men of Persia became familiar with the Old Testament prophecies. Micah 5:2 says that the Messiah would be born in Bethlehem. Daniel 9:24-27, in his noted 70 weeks, even gives the approximate year—the time frame in which the Messiah would be born. Those wise men were Persians. They had the prophecies in their hearts, and that is why they knew to go to the land of Israel and seek out the Messiah—this One, they said, who was born king of the Jews.

Even in exile, God used people to be witnesses for His truth. When all of this is put together—Jews in exile, Esther put on the royal throne, Mordecai exalted to a place of prominence—the believer learns one great truth for life: In all things, God works together for the good of those who love Him. This is the real message of the Book of Esther.

39

Haggai

By David C. Cooper, D.Min.

One of the most magnificent buildings ever constructed was Solomon's Temple in Jerusalem. It was completely destroyed by Nebuchadnezzar and the Babylonian army in the invasion of 586 B.C. After that destruction, the Jews were led into Babylonian captivity, where they lived for 70 years. After that time, the Persian Empire overthrew Babylon. Cyrus, the Persian king, gave the decree for the Jews to return home and for the Temple of God to be rebuilt in Jerusalem. The Temple was very important in Israeli history as the centerpiece of their worship. The word *temple* means "dwelling place or sanctuary." The Temple represented that place where God and man met together in worship and communion. It all began with Moses' Tabernacle, which was a temporary building, then Solomon built the permanent Temple. Therefore, when the Jews returned to Jerusalem, the first order of business was to rebuild the Temple, so once again they would have their sense of identity as the people of God.

Haggai, the Man

One of the men who was very instrumental in helping to rebuild the Temple was the prophet Haggai. God used him as an encourager to Zerubbabel, the governor of Judah, in the construction process itself. Haggai is called the "prophet of the Temple." It is believed that he was born during the Babylonian captivity and exile, and then he returned to Jerusalem with Zerubbabel in the first group of exiles that came out of Babylon (see Ezra 5:1; 6:14).

Crucial Times in Israel

Haggai's ministry came at a critical point in Israeli history—the construction of the Temple. The first order of business, in rebuilding the Temple under the leadership of Zerubbabel, was to build the altar. When they built the altar, the priests began to make the daily sacrifices. Next, they laid the foundation of the Temple, and everyone celebrated that the work was beginning. However, discouragement soon set in. Opposition came from the surrounding peoples, and the people of Israel became afraid. The workers stopped working, and for 14 years, all that stood was the foundation and the altar. Zerubbabel was very discouraged, because as a leader, he felt like he was unable to motivate the people to finish the work.

God stirred the hearts of Haggai and Zechariah. Together, they went and ministered to Zerubbabel and the people to get up and finish the work of rebuilding the Temple. Haggai delivered four messages of encouragement and challenged the people of God. These four messages, or sermons, were delivered over a period of about four months. Haggai was an encourager and a motivator. He was used by the Holy Spirit as a catalyst to cause the people to resume the work on the Temple. In Haggai 2:4 (the key verse), he speaks to the leaders: "'But now be strong, O Zerubbabel,' declares the Lord. 'Be strong, O Joshua son of Jehozadak, the high priest. Be strong, all ye people of the land,' declares the Lord, 'and work. For I am with you,' declares the Lord Almighty" (*NIV*). The message says: "Be strong, and work. For I am with you." Thus, they began the process again of rebuilding the Temple. They now had a sense of motivation that God was with them. They started in the year 520 B.C., and they finished in the year 516 B.C. The Temple was then dedicated to the Lord.

Four Messages

What were the messages that God gave Haggai, this prophet of the Temple, that stirred up the people and motivated them in the work of God? There is one phrase that appears throughout the Book of Haggai that is very important—"consider your ways." In other words, they were to give careful thought to their ways. Haggai challenged them to look very carefully at their lives, at their priorities, at their values, and to ask themselves this question: Am I really seeking first the kingdom of God? One of the reasons that the people had stopped working on the Temple was because the Temple was not that important to them. They were now in their own homes, and life was going good for them; consequently, they were neglecting the house of God. So, he told them to give careful thought to their ways, and to make sure that they were seeking first the kingdom of God. The four messages begin in the first chapter of Haggai.

1. *No excuse (Haggai 1:1-11)*. Now, the first message was very simple—"No excuse." Haggai's message to the people was that there was no excuse that this Temple was not rebuilt. There was no excuse for not doing the work of God. There was no excuse for giving in to fear and discouragement. There was no excuse for getting caught up in their own lifestyles to the extent of neglecting the house of God. Thus, Haggai brought a challenge to them from the Lord:

> Then the word of the Lord came through the prophet Haggai: "Is it a time for you yourselves to be living in your paneled houses, while this house remains a ruin?" Now this is what the Lord Almighty says: "Give careful thought to your ways. You have planted much, but have harvested little. You eat, but never have enough. You drink, but never have your fill. You put on clothes, but are not warm. You earn wages, only to put them in a purse with holes in it" (1:3-6, *NIV*).

God said because their priorities were not in order, everything they did seemed to come up a little short. They seemed to be living beneath their privileges that God had for them. Then, God asked them a very soul-searing question: "Is this the time for you to be living in your house, for you to be living the good life, while this house, this Temple remains a ruin?" (see 1:4). And the people then responded to the Word of God in verse 12: "Then Zerubbabel son of Shealtiel, Joshua . . . the high priest, and the whole remnant of the people obeyed the voice of the Lord . . . and the message of the prophet Haggai, because the Lord their God had sent him. And the people feared the Lord" (*NIV*). They honored the Lord. "Then Haggai, the Lord's messenger, gave this message of the Lord to the people: 'I am with you'" (v. 14, *NIV*).

So, the first message was really a message of confrontation; it was a message of challenge. There was no excuse for the Temple of God to remain in ruins. When Haggai brought that challenge, it seemed to stir a note within them, and they obeyed the voice of God. It started with the leadership of Zerubbabel, and then the priesthood, and then the whole remnant of the people. They began to take the challenge to build a house of God, and they came together and began to work. Verse 15 notes that this took place during the reign of King Darius, king of Persia. Now, the people had a mind to work. Not only did they say they were going to do it, but they followed through and quit making excuses. That is the spiritual lesson to be learned from Haggai. Do not make excuses about why things are not done. Check out priorities and put the things of God first. First things first—that was the message of Haggai to the people, and they responded.

2. A greater glory (Haggai 2:1-9). Now came the second message. This message was very important to these people, but it may have sounded a little strange to them. The second message was a message of a greater glory. He said that there was going to be a greater glory on this new Temple than there was on the Temple of Solomon. Historically, the Temple that Zerubbabel built was much smaller than Solomon's Temple. It was not a magnificent structure in comparison to what Solomon had built; in fact, it took seven years to build that great Temple. It was one of the most magnificent structures ever built. But Zerubbabel's Temple was smaller, and the people who knew the history of the great Solomonic Temple somehow felt as if this Temple just did not measure up. Consequently, God sent Haggai back to them with a second message.

Haggai talked about the greater glory to come.

> This is what the Lord Almighty says: "In a little while I will once more shake the heavens and the earth, the sea, and the dry land. I will shake all nations, and the desired of all nations will come, and I will fill this house with glory," says the Lord Almighty. "The silver is mine and the gold is mine," declares the Lord Almighty. "The glory of this present house, will be greater than the glory of the former house," says the Lord Almighty. "And in this place, I will grant peace" (2:6-9, *NIV*).

Shalom in Hebrew means "the blessings of God." Peace, for believers today, is the absence of conflict or the absence of war or the absence of stress. But peace in the Hebrew is not the absence of something; it is the fullness of the blessings of God. In essence, God is saying that in this place, He will grant His *shalom*—His peace—the fullness of His blessing. What a message of encouragement to these people to know that there would be a greater glory that would enter the Temple of Zerubbabel, even beyond the glory of Solomon's Temple. One can read a fascinating account in 2 Chronicles 5:13, 14 about what happened when Solomon finished building the first Temple. The priests and the Levites came together, and the choirs led an incredible praise service. When they worshiped the Lord, the Bible says, the glory of the Lord filled the Temple. This glory was manifested in a Shekinah cloud with a magnificent brilliance that was so overwhelming the priests could not even stand before that cloud to minister or perform their duties. They fell down before the Lord in the presence of this incredible manifestation of the glory of God. Yet Haggai told them that even though the Temple was smaller, there would be a greater glory.

One might wonder what could be a greater glory. The greater glory comes when the desired of nations comes, and the desire of all nations is the Messiah himself. This was the very Temple that Jesus ministered in. Now, Herod, the king of Israel under Rome, who came to power in 40 B.C., was involved in a lot of construction projects from about 20 B.C.on. Herod did enlarge Zerubbabel's Temple, and it was that Temple where Jesus came, where Jesus taught, where Jesus ministered. It was also here where He delivered His final messages during the week of Passover. It was also here that He confronted the scribes and the Pharisees, and in the Gospels, Jesus was found in the Temple courts. It was here that He came during the Triumphal Entry, and people shouted, "Hosanna, blessed is He who comes in the name of the Lord" (see Luke 19:38). He is that greater glory of which Haggai spoke.

3. *"I will bless you" (Haggai 2:10-19).* In this message, God addressed the priests of the land through Haggai. It was very important that those priests live a holy life and that they lead the people of God in the way that they should walk. This third

message was simple; it was a promise from God: "I will bless you." God said in Chapter 1, in the first message, that they had eaten but were never full. They drank but never seemed to be satisfied. They earned wages, only to put them in a purse with holes. It seemed like every time they were getting ahead, they seemed to fall back. In other words, they were not really experiencing the fullness of the blessings of God. In the third message, Haggai reflected upon that and had the priests reflect upon the fact that they had not really experienced the blessings of God because they were not really living in holiness. Haggai said, "Now give careful thought to this from this day on—consider how things were before one stone was laid on another in the Lord's temple" (2:15, *NIV*). Before the Temple began to be rebuilt, consider how things were in the Babylonian invasion: "'When anyone came to a heap of twenty measures, there were only ten. When anyone went to a wine vat to draw fifty measures, there were only twenty. I struck all the work of your hands with blight, mildew and hail, yet you did not turn to me,' declares the Lord" (vv. 16, 17, *NIV*). They were disciplined, but they still did not repent. But now the people, through the revivals of Ezra and Nehemiah, were once again living as the people of God. They were living in holiness and they were living in obedience. "From this day on . . . give careful thought to the day when the foundation of the Lord's temple was laid. Give careful thought: Is there yet any seed left in the barn? Until now, the vine and the fig tree, the pomegranate and the olive tree have not borne fruit" (vv. 18, 19, *NIV*). They had not really experienced the full blessings of God. But then comes this beautiful

490

statement: "'From this day on, I will bless you'" (v. 19). That was the heart of the Mosaic covenant—the pronouncing of the blessings of God upon His people. Nehemiah led these people in a covenant renewal. They rebuilt the city; they rebuilt the Temple; but now their hearts had been rebuilt. God said, because now that they had returned to Him, not only because they had returned to Jerusalem, but also because their hearts had returned to Him, He would bless them.

4. *Messiah will come (Haggai 2:20-23)*. The fourth and the final message was very brief. However, in this message, Haggai tells the people that the Messiah will come. This is one of the great messianic passages of the Old Testament. "'On that day,' declares the Lord Almighty, 'I will take you, my servant Zerubbabel . . . and I will make you like my signet ring, for I have chosen you,' declares the Lord Almighty" (2:23, *NIV*). God was making a promise to Zerubbabel, the governor in Judah, who was a descendant of King David. He was the last person in the Davidic line to actually occupy a royal position of leadership in Israel, and God gave him a promise. He said, "I will make you my signet ring, and I will bless you, for I have chosen you." This is a messianic passage. God is not only speaking to Zerubbabel, but this blessing is also a blessing about the Messiah. "I have chosen you" is language that he has borrowed from Isaiah, who spoke of the Messiah in Isaiah 42:1. He speaks of the Messiah as "My chosen servant." Zerubbabel here is really the one receiving the blessing, but the blessing is about the Messiah. The phrase "On that day, I will make you my signet ring," means *that day* is the day of the

Messiah—the coming of Jesus into the world. "I will make you my signet ring." This statement means that the signet ring—the ring of the king—was used when a king passed a law. The law, or decree, was sealed with this signet ring. The signet ring, then, was that symbol which declared the authority of the king to fulfill what had been decreed. What God was saying here was that He was going to fulfill the decree to bring the Messiah. God had even raised up Zerubbabel as a descendant of David to remind the nation that there would come that One—that ultimate One—through the line of David, and He would rule as King of kings and Lord of lords. In Luke 1:32, the angel Gabriel appeared to Mary and foretold the birth of Jesus. It was declared that He would be great and be the Son of the Most High, and that God would give to Him the throne of His father David. So, Zerubbabel was symbolically a signet ring—he was a living testimony that God was going to fulfill the covenant given through Abraham, that through Abraham a seed would come, and through Him, all nations would be blessed. A promise of the Messiah, and the message of Haggai in that last verse is very simple—God always fulfills His promises.

Conclusion

Today in the New Testament sense, believers have a signet ring. They have a guarantee of all that God has promised, not only in this life, but also in eternity. That signet ring for the believers is the Holy Spirit. Paul says of the Holy Spirit in Ephesians 1:13, that God marked believers with a seal the same way that a king would use that signet ring to guarantee the decree. In other words, God marked His people with the seal—the promise of the Holy Spirit—that was a deposit, guaranteeing their inheritance. So, the Holy Spirit who lives within believers today is a guarantee—Messiah will come again as King of kings and Lord of lords.

Haggai's message was a message of hope; it was a message of challenge; it was a message to tell people to check out their priorities. They were living in their own homes, life was going along great, but they let the house of God remain in ruins. "Get your priorities in order," he said. "Do what God has called you to do, and God will bless you abundantly." Haggai continued, saying, "Give careful thought to your ways; make sure that you're not putting yourself first; make sure that you're not getting less than what God planned for you." That brings to mind the words of Jesus in Matthew 6:33: "But seek ye first the kingdom of God, and his righteousness; and all these things shall be added unto you." That really was the message of Haggai, the prophet of the Temple.

40 Zechariah

By David C. Cooper, D.Min.

One of the most overlooked prophetic books of the Bible is the Book of Zechariah. Yet, Zechariah contains the largest, single collection of messianic prophecies of any book in the entire Word of God. Zechariah is known as the "prophet of the long-range vision." He looked down the corridor of time, some 500 years before the time of Jesus, and saw with incredible insight and detail, the coming of Jesus. In His first coming, he saw Him in His incarnation as the Suffering Servant. Then in His second coming, he saw Him as the Conquering King.

Zechariah, the Man and His Times

Zechariah came with Zerubbabel and the other exiles back to Jerusalem with the first group that came out of Babylon. Haggai, the prophet, came at the same time. Haggai and Zechariah began their preaching ministries together. They were used by the Lord to encourage the people in the work on the Temple. The Temple altar was built first then the foundation. But because of discouragement, the Temple project stopped for 14 years. It was through Haggai's preaching to Zerubbabel, the governor, and the people, that the work resumed. Zechariah came along at the same time and spoke personally to Zerubbabel, encouraging him that this work would be accomplished "'not by might nor by power, but by my Spirit' says the Lord" (4:6, *NIV*). Haggai's messages spanned only a period of about four months, but Zechariah's ministry continued for many years longer than Haggai's. He ministered in Israel during the reign of Artaxerxes, the king of Persia. Like Jeremiah and Ezekiel, Zechariah was not only a prophet, but he was also a priest. He grew up in Babylon. He learned the ways of Babylon and was familiar with the history. He was a prophet who grew up in exile. But when he returned home, God used him as an instrument in the restoration of the nation and the rebuilding of the Temple.

Again, it is his insight into the coming of the Messiah that makes Zechariah so unique. In Zechariah 1:1, there is an interesting play on the names mentioned in Zechariah's own family line. These names reveal the spiritual theme of Zechariah. "In the eighth month of the second year of Darius, the word of the Lord came to the prophet Zechariah son of Berekiah, the son of Iddo" (1:1, *NIV*). The name *Zechariah* means "the Lord remembers," which means that the Lord remembers His covenant with Israel; God remembers His promises. The name *Berekiah* means "the Lord blesses," and the name *Iddo* means "timely." If the three names are put together, they reveal the spiritual meaning of the book, and that is why it is introduced this way. It is a message to Israel through this prophet that the Lord will remember His covenant and bless His people in a timely manner. God, in His own sovereign timing had brought an end to that 70-year captivity and brought them home. Consequently, one can be assured that God is going to fulfill all the promises of His Word.

Looking back at the history of Israel today, one knows that what Jeremiah said about the 70-year captivity came to pass. They returned home as Jeremiah and others said they would. Looking at the Book of Daniel and all the problems he saw of the coming of the Gentile world powers, one realizes that they too have come to pass. For them, that was future prophecy, today that is past history. But, looking at the prophecies of the second coming of Jesus, one can have that same kind of assurance that is stated in the introduction of this book: the Lord will bless; the Lord remembers; and God does what He does in a timely manner, according to His will. So, the prophecies are undergirded by the understanding that God watches over His Word to perform it and fulfill it in a timely fashion.

Literary Divisions

The Book of Zechariah consists, in its beginning portion, of eight visions that Zechariah experienced. These eight visions are found in Chapters 1 through 8. The Book of Zechariah can be divided into three sections. Section one consists of the eight visions of the prophet: Chapters 1 through 8. Section two describes Christ as the Suffering Servant: Chapters 9 through 11. Section three describes Christ as the Conquering King, the Second Coming, the

Battle of Armageddon, the new heaven and new earth, and New Jerusalem: Chapters 12 through 14.

Eight Visions

Zechariah had eight visions of things to come.

1. *A Man Among the Myrtle Trees (1:7-17).* In the first vision, Zechariah saw a man among the myrtle trees. The vision meant that God would restore and prosper Judah and Jerusalem, but He would also judge the nations that persecuted her. The promise from God that came with this vision was "I am very jealous for Jerusalem and Zion" (1:14, *NIV*). God jealously loves Jerusalem, and He is going to preserve and protect her. Even in recent times, one can read about the rebirth of Jerusalem and the rebirth of the nation of Israel in 1948, when the United Nations declared Israel as an independent state. That also was prophesied in the Old Testament of the final, last days' restoration. God is jealous for His people.

2. *Four Horns and Four Craftsmen (1:18-20).* The four horns represent the four Gentile nations that persecuted and scattered Israel—Assyria, Egypt, Babylon, and Medo-Persia. The four craftsmen represent God's angelic powers to defeat those nations as God preserved Israel even through her exile.

3. *A Man With a Measuring Line (Chapter 2).* The man, or the angel, measuring out the city is a description of God taking a spiritual inventory of the city. It is a proclamation of the restoration of Jerusalem, not only in past history, but also in the future—God's hand is on Jerusalem. Again, there is a promise in Zechariah 2:12, "The Lord . . . will again choose Jerusalem." Jerusalem is the city of

God, and God will use Jerusalem to do great things for His glory.

4. *Clean Garments for the High Priest (Chapter 3)*. The fourth vision in the Book of Zechariah is one of the great stories in the Bible—"Clean Garments for the High Priest." In Chapter 3, Joshua, the high priest, is seen in this vision standing before God, and Satan is standing right next to him to accuse him. The name *Satan* means "accuser or adversary." He is accusing the high priest of not being fit for service—he is dressed in filthy clothes. But God tells the angel to take off his filthy garments and put clean garments on him. Then they put the turban on his head. This is a marvelous portrayal of how even today believers feel something of a Satanic accusation. They feel an inner voice saying they are not qualified, they are not good enough, they are not holy enough. However, all they have to do is remember that they are what they are by the grace of God. It is God's grace that has taken off the filthy garments—the old life. It is God's grace that has clothed them in the righteousness of Christ.

5. *The Gold Lampstand and the Two Olive Trees (Chapter 4)*. The fifth vision seen by Zechariah is the golden lampstand and the two olive trees. The olive supplies the source for the burning lamps. The seven golden lampstands, the menorah, burned in the Holy Place in the Temple. Those lamps represent God's light in the world—Jesus, the light of the world. But in Revelation, the church is described as the lampstand (1:19-20). The oil is symbolic of the anointing of the Holy Spirit. It is the power of the Holy Spirit that supplies the light in the lampstand. This was a message for Zerubbabel who

was discouraged when the Temple project had ceased its construction during the 14-year interval. Zechariah met him on the Temple foundation and gave him the message that God was going to use him to finish this project. But it would be done "'not by might nor by power, but by my Spirit,' says the Lord Almighty" (4:6, *NIV*). Even today, even for the church which is the lampstand, the light of Christ in the world, it is the oil of the Holy Spirit that is the source by which the light can burn in the church.

6. *The Flying Scroll (5:1-4).* The sixth vision is the vision of the flying scroll, which was a solemn word of judgment pronounced on those who had disobeyed the law of God. The prophet tells them that what they have sown, they are going to reap. It is a vision that underscores the principle of sowing and reaping that is found in Galatians. "Do not be deceived: God cannot be mocked. A man reaps what he sows. The one who sows to please his sinful nature, will reap destruction; the one who sows to please the Spirit, from the Spirit will reap eternal life" (6:7, 8, *NIV*). The vision of the scroll is a warning to them about the law of sowing and reaping. They will reap the evil that they have sown.

7. *The Woman in a Basket (5:5-11).* The seventh vision is about a woman in a basket. The woman here represents wickedness, and the basket is a means by which wickedness is being carried out of the land. It represents God taking away the sin of the land, since the people have turned their hearts back to God in real repentance. Perhaps the reason that a woman is used in this figure is because the Hebrew word for wickedness is actually feminine in gender. However, in this vision, two other women

actually carry the basket out of Israel back to Babylon. So, there are two other women that describe this intervention of God to carry wickedness out of Israel. It is a description of a purging of a nation, of the people giving their hearts back to God, of people turning away from their sins, of a deliverance from a nation.

8. *The Four Chariots (6:1-8)*. These chariots were drawn by four horses, which are very similar to the four horsemen of the Apocalypse found in Revelation 6:1 and following. These four horses are angelic messengers, and the bottom line of this vision is that God assures that the nation which has come back home will now enjoy a season of rest and peace from her enemies. Thus, Zechariah is a man of visions, and those visions were messages that he gave to his own people. But beyond seeing into his times and encouraging Zerubbabel and the people and preaching to his times, he again is the "prophet of the long-range vision." Again, the largest single collection of messianic prophecies in any book in the Bible is found in the Book of Zechariah. Zechariah sees something of Jesus that many people missed in the time of Christ—he saw the twofold coming of the Messiah. He saw the Messiah coming as the Suffering Servant that Isaiah said He would be: "Wounded for our transgressions and bruised for our iniquities" (53:5). And, he also saw the second coming of the Messiah as the Conquering King.

Messiah, the Suffering Servant

Zechariah 11:12, 13 tells how the Messiah will be betrayed: He would be sold out for 30 pieces of silver. Then he speaks of the potter's field—a burial place for Jews who did not belong to the city. Judas Iscariot received the sum of 30 pieces of silver from the members of the Sanhedrin who took him up on his offer to betray Jesus. Because Judas hanged himself, that money was actually used to purchase a field—due to the fact that it was blood money. As incredible as it is, Zechariah actually foretold that. Zechariah saw something even more fascinating— the suffering of the Messiah. "And I will pour out on the house of David and the inhabitants of Jerusalem a spirit of grace and supplication. They will look on me, the one they have pierced, and they will mourn for him as one mourns for an only child, and grieve bitterly for him as one grieves for a firstborn son" (12:10, *NIV*). The Messiah actually says, "They will look upon Me, the one they have pierced." The Revelator talks about this in Revelation 1:7 when he announces the second coming of Jesus. "Behold, he cometh with clouds; and every eye shall see him, and they also which pierced him: and all kindreds of the earth shall wail because of him." Not only that, but he also declares something that will happen when Messiah is pierced. In fact, Jesus quoted from this passage in Zechariah on the night of the Last Supper when He talked about His crucifixion and what would happen to His disciples. "Awake, O sword, against my shepherd, against the man who is close to me!' declares the Lord Almighty. 'Strike the shepherd, and the sheep will be scattered, and I will turn my hand against the little ones'" (13:7, *NIV*). And God goes on to talk about the fact that He will bring them through the fire and refine them. That very passage is the passage that Jesus quoted when He talked about the fact that He would be stricken, as the Shepherd in the Crucifixion, and that the sheep also would be scattered. And of course, that was what happened. In Gethsemane, the Bible says that all of the disciples left Him; they fled for their lives. Zechariah 13:1 foretells what will happen when Messiah is pierced. "On that day a fountain will be opened to the house of David and the inhabitants of Jerusalem, to cleanse them from sin and impurity" (*NIV*). That happened on the Cross. That day a fountain was opened when the soldier thrust the spear into His side and out flowed blood and water, symbolic of cleansing. That was Zechariah's vision of Messiah, the Suffering Servant.

Messiah, the Conquering King

Zechariah also saw the Messiah coming as the Conquering King. In fact, Zechariah had a great deal to say about the end times and His glorious return in Chapters 12 through 14.

MESSIAH, THE ROYAL PRIEST

Zechariah foretells that the Messiah will be a royal priest in Chapter 6, verses 9 through15. The Messiah will fill the role of both king and priest. It is interesting to note that there are many scholars who taught before the time of Christ that there would actually be two Messiahs. One would be a priest from the line of Aaron; the other would be a king from the line of David. But the Scripture teaches that the Messiah fills both the role of king and priest. This is typified in the story where Joshua, the high priest, was crowned with a crown of gold and silver. It was placed upon his head and declared that he would be the branch of Jehovah. That was a prefiguring of the fact that the Messiah would be the One who was King of kings, but He would also be the High Priest for the world.

MESSIAH'S TRIUMPHAL ENTRY

It is interesting that Zechariah actually foretells the day that the Messiah would come to Jerusalem riding on a donkey. That was exactly what happened on the Triumphal Entry day when Jesus came into Jerusalem (see Matthew 21:4, 5). The prophet Zechariah said, "See, your king comes to you . . . gentle and riding on a donkey, on a colt, the foal of a donkey" (9:9, *NIV*). When kings came to a city in peace in ancient times, they always rode on a donkey. The king rode on a horse only as a symbol of war. The donkey was a symbol of peace and blessing, and Christ came, declaring the fact that He was the fulfillment of Zechariah's messianic word. When Jesus came into Jerusalem on the Triumphal Entry day, it was an intentional declaration that He was God's Messiah for Jerusalem, and the people recognized it. They understood that prophecy and that was why they waved the palm branches and shouted "Hosanna . . . blessed is He who comes in the name of the Lord" (Matthew 21:9, *NIV*). *Hosanna* means "Lord, save us." They looked to Jesus as their deliverer; they looked to Him as the fulfillment of Zechariah's prophecy.

MESSIAH'S SECOND COMING

In Chapter 14, Zechariah sees a glimpse of the Second Coming, the Battle of Armageddon, the Kingdom Age, and the millennial reign of the Lord Jesus Christ.

1. *The seige of Jerusalem (14:1, 2)*. First, Zechariah saw the siege of Jerusalem: "A day of the Lord is coming when your plunder will be divided among you. I will gather all the nations to Jerusalem to fight against it" (14:1, 2, *NIV*). Thus, he describes that final siege of Jerusalem. That will actually take place during the Tribulation period in the Battle of Armageddon. This final siege of the Holy City is also described in Revelation 16:16-21 as the Battle of Armageddon. "Jerusalem will be trampled on by the Gentiles," Christ said, "until the times of the Gentiles are fulfilled" (Luke 21:24, *NIV*). The last time that the Gentiles, or pagans, will surround and besiege the city is during the Tribulation period.

2. *The return of Messiah (14:3-5)*. Second, Zechariah saw Jerusalem surrounded in the tribulation hour, which is the time when Jesus actually comes from Heaven and returns to earth. Notice how he puts it in Chapter 14: "Then the Lord will go out and fight against those nations, as he fights in the day of battle. On that day his feet will stand on the Mount of Olives, east of Jerusalem, and the Mount of Olives will be split in two" (v. 3, *NIV*). This will happen as a result of a great earthquake. He explains that when the nations surround Jerusalem in that Armageddon portrait, that Christ actually returns to the Mount of Olives as He makes His Triumphal Entry into Jerusalem. He notices that after Jesus returns, that they will enter the Kingdom Age—the age under the reign of Messiah himself. "Then the Lord my God will come," he says, "and all the holy ones with him" (v. 5, *NIV*). That was also what John saw in Revelation 19:11-16, when he saw Christ coming on the white horse and all the armies of

heaven following Him and He treads the winepress with the wrath and fierceness of God Almighty. Written upon His vesture and His thigh is the title King of kings and Lord of lords.

3. *Cosmic changes (14:6-8).* Zechariah also saw that same phenomenon happening when Jesus comes and all the holy ones are with Him. He says that the whole world will change; there will even be ecological and cosmic changes (14:6-8). He says that there will be no more night: when evening comes, there will be light (v. 6). "On that day, living water will flow out from Jerusalem" (v. 8, *NIV*). That same kind of language is found in the Book of Revelation when there is a new heaven and a new earth and a new Jerusalem (see 22:1, 2). All of that is apocalyptic symbolism of the fact that life on earth will be changed. A state of incredible peace and prosperity under the rule and reign of Jesus.

4. *The Messianic Kingdom established (14:9-11).* Zechariah saw the establishment of the Messianic Kingdom. "The Lord will be king over the whole earth. On that day there will be one Lord, and his name the only name" (v. 9, *NIV*). That was exactly what Isaiah said about the coming of the Messiah: "The knowledge of the Lord will cover the earth as the waters cover the sea. And all nations will go up to Jerusalem and they will all worship the Lord and the Word of the Lord will come forth from Zion itself" (see Isaiah 11:9). That says that when Jesus returns, there will be a new Kingdom, a millennial kingdom, and Christ himself will reign as Lord over all.

5. *The judgment of the nations (14:12-15).* Zechariah describes the judgment of the nations in Chapter 14, verses 12-15. Revelation describes the

Great White Throne Judgment and the judgment of the Antichrist's kingdom as the last nation to persecute the people of God.

6. *The universal worship of the King (14:16-19).* In verses 16 through 19 of this last chapter of Zechariah, he says that when Jesus returns and sets as Judge and the Antichrist's kingdom is destroyed, that the whole world will be filled with worship for the living God. "Then the survivors from all the nations that have attacked Jerusalem will go up year after year to worship the King, the Lord Almighty, and to celebrate the Feast of Tabernacles" (v. 16, *NIV*).

7. *The nature of the Millennial Kingdom: holiness (14:20, 21).* Finally, Zechariah describes the nature of the Millennial Kingdom when Christ rules, and that nature is holiness. "On that day, 'Holy to the Lord' will be inscribed on the bells of the horses, and the cooking pots in the Lord's house will be like the sacred bowls in front of the altar. Holy to the Lord. . . . On that day, there will no longer be a Canaanite in the house of the Lord Almighty" (14:20, 21, *NIV*). He does not mean Canaanite in the sense of people or in terms of the geographical location. It is a word that refers to those who are rebellious and wicked and who have turned their hearts away from God and who do not honor the Lord. When Jesus returns, holiness is the order of the day. The wall between the secular and the sacred is torn down in this Messianic Age. Holiness is the quality of public life—that is what is meant by the "bells of the horses." Holiness is the quality of religious life—the "cooking pots in the Lord's house." Holiness is the quality of everyday life—every pot, even the common pots and pans, are holy. What is meant is that

in ordinary life, people live out their lives in a way that is holy before God.

What does it mean to be holy? It means to be set apart from the world and under God for His exclusive use. Today, one does not hear much about holiness anymore, but holiness is a beautiful word. It is not a word of legalism; it is not a word about a long list of rules and regulations; it really means Christlikeness. As Zechariah talked about the holiness of the Millennial Kingdom, he was also saying that if that is going to be the quality of life at that time, then one should also live holy today. Moses said in Leviticus, "I am the Lord who brought you up out of Egypt to be your God; therefore be holy, because I am holy" (11:45, *NIV*). This same verse is quoted in 1 Peter 1:16: "For it is written: 'Be holy, because I am holy'" (*NIV*). *Holiness* really means "to be different." It does not mean to be weird or strange, but it does mean to be different. It means that believers march to a different drumbeat than those in the world who do not know God.

Conclusion

Since the meaning of *holiness* is "to be different," this means that everything in the Messianic Age will be different. The Temple is holy, because it is different from other buildings. The Sabbath is holy, because it is different from other days. The tithe is holy, because it is different from other monies. The Bible is holy, because it is different from other books. The priests were called holy, because they were different from other men. The nation of Israel and the church are called holy, because they are different from other nations. The sacrifices offered in the Old Testament were called holy, because those animals were different from other animals. The people of God are holy, because they live by the holiness of Christ.

Zechariah, the prophet of a long-range vision, prophesied during the time when his nation was trying to rebuild its Temple and get back on its feet. Israel was a nation wondering who they were when God sent the prophets Haggai and Zechariah to encourage them. And Zechariah reminded them that they were the holy people of God, and he gave them a marvelous message of hope.

Zechariah 14:7 makes a simple statement that really is a timeless word of hope to every person. He was talking about the Messianic Kingdom, but it is a spiritual principle: when evening comes, there will be light. When there is darkness, when there is failure, as it had been in the Babylonian exile, when people do not do it right, when they stumble and fall, when they do not even keep the commandments of God, when they have come under pressure and oppression, when they have been attacked, when trouble and difficulties come—when evening comes— there will be light. God always shines the light of His grace and His hope in every situation, and this was the essence of the message of Zechariah—the prophet of the long-range vision.

Joel

By David C. Cooper, D.Min.

One of the most fascinating aspects of the Bible is its prophetic element. In the Old Testament, one can find some 300 plus prophecies of the coming of the Messiah into the world. In the New Testament, there are 318 promises and prophecies about the return of the Lord Jesus Christ. In the Book of Joel and the writings of this prophet, he gives a glimpse of the Day of the Lord and of the return of Christ. Not only did he speak to the times in which he lived, but he also spoke of the last days as well.

The Man and His Message

Dating the Book of Joel is somewhat difficult, and scholars debate as to when exactly he lived and ministered. There are those who see Joel as a contemporary of the prophet Elijah, perhaps ministering to Joash, the king of Judah, between 835 B.C. and 815 B.C. But other scholars date Joel much later in the postexilic period. For the purpose of this study, Joel will be placed in the context of the postexilic period of Israeli history.

511

The name *Joel* simply means "Jehovah is God." Joel called upon the elders and the priests and the people of the land to repent in order to escape divine judgment. He predicted and talked about the outpouring of the Holy Spirit on the Day of Pentecost. He also foresaw the final Day of the Lord, a glimpse of Armageddon, and the Messianic Kingdom to come. The Day of the Lord is a phrase that is used in a variety of ways in the Bible. The Day of the Lord can refer to any kind of divine, dramatic intervention by God—it is God stretching His hand down into history and doing something extraordinary. The Jews referred to that in the Old Testament scriptures as the Day of the Lord. For example, Joel saw a locust invasion, a drought coming to the land. Moses talked about the same thing in the Mosaic law—that one of the results of disobedience and sin would be drought in the land. Joel actually referred to this invasion of locusts as the Day of the Lord, historically (see Joel 1:15).

The Day of the Lord is much larger that just these kinds of breaking into history that God does. The Day of the Lord certainly was the coming of Jesus as the Messiah. However, the Day of the Lord, in a New Testament sense, is the second coming of Christ. Furthermore, there will be an ultimate Day of the Lord when God brings an end to this present age and ushers in the age to come. In the Hebrew thought, the concept of the Day of the Lord always contains two elements: one, a punishment for sin, and two, the peace and prosperity for the people of God. So, the Day of the Lord is always something like a double-edged sword. It is a warning of judgment—there is divine judgment, historically, and there will be a divine judgment, ultimately. But with that judgment comes God's redemption and His grace. The whole purpose of judgment is always to bring men to His heart and to bring men back to Him. So, both punishment and blessing are connected in this idea of the Day of the Lord. So, whether Joel was talking about a drought in his time or whether today's believers are talking about the coming of Jesus at the end of the world, the phrase "the Day of the Lord" always contains the two elements of punishment and peace.

A Call to Repentance

Joel's basic message to his people was repent. Likewise, John the Baptist and other prophets preached "Repent, for the kingdom of heaven is near" (Matthew 3:2, NIV). In other words, men should repent now, because God's power is breaking into their world. God is doing something today the same as He did in Joel's day.

The second chapter of Joel might really be regarded as the heart of Joel's message to his people about repentance. "'Even now,' declares the Lord, 'return to me with all your heart, with fasting and weeping and mourning. Rend your heart and not your garments. Return to the Lord your God, for he is gracious and compassionate, slow to anger and abounding in love, and he relents from sending calamity'" (2:12, 13, NIV). Anyone who teaches that God has some kind of joy in judgment is not teaching accurately. That is not what the Bible teaches. God "relents from sending calamity." Most calamity, most judgment is really the outworking of human sin. The best definition of divine judgment is that man reaps what he sows. In fact, there is an urgency in the following passage to repent:

> "Blow the trumpet in Zion, declare a holy fast, call a sacred assembly. Gather the people, consecrate the assembly; bring together the elders, gather the children, those nursing at the breast. Let the bridegroom leave his room and the bride her chamber. Let the priests, who minister before the Lord, weep between the temple porch and the altar. Let them say, 'Spare your people, O Lord. Do not make your inheritance an object of scorn, a byword among the nations'" (vv. 16, 17, *NIV*).

In other words, the people should pray that they do not fall into obscurity. They should pray that God stirs them and that they remain His people. "Why should they say among the peoples, 'Where is their God?'" (v. 17, *NIV*). Why should they fall again the way that they fell in the Babylonian invasion? Why should the nations even look at Israel as a byword, as something of the past? So, their prayer is that God would stir them and God would minister to them and that God would lead them to repentance so that they might really be the people of God, that they might live out the glory of their name, Israel.

God, through Joel, called His people to a sacred assembly. "Blow the trumpet in Zion, call a sacred assembly" (v. 15). And the whole point of that was repentance. "Return to me with all your heart. . . . Rend your heart and not your garments" (vv. 12, 13, *NIV*). What he meant by that was that real repentance is not external. It does not mean that they just go to the Temple or that they would offer a sacrifice; it is always a matter of the heart. Jesus pointed this out in His own time when he quoted Isaiah. In Matthew 15:8, Jesus said, "Isaiah was right when he said that these people worship Me with their lips, but their hearts are far from Me (see also Isaiah 29:13). Joel said that it is the condition of the heart. The first and greatest of all commandments says: "Love the Lord your God with all your heart" (Matthew 22:37, NIV). That means the sum total of one's personality and whole being. Thus, religion is about one's personal walk and relationship with God; it is about a heart relationship—a love relationship—with God; it is not about the externals. So, Joel called the people to repent, because if they persisted in sin, they would bring a drought upon the land and bring them out from under all that God had planned for them in His blessings.

Now, Joel was a man who interpreted the times in which he lived. Not many people can do that. In fact, there are not many people who can look at history today and make sense of it. We always talk about judgment being something in the future, but judgment happens even now. Just like divine blessings happen, by the same token, men reap what they sow. In fact, it can be seen around the nations of the world. People have sown to communism, they have sown to paganism, and now they are reaping a spiritual and economic drought all around the world—the natural outworking of sin. That is divine judgment.

Joel was able to interpret the times in which he lived and make sense out of it. When he looked at the invasion of the locusts, he saw it as the result of the people's sins. Joel called them the "army of the

Lord" in Chapter 2. And, he says that because this drought is coming, it ought to be a catalyst to motivate the people to repent before God so that the blessing will come and not the drought.

People interpret this locust invasion in different ways. Some see it as an allegory about a spiritual invasion; however, the best and soundest way of looking at this is to see that this was actually a locust invasion. It was a drought, and even Moses talked about the fact that the drought was an act of the discipline of the Lord. Joel used that as a call to repentance for the people, for the priests, and for the elders. He used that in the sense of the Day of the Lord being near. God was breaking in, and He was breaking in with discipline. God was disciplining in order to bring the people back to Himself. He gives an incredible description of the locust invasion: "Blow the trumpet" (2:1), he says. The imagery here is apocalyptic as he talks about the nations and ecological disturbances and the army of the Lord that is coming. And then he makes a statement in verse 11 that John uses in the Book of Revelation. "The Lord thunders at the head of his army; his forces are beyond number, and mighty are those who obey his command" (*NIV*). He is talking about the locust invasion, when he says, "The day of the Lord is great; it is dreadful. Who can endure it?" (v. 11, *NIV*). The ultimate Day of the Lord is the Great Tribulation period and the final judgment. That very same statement and question are found in Revelation 6:16, 17. John saw a seven-sealed scroll, which the Lamb—Jesus—breaks open. He saw history unfolding under the sixth seal: he saw cosmic disturbances, the moon turning to blood, the sun darkened like sackcloth, and the stars falling from the sky. Then, he says that all men, great and small, free and rich, call to the mountains and the rocks: "Fall on us, and hide us from the face of him that sitteth on the throne, and from the wrath of the Lamb: for the great day of his wrath is come; and who shall be able to stand?" The language of the Revelator is the same as the Old Testament. It is important to always connect the symbolism, the imagery, and the language of the apocalyptic writers of the Old Testament with that which is found in the New Testament—in particular, the Book of Revelation.

Foreseeing the Future

Joel also sees into the future. He sees the end times and he sees the ultimate Day of the Lord. In theology, the word *eschatology* means "the study of the last things." Everybody is interested in eschatology and in what happens at the return of Christ and the end of the age. Much debate and differing opinions have been voiced about when all of these events will occur: the Rapture, the Tribulation, the Second Coming, and so forth. It is interesting to learn what the ancient Hebrews believed, because the theology in the New Testament about the return of Christ and the end times is a parallel to what is taught in the Old Testament. Therefore, it is necessary, first of all, to understand the basic Hebrew comprehension of eschatology, the last days, and the Day of the Lord.

Eschatology in the Old Testament, the way the Hebrews looked at the Day of the Lord and the end times, can be explained by a very simple model. First of all, they talked about the present age. Today is the present age—history here and now. It is the day of evil, but it is also a day of divine blessings. It is a day where Satan actually is alive and working. The Book of Job talks about the very presence of evil in the figure of the devil as he accused Job and attacked him. The Book of Genesis talks about how Satan deceived Adam and Eve, and now man lives in a land of thorns and thistles. So, this is the present age. It is a world that is under the curse of sin, yet God has redeemed mankind in the midst of it. Believers live by the power of His Spirit and have the hope of an age to come. So, the Hebrews believed that there would also be an age to come.

The age to come is the Messianic Age, an age of peace, an age of prosperity, an age of blessing, an age where there is an end to the presence of sin, an age where even the earth is delivered from the curse and presence of sin. Isaiah says in Chapter 65: "I saw a new heaven and a new earth," (v. 17). This is the same language that John used in Revelation 21:1: "Then I saw a new heaven and a new earth" (*NIV*). So, the age to come is the age of the Messiah. It is a perfect age, an age of peace and the blessings of God. Ephesians Chapter 1, uses the same terminology. After Paul's prayer in Ephesians 1:17 and following, he says that God appointed Jesus to be the head over everything, "not only in this present age, but also in the one to come" (v. 21, *NIV*). Again, in Hebrews Chapter 6, the same kind of language is used when he says that believers today who have received Christ and the power of His Spirit, have tasted the "powers of the coming age" (v. 5, *NIV*).

What will move mankind out of this present age into the age to come? The Hebrews taught all through

518

the Old Testament that the intervening variable, the climactic event, is the Day of the Lord. This is the great cataclysmic, inbreaking of God; it is the coming of the Messiah to rule as King of kings and Lord of lords that puts an end to the present age, judges sin, and brings mankind into the age to come. That is a very simple way of saying, here is what history is all about. Things are bad now, but Jesus the Messiah will come and usher in the age of the Millennial Reign—the very promises of the living God. If that is all one knows about the future, then he knows enough to have hope. However, believers know from the New Testament that there is a little more to the scheme of things.

Two Comings

This Day of the Lord really is twofold. Jesus came the first time as Savior to die on the cross. Today is the Church Age, which Joel called the last days. Peter quoted this very passage and said, "in the last days" (2 Peter 3:3), the Messiah will come again—at the end of the Church Age. Many believers think that Christ will rapture the church, and then the Great Tribulation period will occur. Afterward will be the Second Coming when Christ returns as King of kings and Lord of lords. And when Jesus returns as King, He will then crush the kingdom of the Antichrist. Following that event, Christ will usher in the age to come—the Millennial Kingdom—after which comes the Great White Throne Judgment. Then the promise will be fulfilled of a new heaven and a new earth. Thus, one can fit his beliefs into a more simple pattern: the present age, the Day of the Lord, and then the age to come.

Pentecost and the Church Age

Joel Chapter 2 continues to talk about the Day of the Lord. He says, "and afterward" (v. 28, *NIV*), whereas Peter quoted this passage on the Day of Pentecost saying, "In the last days . . . I will pour out my Spirit on all people" (Acts 2:17, *NIV*). So, Joel saw the outpouring of the Holy Spirit of God. The Jewish Rabbis taught that when Messiah came, there would come what they call the return of the "quenched Spirit." They saw that even in their own times of backsliding that the power and presence of the Spirit had been quenched, but they looked forward to the time when the Messiah would come and there would come a full outpouring of the power and the blessings of the Spirit. That happened on the Day of Pentecost. When Peter stood up and preached to the thousands at the Temple who had gathered for the great Feast of Pentecost, after the Spirit had filled them, he said, "This is that which was spoken by the prophet Joel . . . In the last days, saith God, I will pour out of my Spirit upon all flesh" (Acts 2:16, 17). So, the last days actually refers to the Church Age. In other words, the last days started with the Day of Pentecost. That was the beginning of the fulfillment of Joel's prophecy. And throughout the entire Church Age, that prophecy is continually being fulfilled. God is pouring out His Spirit in the last days.

THE LATTER TIMES

The phrase *the last days* refers to what might be called "the latter times"—the times that precede the second coming of Jesus. Paul, in 2 Timothy 3:1, said, "In the last days, perilous times shall come." He is talking about the conditions of the world before the return of Jesus. In 1 Timothy 4:1, he says that the Spirit speaks clearly in the latter times. That is the end of the Church Age. "In the latter times some shall depart from the faith, giving heed to seducing spirits and doctrines of devils" (4:1). So, the phrase "the last days" is a phrase that really refers to the Church Age. It began on the Day of Pentecost and extends to the very rapture of the church, the Tribulation, and the second coming of the Lord Jesus Christ.

So, what did Joel really see when he looked down the corridor of history to come? He saw the outpouring of the Spirit on the Day of Pentecost. However, in Joel 2, he saw the cataclysmic upheaval of the Day of the Lord in the Tribulation period. "I will show wonders in the heavens and in the earth, blood and fire, and pillars of smoke. The sun shall be turned into darkness, and the moon into blood, before the great and the terrible day of the Lord come" (vv. 30, 31). That coming of the dreadful Day of the Lord is the return of Jesus at the Battle of Armageddon when sin is judged and mankind enters the kingdom of God. He saw the cosmic upheaval of the Tribulation period. Jesus talked about that fact in Luke 21:26, that men's hearts would fail them for fear after looking at those things which will be coming upon the earth "for the powers of the heavens shall be shaken."

Joel also saw an age, that really began on the Day of Pentecost, when everyone who calls on the name of the Lord will be saved. Also in the last days, the Bible speaks about all of Israel being restored, as discussed in Romans Chapters 9, 10, and 11, when God redeems Israel. When Peter preached on the Day of Pentecost, he made the declaration that whoever "calls on the name of the Lord will be saved" (Acts 2:21, *NIV*). It is stated again in Romans 10:13. Paul said, "If you confess with your mouth, Jesus is Lord, and believe in your heart that God raised him from the dead, you will be saved" (10:9, *NIV*). Then he said, "Everyone who calls on the name of the Lord shall be saved" (v. 13, *NIV*). So, the last days is the Church Age. It began at Pentecost with the out-pouring of the Spirit.

Joel also saw in the last days, a time of cosmic upheaval, which will be in the Tribulation hour. Joel 2:32 says, "For on Mt. Zion and in Jerusalem there will be deliverance" (*NIV*). God is going to bring the present age to an end, and the age to come with the Messiah will be a reality.

In Chapter 3, Joel gets a glimpse of God's judgment on the nations at Armageddon. "In those days and at that time, when I restore the fortunes of Judah and Jerusalem, I will gather all nations" (vv. 1, 2, *NIV*). Zechariah used the same terminology in Chapter 14. He said, "I will gather all nations to Jerusalem" (v. 2, *NIV*). Joel said, "I will gather all nations and bring them down to the valley of Jehoshaphat" (3:2, *NIV*). There is a large valley north of Jerusalem in Galilee, called the valley of Jehoshaphat. It is an ancient battlefield, and it has been the site of many battles. One can stand today on the mountain range and gaze at this massive valley—also called Armageddon or the valley of Megiddo. *Armageddon* means the "mountain of Megiddo." It was called the valley of Jehoshaphat where Jehoshaphat won great exploits for God. This is the site of the last and final battle in human history. The final convergence of good against evil, when Jesus Christ returns in the clouds of glory. Joel catches a glimpse of the nations being gathered together in the valley of Jehoshaphat, and God says, "I will enter into judgment against them concerning my inheritance, my people Israel, for they scattered my people among the nations" (3:2, *NIV*). "Multitudes, multitudes in the valley of decision," he says in verse 14. Not only is he calling this location the valley of Jehoshaphat, but he is also calling it Armageddon, and then the valley of decision. Joel says, "For the day of the Lord is near in the valley of decision" (v. 14, *NIV*). That day is Armageddon and the second coming of the Lord Jesus Christ. The sun and the moon will be dark and the stars will no longer shine. He used apocalyptic language to show the overpowering of the coming of Christ. "The Lord will roar from Zion and thunder from Jerusalem; the earth and the sky will tremble" (v. 16, *NIV*). But in the midst of all that cataclysmic upheaval, in the midst of Armageddon, in the midst of this Day of the Lord and this incredible apocalyptic symbolism, a promise appears. "But the Lord will be a refuge for his people, a stronghold for the people of Israel" (v. 16, *NIV*). And he closes out his message with a word of blessing for the people of God.

What will that day be like—that day of the Lord, the final day of the Lord when Jesus returns, when evil is eradicated, when the Antichrist system is destroyed and Jesus actually rules as King of kings and Lord of lords over the earth? Joel describes it as follows:

> "Then you will know that I, the Lord your God, dwell in Zion, my holy hill. Jerusalem will be holy; never again will foreigners invade her. In that day the mountains will drip

> new wine, and the hills will flow with milk
> . . . a fountain will flow out of the Lord's
> house and will water the valley of acacias.
> . . . The Lord dwells in Zion" (Joel 3:17-21,
> *NIV*).

That is the final word he gives. He wanted them to know that the Lord dwelt with them even now, but when Jesus returns, there will be an age to come that is beyond description, and the Lord will dwell in Zion.

The phrase "the Lord dwells in Zion" embodies the whole promise of the covenant of God that is found in the Old Testament—the God who dwelt with His people. It is also found in the fulfillment of the new covenant. In fact, Jesus said when believers gather together that He is in their midst (see Matthew 18:20). The Lord will live among His people. People will not have to pray to God in heaven; Jesus will actually be here in that new earth in the new age to come. Revelation 21:1-4 makes the same declaration, when John said:

> "I saw a new heaven and a new earth, for
> the first heaven and the first earth had
> passed away and there was no longer any
> sea. I saw the Holy City, the new Jerusa-
> lem, coming down out of heaven from God,
> prepared as a bride beautifully dressed for
> her husband. And I heard a loud voice from
> the throne saying, "Now the dwelling of God
> is with men, and he will live with them.
> They will be his people, and God himself
> will be with them and be their God. He will
> wipe every tear from their eyes'" (*NIV*).

Joel's message is also wonderful: "The Lord dwells in Zion." That is why he told them to repent—God lived in their very presence. They were His people. That is the hope that He gave to Israel and for the world. This present age will one day come to an end, and the Day of the Lord will take place when Messiah comes. This world shall then enter the age to come, and the Lord will "dwell in Zion" among His people.

42 Malachi

By David C. Cooper, D.Min.

The Book of Malachi itself is called an oracle, written in a beautiful prose language. It really consists of a series of dialogues that take place between God and the people of Judah and Jerusalem. The series of questions are sometimes asked by God, and at times, the people ask God questions. The name *Malachi* means "my messenger." Both prophets and priests at times were called messengers of the Lord. Malachi was an anointed prophet of God who is the last in the history of Israel and who closes out the canon of the Old Testament.

The Book of Malachi takes place at approximately the same time as the Book of Nehemiah. When Nehemiah served as governor of Jerusalem, after the wall was rebuilt, Malachi served as a spiritual leader and minister to the people of God. The approximate date of his writing and ministry is 435 B.C. Therefore, it is important to study the Book of Malachi along with the Book of Nehemiah, in particular Nehemiah 13. When Nehemiah first came back from Persia to Jerusalem, he led the construction project of rebuilding the wall. After that time, he went back to Persia for an interim period. When he came back to Jerusalem the second time as governor, there were certain aspects of Israel's life with which he was concerned (see Nehemiah 13). First, the people were breaking the Sabbath—it was just another day of commerce. Second, he was concerned about corruption of some of the priests who were not really living a life of integrity and were not fulfilling the ministry God had given to them. Third, many of the people were neglecting the ministry of tithing and giving. They were not supporting the work of the Temple or the priesthood, and they were keeping all of the monies for themselves. Fourth, he was concerned with the problem of breaking the law of intermarriage. There were certain intermarriages that were taking place that were in direct disobedience to the law of God. Those concerns were the same concerns of Malachi.

Central Theme

The central issue of Malachi's message is found in the key verse in Chapter 3 when he asked a very simple question: "Will a man rob God?" (v. 8). Obviously, this particular question is connected immediately with the whole idea of tithing and offerings. However, the question is concerned with a lot more than that. This is the central question that Malachi is asking the nation of Israel. In other words: Will a man fail to honor God? Will a man deliberately disobey God? Will a man fail to give the Lord the glory and the due He deserves? The answer is "Yes, a man will rob God." People will rob God of worship;

they will rob God of His honor; they will rob God of His glory. Then, there are those who refuse to even acknowledge Him as God. They do not give thanks to God for His many blessings of which Paul speaks in Romans 1:21: "They neither glorified him as God nor gave thanks to him" (*NIV*). A man will rob God. The question is, Why would a person rob God? Why would a person fail to acknowledge God and honor God and glorify him? That question is at the heart of Malachi's message. It is the primary issue that he dealt with—the things in a man's heart that would cause him to rob God of honor, worship, and service.

Eight Areas Where Men Robbed God

Malachi addressed eight primary areas where men robbed God. This was not true of everyone in Israel, but it was certainly true of some. They were hearing Malachi's challenge as he called them to search their hearts and to come back to the place where they really honored the Lord as God.

1. *Men robbed God by neglecting His love.* They robbed God in the sense that they neglected and doubted His love, and neither did they respond to His love.

> An oracle: The word of the Lord to Israel through Malachi. "I have loved you," says the Lord. "But you ask, 'How have you loved us?' Was not Esau, Jacob's brother?" the Lord says. "Yet, I have loved Jacob, but Esau I have hated and I have turned his mountains into a wasteland and left his inheritance to the desert jackals" (1:1-3, *NIV*).

In the story of Jacob and Esau, Jacob was chosen by God, and his name was changed to Israel. God did not choose Esau for that purpose. That is what is meant by the statement that God hated him. It does not mean hate in the carnal sense. It means that God in His sovereignty chose Jacob, or Israel, to be the nation through whom the Messiah would come. And, He talks about the fact that Esau, or Edom, was judged. Obadiah also talked about the fact that one day Edom would be judged because of their rejection of Israel and their gloating over Israel's destruction by the Babylonians. That is the very same issue that Malachi is addressing. He talks about the fact that Edom did experience that judgment and eventually fell into obscurity, historically. But God said, "I loved you. I chose you. I had a calling upon your life." However, the people did not acknowledge that, and they seemed to reject the love of God. They even questioned the love of God—thereby robbing Him of the glory that He deserved, because God loves mankind with an everlasting love. Verse 5 is very interesting. He said, "You will see it with your own eyes and say, 'Great is the Lord—even beyond the borders of Israel" (*NIV*). That is a very important statement, because it verifies the same point that has been made in many of the messages during the postexilic period. When God called Israel, He called them to be a ministering force to all the nations. However, many of the people were exclusive; they wanted to stay to themselves. But God said, "Great is the Lord, even beyond the borders of Israel." In other words, Israel was not the only place in the world where God was at work. That is a very important truth. So, the first way that the people robbed God was that they neglected His love, and they did not acknowledge that God had loved them with a unique love and calling.

2. *Men robbed God by dishonoring His name.* The name of God was to be revered. Verse 6 says, "A son honors his father, and a servant his master. If I am a father, where is the honor due me? If I am a master, where is the respect due me?' says the Lord God Almighty. 'It is you, O priests, who have shown contempt for my name'" (*NIV*). The prophet is confronting some in the priesthood who are just going through the motions of their ministry, but they really did not acknowledge or honor God. They did not really worship the Lord in their hearts, and they dishonored His holy name.

3. *Men robbed God by presenting blemished offerings.* They were not really giving God their best, in other words. The priests asked God, "How have we shown contempt for your name?" (v. 6, *NIV*). God responded by saying, "You place defiled food on my altar" (v. 7, *NIV*). Then they asked, "'How have we defiled you?' By saying that the Lord's table is contemptible . . . You bring blind animals for sacrifice" (v. 7, *NIV*). The explanation goes on talking about the fact that the offerings they brought were not without blemish. They were not the right kind of offerings. In other words, these priests were just going through the motions of ministry, and they were not giving God the best of their lives or the best of their ministries.

4. *Men robbed God by committing acts of idolatry.* Some were actually worshiping idols and some of the priests in the Temple really did not give God honor, thereby committing idolatry. Malachi, Chapter 2 says:

"Have we not all one father? Did not one God create us? Why do we profane the covenant of our fathers by breaking faith with one another? Judah has broken faith. A detestable thing has been committed in Israel and in Jerusalem: Judah has desecrated the sanctuary the Lord loves, by marrying the daughter of a foreign God"(vv. 10, 11, *NIV*).

This terminology says that there was spiritual adultery. Some in the priesthood were actually committing idolatry in their hearts against God.

5. *Men robbed God by insincere worship.* God is a God of the heart, not a God of the Temple. He is not a God of the Sabbath; He is not a God of circumcision; He is not a God of traditions—but He is a God of the heart. Worship was more than going to the Temple, offering a sacrifice, or keeping the Sabbath, worship had to come from the heart. David's confession in Psalm 51 says, "You do not delight in sacrifice, or I would bring it; you do not take pleasure in burnt offerings. The sacrifices of God are a broken spirit; a broken and contrite heart, O God, you will not despise" (vv. 16, 17, *NIV*). Some people in Israel were going through the motions of ritualistic worship. Their worship was insincere—their hearts were not in it. Malachi confronts that issue in Chapter 2 by saying, "Another thing you do: You flood the Lord's altar with tears. You weep and wail because he no longer pays attention to your offerings or accepts them with pleasure from your hands. You ask, 'Why?' It is because the Lord is acting as the witness between you and the wife of your youth" (vv. 13, 14, *NIV*). They came to the altar and flooded it with their tears, but God did not accept their offering.

Why? Because their hearts were not in the worship—it was insincere. Jesus said in John 4, that the Father seeks people who will worship Him in spirit and in truth (see v. 24). He expects honest, genuine, worship from the heart.

6. *Men robbed God by breaking the covenant of marriage.* In Malachi 2:14, there is a very important passage, especially in today's society where a breakdown in the covenant of marriage is seemingly everywhere. In this passage, one sees the fact that the wife is the husband's partner and the word *covenant* is connected with marriage. In the Bible, marriage is a covenant relationship. It is not a contract; it is a covenant. Malachi said, "You ask, 'Why?' It is because the Lord is acting as the witness between you and the wife of your youth, because you have broken faith with her, though, she is your partner, the wife of your marriage covenant" (v. 14, *NIV*). A covenant is a relationship based on unconditional love—it is the love of God, a sacrificial love. It is not a love that takes; it is a love that gives. Listen to what God says about marriage. "Has not the Lord made them one? In flesh and in spirit they are his. And why one? Because he was seeking godly offspring" (v. 15, *NIV*). In other words, the purpose of a holy marriage is this spiritual marriage. In the New Testament sense, in a Christian marriage, the goal is godly offspring. It is the responsibility of every Christian couple, if God blesses them with children, to raise their children "in the nurture and the admonition of the Lord" (Ephesians 6:4). The home exists for the glory of God, in other words. "So guard yourself in your spirit, and do not break faith with the wife of your youth. 'I hate divorce,'

says the Lord God of Israel, 'and I hate a man's covering himself with violence as well as with his garment,' says the Lord Almighty. So, guard yourself in your spirit, and do not break faith" (Malachi 2:15, 16, *NIV*). This verse has been twisted and taken out of context. God does not say, I hate divorced people, He said, "I hate divorce." God actually gave divorce as a concession under the Mosaic law in Deuteronomy 24:1-4, to protect women against the harshness of men, who wanted to put their wives away for any and every reason.

Divorce is not the unpardonable sin. It is, however, a great tragedy. It brings a great deal of hurt and much pain in people's lives. Jesus did sanction divorce on the grounds of adultery, which is the proper interpretation of the Mosaic law. Paul, also talked about it in 1 Corinthians 7. Believers who were abandoned by an unbelieving spouse, were free from that relationship and they could remarry as long as they were with the Lord. As the church reaches out to people, it is very important that ministers understand this passage. Everyone hates divorce—just ask the children whose parents have been divorced; they hate divorce. Ask the people who have lived through the pain of divorce—they hate divorce, as well.

> I had a grandmother tell me after a service recently about the pain that had been in their own family as a result of a divorce. She said, I now understand this verse, I hate divorce. She said, I hate it, too. I hate what it has done to my family, what it has done to my children, what it has done to my grandchildren. And what we have had

534

to learn to do as a family to work through
the pain of it.

The statement, "I hate divorce," is a statement
of compassion, not judgment. God was judging and
disciplining the men of the nation who were putting
their wives away because of their selfishness and
their carnality. God said, "Guard yourself in your
spirit," and do not break the covenant of faith you
have with your wife (see v. 15). But for the people
who have been hurt by divorce, it is a statement of
compassion. God identifies with the pain of divorce.
Thus, the people robbed God of His glory and His
honor. And that was the issue the prophet was
addressing.

7. *Men robbed God by withholding tithes and
offerings.* Malachi 3:8 says: "But you ask, 'How are
we to return?' " Will a man rob God? Yet you rob
me. But you ask, 'How do we rob you?' In tithes
and offerings. You are under a curse—the whole
nation of you—because you are robbing me" (vv. 8,
9, *NIV*). In other words, people are not experiencing
God's blessing because of the way that they are robbing Him. God said, "Bring the whole tithe" (v.10).
The word *tithe* means "one-tenth." It is the first tenth
of one's income. The ancient Israelites under the
Mosaic law had a series of tithes. Some went to the
Temple to support the priesthood; other tithes went
to help with the poor. It was, in a sense, what is
seen in taxation. It provided not only spiritually,
but it also provided socially for the needs of the
underprivileged. The tithe is the first tenth of one's
income, and that is how God blesses financially.
"Bring the whole tithe into the storehouse, that there

may be food in my house" (v. 10, *NIV*). In other words, the tithe provides for the spiritual priesthood. "'Test me in this,' says the Lord Almighty, 'and see if I will not throw open the floodgates of heaven and pour out so much blessing that you will not have room enough for it'" (v. 10, *NIV*). This word, *floodgates*, comes from the same Hebrew word found in Genesis during the Flood when the floodgates of the deep were opened and the earth was flooded. God says, "Test me in this, and see if I will not throw open the floodgates of heaven and pour out so much blessing that you will not have room enough for it" (v. 10, *NIV*). The land was under a curse, but He said, "if you obey Me," the floodgates of heaven will be opened. This is the only place in Scripture where God says "Test Me." The blessing will be that "'I will prevent pests from devouring your crops, and the vines in your fields will not cast their fruit,' says the Lord Almighty. 'Then all the nations will call you blessed, for yours will be a delightful land' says the Lord God Almighty" (vv. 11, 12, *NIV*).

8. *Men robbed God by serving Him with carnal motives.* There were those who served God for what they could get out of Him. "You have said harsh things against me,' says the Lord. 'Yet you ask, What have we said against you?'" (v. 13, *NIV*). Malachi 3 says, "You have said, 'It is futile to serve God. What did we gain by carrying out his requirements and going about like mourners before the Lord Almighty? But now we call the arrogant blessed. Certainly the evil-doers prosper, and even those who challenge God escape'" (vv. 14, 15, *NIV*). The people were saying that it was futile to serve God. They thought if they served God, then that meant they would never have

any problems. There are some people today who think that. But that is not why people serve the Lord. They serve God and honor Him because He is their Creator and Redeemer. Believers should not serve God because of what they can get out of Him, they should serve God because of who He is and because they have been redeemed by the blood of the Lamb. They belong to Him, and in that relationship of worship, comes the blessing of God. But the people robbed God. And Malachi called them back to a relationship of loving the Lord with all their hearts and living as the holy people of God, so that they could be a witness to all nations.

Closing the Canon

Malachi closes out the Old Testament canon and the body of Old Testament scriptures. How does he close it out? He announces the coming of the Messiah. The final message of Malachi prepares for the coming of Jesus in the New Testament. He says, the Messiah shall arise "as the sun of righteousness . . . with healing in its wings" (4:2, *NIV*). And then he makes a very fascinating statement: "See, I will send you the prophet Elijah before the great and dreadful day of the Lord comes" (v. 5, *NIV*). How could God send Elijah before the Messiah? Malachi is giving this word roughly 400 years before the coming of Jesus. Elijah lived 800 years before the coming of Jesus. He had already been deceased for 400 years. The Bible says in Luke 1:17 that John the Baptist came in the "spirit and power of Elijah" (*NIV*). And Jesus said in Matthew 11:13, 14, that John the Baptist was the Elijah that would come. John came in the "spirit and power of Elijah."

Intertestamental Period

After the period of Malachi and the ministry of Nehemiah, the ministry of the prophets, as they were seen in the Old Testament, ceased. It does not mean that God did not speak to Israel. It does not mean that God was not working in Israel. It does not mean that God never had prophetic messages. It means that the strong prophetic office in ministry in the intertestamental period was no longer seen or experienced as it was in the Old Testament. For example, there were strong prophetic ministries like Moses, Elijah, and Elisha who established the school of the prophets. Then, as a result of that, throughout the Old Testament record, there were also strong literary prophets like Isaiah, Jeremiah, Ezekiel, Daniel, and the minor prophets. Thus, Malachi was the last of these great literary prophets.

Then history moves into the intertestamental period. Some call this period the silent years, but it was not really silent. To call it the silent years, implies that God was not speaking and God was not working. But that certainly was not the case. What happened between Malachi and the voice of John the Baptist thundering, "Repent, for the kingdom of heaven is at hand"? Was everything really silent in Israel? Not at all. Much happened politically during the silent years after the Medes and the Persians and the rule of the Persian Empire. First, came the swift and mighty conquest of Alexander the Great. Then, came that period of the Syrians that tried to dominate Israel, but God gave them great deliverance. Then, came the Maccabean revolt, discussed earlier in the section on the postexilic period. They rededicated the Temple; they defeated Antiochus

Epiphanes; and they celebrated that great work of God, known today as the great Festival of Dedication, Hanukkah. Rome came to power and dominated Palestine in 63 B.C., and Rome was still in power when Jesus came. It is interesting that Daniel foresaw the coming of all of these empires. So, this intertestamental period was a time of great political change.

From a literary standpoint, a great deal happened as well. The Rabbis and the Scribes took the Old Testament scriptures and translated them into the Greek language. After Alexander the Great and the process of Hellenization, Greek became the major language of the world. He tried to unify cultural language. So it was during the intertestamental period, roughly 200 years before the time of Jesus, when the Old Testament scriptures were translated into the Greek language, known as the Septuagint. The translation was done by the great scribes of Israel.

Religious developments also took place during the intertestamental period. Synagogues were built and synagogue worship continued to be developed as Israel repopulated the Holy Land. While in exile in Babylon, the Jews did not have the Temple; therefore, they learned to worship around the Torah. When they came back to the Holy Land after the captivity was over, even though they had the Temple, they still had it in their hearts that wherever the Torah—the law of God and the scriptures—was present they could gather and worship. So, synagogues filled the landscape of Israel. Therefore, when Jesus came, He went into every town and entered the synagogue and proclaimed the kingdom of God.

So, the intertestamental period was anything but silent.

It was also during this period that certain schools of theology developed in the religion of Judaism. The name *Pharisee* means "pious one or holy one." This group had its beginning during this period. They held to strict Rabbinical traditions. Then the Sadducees also came into being, and they did not really accept Rabbinical tradition. They did not believe in supernatural phenomenon, angels, demons, or even the resurrection of the dead. They were the party of priests in the time of Jesus. They were the aristocracy of Israel who were in collusion with the Roman government. The Essenes also developed during the intertestamental period. In 1947 and 1948, the great discoveries of the Qumran community and the Dead Sea Scrolls that were found were developed by many of these Essenes. They lived an aesthetic lifestyle, and they pulled out of Israel because they saw the corruption of religion, even in the time of Jesus. All these groups and sects developed during the intertestamental period.

This material helps to give an understanding of the New Testament times in which Jesus lived. The last and great promise of the Old Testament is the coming of the Messiah "unto you that fear his name shall the sun of righteousness arise with healing in his wings" (Malachi 4:2, *NIV*). That great prophetic office, that seemed to come to a silent place, made a transition the day that John the Baptist, the son of a Levite priest, stood in the Judean wilderness and began to preach, "Repent, for the kingdom of heaven is at hand." Crowds came to be baptized and to confess their sins. It was a time of revival like the one under Malachi and the other prophets. However, the day came when Jesus entered the Jordan River. When he came up out of the water, John proclaimed to the people and to the world, "Behold the Lamb of God which taketh away the sin of the world." Everything from Genesis to Malachi points to Him— the Lamb of God. He is the fulfillment of the Law and the prophets. Romans 15:4 says, "For everything written in the past was written for our learning so that we through the endurance and the encouragement of the Scriptures might have hope."

APPENDICES

GLOSSARY

GLOSSARY

1. **Allegory** — A narrative wherein abstractions (such as virtue, fear, love) are made concrete (Ms. Virtue, etc.), for the purpose of effectively communicating a moral. The characters and their actions interest us, and we absorb the moral ideas they embody. Example: In Bunyan's *The Pilgrim's Progress*, a man named Christian journeys to the Celestial City, encountering on his way Mr. Worldly Wiseman, the Giant Despair, and so forth.

2. **Analogy** — A resemblance in some particulars between things otherwise unlike: similarity.

3. **Antithetical** — Relating to Hebrew poetry—two lines which have opposite meanings. Example: Proverbs 10:7.

4. **Apocalyptic** — To uncover, disclose or reveal; derived from the Greek word *apokalyptein*.

5. **Canon** — An authoritative list of books accepted as Holy Scripture; a sanctioned or accepted group or body of related works.

6. **Characterization** — The means whereby an author establishes a character with traits and personalities which a reader can recognize and analyze. The character may be developed by means of several techniques; for example, physical description, actions, words, a character's innermost dreams, feelings, and thoughts, and so forth.

7. **Characterize** — To analyze (describe) a character by his distinguishing traits; for example, his integrity (or lack of), impulsiveness, fear, love, patience, and so forth.

8. **Covenants** — Abrahamic: Genesis 12:1-3
   Davidic: 2 Samuel 7:12-16
   Palestinian: Deuteronomy 30:1-10

9. **Creation Era** — The time period in Genesis, Chapters 1 through 11.

10. **Disputation** — Verbal controversy. In the Book of Malachi, God accuses Israel of various things. Each of Malachi's prophecies begins with God's pointed and stern accusation. Israel's response is usually a pretense of innocence. The reader gets the sense of listening in on a conversation.

11. **Dualism** — The theory of two infinites.

12. **Ebla Tablets** — Discovered in northern Syria in the mid-1970s, dating back to 1400 B.C., they confirm the advancement of language and written communication which allows for a 14th-century date of the Pentateuch.

13. **Emanation theory** — Pantheism.

14. **Epitomize** — To serve as the ideal or typical example of something.

15. **Eschatology** — A branch of theology concerned with the final events of the world or mankind. Any of the various Christian doctrines concerning the Second Coming, the resurrection of the dead, or the Last Judgment.

16. **Evolution** — The theory of spontaneous generation; unfolding; a process of continuous change from a lower, simpler, worse to a higher, more complex or better state.

17. **Exodus Era** — The time period covered in the Books of Exodus, Numbers, and Deuteronomy.

18. **Foreshadow** — A hint of something to come. To indicate or typify beforehand; prefigure.

19. **Imagery** — May be considered as either a direct sense appeal and/or a figure of speech which enables the reader to visualize a concept.

20. **Law of Causality** — Every effect is the result of a cause, and no effect is greater than its cause.

21. **Law of Uniformity** — Whatever caused some effect in the past will cause that same effect in the future.

22. **Levir** — The man who performed the levirate custom.

23. **Levirate custom** — An Israelite law which stated that if a man died without leaving an heir, the man's brother or closest of kin would marry the widow to raise up an heir and purchase their land to keep it in the family.

24. **Microcosm** — A little world; a miniature universe. Example: A camp becomes a city in microcosm.

25. **Names of God** —
     Adonai: The Lord, the owner and ruler of all things, the most frequently used name when addressing God.
     El-Elyon: The exalted one, the Most High, the object of reverence and worship.
     Elohim: The Hebrew word for God. The "el" means "like God."
     El-Olam: The everlasting God
     El-Shaddai: The Almighty God, the great God who brings blessings and comfort to His people.
     Jehovah-Jireh: God who sees ahead of time; our provider.
     LORD (All caps): Means Jehovah
     Lord: Means *Adonai*
     Yaweh: God's proper name, His most sacred and holy name, the God of grace and covenant, formed from the Hebrew verb translated I AM. In English, Jehovah.

26. **Pantheism** — A doctrine that equates God with the forces and laws of the universe.

27. **Parable** — A short story that illustrates a moral attitude or a religious principle.

28. **Parallelism** — Denotes the balancing of equal parts of a sentence, the repetition of a sentence pattern, or the repetition of words at the beginning of lines of poetry. Such use of parallelism

contributes to the musical quality of prose or poetry. Relating to Hebrew poetry—two lines that make the same point. Example: Proverbs 4:9.

29. **Particularism** — A theology which concerns God's relationship to Israel "in particular."

30. **Patriarch Era** — The time period covered in Genesis, Chapters 12 through 50.

31. **Pentateuch** — Literally means "five books." The first five books of the Bible: Genesis, Exodus, Leviticus, Numbers, Deuteronomy comprise the Pentateuch.

32. **Prophetic Stories** — Stories that focus on the prophets of Israel and Judah which do not follow a predictable pattern.

33. **Prototype** — A standard or typical example. A first full-scale and usually functional form of a new type or design of construction.

34. **Ras Shamra Tablets** — Discovered on the coast of Syria in 1929, dating back to 1400 B.C. They contain historical data that confirms the information found in the Pentateuch.

35. **Rhetorical** — Asked merely for effect with no answer expected—a rhetorical question.

36. **Royal Reports** — Stories that focus on the kings of Israel and Judah which follow a predictable pattern.

37. **Scenario** —A sequence of events, especially when imagined.

38. **Soliloquy** — A speech, most often in drama, wherein a character speaks his thoughts aloud while alone—a monologue (denoting an extended speech delivered by one character).

39. **Specified Complexity** — Anything complex must have intelligent intervention.

40. **Syncretism** — A mingling of beliefs. Example: Mixing Canaanite religion with Judaism.

41. **Synopsis** —A condensed statement.

42. **Theistic Evolution** — The belief that God created the world through evolution.

43. **Theme** — The essential meaning or main concept of a literary work.

44. **Theophany** — An appearance of God: God manifested in a human way.

45. **Torah** — In Hebrew, the first five books of the Bible, meaning the Law.

46. **Transcendent** — Exceeding usual limits; surpassing. Example: God is *transcendent*.

47. **Typology** — A study of or analysis based on types or categories.

48. **Universalism** — A theology which deals with God's relationship to the whole world.

SELECTED
READING

Selected Reading

Amit, Yairah. *History and Ideology: An Introduction to Historiography in the Hebrew Bible.* Sheffield, England: Sheffield Academic Press Ltd., 1999.

Arnold, Bell T. and Bryan E. Beyer. *Encountering the Old Testament: A Christian Survey.* Grand Rapids: Baker Books, 1999.

Brueggemann, Walter. *A Social Reading of the Old Testament.* Minneapolis: Fortress Press, 1994.

Brueggemann. *Hopeful Imagination: Prophetic Voices in Exile.* Philadelphia: Fortress Press, 1986.

Brueggemann. *The Land.* Philadelphia: Fortress Press, 1977.

Brueggemann. *Old Testament Theology: Essays on Structure, Theme, and Text.* Ed. Patrick D. Miller. Minneapolis: Fortress Press, 1992.

Brueggemann. *Theology of the Old Testament.* Minneapolis: Fortress Press, 1997.

Brueggemann and Hans Walter Wolff. *The Vitality of Old Testament Traditions.* 2nd ed. Atlanta: John Knox Press, 1982.

Collins, John J. *The Apocalyptic Imagination: An Introduction to Jewish Apocalyptic Literature.* 2nd ed. Grand Rapids: Wm. B. Eerdmans Publishing Company, 1998.

Cook, Edward M. *Solving the Mysteries of the Dead Sea Scrolls.* Grand Rapids: Zondervan Publishing House, 1994.

Crenshaw, James L. *Old Testament Wisdom: An Introduction.* rev. ed. Louisville: John Knox Press, 1998.

Spurgeon, Charles H. *Men and Women of the Old Testament.* World Classic Reference Library. London: AMG Publishers, 1995.

BIBLIOGRAPHY

BIBLIOGRAPHY

Alexander, David and Pat Alexander. *Eerdmans Handbook to the Bible.* Grand Rapids: Wm. B. Eerdmans Publishing Co., 1973.

LaSor, William S., David A. Hubbard and Frderic W. Bush. *Old Testament Survey.* Grand Rapids: Wm. B. Eerdmans Publishing Co., 1982.

Pfieffer, Charles F. *Old Testament History.* Grand Rapids: Baker Book House, 1973.

Pfieffer. *Baker's Bible Atlas.* rev. ed. Grand Rapids: Baker Book House, 1979.

INDEX

Index

F

Festival of Firstfruits,   105
Festival of Lights (Hanukkah),   107, 431, 447, 539
Festival of Pentecost,   106
Festival of Purim,   107, 471
Festival of Tabernacles, 106
Festival of Trumpets, 106
Festival of Unleavened Bread, 105
Flood, 16, 61, 62, 63, 65, 536

G

gap theory, 35, 36
Genesis, 14, 15, 16, 18, 19, 21, 23, 24, 25, 26, 28, 29, 31, 33, 35, 36, 37, 39,
    41, 42, 43, 44, 45, 47, 49, 51, 53, 55, 56, 57, 58, 59, 60, 61, 63, 65, 66, 67,
    68, 69, 70, 71, 72, 73, 75, 76, 77, 79, 80, 81, 83, 84, 85, 86, 87, 88, 89,
    91, 95, 392, 411, 412, 444, 518, 536, 541, 548, 551
Gibeon, 119, 120
Great Commission, 18, 47

H

Habakkuk,   357, 359, 361, 362, 363, 364, 365, 366, 367, 369
Haggai, 446, 483, 484, 485, 486, 487, 488, 489, 490, 491, 492, 493, 495, 509
Haman, 472, 474, 475, 477, 478, 479, 480
Hanukkah, 07, 431, 447, 539
Hebrew(s), 23, 29, 30, 34, 36, 39, 42, 43, 46, 65, 67, 68, 72, 80, 81, 92, 96, 101,
    103, 118, 129, 133, 144, 145, 162, 167, 207, 215, 219, 224, 227, 235, 236,
    237, 240, 250, 253, 263, 279, 280, 294, 295, 299, 303, 305, 310, 313, 323,
    358, 359, 360, 361, 362, 370, 381, 382, 412, 415, 422, 423, 447, 448,
    451, 465, 469, 472, 488, 500, 512, 517, 518, 536, 547, 550, 551, 552, 555
Hezekiah , 309, 310, 311, 317, 318, 336, 337, 338, 339, 340, 341, 344, 345, 368
Holy Spirit, 15, 18, 23, 45, 182, 198, 233, 271, 410, 415, 416, 439, 454, 485,
    492, 493, 499, 500, 512, 520
Hosea, 245, 259, 280, 281, 291, 292, 293, 294, 295, 296, 297, 298, 299, 301,
    330

I

I AM, 550
imagery, 213, 322, 346, 372, 374, 405, 516, 517
incarnate, 15, 18, 150
intermarriage, 451, 467, 528
Isaac, 25, 66, 70, 71, 72, 73, 76, 77, 80, 83, 84, 85, 86, 90, 272, 435
Isaiah, 17, 30, 235, 242, 247, 248, 249, 250, 252, 279, 308, 310, 317, 318,
    319, 321, 322, 323, 324, 325, 326, 327, 328, 329, 330, 331, 333, 339,
    340-345, 351, 352, 366, 374, 385, 386, 395, 400, 413, 427, 429, 440,
    491, 501, 506, 515, 518, 538

J

K

L

M

N

Q

R

S

T

U

V